MW01055652

FAMINE IN THE REMAKING

Famine in the Remaking

Food System Change
and Mass Starvation
in Hawaii, Madagascar,
and Cambodia

STIAN RICE

West Virginia University Press
Morgantown

Copyright © 2020 by West Virginia University Press
All rights reserved
First edition published 2020 by West Virginia University Press
Printed in the United States of America

ISBN
Cloth 978-1-949199-33-8
Paper 978-1-949199-34-5
Ebook 978-1-949199-35-2

Library of Congress Control Number: 2019044495

Book and cover design by Than Saffel / WVU Press
Cover image: A Cambodian refugee mother holds her child and a pail for
water as they wait to collect their daily rations in 1979, at a camp north of
the Thailand town of Aranyaprathet. (AP Photo)

Revenge, shame, fire
The horror has made us all so brave
But moved us only to narrate.

—Nasib Arida

Contents

Preface

Famine is a big word. It conjures images of desiccated and fly-covered bodies packed into relief camps. It recalls vast, arid swathes of the earth—dustbowls littered with scorched fields, cattle carcasses, and swollen bellies. For some, famine invokes indictments of communism; for others, colonialism or capitalism (cf. Sen 1999; Davis 2002). It has initiated and terminated social movements, foretold the collapse of governments, and preceded the conquest of nations (Brunel 2002). Famine consorts with concepts like genocide and holocaust, and has marked watersheds in social and cultural history. But, always, *famine* is a word that prefaces a body count.

This book is not only about "big" famine, but the big things that cause it: societies, economies, ecologies, climate, and war. As such, I tend to speak in broad and abstract terms. I talk about slow and irresistible forces of change, discuss the impacts of these changes on amorphous populations, and describe the consequences in broad generalizations. Indeed, to analyze famine is to invoke a conceptual scale that makes it easy to lose sight of the victims. This book attempts to maintain a depth of field that keeps continents and centuries in focus and still resolves crops, cows, and corpses. But overcoming the tremendous scale implicit in famine analysis is an extraordinary challenge.

For this reason, I start with the fundamental unit of all famines: the human body. After all, it is the body that connects every victim of starvation to every other. It is the body's adaptations to hunger that serve as the last defense against death, and it is the body's physiological strategies for resisting starvation that provide the best counterpoint to the socioeconomic and socionatural systems examined throughout this book.

Starvation and the Body

It is hard to die from hunger. Through a ceaseless negotiation between needs and resources, a healthy body will go to extraordinary lengths to keep itself alive. When the supply of food is first interrupted, the body metabolizes whatever remains in the digestive tract before switching to the consumption of glycogen in liver cells. The conversion of glycogen is important for making glucose: unlike other tissue, brain cells require glucose to function. But after two to three days, glycogen is depleted, and the body's tactics must change. Metabolism switches to the consumption of free fatty acids from stores of fat. Other tissues help out: for example, when muscle cells receive fatty acids through the bloodstream, they switch off their consumption of glucose, reserving this precious sugar for the brain.

Around the four-day mark, the body's options for producing glucose are gone. Once again, the liver changes tactics, this time converting fatty acids into ketone bodies—simple, water-soluble molecules that can be consumed by brain tissue (Coffee 1999). Human beings are the only animal with a brain that can function on both glucose and ketones, a remarkable adaptation that prolongs survival by delaying the final stage of starvation: the consumption of the body's own muscles and organ tissue (Cahill and Veech 2003). But this adaptation comes with physiological costs. Ketosis, the metabolic state in which ketone bodies are produced and consumed is frequently accompanied by weakness, exhaustion, extreme thirst, dry mouth, and cramping in the extremities. In some cases, ketosis can lead to ketoacidosis, a condition in which the acidic ketone bodies have pushed blood pH dangerously low. Ketoacidosis can lead to nausea, vomiting, hyperventilation, and death (Mostert and Bonavia 2016).

Once fat stores have been depleted, the body begins to break down protein-rich muscles, releasing amino acids into the bloodstream. The liver switches back to producing glucose through the conversion of these amino acids. The cost of survival is extreme: the body has started to eat itself to stay alive. Over time, key organ functions suffer as muscle tissue is consumed (Coffee 1999). The hungry become listless, withdrawn, and apathetic. They also become increasingly vulnerable to disease (Young and Jaspars 1995).

With the loss of key vitamins and minerals, the body's immune system begins to fail. Skin begins to flake and hair can change color. Red spots may form under the skin from subcutaneous bleeding, a condition known as purpura that results from a lack of Vitamin C. Corneal lesions and night blindness may develop due to Vitamin A deficiency. The body becomes more susceptible to skin and respiratory infections. Crowded conditions increase the chance of infectious diseases like measles, typhoid, and cholera. Now that the body is consuming its own amino acids, tissue begins to absorb water (edema). Symptoms of protein deficiency emerge, like kwashiorkor (a swelling of the belly and liver), marasmus, and dehydration. All are accompanied by severe pain (Checchi et al. 2007). Body temperature may fluctuate and victims may suffer from hyperventilation and pneumonia. In the end, death usually comes from cardiac arrest or arrhythmia resulting from electrolyte imbalance or the degradation of cardiac tissue.

This process can take up to *12 weeks*, a testament to the body's remarkable ability to turn its own matter into time. It accomplishes this feat by continuously balancing the metabolism of energy sources with the needs of key organs. By contrast, the socioeconomic and socionatural food systems designed to provide sustenance to these bodies can fail within minutes—through a wildfire that destroys crops, a tsunami that floods essential fields, a financial market collapse, or the passage of new legislative measures (cf. Kondo 1988; Davis 2002; Garenne 2002; Brinkman et al. 2010). Rather than balancing resources with needs, these systems invariably do the opposite: markets move food away from the hungry and toward the wealthy, land reforms accelerate the expropriation of capital and increase vulnerability, and worker programs jeopardize food production by redirecting labor toward cash crops. Unlike the body's unwavering focus on self-preservation, the systems we depend upon for food are often designed to serve other masters than the hungry, and satisfy other needs than survival.

Mass Starvation and Society

It is hard to die from hunger; yet, millions do. Over 110 million died from famine in the 20th century, more than in any previous century.[1] In 2002, a food crisis in southern Africa put 14 million people at risk of starvation before aid arrived (Devereux and Tiba 2006). As of this writing (May 2018), as many as 16 million face starvation in East Africa, especially communities in Somalia, Ethiopia, and Sudan. Half the population of Somalia is currently classified as "food insecure" (FAO 2017) and Save the Children reports that up to 85,000 children have starved to death in Yemen where hunger has increasingly become a weapon of war (McKernan 2018; Mohareb and Ivers 2018). This comes at a time of unparalleled abundance: total global grain production in 2016–17 was over 2.5 billion metric tons, the most in history (Statista 2017).

This paradox of mass starvation and mass food production has inspired prolific literature, funded a multibillion-dollar aid industry, and motivated extensive scientific research (including this book). If we are producing enough food to feed the planet, why does mass starvation persist? What is it about the way our global food systems are organized that makes it difficult—or undesirable—to eradicate hunger? Theories about the causes of famine have been topics of vigorous debate for decades. What have we gotten right? Where have we gone wrong? Finally, how do we begin to reorganize our food systems to make hunger obsolete? These questions occupy the heart of this study.

Global food systems are experiencing unprecedented transformation. Population growth, changing diets, shifting geopolitical and trade regimes, social movements, civil unrest, land and labor reform, agrarian transition, climate change, and global market penetration are combining to reshape food provisioning, rearranging the complex network of actors and processes that link producers (farmers, ranchers, and fishers) with an increasingly diverse set of consumers. Historically, these changes have had mixed results: some technological improvements and political reforms have increased abundance while others have created new barriers to access and new forms of exploitation. Some changes have precipitated food system collapse and led to mass starvation. This book examines three of these violent failures: Hawaii in the 1820s, Madagascar in the 1920s, and Cambodia in the 1970s. These are stories of economic collapse, social revolution, species introduction, disease epidemics, market reform, imperialism, embargoes, and war. They are also stories of well-intentioned but, ultimately, destructive rescue attempts. Indeed, despite the intervening decades and centuries, the through-lines of these narratives bear an uncomfortable similarity to the causes of food crisis today.

The use of the word *remaking* in the title reflects two simultaneous objectives for this book. On the one hand, the three case studies examine the relationship between reorganization (the remaking of food systems) and famine. After all, knowing what kinds of transformations have precipitated past failures is essential for avoiding future disaster. On the other, this book reflects on the state of the famine scholarship, offering a perspective that highlights the large-scale and slow-moving processes of social and environmental change constantly reshaping our food provisioning systems. There is still much to learn about what causes famine at these temporal and spatial scales. In this regard, I hope this book contributes to remaking our theories of famine genesis.

In the end, understanding the actors and mechanisms that drive reorganization can do more than prevent future crises; it can help direct food system reform and transformation. Today, we face the challenge of remaking modern food systems in ways that increase agricultural resilience, promote environmental justice, provide equitable access, and—critically—prevent hunger. To achieve these goals, we need to make the systems that provision food as irrepressible as the living bodies that depend on them.

Acknowledgments

Historical reconstructions like this could not exist without the painstaking and sometimes perilous work of countless eyewitnesses, journalists, historians, and scientists. In this case, that list includes the victims and survivors of mass starvation and its accompanying violences—exposure, dehydration, disease, dispossession, exploitation, sexual assault, enslavement, and genocide. Without their contribution to knowledge, the opportunity to learn from our collective past would be irreparably harmed. I owe a profound debt to all those who have lived and breathed the histories I recount here: it is both a privilege and a duty to hear and repeat their stories.

This book is the culmination of an eight-year-long conversation with James Tyner—my mentor and friend—on the structural origins of famine and genocide. His originality, knowledge, and unwavering support was essential for this work. During my tenure at Kent State University, I benefited greatly from the guidance and encouragement of advisors and colleagues, notably V. Kelly Turner, Mandy Munro-Stasiuk, Joshua Stacher, and Babacar Mbaye. In particular, I credit Kelly Turner with inspiring my interest in socioecological synthesis, an indispensable tool for this research. This book would not exist without the constructive support of Judith Watson, David Correia, Salvatore Engel-Di Mauro, Mazen Labban, Derek Krissoff, and the readers and editors at West Virginia University Press. For their insight, rigor, and patience—especially their patience—I owe them an enormous debt.

Throughout this research, I relied upon the help of countless people, in particular: Rebecca Niemiec for her assistance locating Hawaiian GIS data and historical sources; Savina Sirik and Sokvisal Kimsroy for their knowledge and guidance during fieldwork in Cambodia; the staff and student archivists at the Hawaiian/ Pacific Collections, University of Hawaii at Manoa; John Barker and the staff at the Hawaiian Mission Houses Archive in Honolulu; the staff at the USDA National Agricultural Library in Silver Spring; the Archive d'Outre-Mer in Aix-en-Provence, and the Documentation Center of Cambodia in Phnom Penh. No less important were the programmers and technicians who developed and maintained the numerous archival search tools I depended on, most notably the exceptional Persée Catalog of the University of Lyon and the Bibliothèque National de France.

For better or worse, a project like this becomes a close family member, and I am profoundly grateful to all of those who welcomed this demanding visitor into their lives. I am indebted to friends, colleagues, and co-agitators: Veronika Archer, Alex Peimer, Alex Colucci, Peggy and David Giltrow, Emily Midgley, José Díaz-Garayúa, Brad Austin, and Crista Johnson. I am deeply grateful for the unwavering support of my family—Bill, Jo, and Sonja—and my partner, Erin. More than anyone, she has carried the weight of my dedication to this work and borne witness to both my fascination for this subject and my frustration with a world that keeps making it relevant. To all of you—and the many I have neglected to mention—thank you. You have made these last few years a true delight.

Most importantly, I wish to thank Will, who sacrificed innumerable hours of play so that his father could work. He is the inspiration behind this study, for it is in his world that our theories will become practice. I hope that someday his children and their contemporaries will find books like this one wholly unnecessary.

Introduction

Brother, if when the war is over
The west clamors for glory
And sanctifies its dead and glorifies its heroes,
Do not sing the praises of the victors
Or despise those who lost the war.
Instead, like me, kneel silently
And in reverence
To weep over our dead.

. . . .

Brother, if when the war is over
Soldiers go home to shelter in loving arms,
Do not expect love when you go home.
For hunger has left us no friend to love
Other than the ghosts of our dead.

. . . .

Brother, who are we? Without a home or clan or neighbor
Humiliated day and night
The world cares not for us as it never cared for our dead
Grab a shovel and follow me
So we may bury our living.

—Mikha'il Na'ima, *Brother*

Na'ima's wartime poem *Brother* captures the disillusionment, loss, and shame felt by many who survived the Lebanese and Syrian famine of 1915–18. In the poem, Na'ima conjures the image of Lebanese men returning home from the Great War, encountering the remains of farms, homes, and family members (Fraser 2015). Unlike the victorious Western soldiers who returned to nationalist glory, these men arrived home to witness the aftermath of societal collapse: the degradations of prostitution and rape, murder, and gruesome cannibalism. The horrors visited on the victims and survivors of this famine that killed 300,000 mark an unforgettable juncture in cultural memory, what Najwa al-Qattan (2014, 719) refers to as a "remembered cuisine of desperation."

Brother reveals the dark and complex ties of kinship that bind mass starvation to war, geopolitics, economics, culture, community, home, and bodies. It speaks of a social breech too wide to fit within the bounds of a single discipline and too deep to be captured by simple theorization. Indeed, the recurring significance of famine in human history has produced abundant interest and ensured ample data and analysis. Its far-reaching impacts have encouraged contributions from anthropologists, sociologists, economists, legal scholars, religious leaders, politicians, psychologists, geographers, scholars of public health, and development theorists. It has both defied explanation and been readily explained away—as divine will, the wages of sin, or the fault of the promiscuous poor. But it has always been a subject of vigorous debate.

Over the last 50 years, scientific scholarship around famine has grown significantly, evolving through three broad phases of interpretation (Devereux 2006). The first phase, known as food availability decline (FAD), assumed that starvation is caused by a lack of food, usually a consequence of production failure (Atkins 2009). Production failure was traditionally attributed to natural interference with human systems of subsistence. This interference might be sudden—droughts, floods, fires, earthquakes, tsunamis, and eruptions—or slow-moving processes of resource depletion and climate change that combine with increasing resource demand (see Kondo 1988; Diamond 2007).

One well-known FAD-oriented theory is presented in Thomas Malthus's (1993 [1798]) *An Essay on the Principle of Population*. Malthus noted that while the rate of growth in food production was generally linear, the rate of human population growth was exponential. At various points in history, the number of mouths that required food exceeded the capacity to feed them, leading to starvation, a reduction in population, and a return to sufficient provisioning. Malthus argued that famine would continue as an inescapable consequence of this relationship unless rapid population growth—a crisis he blamed on the poor—was curbed.

Malthusian ideas helped motivate the development of Green Revolution policies and technologies in the 1940s to 1960s that sought to alleviate world hunger through increased food production (Kloppenburg 2005). Despite a long history of criticism (for example, Boserup 2005), forms of Malthusian theorization persist today, especially in development and relief sectors where policy makers extol increases in food production to support the demands of the world's burgeoning population and changing diets (cf. Brown 2011, 2012; Heinberg 2011).

In the early 1980s, the second phase of famine theorization moved almost exclusively toward analysis of economic, political, and demographic drivers—an evolution Stephen Devereux (2006, xi) refers to as a shift from "old famine thinking" to "new famine thinking." This shift emerged in response to FAD's perceived failure to incorporate political actors and processes; that is, FAD failed to explain how *access* to food might be disrupted in situations where food is plentiful, where life and death often follow lines of race, class, gender, or political visibility (Devereux 2006). Amartya Sen (1981, 1, emphasis added) expressed this in the now-famous opening sentence of *Poverty and Famines*: "Starvation is the characteristic of some people not having enough to food to eat. It is not the characteristic of there not *being* enough food to eat." Histories of the literature point to Sen's 1981 publication as a turning point in the politicization of famine studies and the introduction of the influential entitlement approach. However, it was not the first time that socioeconomic factors were implicated in famine causation. Sociopolitical involvement was acknowledged in the Indian Famine Codes of 1883 (Rangasami 1985), government responses to 19th century famines in northern China (Mallory 1926; Edgerton-Tarpley 2008), and research into Sahelian famines in the 1970s (Meillassoux 1974; Franke and Chasin 1980).

Political approaches opened up an enormous range of research areas, including entitlement collapse (Sen 1981; Drèze and Sen 1989), regime type (Sen 1999), urban social stratification (Garenne 2006), geopolitics (Gazdar 2002, 2006; Zerbe 2004; Lautze and Maxwell 2006; Watson 2006; Mackintosh 2011), HIV/AIDS (de Waal and Whiteside 2003), resource booms (Sen 1981), neoliberalism (Jarosz 2011), incomplete democratic transition (Devereux and Tiba 2006), failure of accountability (Lappé et al. 1998; Baro and Deubel 2006; Edkins 2006; Lappé 2011), centralization of agricultural policy (Haggard and Noland 2007), decentralization of agricultural policy (Meillassoux 1974), failure of response (de Waal 1997; Edkins 2000), and war (Maddox 1990). This work has engaged new scholars and significantly expanded our understanding of famine causation.

But as with FAD, political approaches present several shortcomings that challenge an integrated understanding of famine causation. First, many studies do not adequately account for long-term or large-scale structural precursors. There is a tendency to apply strict spatiotemporal constraints to the analysis of food systems, ignoring or excluding exogenous factors (like trade sanctions) and environmental conditions that are slow to materialize.[1] By geographically bounding the causal narrative of famine, these approaches tend to ignore relationships between actors that span spatial scales or bridge institutional levels. Second, with few exceptions, famine research has not addressed the interplay between social and environmental actors and processes. Situated squarely within the development literature and directed towards a policy audience, theorization around food crises has not embraced contemporary work on nature-society interactions (see Castree 2001, 2005; Bakker and Bridge 2006). Third, neither FAD nor political approaches effectively account for violence, expropriation, or extralegal activities during the evolution of a crisis (Edkins 2006). Fourth, there is a tendency among analysts to view complex food systems through disciplinary lenses, privileging certain explanations for failure over others. FAD assumes the problem starts with a failure of production and that institutions for distributing food are otherwise effective. Political approaches assume institutional failure is responsible for starvation and that changes to production have little overall impact. Those political approaches concerned with household access (for example, entitlement theory) tend to view hunger as a matter of poverty (see de Waal 1990), while macroeconomic perspectives tend to blame starvation on state-level economic policies. Disciplinary specialization has encouraged a "one-size-fits-all" approach to theorization.

Most recently, research has turned away from questions of famine genesis and toward famine response—that is, the best ways to detect and mitigate emerging crises once in progress (Howe and Devereux 2006; Watson 2006). This scholarship explores a wide range of topics, including the logistics of delivery (Long and Wood 1995), management (Mayer 1975), models of distribution (Hwang 1999), the ethics of relief for victims (Singer 1972), and the ethics of charitable giving (Kahneman and Ritov 1994), among others. Although the focus on response has been well received by a burgeoning aid industry, it draws attention away from underlying causes, especially the long-term and large-scale social and natural processes that continue to reproduce crises. Such a focus creates the impression that mortality prevention is more important than crisis prevention: persistent, "everyday" subsistence threats created by dysfunctional (even profitable) food systems are acceptable so long as *mass* mortality does not occur. As such, a response-centered approach offers few benefits for understanding the origins of food system failure.

Over the last 50 years, the academic understanding of food system failure has tended toward simplification even as our food systems become increasingly complex. Missing from contemporary analyses is an acknowledgment of the diversity of actors and processes involved in food provisioning, the deep integration of social and ecological factors, the interaction of short-term stresses with long-standing historical conditions, and the interplay between actors across spatial scales and institutional levels.

Hunger and Regime Type

During this time, there has been a growing fascination with the connection between mass starvation and system of government. Following Sen's *Development as Freedom* (1999), some have argued that the problem of famine is essentially a lack of capitalism and democracy: communist policies produce famine while free market economies do not.[2] To support this argument, proponents point to the famines of Ukraine (1932–33), China (1958–61), Cambodia (1975–79), Ethiopia (1970s and 1980s), and North Korea (1998, 2002), all of which occurred under ostensibly communist regimes. But this form of reductionism fails to account for the vast differences between regimes in terms of the organization of food production and consumption—differences that are conveniently obscured by the categorical term "communism." It also fails to account for numerous famines under noncommunist governments—for example, South Asian and African famines during the colonial period; postcolonial famines in Uganda, Rwanda, and Indonesia; and the most recent famines in Malawi, Zambia, Mozambique, and Iraq after US occupation (see also Bassett and Winter-Nelson 2010). Finally, it tends to discourage a more detailed analysis of the *specific* policies, structures, and dynamics that participate in the production of crisis.

In a similar vein, some Marxist authors and critics of colonialism have blamed colonial-era governments for the famines that occurred in the Sahel, East Africa, India, and China between the 18th and 20th centuries (cf. Meillassoux 1974; Franke and Chasin 1980; Davis 2002; Edgerton-Tarpley 2008). For many of these authors, exploitative land and labor policies, "free" markets (Garenne 2006), and the legacy of dependency theory (Blaney 1996) explain the collapse of food provisioning. But, as with communism, not all colonialisms were the same: French, English, Spanish, and Dutch governance systems differed dramatically between locales, especially at the level of food production. Ironically, throughout the colonial period, European observers regularly blamed famine on the laziness, savagery, and backwardness of native society (cf. Petit 1929; Olivier 1931; Bathie 1934), a position widely discredited today.

If communism, capitalism, colonialism, marketization, globalization, and "native sloth" can all be blamed for mass starvation, there must be more to the story. Indeed, many of these explanations seem to be attempts to simplify complex and multidimensional histories into critiques of an already *en vogue* "evil," one whose defects are presupposed. But behind these simplifications there are *structures*—social, cultural, economic, and environmental arrangements of actors and processes—that make our food systems work and fail. The intent of this book is to understand these structures without first condemning them with a name.

It makes little sense to pin starvation on any single form of government. But a cursory investigation of the famines mentioned here reveals one important similarity: in each case, the food provisioning system experienced a significant reorganization prior to failure. Agricultural reorganization was essential to the Soviet (1932), Chinese (1958), Cambodian (1975), and North Korean (1998, 2002) famines. The incorporation of new food markets and export arrangements was involved in the Indian famines during British rule (1866, 1876, and 1899) and the Great Irish Famine in 1845 (Ó Gráda 1995; Davis 2002; Nally 2011). Reorganizations associated with warfare occurred in Iraq in 1991, East Africa in 1917, the Levant in 1915, and Ethiopia in the 1970s (Maddox 1990; Gazdar 2002; Lautze and Maxwell 2006; Thompson 2013). Devolution of government control played a role in Madagascar in 1985 (Garenne 2006) and conversion to cash crops led to starvation in Java in the 18th century (Hugenholtz 1986). The reorganization of food systems—and the role these transformations play in collapse—is a primary concern of this book.

The Slow-Moving Socioecology of Famine

Our food comes to us through complex systems that connect consumers to farmers, ranchers, pastoralists, and the vegetable and animal products of their labor. Between us and them are myriad social and natural systems—the biophysical environment, seed and chemical markets, pesticides, herbicides, weeds, insects, land-tenure systems, labor organizations, transportation networks, commodity markets, and retailers. At different times and places, these *food provisioning systems* have been organized in different ways. To support long-term subsistence needs, such systems have evolved to withstand environmental and social shocks with diverse cultivars, stockpiles, trade, price controls, and moral economies (Scott 1976; Rindos 2013). Of course, these systems do not stand alone, but are connected to—and integrated into—other social, economic, and environmental systems: indeed, identifying and untangling the processes that link these overlapping arrangements of production and consumption is a substantial part of understanding how food provisioning systems work.

Food provisioning systems may fail under stress. *Failure* is the moment when a segment of the population is no longer able to acquire basic subsistence through the system. Provisioning systems may fail completely, affecting whole societies, or partially, impacting only a segment of society, often distinguished by age, class, race, political affiliation, or role in the system. Failure may occur suddenly or progressively, in isolation or in repetition. As circuits of both food and capital, provisioning systems establish and participate in social relations of production and consumption that unevenly distribute wealth. As such, failure consistently creates both winners and losers: in some historical cases, the winners initiated the failure for personal or political gain (Keen 1994). The consequences of failure may range from localized impoverishment and malnutrition to mass starvation and civil war.

The organization, or structure, of a food provisioning system changes over time in response to social, economic, and environmental factors. For example, rice cultivators in the highlands of South East Asia switched between swidden and paddy cultivation in response to the condition of local soils and the changing availability of labor (Hanks 1992). Over the last forty years, American meat consumption has increased as farmers have expanded corn production, a response due in part to pro-corn subsidies and technological innovations that allowed efficient conversion of corn to ethanol and animal feed (Albritton 2009). Some of these changes may end up being "successful" (or, at least, benign) responses to changing circumstances. Others, however, are not. The two largest famines in history, the Ukrainian famine (1932–33) and China's Great Famine (1958–61), occurred during periods of agrarian restructuring (Wemheuer 2014). Such reorganization may bring about failure by itself or increase the system's vulnerability to socioecological stress. For example, the Indian Famines of the late 19th century (1866, 1888, and 1898) arose from the combination of El Niño–related droughts and a provisioning system evolving to address the demands of a new, international grain market (Davis 2002; Fagan 2009).

In the cases that follow, *reorganization* is defined as a functional change to the social and material relations of production, distribution, and consumption within a food provisioning system; for example, food rationing, price controls, changes to land tenure, decentralization or recentralization of state regulation, the introduction or exclusion of actors, and changes to the kinds of crops or the methods of cultivation. Reorganization is distinct from other adjustments that are essentially changes in the value of flows between actors, such as variations in productivity or consumption, the price of a commodity, or the availability of a natural resource (e.g., rainfall). These fluctuations are not considered instances of reorganization as they do not alter the underlying structure of the system.

How, then, is the reorganization of food provisioning systems associated with failure? Are there similarities in the forms of reorganization that have precipitated past famines? And are there similarities in the processes that have propelled reorganization? To answer these questions requires a strategy that differs markedly from past approaches to famine theorization. First, it must account for food provisioning systems as dynamic and complex arrangements of diverse social, cultural, economic, and ecological actors and processes. Second, it must account for interactions between these actors and processes across spatial scales and institutional levels: global markets, geopolitical imperatives, and climate teleconnections must be integrated into the same analytical frame as cassava, cows, and corpses. Finally, to capture the slow-moving processes of social and environmental change that make food provisioning vulnerable to failure, the analysis must identify changes taking place over decades and centuries, not the months and years that are common to contemporary studies.

Three Historical Failures

This book pursues these questions through a comparative historical analysis of three famines: Hawaii in the 1820s, Madagascar in the 1920s, and Cambodia in the 1970s.

Hawaii, 1820s—Traditional subsistence cultivation on the Hawaiian Islands was severely disrupted in the early 19th century with the rise of the Pacific Trade in sandalwood, a timber product with a large market in East and South Asia. To support increasingly lavish lifestyles, Hawaiian chiefs required households to commit labor to sandalwood extraction. In time, extraction quotas were so high that food production dropped precipitously, leading to mass starvation. Famine intensity fluctuated over several years as ruling elites adjusted social and religious practice in an effort to balance export profits with "acceptable" levels of mortality (Schmitt 1970). The Hawaiian case study provides a unique opportunity to reconstruct a little-known famine from primary source material. Prior to the 1820s, famines on the islands had occurred in conjunction with warfare, outbreaks of disease, and infrequent droughts. But this event is the first famine associated with economic precursors. It also takes place at a time of considerable upheaval in Hawaiian politics and social organization.

Madagascar, 1920s—Known as the "Cactus War," the collapse of food provisioning in Madagascar's Mahafale and Antandroy communities resulted from French colonial efforts to consolidate control over the pastoralists of the island's arid South.[3] Local villages had come to depend upon abundant prickly pear cactus as a source of food, physical security, and fodder for large cattle herds. Beginning in 1924 and aided by renowned scientists, French officials waged a campaign of biological warfare to eliminate the cactus and end local self-sufficiency. The resulting destruction of prickly pear led to the deaths of up to 300,000 cattle and tens of thousands of people. The lead-up to this event has been portrayed as a typical colonial-era conflict between subsistence society and an empire intent on producing wage laborers. But it is also an ecological story: the famine occurred because of an unexpected botanical collapse and followed a trajectory shaped by over 150 years of environmental and political change.

Cambodia, 1970s—Over a ten-year period, Cambodians experienced a sustained bombing campaign by the United States, the culmination of a civil war, the systematic transformation of both agricultural production and consumption under the Khmer Rouge, the collapse of the Khmer Rouge regime through war with Vietnam, and the installation of a new government. Declines in food production coupled with oppressive rationing and a provisioning system geared toward production for export led to as many as a million deaths from starvation, exposure, and disease (Tyner and Rice 2015). Cambodia offers perhaps the most clearcut case of food system reorganization. But many of the common explanations given for the failure suffer from oversimplification; for example, the claim that famine resulted from the implementation of an idealized, autarkic, communist state (cf. Vickery 2000). This study suggests that the failure of food provisioning in Cambodia was considerably more complex. Furthermore, whereas many commentators assume food provisioning failure was a secondary consequence of a brutal regime, this analysis reveals the inverse: that the demands of the food provisioning system drove the shape of Cambodia's political superstructure.

Unlike other chronicles of mass starvation, I do not address the "great" 19th century famines of Ireland, India, and China, nor the 20th century famines of Ukraine, China, and Bengal. These famines have already received significant scholarly attention (see Drèze and Sen 1989; Davis 2002; Ó Gráda 2009; Nally 2011) and debates over their causes form the basis for distinctly economic and political theories of famine. As such, I hope that a focus on less-analyzed cases, developed from primary sources, provides a better foundation for multidisciplinary analysis. Furthermore, the great famines have received heightened attention largely due to *high mortality*. But when it comes to causation, it is not clear that high mortality makes the great famines worthier of study: a high body count in these instances may have more to do with a failure of response than a fundamental difference in how these big crises emerged.[4]

Instead, the three famines examined in this book were selected based on five criteria. First, there was enough available historical data to ensure a sufficient representation of the food system could be devised, changes identified, and consequences modeled. Second, the case had not received extensive scholarship: by focusing on lesser-known crises I hoped to contribute to historical knowledge. Third, the case involved socioecological conditions or processes that have received less attention in the famine literature; for example, the roles played by interstate violence, invasive species, or environmental perceptions. Finally, the case involved interaction between ecological and political actors.

Each of these stories is distinct in terms of its sociohistorical and ecological *context*—for example, the organization of the global economy, the local environment and food culture, the primary forms of cultivation, and the organization of the state. But this is where the distinctions end. When it comes to *causal mechanisms*—structural reorganization, response to stress, and failed adaptation—these famines, spanning three continents and 150 years of history, look all too similar.

A Geography and Historiography of the Big and Slow

To identify and understand the large-scale and slow-moving drivers of famine, the analyses that follow draw heavily from approaches in comparative historical analysis, the Annales School of historiography, political ecology, and Marxist political economy.

Scholars of the French Annales School of historical writing emphasized the role of long-term historical processes over short-term events. Detecting a tendency among historians to focus on *histoire événementielle* ("event history") that exaggerates the role of individual actors, Marc Bloch, François Simiand, Lucien Febvre, and Fernand Braudel developed a three-part approach to historiography that helped provide insight into slow-evolving structures (Braudel 1982). At the largest temporal scale, emerging over the span of centuries, the *longue durée* refers to processes of social evolution that may exhibit considerable "inertia" and result in dramatic changes in social organization, but move so slowly that they are barely perceivable over the span of a human lifetime (Braudel and Wallerstein 2009). The transition from feudalism to mercantilism to liberal capitalism, the steady development of drought-resistant varieties of maize, or the slow deposition of sediment in a river estuary are all examples of processes taking place in the longue durée. Braudel (1982) argued that such processes can have profound consequences without ever being acknowledged.

At the shortest temporal scale, events are brief periods of upheaval that tend to capture disproportionate attention in the historical narrative. That said, events such as military battles, riots, stock market crashes, elections, hurricanes, and volcanic eruptions can all have profound effects on food provisioning. Whether the effect is lasting may depend on the organization of the provisioning system: resilient systems may be able to survive strong, negative shocks by maintaining surpluses or by temporarily reorganizing along adaptive pathways, whereas less-resilient systems may fail or be permanently reorganized.

Between events and the longue durée is the conjunctural scale (Braudel 1982). Conjunctural processes take hold more slowly and less dramatically than events (usually emerging over the span of decades), but also exhibit a definable beginning and end. Forces operating at this scale tend to be noticed by those experiencing them, though the full effect may not be obvious for some time. The three case studies direct the most attention to conjunctural processes: it is at this scale that large social structures experience and respond to transformative tension. Colonization, decolonization, economic takeoff, economic depression, soil nutrient depletion, forest clearing, various forms of demographic transition, and decadal oscillations in climate all operate at the conjunctural scale. How these slow-emerging processes interact to alter the organization of food provisioning systems is critical to understanding the emergence of mass starvation.

The analytical traditions of political ecology offer three critical contributions to famine studies in general and this study in particular. First, food provisioning systems are complex arrangements of socioecological actors and processes, and there is growing recognition that famine research must account for the myriad interactions that take place between nature and society (see Collet and Schuh 2018). By incorporating nature into social systems, political ecology allows for the interaction of short- and long-term processes across both sides of the nature-society divide (Zimmerer and Bassett 2003). Crop failure can be understood as an outcome of extreme events like fire, gradual changes in rainfall, sudden mass migration, or the legacy of decades-long land policy.

Second, political ecology encourages an understanding of how power is articulated through ecological change (Bryant 1998). Modifications to the environment become telltales of social intervention and political intention. Attention to power introduces the possibility that vulnerability is produced not just through the elimination of social safety nets and the loss of various forms of social, cultural, and human capital, but also through the deliberate manipulation of the environment and the expropriation of natural capital (Watts and Bohle 1993; Smith 2008). These ecological expressions of structural power are crucial to understanding provisioning system failure.

Finally, emerging in part from this attention to socionatures, recent scholarship in geography and other disciplines has encouraged a reengagement with the materiality of physical objects and substances that participate in our social existence. This "material turn" (Bakker and Bridge 2006; Anderson and Wylie 2009; Barnes 2014; Fadani 2018) serves as a reminder that the "things" we interact with on a daily basis—water, food, air, and bodies—are not "invariant essence" but dynamic, socionatural constructions with both material and representative forms (Linton 2010, xi). Food provisioning systems operate in ways that involve material things. In fact, these systems exist to transform and reproduce numerous, intersecting materialities: bodies, foods, nutrients, plants and animals, soils, and microbes, among others. Similarly, the failure of these systems leaves material traces in the form of altered bodies and environments (Fadani 2018).

This study does not categorize food crises into types, nor does it assume that starvation is associated with specific forms of government. It expressly considers the possibility that food system failure emerges from *particular rearrangements of labor, nature, and capital* within the dominant mode of production. But these rearrangements need not be associated with a kind of economy, nor any specific philosophy or system of governance. In a strictly historical sense, the crises that struck Hawaii, Madagascar, and Cambodia were capitalist famines in that they occurred within the last 200 years, a period when capitalism was the emergent or dominant global economic system. But the local forms of production that conspired to produce starvation could hardly be called capitalist: feudalism, traditional economies, and moral economies interacted with capitalist and colonial imperatives in complex and sometimes unpredictable ways. It is these mechanisms and interactions that pushed millions of victims toward starvation, not archetypal capitalism, colonialism, or communism per se.

Organization of This Book

Chapters 1 through 3 narrate, interpret, and analyze the three historical case studies: Hawaii in the 1820s, Madagascar in the 1920s, and Cambodia in the 1970s. Beginning with the human body and moving outward in space and time, each chapter provides a reconstruction of the pre-failure food provisioning system, a brief history leading up to the failure, and a reconstruction of the failing food system before concluding with an analysis of the forms of transformation associated with the famine. Chapter 4 brings together the structural analyses conducted for each case study, develops a framework for food crisis evolution, and discusses the significance for famine theorization and related literatures. In this final chapter, I discuss the question of personal responsibility, the implications for the prevention of future famine, and the positive potential of food system reorganization in pursuit of social and environmental justice.

The Past in the Present

It is hard to die from hunger, but millions do, and the reasons have resisted easy theorization. Indeed, "explanations" of famine have simplified even as provisioning systems have grown increasingly complex. Meanwhile, the world produced more food this year than ever, yet the current crisis facing Africa and the Middle

East may be the largest in half a century. Scholars of famine have turned—as if in retreat—from prevention to relief, a rear-guard action designed to assist a burgeoning aid industry dependent on the constant supply of precarious lives. In some ways, this shift is understandable: famines are big, politically contentious, emotionally entangled, distinctive, and notoriously complex. The case studies that follow demonstrate this complexity and distinctiveness—at first glance, they seem to have little in common beyond dead bodies. But comparative historical analysis reveals something else: there are similar conjunctures, similar arrangements of actors and processes, and similar forms of reorganization. The famines that looked so different when viewed from the "near" and "recent" look remarkably alike with time and distance. Most importantly, these common forms of structural reorganization—precursors of failure in the 1820s, 1920s, and 1970s—are all at work today on the increasingly interconnected global food system.

Food provisioning systems throughout the world are undergoing significant change. On the production side, high-yielding varieties are replacing traditional cultivars (Scoones and Thompson 2011; Nabhan 2012), smallholder agriculture is giving way to large-scale farms, economies in the Global South are being radically reshaped to promote agriculture-led economic take-off (Norton, Alwang, and Masters 2014), and state deregulation is exposing more producers to the vagaries of global markets (Jarosz 2011). On the consumption side, middle class growth is increasing preferences for meats and processed foods, while commodity speculation and growing income disparity are exposing poor consumers to price volatility (Norton, Alwang, and Masters 2014). Recent changes in the geopolitical landscape are increasing food availability for some even as others suffer under trade sanctions, political brinksmanship, or civil war (Gazdar 2006). Finally, climate change is bringing damaging rainfall variability to once-dependable agricultural regions and displacing agricultural producers both geographically and economically.

Every one of these elements—from the socioeconomic to the biophysical—has been implicated at some point in the collapse of a historic food provisioning system. The combination of these elements today poses a unique challenge: global food security is no longer a question of what types of systems are effective or efficient, but how systems can be rearranged to respond to changing geopolitical and biophysical landscapes. It is imperative that policy makers learn to distinguish between those forms of restructuring that improve system resilience and those that have led to collapse. To the extent that this analysis furthers such an understanding, it will have accomplished more than just historical narration: past horrors will have been put to important work.

CHAPTER 1

The Hawaiian Sandalwood Famines: 1820s

As darkness fell, Beckervaise, a quartermaster on the expeditionary ship HMS *Blossom*, caught sight of the sandalwood cutters. Having made the arduous ascent from the shore that afternoon, he found the cutters preparing to traverse the mountainous terrain: "There stood a vast number of men assembled, each with a torch made from sandal wood, which burns bright and clear" (Beckervaise 1839, 220). In the glow of the torchlight, he watched as the men dispersed into the hills to search for precious—and increasingly rare—stands of timber. The trees these native cutters sought had forested the Hawaiian highlands for millennia but had only been valued by foreign merchants in the last twenty years. With growing demand 8000 kilometers away in East Asia, global markets had ratcheted up the pressure on trees and Islanders, one merchant vessel at a time. As the night advanced, each man cut as much as he could carry before strapping the timber to his back and beginning the long trek down to the shore and waiting ships.

Beckervaise depicts this scene in early 1827 with a sentimental flourish. He describes how the men sing as they cut and collect bundles of the sweet-smelling wood: "each accompanying his labour with a song, to which the whole band within hearing join in chorus; the song we understood not, but in the calm of a beautiful night it was calculated to inspire delight" (1839, 220). Missing from his narrative—perhaps missing entirely from his field of view—were less idyllic truths. The labor was forced. The men who brought this most valuable commodity to the market would receive none of its value. Most importantly, unlike many of the men and women forced to hunt for sandalwood in the 1820s, these cutters were fortunate to be alive.

The political and cultural upheaval sweeping these islands would have been well known to the men in the forest. Two kings had died in quick succession: Kamehameha in 1819, who unified the islands under a single throne, and Liholiho in 1824, who sent the monarchy spiraling into debt. Centuries-old political hierarchies were being discarded and replaced with Western philosophies of governance. Ships from Britain and America were arriving with growing frequency bearing muskets, measles, and missionaries. They set sail with vegetables, pigs, and sandalwood. Like all the Islanders, the cutters would have witnessed the recent destruction of traditional idols and, with them, the collapse of cultural practices that governed land tenure, taxation, and welfare. They would have watched tens of thousands die from unexplained disease.

Added to this mix were distant cataclysms these cutters could not have known about. The Panic of 1819 damaged U.S. banking and trade. Tambora, the largest volcanic eruption in recorded history, destroyed agricultural production across much of the Northern Hemisphere during 1816—the infamous "year without a summer." Other circumstances unfolded slowly enough to be overlooked. Since the arrival of foreign merchants, conspicuous consumption by chiefs and kings had created stockpiles of Western luxuries that no one used. Wild cattle and horses, brought to the islands by early explorers, were multiplying in the interior and consuming local flora. The population of the islands had been in steady decline for at least 50 years. And the forests were running out of sandalwood.

That night, as Beckervaise listened to the cutters "inspire delight" with their song, the Hawaiian island chain—one of the most geographically isolated places on earth—was being grappled into a global political economy on the starting block of the industrial revolution and unprecedented colonial expansion.[1]

In its most basic expression, the collapse of Hawaiian food provisioning is a story of failed labor allocation. Upon discovery of sandalwood in the early 1800s, American and British companies saw an opportunity to make a fortune carrying timber from the islands to East Asia. Merchants purchased sandalwood from Hawaiian chiefs who conscripted their subjects—under penalty of banishment or death—to locate and extract the trees from the forested interior. For a time, the profits from this trade supported increasingly lavish lifestyles for chiefs. But eventually, with timber extraction taking a toll on the wild-growing tree, sandalwood became harder to find. In a desperate attempt to maintain the trade, chiefs forced increasing numbers of laborers away from agriculture and into the interior to hunt for the elusive tree. The labor shortage led to a decline in food production and mass starvation.

But below the surface, this history is three, interwoven stories. The first is about *arrivals*, of merchant ships, infectious diseases, and money—extraordinary amounts of money. The second is about *departures*, of sandalwood, religious idols, and laboring bodies. And the third story traces the decades-long *transformations* that connect the two: the decentralization of royal authority, the abrogation of social safety nets, deforestation, population decline, conspicuous consumption, expanding imperial interests, and the unexpected harmonization of two contrasting modes of economy—feudalism and merchant capitalism. Within Hawaiian feudalism, capitalism found a conspirator willing to embrace Western philosophies of governance, and a ruling class eager to exploit its subjects in new ways. This hybrid economy was characterized by two opposite forms of decision-making: embracing radical change, and doubling down on a commitment to old ways. In the early decades of the 19th century, Hawaiian leaders, prodded on by British and American interests, tried both strategies at the same time. The rupture this created not only altered the direction of Hawaiian society, it established opposite trajectories for nobles and commoners. At the turbulent interface of "traditional" practices and "modern" markets, chiefs, kings, and merchants amassed extraordinary wealth as commoners starved.

This chapter is organized into four sections. The first provides a brief history of mass starvation in Hawaii, the standard narrative of the sandalwood famine, and the challenges inherent in reconstructing this event from the historical record. The second section describes the state of Hawaiian food provisioning before Cook's arrival in 1778: diets and food practices, cultivation systems, land tenure arrangements, social and political organization, and environmental conditions. In the third section, I trace the history of this food system between 1778 and the estimated peak of the crisis in 1827. This history includes the arrival of Europeans and Americans, growth in the Pacific Trade, the reign of Kamehameha, the ascension of Liholiho, and the catastrophic transformations wrought by the sandalwood trade. The final section assembles these pieces to trace the mechanisms—events, conjunctures, and shifting perceptions—that precipitated food system failure.

A Brief History of Hawaiian Famines

Wi is the Hawaiian word for famine and broadly describes any shortage of food that leads to starvation. Following local tradition, some of the larger famines— *Hi-laulele, Haha-pilau, Laulele, Paulele, 'Ama'u,* and *Hapu'u*—were named after the wild plants that provided sustenance during the crisis (Kamakau 1961, 204). For 19th century Hawaiian historians like Malo and Kamakau, famine is portrayed as a common feature of the precontact period, an unfortunate but inescapable consequence of warfare and weather.[2] Malo (1903, 253) notes that people living in the sunny leeward region of Hawai'i "frequently suffer from famine," while Kamakau (1992, 31) observes that "sometimes famine, bitter famine, came over the land because it had become parched through the excessive heat of the sun and the lack of rain." This narrative of precarious subsistence was repeated by American and European visitors to the islands, many of whom saw famine as the obvious accompaniment to the savage life. For missionaries, a self-reinforcing link between violent kings and uncertain survival was seen as the ultimate barrier to social evolution. James Jarves (1843, 32), an early American missionary, exemplifies this view: "It is probable that the political condition of the country during this period, was much the same as when first visited by Captain Cook: wars and famine, peace and plenty, alternating according to the dispositions of the ruling princes . . . The prevalence of such a system must effectually have checked any tendency to mental or physical advancement." For Jarves and others, without foreign intervention, the future of Hawaii—known to Westerners at the time as the Sandwich Islands—would continue to be one of suffering and hunting wild plants.

Despite the reported persistence of famine, few authors of the period devoted much effort to describing or understanding its causes. Explanations were limited to single causes, invariably the most proximate in space and time. This lack of detail—beyond mere mention of famine's presence—may help explain the subsequent lack of interest among 20th century scholars. Indeed, historical famine in Pacific societies has received far less academic attention than famines in Europe, Asia, or Africa (see Currey 1980; Schmitt 1970, 1969). Schmitt (1969, 67) notes that famines in Hawaiian history "have been largely ignored by serious historians," adding that "virtually nothing is available on famine mortality" even though considerable work has been directed toward calculating other forms of population decline.

When historians have addressed causation, the consensus is that Hawaiian famines were primarily the result of two factors: warfare between chiefs, and drought. The human toll from destruction of food and agriculture during war often exceeded the toll from battle. As William Shaler (1935, 163), a visitor to the islands in 1804 writes, "The slaughter is not usually great in the field, but the unrestrained license, and the waste and destruction of provisions by the conquerors, generally causes a famine in the conquered territory." The practice of seizing crops and livestock is noted as far back as 1778 when chiefs from the island of Hawai'i launched a series of raids against the island of Lanai that "stripped the island bare of food, leaving the inhabitants nothing to eat but fern roots" (Schmitt 1970, 110). Starvation was sometimes used to force submission: in 1772, King Kahekili held rebel territory on Maui under siege until the enemy had been sufficiently weakened by hunger. Those who survived were then rounded up and massacred. In other cases, food crises were initiated by the demands of occupying chiefs and their armies. The British explorer, Vancouver, observed such an event on Maui in 1795 following King Kamehameha's conquest of the island. He noted that the invading armies had consumed "vast quantities" of food and that "all the hogs, dogs, and fowls, that could not be carried away, were killed, or dispersed over the country" (Vancouver 1801, 110–11). Three years later, the impact to agriculture on Maui was still being felt through persistent food shortages.

Most war-related famines in the historical record were associated with the wars of unification that brought all the major islands under Kamehameha's control between 1780 and 1805. As Kamehameha's armies moved from Hawai'i through Maui, Molokai, and Oahu, they consumed enormous resources and left agricultural production in disarray. William Broughton, a captain on Vancouver's 1795 expedition, recorded that residents on Oahu were starving in the wake of

Kamehameha's recent conquest. He noted that fields had been abandoned in advance of the arriving armies and suggested that locals may have destroyed their own livestock to deprive Kamehameha of supplies (Broughton 1804, 71). Before sailing from Oahu on his first attempt to capture the island of Kauai, Kamehameha's army seized the remaining food, and "owing to the neglect of the lands, a famine of great severity threatened the inhabitants with starvation" (Twombly 1899, 145). Common people—caught between hunger and the impositions of unfamiliar chiefs appointed by Kamehameha—found themselves with few options: "Many of the people, to relieve their hunger, stole from the chiefs, and were cruelly punished, several being burned alive to terrify the rest" (Alexander 1891, 147). In general, the long-term repercussions of Hawaiian war-

Figure 1. Waimea, Kauai, in the 1820s. (Bingham 1855, 217)

fare on human well-being appear to have exceeded the warfare itself: firsthand accounts broadly agree that the greatest loss of life occurred as a result of starvation and disease in the aftermath of invasion and the destruction of agriculture (Schmitt 1969).

In addition to war, drought has been blamed for a history of recurring food shortages on the islands. Major droughts resulting in famine were recorded on Niihau (1793–94), Maui (1806–07), and Hawai'i (1811–12), among others (Menzies and Wilson 1920; Schmitt 1970; Cordy 1972). Severe drought, usually involving a failure of late winter or spring rains, invariably led to crop failure and loss of livestock. In many instances, affected populations would migrate: the unique topography of the islands produced considerable variation in rainfall between nearby regions, enabling subsistence cultivators to avoid starvation by temporarily moving food production to unaffected areas (see the discussion on Ahupua'a in this chapter). This geographical variation in rainfall also ensured that life-threatening droughts were usually localized: early explorers regularly noted vast differences in the availability of food or the condition of fields between neighboring valleys or ports (cf. Vancouver 1801; Alexander 1891; Menzies and Wilson 1920).

For nine hundred years, this interplay of war and drought was the primary cause of mass starvation on the Hawaiian Islands. But by the early 1800s, the "discovery" of sandalwood by European merchants brought dramatic social and ecological change, and with it, a new kind of food crisis. Sandalwood is a slow-growing and sweet-smelling tropical evergreen that can be found throughout archipelagic Southeast Asia and in several Pacific island chains. The tree is a poor source of firewood and charcoal—in Hawaii, local use was generally limited to grinding the timber into a fine powder to scent fabric. But in China, Burma, and India, sandalwood was an essential component of religious practice, and high demand drove traders and explorers to search for the scented wood in Indonesia, the Philippines, and southern Polynesia. By 1810, a lucrative trade in sandalwood was hitting its stride as demand for the fragrant timber in Macau and Canton drove a vigorous extraction industry across the Pacific (Hammatt and Wagner-Wright 1999). Sensing profit, Kamehameha ordered his chiefs to conscript labor for sandalwood collection, sending commoners into the mountains to cut trees and carry the timber to shore where it was sorted, bundled, and sold to China-bound merchants.

By the middle of the decade, foreign visitors noticed a troubling change. Otto von Kotzebue (1821, 200), captain of a Russian expedition to explore opportunities for trade with the islands, noted of his 1817 visit to Oahu that "many fields . . . lie uncultivated, as the inhabitants are obliged to fell sanders-wood." The first missionaries to arrive in 1819 corroborated Kotzebue's observations. On a visit to Pearl River for provisions, missionary Hiram Bingham (1822, 281) found that scarcity had driven up the price of food: "The reason why provisions are so scarce on this island is the people for some months past have been engaged in cutting sandal-wood & of course neglected cultivation of the Land." William Alexander, another American missionary, would later reflect on the growth of trade in sandalwood: "Soon after this there was a famine in Hawai'i, caused by the neglect of agriculture while the people had been forced to spend their time in cutting sandal-wood" (Alexander 1891, 151). Kamakau (1961, 204) reported that "[Kamehameha] ordered men into the mountains of Kona and Ka'u [Hawai'i] to cut sandalwood, paying them in cloth and in tapa material, food, and fish . . . Rush of labor to the mountains brought about a scarcity of cultivated food throughout the whole group [of islands]." Sir George Simpson, British Minister Plenipotentiary, noted the "great waste of life caused in obtaining sandalwood from the mountains" (in Hopkins 1862, 373). Other contemporary observers— Ellis (1826), Dibble (1843), and Wilkes (1845)—tell a similar story.

In fact, accounts from the early 19th century, though generally lacking in detail, are remarkably consistent with respect to three claims: first, the famine occurred during the boom in sandalwood extraction, roughly 1811 to 1830; second, the famine occurred *because* of this trade; and third, the proximate cause of starvation was a decline in food production driven by a redirection of labor. Later historians (cf. Kuykendall 1938; St. John 1947; Schmitt 1970; Cho, Yamakawa, and Hollyer 2007) would repeat the findings of earlier authors (see also Porter 1930). These three claims establish the basis of the narrative in Potter's (2003, 26) textbook *History of the Hawaiian Kingdom*: "Travelers to the islands reported that whole villages were deserted while the people were in the mountains cutting sandalwood . . . This labor weakened the workers and left them little time to cultivate their fields."

If we accept these assertions—and there appears to be no reason not to—then the food crisis associated with sandalwood extraction is the only Hawaiian famine in the historical record attributed to something *other than* warfare or drought. It marks the first instance of a famine with an *economic* precursor. And, if Kamakau (1961) is to be believed, it is the first famine to extend across all of the major islands. Such a reading of the record suggests that the sandalwood famine was an unprecedented event in Hawaiian social history.

Despite some consistency in the basic sandalwood narrative, information about famine conditions is essentially nonexistent.[3] There are no mortality estimates and few geographic clues that might suggest which areas were worst hit. Some firsthand observers during this period make no mention of food stress, even when detailing the obvious demise of local agriculture (for example, Kotzebue 1821). As for timing, no author specifies when people started to die of starvation. Unlike other famines for which dates are clearly identified—by the failure of predicted rain or the moment of enemy invasion—this famine seems to have occurred sometime between 1811 and 1830, a period defined not by observations of starving people but by its association with the growth in sandalwood extraction. In most cases of historical famine, basic questions of when, where, and how bad are usually the most readily answered, even in Hawaii. But that is not the case here, once again making the sandalwood famine somewhat unique. Later in this chapter I offer reasons for the lack of specificity, finding that this dearth of information is itself a clue to the trajectory of the crisis.

The story begins with a famine explained as a collapse of agricultural production caused by sandalwood extraction. This narrative is not wrong so much as incomplete: indeed, through the remainder of this chapter I attempt to show that there was not one sandalwood famine, but two; that starvation was most likely concentrated on the southwest coast of Hawai'i; and that the failure of food provisioning cannot be explained by sandalwood alone, but by a confluence of numerous, slow-emerging processes of social change initiated four decades earlier by the arrival of Captain James Cook.

Food Provisioning

They ate the flesh of nearly everything living in the sea, as well as that of swine, dogs, and fowls, yams, sweet potatoes, fruits, berries, and several kinds of seaweed, besides the staple of their foods, poi, *a sort of fermented paste made from taro, a bulbous root very similar to an Indian turnip. They drank an intoxicating beverage made from the sweet root of the ti plant, and a stupefying liquor from the awa root.*

—George Waldo Browne, *The Paradise of the Pacific*

The written records upon which a study like this must rely do not appear until the arrival of Europeans—in this case, the "discovery" of Hawaii by the British captain James Cook on January 18, 1778.[4] Located 3600 kilometers from the nearest continental landmass, the island chain is one of the most remote places on earth. Even so, the discovery of the islands in 1778 is somewhat late by European standards. Spanish, Portuguese, French, and British explorers had been crisscrossing the Pacific for centuries. In 1568, the Spanish explorer Mendaña passed to the northwest of Midway Island before turning east toward what is now Mexico—a near miss. Ten years later, Francis Drake passed to the southwest of Hawai'i on his way to the Gilbert Islands and the Philippines. Most Polynesian archipelagoes in the south and western Pacific had been known to Europeans since Magellan in the 1520s, but the Hawaiian Islands (or Sandwich Islands, as Cook would name them) were absent from nautical charts for an additional 260 years.

Not only was the discovery of the Hawaiian Islands rather late by European standards, the settlement of the islands around AD 900 was late by Polynesian standards. The people who paddled out to meet Cook's ships in 1778 were the descendants of one of Polynesia's last—and most extraordinary—waves of expansion, a journey of 3500 kilometers from the Marquesas Islands. Tahiti had been settled by AD 700, Samoa by 800 BC, Fiji by 900 BC, and the Solomon Islands as early as 2000 BC (Bellwood 1987). Between AD 900 and 1200, Polynesian seafarers expanded their reach from the Marquesas to the north, east, and south, establishing settlements on Hawaii, Easter Island, and New Zealand. Like European colonists centuries later, the first human settlers brought with them the appurtenances to reproduce society: animals and plants, seeds, tools, cultivation techniques, cultural practices, and forms of governance. In fact, all the plants and animals that would eventually make up the common

Hawaiian diet crossed the Pacific packed into canoes (Culliney 2006). All the settlers needed was land.

The land they found would have borne a striking resemblance to the lands they had left. Like the Marquesas, Tahiti, and Fiji, the Hawaiian Islands are of volcanic origin. The largest, Hawai'i, is home to Mauna Kea, Mauna Loa, and Kilauea, active shield volcanoes that regularly erupt and add new land to the island's coast. The

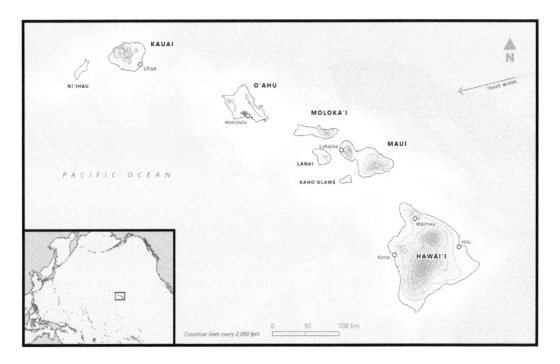

Figure 2. Map of main Hawaiian Islands with selected places identified.

first settlers would have encountered rich, volcanic soils to which their favorite cultivars were already well suited. The five large islands and three lesser islands (fig. 2) would have offered sufficient resources for agriculture, fishing, and hunting. Between these islands, early settlers would have discovered great variation in topography: the older islands (Kauai, Oahu, and Moloka'i) are crosscut by deep valleys and eroded cliffs while the youngest (Maui and Hawai'i) still resemble the sloping shield topography of their volcanic origin.

Early European explorers noted the pleasant and "salubrious" climate afforded the islands by the mediating effect of the Pacific (Jarves 1843, 18). Between 1820 and 1832, Hopkins, an early missionary to Hawaii, kept detailed temperature records. Over that 12-year span, the maximum range of temperatures was 37°F with an average diurnal range of 12°F. Hopkins (1862, 32) saw in the pleasant climate an opportunity to moralize, ascribing to the "very beauty of the weather" a corresponding "lotus-eating condition of mind" on the part of the native population.

But consistency in temperature did not carry over to rainfall. The islands are located between 18° and 23° north latitude, at the southern edge of the northeast trades. These winds bring heavy, consistent rainfall to the windward (ko'olau) sides of the islands, while high elevations in the interior create significant rain shadows to leeward (kona). Depending on topography, annual rainfall variation can exceed 100 inches over a distance of 20 miles (Schmitt 1970). Within the same island, streams emptying to windward will flow year-round while large rivers on the leeward side may be seasonally dry. In fact, droughts have historically had the greatest impact on leeward areas, particularly on Hawai'i (Cordy 1972). Malo (1903, 253) notes that people in the Kona region of Hawai'i are the most exposed to the sun, experience the longest periods of dryness, and "frequently suffer from famine."

The Hawaiian calendar was divided into dry (kau) and wet (ho'oilo) seasons. In most areas, the dry season runs from May through October, with the first showers in October and November announcing the start of the wet season (Hommon 2013). Windward regions are more likely to see consistent rainfall throughout the year, while disruptions in seasonal rainfall patterns are more likely to affect leeward areas: Kamakau (1992) observes that drought in leeward regions often resulted from excessive heat and lack of rain between November and January, or a failure of the spring thunderstorms that visit the leeward coast between February and May.

At the end of the 18th century, Hawaiian bodies were still nourished by the same array of foods that had sustained them for a millennium. All of the staples and vegetables in the common diet were introduced to the islands by early Polynesians (Hommon 2013): taro, sweet potatoes, yams, sugar cane, breadfruit, coconuts, and bananas were common to Polynesian culture at the time of Hawaiian settlement (Cordy 1972). Taro and sweet potato were the primary staples and formed the basis of most agricultural production on the islands. During periods of food stress—invariably the result of crop failure—Islanders turned to local wild plants. Malo (1903, 50) notes the use of ferns: "The following articles were used as food in the time of famine: ha-pu-u fern (the fleshy stem of the leaf stalk); the ma'u and i-i-i (the pithy flesh within the woody exterior). These [ferns] grow in that section of the mountain-forest called wao-maukele . . . But one is not really satisfied with such food." Other famine foods included bitter yam, Polynesian arrowroot, and cabbage palm (Handy, Handy, and Pukui 1972; Hommon 2013).

The majority of protein consumed by commoners came from fish (Hommon 2013). Extending outward from shore, Hawaiian fishers exploited three partially overlapping ecological regions: inshore, pelagic, and benthic zones. In each zone, different techniques and technologies were used to lure and catch prey (Kirch

1982). The inshore zone (from tidal pools to an offshore depth of 20 meters) provided an abundance of sea life—as much as 100 times as many species as in the other zones. In addition to fish, men and women collected sea urchins, mollusks, octopus, and crustaceans. In the pelagic zone (from 20 to 100 meters in depth), specialized hooks were employed to catch tuna, scad, jacks, dolphinfish, and various sharks. In the benthic zone (to a depth of 365 meters), fishers used long lines and hooks to catch bottom-dwelling amberjacks, snappers, groupers, and bonefish. In fact, Hawaiian hook and lure technology had advanced to such a point that skilled craftsmen usually specialized in this trade, devoting their labor to the production of fishing equipment and trading their wares for food and other necessities (Hommon 2013).

Before Cook's arrival, the only other sources of meat protein were pigs, dogs, and chickens. Pork was regularly eaten by the nobility but only consumed by commoners during religious ceremonies or in the company of a chief (Hommon 2013). Even then, only men were permitted to eat it. Women were responsible for raising pigs but were forbidden from consuming pork under penalty of death—one of many dietary prohibitions placed on women under Hawaiian religious custom. By contrast, dogs were a more common part of the diet and could be eaten by women and commoners on a regular basis (Cordy 1972; Culliney 2006). Unlike pigs and dogs, much less is known about the role of chickens in the Hawaiian diet. Hommon (2013) suggests that chickens may have been used during religious rituals but otherwise the meat was not prized by the ruling class. Most chickens were probably free-range, as there is little mention of husbandry.

Class and gender strongly influenced the diet. Males in the nobility ate whatever they wished, unless a temporary prohibition had been established by a higher-ranking chief or priest. Among male chiefs, the protein of choice was pork (Hommon 2013). Women were forbidden from eating pork, chicken, coconuts, bananas, several kinds of fish, and any foods currently being offered in religious sacrifice. Furthermore, meals for women could not be cooked using the same fires as meals for men, nor could food be "eaten off the same board" (Donne 1866, 109). These prohibitions extended to children: Jarves (1843, 95) notes that the "choicest of animal and vegetable products were reserved for the male child, poorest for the female, with many food items prohibited from girls."

Early writers were fond of noting the physical differences between the bodies of chiefs and commoners. Members of the nobility were tall and stout, "to the point of being obese" (Jarves 1843, 86), while the common people were generally short and lean. Bingham (1855, 82), upon meeting a young prince, writes "on coming to maturity, [he] balanced in the scales two peculs of their sandal wood, 266 and 2/3 lbs . . . this was about the weight of Kalanimoku, and may be regarded as the average weight of the chiefs of the islands, male and female."[5] Historians attribute this stark disparity in size to differences in diet and exercise: it was common practice for members of the nobility to be carried by attendants and perform no manual labor (Jarves 1843, 87).

Taro and Sweet Potato

Taro (*Colocasia esculenta*) is the 14th most consumed vegetable in the world and the primary staple among Pacific people (Cho, Yamakawa, and Hollyer 2007). Archeological evidence suggests this perennial root crop was domesticated in multiple locations approximately 50,000 years ago, in or around the Malay Peninsula. From there, taro accompanied human migration through the Indonesian archipelago and the Solomon Islands around 28,000 years ago. As populations moved east, taro became the centerpiece of Pacific agriculture before arriving in Hawaii with the first settlers around AD 900–1000. As in the rest of Polynesia, taro was the favorite staple among Hawaiians and played an important role in religious ceremonies and narratives of origin.

The taro plant (*kalo* in Hawaiian) is harvested for its corm, a thick, subterranean stem that is used by the plant to store energy. The starches in the corm are 98.8 percent digestible and have a granule size one-tenth that of potato, making taro one of the most easily digestible staple crops. It contains significant potassium (more than banana), carbohydrates, calcium, and enough iron to have dietary significance when eaten regularly. The leaves of the plant are rich in calcium, fiber, provitamin A carotenoids, and Vitamins C, B2, and B1. This nutritious bounty comes with a price: like other plants in the *Esculenta* family, taro contains toxic oxalic acid and must be steamed or boiled before being eaten (Cho, Yamakawa, and Hollyer 2007). As with other foods, the need to cook taro would place demands on another resource: firewood.

Taro was the basis of *poi*, the most common dish in the Hawaiian diet. The traditional process of making poi began by baking the taro corms in underground ovens packed with soil, rocks, and charcoal. Once cooked, the softened corms were mashed using a large pestle before being mixed with water. The resulting, dense "paste" was usually set aside to ferment: Jarves (1843, 76) notes that eating unfermented poi, though "nutritious," usually led to "acrid humors." Fermented poi was often served with vegetables and fish, or other meats. Blocks of "hard" poi (*pa'i'ai*)—mashed taro not yet mixed with water—could be stored for later use as gifts or payment of tax and tribute. Hard poi could keep for up to six weeks (Hommon 2013).

The strong preference for taro among Islanders, especially the nobility, ensured that taro cultivation and consumption was a common subject for early writers. Meanwhile, far less has been written about the other primary staple food, sweet potato (*Ipomoea batatas*). Among Islanders, sweet potato was considered the food of commoners and—like taro—was carried to Hawaii by the first Polynesians who had cultivated the crop for centuries (Kirch 1994). Sweet potato and taro required different environmental conditions for growth and benefited from different forms of cultivation. These contrasts ensured that sweet potato and taro cultivation occupied somewhat distinct geographical spaces and coevolved with different forms of political economy. The following sections examine the relationships between cultivar, cultivation system, and social structure to understand how variations in the organization of food provisioning would have responded to socioecological change. Indeed, these variations suggest that taro and sweet potato cultivation systems experienced substantially different impacts from the sandalwood trade.

Cultivation Systems

Food was a child to be cared for, and it required great care.

—David Malo, *Hawaiian Antiquities*

Like Cook before him, Vancouver was repeatedly impressed by the state of agriculture on the islands. Unlike the haphazard mosaic of rotating cultivation in the East Indies, Sandwich Islands agriculture appeared highly organized to the Western eye, especially the sophisticated pond-field systems used for growing taro. The deliberate, interlocking patterns of flooded terraces and irrigation canals may have reminded early visitors of the "civilized" row monocultures of Europe and North America. Vancouver (1801, 366) writes of a trip into the interior of Oahu in 1791: "we found the land in a high state of cultivation, mostly under immediate crops of taro . . . The plains, however, if we may judge from the labour bestowed on their cultivation, seem to afford the principal proportion of the different vegetable productions on which the inhabitants depend for their subsistence." In his journal, the seasoned captain wrote with admiration of the canals and dams used to control water (Culliney 2006), the planning and preparation of fields, and the work ethic of cultivators who tended to their young plants for long hours, waist-deep in dark, fertile mud.

Early visitors had reason to be impressed. Hawaiian agriculture at the turn of the 19th century was intensive and productive, successfully supporting population densities that were unusual for the Pacific and high even by modern standards (Kagawa and Vitousek 2012). The irrigated systems used on the islands were the largest and most complex in all of Polynesia (Kirch 1994). Over the centuries, early settlers had succeeded in transforming the landscape to support the crops they carried with them: a pattern repeated throughout Polynesian expansion. In Hawaii, these systems were adapted and intensified, reaching unprecedented levels of productivity and supporting a population of around 300,000 by the time of Cook.[6]

Most authors (cf. Handy, Handy, and Pukui 1972; Ladefoged et al. 2009; Kagawa and Vitousek 2012) divide Island agriculture into two main types: irrigated and dryfield. Irrigated systems, like those that dominate the accounts of early explorers, involved complex arrangements of canals, aqueducts, and flooded fields to grow taro as a high-density monoculture. Dryfield (or rainfed) systems were implemented in places where irrigation was impossible but sufficient rainfall—and significant mulching—allowed seasonal harvests. Both irrigated and dryfield types were fixed-field, short-fallow systems; that is, nutrients were returned to the soil hydraulically (through the flow of water in an irrigated system), or by mulching and limited fallowing.[7]

The irrigated cultivation systems (*'āina wai*) that impressed early visitors may have been typical of Polynesia in their form but were unique in productivity and extent. By the time Kamehameha captured Oahu in 1795, visitors reported that the island was "a great prize, a flourishing island with well-stocked fish ponds on the lower plains and inside the reefs, and rich valleys planted in taro" (Daws 1968, 41). These large-scale, interconnected arrangements of canals, fields, and field-ponds were usually established along valley floors and coastal wetlands, primarily on the windward sides of geologically older islands like Kauai and Oahu where increased rainfall to windward established perennial rivers and broad valleys. On Kauai and Oahu, extensive irrigated agriculture could also be found on the leeward sides, in wide valleys with rivers fed by convectional montane precipitation. Out of necessity, these leeward systems exhibited some of the most ambitions irrigation schemes (Culliney 2006) to offset inconsistent lowland rainfall.

The most common cultivar in irrigated systems was taro. Floodable fields (*lo'i*) with high embankments were built alongside canals and sluices that moved water into and between fields. To protect the embankments from erosion, commoners planted sugarcane, bananas, and cabbage palm along the edges of fields as protective hedges (Kamakau 1992). As with wet rice cultivation in East and Southeast Asia, wet field taro demanded precise control over the timing and amount of water that is available to the crop. The variety of wet field taro used in Hawaii needed a nearly continuous supply of flowing water during its growing season, as stagnant water could lead to basal rot. The amount of water in each field had to vary during the plant's period of growth, from flooded, to dry, and back to flooded (Hommon 2013). To meet these demands, wet field taro could only be used in places with favorable topography and hydrology, usually along the bottom of gently sloping valleys. In any given location, these irrigated systems often expanded to fill the available space. Despite these limitations, it is estimated that wet taro cultivation covered more than 8000 hectares across all islands at its peak (Cho, Yamakawa, and Hollyer 2007).

Wet field taro cultivation placed high demand on labor during field preparation, planting, and harvesting. Kamakau (1992, 34–35) describes this process: Before planting, the field is flooded and "trampled out," a task that involves men, women, and children from multiple households "stirring the mud . . . dancing, rejoicing, shouting, panting, and making sport." Trampling helps to break up the topsoil and balance soil pH. The following day, taro cuttings are planted. These cuttings were selected from last season's crop based on the perceived vigor of each plant. When the planting is completed, fish are released into the field (in the case of a pond-field) and weeding begins. Once the taro plants start to grow, a prohibition (*kapu*) is placed on the field forbidding anyone from disturbing it until the taro is mature, a period of 9–18 months (under poor conditions it may take 3–4 years). Taro leaves turn yellow when mature, at which time the corms are visible above the surface. The harvesting of the field is accompanied by a feast that includes poi made from the taro, crops grown on the embankments, and pond fish (Kamakau 1992, 34–35).

As for labor, perhaps the single largest outlay of work involved building and maintaining the canals, terraces, and pond-fields—what Harold Brookfield (1984) calls "landesque capital." Landesque capital refers to "any investment in land with an anticipated life well beyond that of the present crop, or crop cycle" (Blaikie and Brookfield 1987, 9).[8] In this case, that includes the material modifications to terrestrial forms necessary to move, contain, and otherwise control water along with its nutrient and biological loads. For a system as extensive and complex as wet taro cultivation, the production of landesque capital factored prominently in labor calculations and required special arrangements for amassing and managing the workforce.

The production of landesque capital for irrigated cultivation can be divided into two categories: field construction (benefiting those households with rights to that field), and irrigation system construction (benefiting all households within the system). In both cases, labor was amassed from the larger community to support the project. Kamakau (1992) describes the process of field construction: Water is directed over the selected land for several days. Once the soil has softened, several hundred laborers are assembled along the edges of the field to begin construction of the retaining walls. Embankments are raised by excavating dirt and heaping it into a high mound along all edges of the field. The tops are leveled and the sides of the embankment that face the field are tamped down to increase water retention. Sugar cane stalks and coconut shells are pushed into the soil to reinforce the bank and improve erosion resistance, and the foundation of the wall is set with large stones. Workers then proceed to dig out and flatten the field, a process that "could take from a month to some years, depending on the size" (Kamakau 1992, 33–34). Pond-fields required the most time and labor due to their spatial extent. In fact, the biggest pond-fields belonged to kings and chiefs who had enough power to assemble the labor force necessary for construction and maintenance.

The design of each irrigation system was closely related to topography, the pattern of irrigated fields, and local politics. The construction of channels and dams had to be authorized by the king or by regional chiefs. For large-scale irrigation schemes, the authority for construction was ultimately bestowed on the chief who provided the most laborers: in fact, once completed, water within the system was distributed to each chief in a manner relative to their labor contribution (Morgan 1948). Thus, tenants of chiefs who provided fewer laborers would see their fields filled last and least, while tenants of chiefs who contributed many laborers would be the most protected from water shortages.

The steady expansion of Hawaiian irrigated cultivation between AD 1100 and 1650—particularly in the leeward valleys of the older islands—supported a period of population growth and environmental transformation unseen anywhere else in the Pacific (Culliney 2006). The administration of these irrigation systems was tightly integrated into a political hierarchy that managed the mobilization of labor and governed the distribution of resources. Karl Wittfogel (1957) uses the example of Hawaiian irrigation to support his now famous "hydraulic society" hypothesis in which he argues that societies dependent on irrigation require centralized coordination and authority, making them more likely to emerge as states.

The preeminence of Hawaii's irrigated systems would not last. Indeed, the extensive terraces, pond-fields, dams, and canals so admired by Vancouver's contemporaries were already at or past their peak by the time of European contact (Handy, Handy, and Pukui 1972). By 1820, outlays of labor for new landesque capital were low: new irrigation systems were no longer being constructed (Cho, Yamakawa, and Hollyer 2007) and decades of peace following the consolidation of the islands eliminated the need to rebuild agricultural infrastructure destroyed by war. But with the Hawaiian population in steady decline, the extensive irrigated systems that had supported settlement on the leeward islands for hundreds of years were set to experience a slow retreat. The trajectory for dryfield systems, by contrast, would be much more dramatic.

Wittfogel's (1957) inclusion of Hawaii in his hydraulic society hypothesis helped reinforce a long-standing "hydraulic bias" on the part of archeologists and anthropologists (Kirch 1994, 8). When compared to other forms of agriculture, the irrigated systems of Hawaii have received a disproportionate amount of attention, even though the work of Hawaiian scholars like Malo and Kamakau in the mid-19th century stressed the importance of dryfield systems (cf. Malo 1903; Kamakau 1961, 1992). Case in point: William Bryan's (1915) extensive manuscript, *Natural History of Hawaii, Being an Account of the Hawaiian People, the Geology and Geography of the Islands, and the Native and Introduced Plants and Animals of the Group*, dedicates five pages to taro production and only four sentences to sweet potato, with no description of how it is cultivated. This oversight is unfortunate given that these dryfield systems—unlike irrigated ones—existed nowhere else in Polynesia. As a subject of study, dryfield agriculture provides insight into unique forms of production particular to the intersection of Hawaiian society and environment (cf. Kirch and Zimmerer 2010; Kirch 2011).

Dryfield cultivation (ʻāina malo ʻo) was used in locations that lacked suitable valleys for irrigation and where rainfall was sufficient to support basic agriculture. The timing and amount of rainfall had to fit within tight constraints: too little and crops would not grow, too much and soil nutrients would be lost to leaching (Kagawa and Vitousek 2012). For the most part, these conditions tended to occur on the mesic, leeward slopes of the younger islands—Hawaiʻi and Maui. The primary dryfield cultivar was sweet potato, best grown below 900 meters on land that received between 750 and 1750 millimeters of rain a year (Hommon 2013). Growers used different varieties to distribute risk: fast maturing varieties could be ready for harvest 4–5 weeks after planting and were grown to protect against crop failure, while slow-maturing varieties tended to produce harder fruit that could keep for up to a year after harvest (Kamakau 1992). Dryfield varieties of taro were sometimes grown alongside sweet potato where soil fertility was high and annual rainfall exceeded 1270 millimeters (Hommon 2013), though Hopkins (1862, 36) observed that this "mountain taro" was considered less desirable than the varieties grown in the irrigated bottomlands.

In the last 50 years, extensive research in archeology and anthropology has attempted to reconstruct Hawaiian dryfield cultivation (Handy, Handy, and Pukui 1972; Kirch 1994; Ladefoged et al. 2009). Much of this effort has focused on the large-scale dryfield systems on the leeward side of Hawai'i, like the Kona Field System (KFS) and the Leeward Kohala Field System (LKFS). At their peak around the time of Cook's arrival, these systems were enormous: the KFS covered 21 square miles of rocky terrain on the southwestern slopes of Hawai'i, while the LKFS, located to the north near Waimea, covered 55 square miles. Archibald Menzies, naturalist and surgeon for Vancouver on HMS *Discovery*, remarked on the extent of dryfield cultivation above Kealakekua Bay: "For several miles around us there was not a spot that would admit of it but what was with great labor and industry cleared of loose stones and planted with esculent roots or some useful vegetables or other" (Menzies and Wilson 1920, 75). These enormous dryfield systems emerged around a "sweet spot" for rainfall and soil quality during a resurgence and expansion of Hawaiian agriculture around the 15th century (Hommon 2013, 71).

The KFS and LKFS involved an extensive matrix of fields extending up the leeward slopes. Each field was delineated with stone walls and bordered with sugarcane hedges to protect crops from wind, prevent sheet erosion during heavy rain events, and reduce evaporation (Hommon 2013). A key requirement of dryfield cultivation was managing soil moisture. To this end, considerable labor was dedicated to mulching the growing beds. There is evidence that cultivators used the abundant supply of loose stones as lithic mulch, spreading the stones in an even layer over the newly planted fields. Lithic mulch has been shown to reduce soil moisture loss by 50 percent and may have helped regulate soil temperature during periods of abundant sunshine (Hommon 2013). At the other moisture extreme, sweet potato is vulnerable to flooding: when heavy rainfall threatened to inundate fields, cultivators were forced to pull up the immature sweet potato in an effort to rescue some of the crop before it was destroyed by rot (Kamakau 1992).

The enormous extent of Hawaii's dryfield systems meant that farmers could take advantage of a continuum of growing conditions. In the KFS, farmers planted sweet potato in the lowest zone (0–150 meters), a region receiving 800–1300 millimeters of rain. At higher elevations (150–300 meters), breadfruit was added to sweet potato. Between 300 and 750 meters, an area that received up to 2000 millimeters of rain, dryland taro was added to sweet potato. Increasing rainfall gradients at higher elevations were more suitable for dry land taro than sweet potato, which was generally grown on lower and drier slopes. Bananas and plantains were planted in the highest fields and along the forest margin (600–900 meters), an area receiving upwards of 2000 millimeters of rain (Handy, Handy, and Pukui 1972). The variety of agroecological regions within the KFS and LKFS allowed the food provisioning system to distribute risk across cultivars and avoid wholesale collapse during times of environmental stress. After all, these leeward systems were the most prone to environmental variations and soil nutrient depletion (Hommon 2013).

Dryfield cultivation required high labor inputs for most of the growing season. Unlike wet taro, in which continuous inundation reduced competition from other plants, rainfed fields had to be constantly weeded. Once again, Kamakau (1992) provides the best description of dryfield sweet potato cultivation. Prior to the first winter rains, the field is prepared by stirring up the soil, spreading mulch, and removing weeds. The weeds are inspected to see if any of the leaves are torn or eaten—an indication of cutworms or other pests. If pests are active in the field, the farmer does not plant but fallows the field for a season. Planting of the sweet potato slips, sprouts, and old vines begins with the arrival of the first winter rains. As the potato plants form runners, the field is continuously maintained to prevent weed growth. With the arrival of sunny days, some farmers build nearby fires so that the smoke might shade their fields and prevent desiccation. After sufficient rain has fallen, dirt is mounded up over the young plants to prevent excessive drying. Between three and six months after planting, the potatoes are harvested and a feast is prepared to "honor all who had helped in the growing of the food" (Kamakau 1992, 27). The demand for labor throughout the growing season meant that in dryland areas of Hawai'i and Maui, both men and women performed agricultural work: on Kauai and Oahu where wet taro dominated, only men worked the fields.

Labor allocation varied depending on which agroecological zone was being cultivated. In the wet and fertile bottomlands (*palawai*), soil preparation and planting required less effort: high moisture content meant there was less need for mulching, though fields in these areas were more vulnerable to flooding (Kamakau 1992). These regions tended to produce more—and larger—produce. Kamakau (1992, 25) relates the story of "the great sweet potato of Hinauone" that "grew as large as a house, so that four men could sit within it and light an oven." Potatoes from this area were so big they were used as "rollers under their boats" (Kamakau 1992, 25).[9] Despite the productivity of palawai lands, they formed only a small part of the dryfield production systems that supported the majority of people on Hawai'i and Maui.

As for landesque capital, historians have generally discounted the labor involved in producing dryfield infrastructure. After all, the flat, rocky fields of dryfield systems did not leave quite the same impression on early visitors as the intricate network of valley terraces and canals used in irrigated lands. Nevertheless, extraordinary effort and labor organization was needed to clear vegetation, remove stones, build retaining walls, and distribute lithic mulch. The removal of stone alone would have been a monumental undertaking accomplished only through the mobilization of a large labor force: Hommon (2013) estimates that the construction of the KFS would have required the removal of 2.28 million metric tons of material.

By the time of European contact in 1778, the KFS and LKFS were the pinnacle of agricultural technology, helping Hawai'i sustain the largest population of any of the islands. As sedentary systems go, the short-fallow, mulched, and intercropped fields extracted remarkable potential from poor soils and fickle rains—conditions far less conducive to agriculture than the wet bottomlands of windward valleys. But by 1830, dryfield agriculture was in steep decline and the KFS and LKFS were in disrepair (Handy, Handy, and Pukui 1972). By contrast, irrigated cultivation continued well into the 20th century. Researchers have forwarded several theories to explain this conjuncture (cf. Cordy 1972), but the rapid disappearance of dryfield agriculture remains a mystery. The history of the sandalwood famines may offer insight, for it is during these events that Hawaiian agriculture encountered the one thing these stress-tolerant systems had never experienced: a shortage of labor.

The Two Systems Compared

Irrigated taro and dryfield sweet potato—the two most common arrangements of cultivar and production system—offer stark contrasts in productivity, food energy, and inputs of labor and land (table 1). The production estimates shown in this table are from Hommon (2013) and include data from Handy et al. (1972) and Ladefoged (2009). Where Hawaiian data was unavailable, figures are derived from other Polynesian sites in Vanuatu and the Solomon Islands.

At first glance, taro has distinct advantages over sweet potato. For example, irrigated taro is between 2.19 and 8.68 times more efficient in its use of labor at producing calories, and between 0.92 and 4.34 times more efficient in its use of land. Donne (1866, 62) comments on this high productivity: "The taro is so productive that, it is said, a square mile cultivated with it would keep fifteen thousand people in food the whole year through. You will find . . . that an average crop from a square mile of wheat will scarcely feed two thousand people for the same time." Morgan's (1948) economic analysis of Hawaiian agriculture makes a similar claim, though it is possible Morgan was using Donne's numbers as a guide. Hopkins (1862, 36) observes: "under diligent culture [irrigated taro] is so productive that it has been said, a taro pit a few yards in length will supply food for one man throughout the year." Taro responds better to short-term variations in rainfall (thanks to irrigation) and was preferred by taste. In fact, the preference for taro among the nobility suggests that in places with high potential for both taro and sweet potato, political influence may have encouraged taro cultivation over "common" sweet potato.

Taro's primary disadvantage is its long time to maturity: the loss of a single crop at the wrong time could delay harvesting by up to two years. In addition, taro cannot be kept as long as sweet potato after harvest, six weeks at most (Hommon 2013). This, coupled with long maturity times, meant that farmers needed to stagger planting across multiple fields, or risk long periods without harvest. Early observers recorded the frequent destruction of agricultural infrastructure during times of war, disrupting food production and initiating localized famine. It is

Table 1. Comparison of productivity, food energy, and labor inputs between irrigated taro and dryfield sweet potato cultivation.

	Taro (Irrigated)	Sweet potato (Dryfield)	Ratio (taro/sweet potato)
Crop yield (mt/ha), no fallow	25	5	5:1
Crop yield (mt/ha), 60% fallow	10	2	5:1
Food energy (kcal/mt)	1.12 million	0.86 million	1.3:1
Planting to maturity period (mo)	9–18	3–6	1.5:1 to 6:1
Productivity (mt/ha/mo)	0.56–1.11	0.33–0.67	1:1.2 to 3.36:1
Productivity (mt/ha/yr)	6.72–13.32	4–8	1:1.19 to 3.33:1
Food energy (kcal/mt/yr)	7.53–14.92 million	3.44–6.88 million	1.09:1 to 4.34:1
ACEs (ha/yr)	9.41–18.65	4.3–8.6	1.09:1 to 4.34:1
Work-days required (ha/yr)	435	870	1:2
Effort to supply one ACE (work-days)	23.3–46.2	101.2–202.3	1:2.19 to 1:8.68

Definitions: mt = metric tons; ha = hectare; kcal = kilocalories; mo = month; yr = year; ACE = Annual Caloric Equivalent (800,000 kcal)
Source: Hommon (2013)

reasonable to assume that famine resulting from war was more likely to happen under irrigated cultivation where infrastructure is directly exposed. The destruction of a large-scale pond-field system immediately before harvest would have had severe impacts on local food provisioning and placed considerable demands on a labor force recovering from war.

Sweet potato's primary advantage—the reason it could be cultivated on the leeward slopes without irrigation—is its ability to grow under less favorable rainfall and soil conditions. Sweet potato matures in one-third the time of taro and can be stored for longer periods without spoiling. The possibility of planting and harvesting a crop quickly, in makeshift conditions and with good storage potential, may have helped support temporary migration in the face of war or drought. These benefits come primarily at the cost of labor. As Malo (1903, 251) notes, "On the Kula [dry] lands farming was a laborious occupation and called for great patience, being attended with many drawbacks. On some of these were grubs, or caterpillars, or blight, *hauoki* [frost], or *hake* [flash floods], or the sun was too scorching; besides which there were many other hindrances." The additional labor costs of sweet potato were related to mulching, weeding, and mounding for moisture retention.

Irrigated and dryfield cultivation were suited to vastly different arrangements of topography, leeward/windward position, and age of terrain. Neither taro nor sweet potato could be adapted for planting above 800 meters; as a result, little attempt was made to establish settlements above that elevation. Taro and sweet potato may have occupied the same elevation range, but differences in rainfall between leeward and windward tended to separate agricultural strategies to different sides of the islands. Higher and more consistent rainfall to windward supported irrigated cultivation of taro, while drier conditions and greater variability along leeward slopes could only support agriculture under dryfield practices. Cultivation systems were also separated by island, a function of geologic age. The long, well-watered valleys that supported irrigated cultivation were primarily located on the older, western islands of Kauai and Oahu. To the east, the younger, shield topography of Hawai'i and Maui lacked deep valleys, providing few opportunities for irrigated systems.

Table 2 compares the difference in the area of high potential (HP) land for agriculture on each island. Overall, less than 10 percent of land on the islands had high potential for agriculture based on technologies of the period (Hommon 2013). But of this 10 percent, the stark contrast between western and eastern islands is made clear by comparing the percentage of HP land suitable for irrigation between Kauai (100 percent) and Hawai'i (2.7 percent). During the early archeological period, almost all irrigated cultivation—and, therefore, human settlement—was restricted to the windward sides of each island. As irrigation technologies improved during the period of agricultural expansion (approximately AD 1400–1700), large valley systems on the leeward sides of Kauai and Oahu were developed, expanding settlement to the southern and western shores of these islands. Frederick Beechey (1831, 231), captain of HMS *Blossom* on which Beckervaise was quartermaster, reported that from the vantage point of the heights, "extensive ranges of taro plantations are seen filling every valley," a sight that justifies Oahu being called the "garden of the Sandwich Islands." As irrigated agriculture flourished to the west, large-scale dryfield cultivation started to appear on Hawaii and Maui for the first time in Polynesia (Kirch 1994; Culliney 2006). The intensification and extensification of both dryfield and irrigated systems during this period supported growth in population and expansion of settlement across the islands.

Table 2. Comparison of high potential irrigated and dryfield land by major island.

Island	Total area	HP area (% of total)	Irrigated HP area (% of HP)	Dryfield HP area (% of HP)
Kauai	1,431	57.6 (4.0%)	**57.6 (100.0%)**	0.0 (0%)
Oahu	1,547	120.6 (7.8%)	86.5 (71.7%)	34.1 (28.3%)
Molokai	674	36.0 (5.3%)	9.5 (26.4%)	26.5 (73.6%)
Maui	1,884	167.5 (8.9%)	28.1 (16.8%)	139.4 (83.2%)
Hawai'i	10,433	572.0 (5.5%)	15.4 (2.7%)	**556.6 (97.3%)**

Definition: HP = high potential
Note: All values are in square kilometers. Highest HP percentages for each cultivation type shown in bold.
Source: Hommon (2013)

Division of Land

Hawaii's ancient system of land division—like its politics—was hierarchically organized. From the entire island chain down to the estate, units of land were associated with a corresponding political authority (table 3). Before the consolidation of the islands under Kamehameha around 1810, each island (*mokopuni*) was ruled by a separate king.[10] After consolidation, Kamehameha was declared king and each island was assigned a governor who reported to him (Morgan 1948). In a fitting reflection on the subsistence origin of all land division, the Hawaiian word for governor was *ali'i ai moku*, literally "the chief who eats the island" (Culliney 2006). Islands were divided into several pie-shaped districts (*moku*) with the apex of the pie at the highest point in the interior. This arrangement ensured that each district was an ecological transect; that is, it had access to the full continuum of ecological zones from coastal to alpine.

Districts were divided into several *ahupua'a*, each ruled by a single chief. As a way to link administrative authority to environmental outcomes, the ahupua'a was a socioecological unit uniquely suited to Hawaii. Extending inland from the coast, each ahupua'a enclosed a range of ecological zones, including swampy bottomlands, grassy plains, forested highlands and—in places—rocky montane landscapes. Outwards from the shore, inhabitants of an ahupua'a claimed rights to all fish and marine products from the inshore, pelagic, and benthic zones. This division of land ensured that each ahupua'a had access to the environmental resources necessary for a diverse economy: rainfall and soil regimes, sources of food, and forested environments for craft production (Hommon 2013). In a few instances,

Table 3. System of land division and political organization.

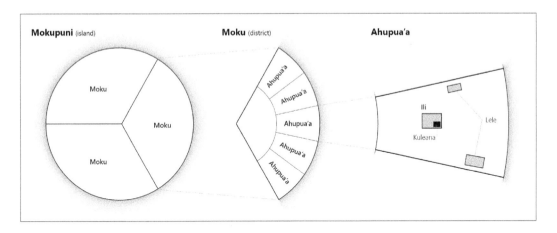

Unit	Description	Authority
Mokupuni	Island	King (or governor by 1810)
Moku	District—largest division of an island	No specific authority Overseen by king and chiefs
Ahupua'a	Subdivision of a district, usually along watershed boundaries	Chief, sometimes with an appointed *konohiki*
Ili	Estate—land and associated households of the chief	Chief
Lele	Noncontinuous tract of land associated with an estate	Chief
Kuleana	Peasant holding (farm)	– – – –

the production of specialized items like stone adzes (quarried on Hawai'i) and canoes (dependent on *koa* trees) was limited to specific places (Morgan 1948). Such specializations formed the basis of trade between districts and islands. For the most part, ahupua'a did not extend inland to the apex of each district; rather, the higher elevations of each district were set aside for the use of the king (Morgan 1948). Given the inability to grow staple crops above 800 meters, there would have been less interest in establishing settlement or competing for resources at these elevations.

For the most part, ahupua'a were established to provide inhabitants with the greatest opportunity for self-sufficiency. The borders between ahupua'a generally followed watershed boundaries, allowing water-dependent activities downstream to maintain control over their sources. The growth of large-scale irrigation schemes in the western islands was perfectly suited to this form of land division: each system could be contained entirely within a single ahupua'a and managed by a single ruling chief with authority over the flow of water from forest to coastal fishponds (Kagawa and Vitousek 2012). In places more suited to dryfield cultivation, the vertical strips of land characteristic of ahupua'a provided opportunities to grow a diverse array of crops at different elevations and at different times of the year (Kagawa and Vitousek 2012). However, in and around the large dryfield systems of leeward Hawai'i, it seems that ahupua'a may have been defined with greater flexibility: after all, the Kona Field System spanned more than 40 ahupua'a (Hommon 2013). To assemble the labor for field construction would have required a degree of coordination between chiefs that was not necessary with irrigated systems (Kagawa and Vitousek 2012).

In determining the absolute size of each ahupua'a, the king generally sought to divide productive capacity evenly. To simplify taxation and reduce competition between chiefs, kings divided districts into units that had roughly similar populations and productive resources. This principle of even division resulted in smaller ahupua'a to windward (where higher rainfall produced greater resources) and larger ahupua'a to leeward. By the 18th century, ahupua'a ranged in size from 40 to 40,000 hectares depending on the island and the productive capacity of the local environment (Morgan 1948). Of course, the principle of even division was not always obeyed: ahupua'a boundaries had to conform not only to landforms but also to the contours of nobility politics (Kagawa and Vitousek 2012). Nevertheless, there was strong incentive for kings to maintain relative balance between chiefs to weaken any threats to the throne. To this end, the careful adjustment of political influence through boundary making was key to maintaining power. Indeed, the importance of the ahupua'a as a political-ecological unit ensured that boundaries were "definitely marked, well-understood, and permanent" (Ellis 1826, 352).

Within each ahupua'a, chiefs established estates (ili), each of which comprised one or more tracts of land (lele) (Morgan 1948). Usually, estates were fiefs of the chief that ruled the ahupua'a; however, in some cases estates were claimed by the king (ili kuponos) and kept as a reminder of the absolute authority of the monarch. These royal estates held no allegiance to the chief, paid dues only to the royal family, and were not affected by changes to the political leadership of the ahupua'a. As a result, the small number of commoners fortunate enough to work on royal estates enjoyed some degree of security over their counterparts.

Each estate comprised multiple *kuleana*, or tenant's holdings—the basic unit of land tenure for commoners. Morgan (1948, 21) defines kuleana as the "functional unit of soil cultivation, corresponding to the peasant's holding in Europe." Within irrigated cultivation, a kuleana may have included one or more pond-fields or terraces, depending on size. In the case of dryfield cultivation, a kuleana might range from 2.5 to 5 hectares depending on environmental conditions, in particular, the fallowing time needed to replenish soil fertility (Lyons 1875). Households usually clustered in small settlements around the numerous kuleana that comprised the chief's estate (Cordy 1972).

Land tenure was assigned by the ruling chiefs to commoners on the basis of birthright (Kamakau 1992). The right to use land and extract its resources was granted to commoners on the condition that taxes were paid and households obeyed calls for labor to build landesque capital or wage war (Morgan 1948). As with other feudal systems, land was inherited from parents: it was the obligation of chiefs and their administrators to memorize the boundaries of all estates and kuleana within the ahupua'a for the purpose of assessing taxes and assembling labor (Cordy 1972). Ultimately, the customary relationships that guaranteed tenants the right to land depended on the whims of the ruling chief. However, long-standing religious and political practices helped mitigate chiefly excesses and served as a corrective for flagrant violations of custom.

The chiefs who ruled each ahupua'a were appointed by the king and had authority to manage infrastructural projects, collect taxes, conscript labor, and wage war. In some instances, administrative tasks like tax collection were delegated to a land manager (*konohiki*). It was customary for konohiki to establish bonds of trust with commoners by marrying into one of the commoner households and cultivating ahupua'a land—what Cordy (1972, 397) calls a "kinship bridge." As tax assessors, konohiki were responsible for fixing the amount of tax for each land division, with larger, more productive divisions paying greater tax than smaller, less productive ones (Kamakau 1961). To accomplish this, konohiki had to have an extensive—and long-standing—knowledge of the production capacity in each land division, along with a rough census of the division's population (Hommon 2013).

Commoners paid taxes to their immediate chiefs, who paid a percentage of their take to higher chiefs, on up to the king. Commoners paid their taxes yearly with crafts, food, livestock, and other extracted resources: "*tapasi* [cloth], skirts, loin cloths, swine, dogs, chickens, mats, *olona* fiber, nets, fish lines, 'o'o and *mamo* feathers, and pearls" (Kamakau 1961, 177). The actual amount paid by any household was ultimately determined by the konohiki, but over time, certain quantities came to be broadly recognized as "normal" amounts for a specific area. In addition to taxes, "gifts" to the chief were expected at times during the year, notably the first harvest or first take of fish during the season (Jarves 1843). According to Morgan's (1948) estimates, commoners retained one-third of their produce on average, with two-thirds going to the chiefs in the form of gifts and taxes.

Every year, the taxes collected from each ahupua'a were presented to the royal court where the lot was tallied and redistributed back down the hierarchy of chiefs (Sahlins 1990). If the take from any given ahupua'a was not deemed acceptable, chiefs could order that the ahupua'a be raided until enough material had been amassed to satisfy the leadership. Hawaiian kings built large storehouses to contain the yearly tribute while it was being tallied and sorted (Hommon 2013). Over time, these storehouses came to hold vast assortments of items that were paid to the king as tax but never used. This practice of hoarding tribute would play a central role in the growth of conspicuous consumption during the sandalwood trade.

This system of taxation existed in the same basic form across all islands, with one key distinction. On Hawaii and Maui where dryfield cultivation dominated, both sexes participated in agricultural labor. As a result, the chiefs and konohiki of Hawaii and Maui, when calculating the expected tribute from each kuleana, imposed taxes on both men and women. By contrast, under the irrigated systems of the eastern islands, women were forbidden from doing agricultural work and were not taxed. Kamakau (1992) claims that this custom of taxing women earned Hawai'ian chiefs a reputation for being oppressive—a sentiment that is hard to dispute. After all, if Hommon's (2013) labor calculations are right, adding women to the agricultural labor pool appears to have been a *requirement* of dryfield cultivation, not a convenient way for households to amass wealth.

Other than taxes, the primary imposition placed on commoners was the requisition of labor. In the event of war, chiefs could conscript both men and women to serve as soldiers. Under peaceful circumstances, chiefs demanded that commoners work one day out of five on the chief's fields as part of their rent. When there was need for workers to build infrastructure, support ceremonial practices, or otherwise satisfy the needs of the nobility, *corvée* labor could be summoned immediately and arbitrarily.

Social and Political Organization

Hawaii's different cultivation systems influenced the emergence of distinct political economies and forms of social organization—after all, irrigated and dryfield agricultural regimes required "different sets of technologies, knowledge, skills, and strategies" (Hommon 2013, 61). Accompanying these differences in production were political tensions between islands, and between districts of the same island—a nearly continuous state of conflict well documented in other parts of Polynesia (Kirch 2011).

Of the two dominant cultivation systems, Kirch (2011, 10) finds that the most hierarchical and "hegemonic" polities were those centered around dryfield cultivation, not irrigation. Such a finding tends to dispute Wittfogel's (1957) hydraulic society hypothesis, that the demands of irrigated cultivation established the basis for state-like political hierarchies. In Hawaii, at least, the idealized, state-like chiefdoms were dryfield, not irrigated. On the island of Hawai'i, where dryfield cultivation proliferated, polities were vulnerable to both internal discord and invading neighbors (Kirch 2011). Political relationships and practices were characterized by competition between chiefs—conflicts that Sahlins (1967) attributes to competition for labor. Ultimately, such conflicts did not alter the organization of government; instead, leaders were replaced, new administrators appointed, and the relationship between nobles and commoners resumed unchanged. Following Sahlins's (1967) labor thesis, one could argue that irrigated systems were less expansionist because large-scale outlays of labor were intermittent and rare: the greatest need for labor occurred during the production of landesque capital, which happened rarely (on a large scale) and generally did not require access to resources outside of the ahupua'a.

On most of the islands, commoners and chiefs were generally sedentary. But in Hawai'i, it was common for chiefs and some attendant commoners to travel for work. A culture organized around travel, whether for work or military expansion, would derive significant benefit from sweet potato cultivation. Taro spoils soon after harvest and must be eaten quickly, discouraging storage and transportation. At best, hard (desiccated) poi will keep for up to six weeks. Sweet potato, on the other hand, can be stored for longer periods and is more convenient to transport, supporting what Kirch (1994, 14) calls a "magazine economy" in Maui and Hawai'i in which people moved between locales for work and brought staples with them. Wet taro solves the storage problem through year-round cultivation, enabled by irrigation. Year-round cultivation encourages labor to stay in place.

Most analysts describe the relationship between environment, agricultural system, and sociopolitical form as a causal progression: environmental conditions drive cultivation decisions which, in turn, make certain forms of social organization and patterns of settlement more useful, obvious, or necessary than others (cf. Wittfogel 1957; Sahlins 1967; Kirch 1994). In all likelihood, this relationship is less deterministic than assumed. The evolution of Hawaiian agriculture suggests that cultivation systems and sociopolitical forms are mutually reproducing: cultivar ecology may have shaped differences in local political economy, but political economy also influenced the selection of cultivars. In fact, it is reasonable to assume that early settlement on the islands would have experimented with diverse combinations of cultivars and agricultural techniques across a range of environments. Only later did political-ecological feedback help drive the profound spatial differences between eastern and western islands.

The organization of Polynesian societies has been a long-standing subject of interest to anthropologists, one based in part on the perception that these societies represent the idealized political "chiefdom." Many anthropologists (cf. Sahlins 1967; Goldman 1970) consider Hawaii to be one of "Polynesia's most highly stratified, intensely competitive chiefdoms" (Kirch 1994, 251). As such, considerable scholarship has addressed the organization and operation of the political hierarchy, while less work has addressed the material basis for this hierarchy, both ecologically and economically.

The Hawaiian noble class was divided into three "orders": (1) kings, queens, members of the royal family, and chief advisors not of royal birth; (2) governors of islands and chiefs of large ahupua'a; and (3) lesser lords, priests, and other estate-holders (Jarves 1843, 36–37). The king had absolute authority and could take anyone's life and property at any time. By 1810, King Kamehameha had expanded the power of his throne to include all the islands. The authority of the monarch was then delegated to island governors and lesser chiefs on down the line. Chiefs had nearly absolute authority over their own subjects, including the taking of life and dispossession of property. However, those accused of capital offenses by their chief could appeal to the king for leniency. No chief could exert authority over another chief's subjects—for example, requisitioning their labor—unless the chiefs had reached an agreement. The everyday, administrative functions of government were executed by the chief's attendants, many of whom were personal friends or relations and formed the chief's full-time entourage.

As with other feudal arrangements, commoners were considered "attached to the soil" and were "transferred with the land" in the event that a chief died or was overthrown (Jarves 1843, 37). For commoners, everyday life was conducted within the constraints of numerous prohibitions, a fluid legal landscape shaped by both long-standing customary practice and the whims of the current leader. Ellis (1826) notes that the quality of life experienced by commoners depended in large part on the personality of the king, whose character tended to permeate the political hierarchy.

Kapu System

The English word *taboo* comes from the Polynesian word *tapu* meaning "forbidden." Early visitors to the Hawaiian Islands transliterated *tapu* as "kapu." Here, *kapu* was used to denote behaviors and things that were reserved for spiritual purposes and forbidden from use. In practice, kapu amounted to codes of conduct that governed everything from what foods could be eaten to the way water was distributed from a shared canal. The kapu system regulated the interactions of all Hawaiians regardless of class, an extensive system of social practice that was "penetrating and complete" (Jarves 1843, 56). Daws (1968, 54) offers this description: "*kapu* pervaded all of life—politics, religious worship, sex, landholding, the cultivation and eating of food, even play. It was a fixed principle, always there, just as shadow was an inevitable part of a sunlit day. To step into the shadow to violate the *kapus*, even accidentally, was to forfeit the right to live."

The kapu system was administered by the priesthood, a social class with broad authority to establish or suspend prohibitions on essentially any object or behavior (Jarves 1843). In this regard, the priesthood wielded considerable power: priests owned estates and subjects, received rents and taxes, and worked alongside chiefs (Hommon 2013). Many chiefs had "family priests" responsible for protecting the connection between divine and mortal authorities. Priests often acted as judges tasked with resolving disputes, though Jarves (1843, 39) notes that the execution of justice was more "sorcery and witchcraft" than any reflection on the concerns of the disputants: "the religion of the Hawaiians . . . was rather a system of worldly despotism, better calculated to perpetuate the power of the priests, than to direct the ideas of the people to concerns of eternal interest" (Jarves 1843, 41). His negativity is understandable given his position: as a missionary, Jarves saw Hawaiian idols and "superstitions" as a manifestation of the evil he had been sent to cast out. Later historians, particularly those writing in the 20th century, would take a different view, finding in the kapu system a corrective to chiefly excesses.

The kapu system placed constraints on everyday life well beyond labor, food, and cooking. Men and women were not allowed to eat together or sleep under the same roof. Temporary ("common") restrictions were often placed on specific activities—such as fishing or hunting—for a period of time. "Strict" kapus, like those declared to commemorate the end of each year, required all people to pray, abstain from productive activities, and remain completely silent. Jarves (1843, 58) notes that under strict kapus, animals were corralled and dogs' mouths were tied shut to prevent them from barking. The kapu system was used to regulate the distribution of water from irrigation canals, define the terms under which goods and services could be bartered, and establish how damages would be remediated and how criminals were to be punished. In this regard, kapu functioned as both a religious framework and a system of common law. Punishments ranged from light fines to banishment or death. In the event that a commoner stole property from a chief, the thief was to be "bound hand and foot, put in a 'decayed' canoe, and set adrift" (Jarves 1843, 34). Several early authors mention the use of human sacrifice in kapu practice (Ellis 1826; Jarves 1843; Hopkins 1862; Donne 1866). But it is not clear whether this constituted religious ritual, legal practice, or a combination of both.

With respect to food provisioning, the kapu system was a mixed bag. On the one hand, prohibitions against labor and restrictions on consumption may have exacerbated food stress during shortages. On the other, kapu not only helped to curb excesses and regulate extractive demands, but provided opportunities for both formal and informal redistribution of material from chiefs to commoners—a form of moral economy (see Scott 1976).

As a buffer against chiefly impositions, the kapu system codified land tenure, personal security, the right of property, and the right to barter. With few exceptions, chiefs did not infringe on these provisions (Jarves 1843). Those who did risked alienation from both their subjects and fellow chiefs. For example, chiefs rarely exercised the right to arbitrarily dispossess commoners from the land. In his letter to Captain Wilkes, William Richards (March 15, 1841, 16–17) notes that "it was considered improper to eject the direct cultivators of the land and hence it was often the case that all the different ranks of chiefs were dispossessed, while the last dependents, the cultivaters [sic] of the soil, were continued in their possessions." Even though commoners were considered "attached to the soil" and, therein, attached to their chief, under conditions of severe oppression commoners retained the right to move to a different ahupua'a. In fact, the kapu system maintained a long tradition of welcoming and supporting these migrant commoners in their new home (Morgan 1948). Finally, the kapu system established safe, "retreat villages" (*pahonua*) in which criminals and noncombatants escaping war could find protection (Jarves 1843, 58). It is not clear what happened to the pahonua: by the 1830s the only mention of these retreat villages is as a precontact custom.

Perhaps the most significant practice of material exchange—other than taxation—was *Makahiki*, a series of festivals commemorating the end of the year and coinciding with the payment of tribute. Makahiki celebrations lasted for seven days during which time warfare was suspended across all the islands (Kamakau 1961; Hommon 2013). The festivals combined both ceremonial and practical purposes, reinforcing numerous reciprocal relations within the chiefdom and between chiefs and commoners. For the common people, these festivals offered food and entertainment, including "ceremonies, dancing, sporting events, and gambling" (Hommon 2013). Food was provided by the chiefs from collected taxes. Most importantly, the festivals offered a reprieve from work thanks to a kapu placed on all forms of labor, requisitioned or otherwise (Kamakau 1961). For the king and chiefs, Makahiki offered several administrative benefits. Hommon (2013, 100) describes how the festival cycle could "enable a Hawaiian ruler to . . . collect information on the economic resources of the kingdom, apply an equitable regularly scheduled system of revenue collection, plan information-based government policy, engender loyalty in government officials through the distribution of tax receipts, and encourage group solidarity among the people in general."

Beyond the provisions of the kapu system, long-standing cultural practices helped normalize exchange between commoners, and reduced household risk during times of stress. Early writers noted the Hawaiian tradition of hospitality to household visitors (Hopkins 1862). It was commonplace to exchange gifts, including food. Visiting relatives could expect to be fed and housed indefinitely, a practice that helped ensure survival during times of localized production failure. As noted in other agrarian contexts during this period, these informal practices of exchange were symbols of affinity, helping to reinforce social cohesion even as they materially kept bodies alive (Scott 1976).

That night in 1827, as Beckervaise watched the sandalwood cutters spread out into the forest, he witnessed the performance of a long-standing tradition: the requisition of labor by chiefs. Failure to respond to their call could have had severe consequences for one's health and well-being. This tradition of labor conscription profoundly influenced the islands: it was responsible for the expansive dryfield systems on Hawai'i and the pond-fields of Oahu that so impressed early visitors. Conscription had enabled Kamehameha to assemble an army capable of unification. But behind the scenes and beyond Beckervaise's view, the bonds of reciprocity that linked chiefs to laborers were missing. Indeed, by 1820, the parts of the kapu system that had explicitly countered the excesses of the nobility were in full collapse.

Natural Resources

Abundant firewood was needed to prepare the primary staples of Hawaii. According to kapu, every male adult was responsible for collecting enough wood each day to fuel two ovens. Hommon (2013) estimates that a family of six, under this requirement, would have consumed 10 kilograms of wood per oven every three days, or 2.4 metric tons per household per year. At the scale of an average ahupua'a on Hawai'i, this consumption would amount to approximately 244 metric tons per year, or 104,000 metric tons for the entire island (Hommon 2013, 53). Early visitors noted that Hawaiians did not travel long distances for wood: most firewood was collected from a band of low scrub that ringed each island and extended 6–8 kilometers inland from the shore. Extractive pressure in this zone may have been significant, particularly in areas with high population density. In 1779, Cook's surgeon noted that all of the trees along Molokai's shoreline had been cut (Culliney 2006). Ironically, it would be sandalwood—a tree that is useless for cooking—that would form the basis of Hawaii's first natural resource boom.

In addition to firewood, clearing was undertaken for other forms of production: fires were sometimes set to clear foliage and encourage the growth of grasses for house thatching, or ferns and arrowroot for pig fodder (Hommon 2013). The removal of trees at lower elevations would have increased desiccation, erosion, and topsoil loss, negatively impacting soil quality in the ideal zone for dryfield cultivation of sweet potato: the palawai bottomlands. By contrast, irrigated cultivation, though vulnerable to deforestation in the watershed above a pond-field system, would have experienced *less* impact from lowland deforestation due to its reliance on flowing water for nutrient transport. As such, the steady deterioration in soil quality across islands—well underway by 1800—is a conjunctural process that could have affected irrigated and dryfield cultivation to varying degrees and helped solidify different trajectories for the eastern and western islands.

Culliney (2006) and Kirch (1994) argue that Hawaiian agriculture had reached its peak shortly before the arrival of Cook in 1778. Kirch (1994, 255) refers to the vast dryfield complexes on Hawai'i as the developmental "endpoint of the process of short-fallow intensification." Many of the systems constructed during the previous 200 years of agricultural expansion had reached ecological carrying capacity, leading some archeologists to speculate that Hawaii's population was in decline before the arrival of Western diseases (Culliney 2006).[11] If these authors are correct, the sandalwood-related crises took place immediately following the period of greatest agricultural extent, diversity, and intensification. At first glance, the islands' food provisioning system should have been highly productive; after all, warfare had come to an end and population pressure was in decline. Agricultural extensification had peaked, reducing demands on conscripted labor for landesque capital. A decrease in population would have reduced total labor, but this decline would have accompanied a similar reduction in caloric demands per hectare. With less demand per hectare, cultivators could have switched to longer fallow times, helping to replenish soil resources.

How, then, can we account for the food crises that emerge between 1811 and 1830? Part of the answer will come from the historical record and the conjunctures influencing agricultural production. The other, from the distinct spatial distribution of wet and dry cultivation and its accompanying polities.

Transformation: 1778–1827

We were charmed with its appearance as we came near it, observing it to abound with rivers, and to exhibit a prospect so full of plenty, that we anticipated the pleasure we expected, by supposing ourselves already in possession of a most seasonable supply. We had been for several days reduced to the scanty allowance of a quart of water a day . . . and now that we saw whole rivers before us, our hearts were dilated with joy; yet we had still much to suffer.

—Officer John Rickman, on seeing the island of Kauai for the first time, January 20, 1778, *Journal of Captain Cook's Last Voyage to the Pacific Ocean*

In his comprehensive journal, John Rickman—an officer on Captain Cook's third voyage to the Pacific—relates the exhilaration of finding land. The day before, the parched crew had been battered by a severe storm, only to emerge from it within eight leagues of an island brimming with water. But Rickman's account of this moment is replete with trepidation and fear. Would the natives be friendly? The first Islanders to paddle out to the British ships *Discovery* and *Resolution* behaved with "great civility," bearing plantains, dried fish, and pigs (Rickman 1781, 216). But matters quickly turned. The next day, one of Cook's lieutenants shot an Islander dead during a quarrel. A year later on Hawai'i, Cook himself would be killed along with some of his crew.

We have no record of what was going through the minds of those Hawaiians who paddled out to meet Cook for the first time, but it would be little surprise if they shared Rickman's sense of excitement, wonder, and trepidation. After all, their storm was about to begin.

Cook, Vancouver, and Early Visitors

The first encounters between Hawaiians and early explorers had mixed success. During Cook's time on the islands (in early 1778 and again in early 1779) he encountered hospitality and hostility. He and his crew returned both in equal measure. Cook was impressed with the level of interest in trade: Islanders readily approached the British with fruits, vegetables, and pigs in exchange for bits of iron, nails, and other trinkets (Jarves 1843). Wherever the expedition sailed in the archipelago, canoes from nearby villages came out to greet the ships and some, mostly chiefs, were welcomed on board. But local curiosity with the newcomers quickly turned oppressive. Cook and his crew became increasingly concerned with the occasional theft of items from their ships. Their attempts to

44

correct these "injustices" frequently brought the crew into direct conflict with local chiefs. At times, Cook and his crew seemed less concerned with returning stolen property than educating a savage population on the proper behavior of civilized people—a paternalism that cultivated hostility. In February 1779, while anchored off Kealakekua Bay, Hawai'i, Cook attempted to recover a small boat that had been stolen from the expedition. When he failed to locate it, Cook decided to kidnap the king, Kalani'ōpu'u, and hold him for ransom until the boat was returned. But in his attempt to spirit the hostage to the ship, Cook and his retinue were confronted by a large crowd at the shore. A skirmish ensued and Cook, along with four of his crew, were killed (Rickman 1781).

One of the surviving crew members, George Vancouver, would lead his own expedition to the North Pacific and the Sandwich Islands 11 years later. By the time of his return, several European and American ships had visited the islands. Tensions between Islanders and foreign crews had increased, with repeated thefts, kidnappings, and massacres. With expanded contact came expanded trade: visitors during this period admired how quickly the Islanders took to the business of exchange (Morgan 1948). Indeed, despite the growing pains of first contact, early visitors to the islands generally succeeded in their objective, namely, to create opportunities for future trade. For British expeditions sailing under the orders of King George III, these objectives included laying the groundwork for territorial accession. But of all the changes in the decade since Cook, perhaps the most important was the emergence of a new, powerful chief on Hawai'i—one who would use Vancouver and foreign trade to achieve his dreams of conquest.

King Kamehameha: Foreign Allegiance, Conquest, and Consolidation

For the ambitious Kamehameha, the arrival of British explorers like Vancouver could not have been more perfectly timed. Vancouver landed on Hawai'i in 1792 as Kamehameha was consolidating his control over the island and making plans to attack the islands to the west. The two leaders became quick friends: for Vancouver's part, he sought to repair some of the damage done since Cook's fatal visit and work to convince Islanders that the intentions of the British were peaceful. For Kamehameha, he saw in Vancouver a powerful ally. The two leaders shared one important goal: both wanted to see the islands unified under a single leader. For Kamehameha, conquering all the islands would make him the greatest king in Hawaiian history and prove the superiority of his chiefly line. For Vancouver, a unified archipelago would simplify royal accession of the territory by establishing a single authority: by the late 1700s, the British strongly preferred dealing with a government or monarch over a morass of frustrated warlords. In 1792, in exchange for British support for his island conquest, Kamehameha agreed to grant possession of the islands to King George III. The support that Kamehameha needed most took the form of military advisors, firearms, and—eventually—ships.

Kamehameha's close ties with the British not only provided the material basis for his westward conquest, they served to isolate other chiefs who had been vying for foreign alliances (Daws 1968). As Kamehameha's influence grew, he ratcheted up the pressure on foreign merchants, making it kapu for Islanders to exchange goods with traders unless they received weapons in return. For their part, traders were desperate for provisions and few had qualms about providing muskets to warring neighbors (Daws 1968). Kamehameha's influence with foreigners earned him the respect not only of chiefs and subjects but also of the small group of foreigners that lived on the islands and served as the new king's advisors (Jarves 1843).

Supported by foreigners and guns, Kamehameha moved his armies west through Maui and Molokai before capturing Oahu in 1796. Pushing the advantage, the invigorated king immediately set sail for Kauai—the last major island to the west—but was forced to turn back after his fleet was nearly destroyed in a storm (Jarves 1843). Over the next eight years, Kamehameha prepared for another assault on Kauai, enlisting carpenters to build 800 *peleleu* (double-hulled) canoes. By 1804 he had amassed 5000 men and was about to leave for Kauai when "an epidemic broke out . . . of a peculiar character," killing much of Kamehameha's army (Jarves 1843, 191). Daws (1968) speculates that the epidemic may have been cholera or typhoid. Though the king survived, he made no other attempts to capture Kauai. Over the next several years, Kamehameha and the king of Kauai (Kaumaulii) reached an agreement wherein Kaumaulii would retain control of the island but as Kamehameha's vassal, effectively granting Kamehameha absolute authority over the entire island chain.

The period of conquest between 1780 and 1796 had been bloody. Bingham (1855, 49) writes, "It is supposed that some six thousand of the followers of this chieftain [Kamehameha], and twice that number of his opposers, fell in battle during his career, and by famine and distress occasioned by his wars and devastations." For the first time in Hawaiian warfare, firearms had been widely used, a development that hastened victory but greatly increased the bloodshed. The accession of Kauai to Kamehameha by 1810 brought large-scale warfare on the islands to an end.

With all the major islands under his control, Kamehameha set about reorganizing the government and improving infrastructure. He appointed his most trusted chiefs as governors, who then distributed the ahupua'a to their favored chiefs on down the political hierarchy to the level of individual estates (Morgan 1948). To assist with the communication of law and policy, the king created a network of expert canoers tasked with traveling regularly between islands (Daws 1968)—a state function that had not been necessary before consolidation. Finally, he turned his attention to agriculture, amassing labor "to work terracing hills, banking up taro patches, digging long irrigation ditches, and building fishponds," projects that helped cement his reputation with the common people (Potter, Kasdon, and

Rayson 2003, 23). Stories were told of Kamehameha regularly joining commoners in the muddy, flooded fields to help with the harvest (Kamakau 1961).

Kamehameha died on May 8, 1819, in Kailua, Hawai'i, in the company of his family. His impressive military career earned him the nickname "Napoleon of the Pacific" (Jarves 1843, 206), but it was his approach to governance for which he is most remembered. He was widely admired by his own subjects for establishing substantive peace, eliminating oppressive chiefs, and bringing a more just and stable character to the political hierarchy. He was admired by foreign traders and diplomats for creating a form of centralized government that was rational to Western economic interests, even though this government was wholly different than the Western ones with which it was aligned. Most importantly, Kamehameha helped protect long-standing practices of food provisioning from an array of mounting challenges, ones that were arriving in greater numbers with each foreign ship.

The Pacific Trade

By the time Kamehameha died, commerce between North America, Hawaii, and China was in full swing. Like its counterpart in the Atlantic, the so-called Pacific Trade was propelled by growth in demand for both natural commodities and manufactured goods (Porter 1930, 500). What started as an exchange of fur between the northwest coast of North America and Canton quickly expanded to include major ports in Europe and the eastern seaboard of the United States, with growing demand for goods of Chinese manufacture. The inclusion of Hawaii on nautical charts after 1779 brought merchants and whalers to the islands. At first, ship captains found Hawaii a convenient place to acquire provisions (including fruits and vegetables to ward off scurvy), rest weary crews, and refit ships. But by 1810, Hawaii had become a place of trade in its own right. Merchants were arriving in increasing numbers to sell various items of western manufacture in exchange for sandalwood. Sandalwood was not the basis of the Pacific Trade, but a commodity that could be conveniently added to the portfolio of commerce for trading houses in New York, Boston, and London (Porter 1930).

Kenneth Porter (1930), an economic historian who studied the trading patterns of New York's merchant houses, describes the sequence of trade. Ships arrived in Hawaii laden with manufactured goods from North America and Europe. These goods were sold to chiefs in exchange for promises of sandalwood that had yet to be cut. While the sandalwood was being collected, the ships left Hawaii for the Pacific Northwest to purchase beaver and otter furs. With half a hold full of furs, the ships returned to Hawaii to load the consignment of sandalwood. Now laden with fur and sandalwood, ships set sail for Canton, Macau, and other Chinese ports. Proceeds from the sale of these luxuries went directly to the purchase of Chinese porcelain, tea, rice, and other commodities. From China, ships returned to Europe or the U.S. East Coast to sell Chinese goods and purchase

Western manufactured items, completing the cycle. When timed correctly, crews could take advantage of the northeast trade winds, avoid stormy weather in the Pacific Northwest, and ride out the winter in the comfort of a Hawaiian port town. As the trade expanded, voyages out of Boston increased from one year to over three years at sea (Morgan 1948).

Traders exchanged an impressive assortment of products. Hawaiian chiefs traded sandalwood for everything from flour, rice, and olive oil to schooners. In fact, Kamehameha acquired six ships through the sale of sandalwood (Hammatt and Wagner-Wright 1999). Receipts of trade from March 1819 indicate that the king "paid 850 piculs of wood for 16 kegs of rum, a box of tea, and $8000 worth of guns and ammunition" (Hammatt and Wagner-Wright 1999, xx). With barter as the only form of exchange on the islands, Hawaiians took quickly to the practice of trade. During the early years, foreign merchants reported that Hawaiian chiefs were able to gain the upper hand in negotiations and force competitive terms of trade from merchants at every turn (Daws 1968).

British merchants had a monopoly on the Pacific Trade until 1791, when U.S. merchants began to appear on the islands. Two decades later, the tables had turned: by 1810, the trade was broadly controlled by U.S. companies, though Kamehameha still gave preference to the British when he could, thanks to his friendship with Vancouver and a debt of gratitude he felt to the British. For their part, U.S. merchants after the Revolutionary War suddenly found themselves isolated in a world dominated by British commerce—a circumstance that would recur after the War of 1812. Westward expansion into the Oregon Country during the early 19th century helped the United States capture an increasing part of the fur trade, launching American interests into the Pacific and on to China. Between the constraints of competition and rapid growth in demand, U.S. merchants were desperate to outsell the British in the fur trade and acquire goods like tea, cotton, and silk from China. Control over Hawaii—with its advantageous location and valuable sandalwood—was becoming a question of national economic security.

The growing desperation of U.S. merchants was exacerbated in 1819 with the first financial crisis in U.S. history. The Panic of 1819 and the collapse of American banks led to a shortage of money, curbing domestic consumption and forcing traders to seek profits in other parts of the Pacific Trade. Merchants were increasingly motivated to buy and sell goods between Hawaii and China, a trade that led to fierce competition for sandalwood and encouraged new and creative forms of financing (Hammatt and Wagner-Wright 1999, xxii). By 1820, sandalwood traders were encouraging chiefs to pay for their luxuries on credit, a development that would push the monarchy into debt, push commoners into the mountains, and draw American warships into Hawaiian waters for the first time.

The Pacific Trade involved much more than the exchange of timber and manufactured goods. *Haole* is the Hawaiian word for any non-Polynesian, especially a white person. Today, the term retains a mild derogatory connotation, no doubt the byproduct of centuries of strained relations. At the height of the Pacific Trade, the influx of foreign goods, customs, and bodies transformed Hawaii's port cities. Places like Kealakekua, Kailua, Waikiki, and Lahaina quickly grew from seaside villages into bustling towns, drawing waves of commoners and chiefs into surrounding areas to support the growing port economy (Morgan 1948). Honolulu, situated at the mouth of the finest natural harbor on the islands, quickly became the most important port town. By 1805, it was known throughout the Pacific and attracted the majority of trade and foreign visitors (Daws 1968). Beckervaise (1839, 191) made note of the Western amenities near Diamond Head, Oahu, in May 1826: "There are in this small town not less than sixteen public houses . . . one of these houses in particular surprises the stranger . . . for in it you see mahogany tables, flint glass decanters, and tumblers . . . this is called the London Tavern, and in another or two are billiard tables."

The principal economic activity supporting port towns was the provisioning of ships. In the 1780s and 1790s, the arrival of foreign vessels offshore placed extraordinary stress on local production. Jarves (1843, 120) reported that some villages feared the onset of famine due to "the voracious appetites of Cook's retinue." Donne (1866) expressed a similar concern, voiced by local chiefs, that foreign ships might leave them with nothing. Demand was greatest for pigs, especially on Hawaii and Kauai (Cordy 1972). In fact, by the early 1820s, Hawaiian pigs were single-handedly keeping the American whaling fleet alive at sea. Whalers picked up provisions in early spring before the summer hunt, and again in the fall before sailing home. Ellis (1826, 390) observed both the demands on production and the profits to be made: "Seen upwards of thirty [whaling ships] lying at anchor off Oahu at one time. The farmers in many places dispose of the produce of their land to these ships; but in Oahu and some other harbours, this trade is almost entirely monopolized by the king and chiefs."

One haole trade for which Hawaiians were in high demand was serving as crewmembers. Foreign captains found locals to be hardworking, strong swimmers, and excellent seafarers. As early as 1793, American ships were actively recruiting Hawaiian men for the Pacific Trade (Jarves 1843). In many cases, these men filled spaces opened up by deserters: the bucolic islands were notorious for luring U.S. and British sailors away from their contracts. In fact, one of the official reasons for the visit of the USS *Peacock* in 1826 was to sort out an array of social problems caused by a sizeable population of deserters living in Honolulu (Jarves 1843).

One consequence of haole interaction commonly cited in early histories concerns the relationship between foreign sailors and local women. In this regard, writers frequently relate the apparent eagerness of women to visit ships and consort with foreign men, going back as far as Cook. Citing a seaman by the name of Mr. Damon, Dibble (1843, 457) writes: "Boat loads of lewd women have been seen going and returning from vessels, which have recently touched at this harbor for supplies." Dibble (1843, 127) speculates that such promiscuity and licentiousness were cultural traits: "For a man or woman to refuse a solicitation for illicit intercourse, was considered an act of meanness." Jarves (1843, 263) is somewhat less generous, referring to "universal licentiousness" as their "most repulsive trait." When missionaries began arriving in 1819, the sexual behavior of women became a subject of broad discussion—curbing such behavior became a primary objective of missionary efforts. In later years, kapus were established to prevent consort between women and visiting ships, though it seems these prohibitions operated primarily to keep a burgeoning sex trade under chiefly control (see Daws 1968).

Questions of morality aside, consort between Hawaiians and haole was inevitable and widespread. Venereal disease was brought to Hawaii by Cook's 1778 expedition and continued to be a concern well into the 19th century (Jarves 1843). Some analysts have suggested that sterility from sexually transmitted diseases was so widespread that it impacted the birthrate (Schmitt 1969; Cordy 1972). Characteristic of patriarchal thinking during this period, responsibility for the spread of disease—and the demise of society in general—was placed squarely on the shoulders of women.[12] Writing in 1857, the Minister of Foreign Relations reported, "It is my frank belief that unless Hawaiian females can be rendered more pure and chaste, it is impossible to preserve the Hawaiian people in being." How, exactly, to execute such rendering would become a central objective of mission work.

Whether or not venereal disease played a significant role in overall public health, other diseases brought by foreigners most certainly did. Between 1804 and 1845, reports of mumps, influenza, measles, dysentery, and whooping cough were common (Hopkins 1862). As with venereal disease, authors tended to place responsibility for outbreaks on the victims: "Their diseases are greatly to be attributed to their wretched manner of living—damp habitations, insufficient clothing, poverty, prevalence of quackery, and general low estimate of life" (Jarves 1843, 18).

One particular epidemic is worth special note. The *mai okuu* of 1804 was an outbreak of unknown origin that struck Oahu as Kamehameha was preparing to attack Kauai. Kamakau (1961, 189) repeats the account of eyewitnesses: "It was a very virulent pestilence, and those who contracted it died quickly. A person on the highway would die before he could reach home. One might go for food and water and die so suddenly that those at home did not know what had happened. The body turned black at death." Eventually, the epidemic spread to other islands where it was equally destructive. Estimates of mortality from mai okuu are wide-ranging: some early writers claim that as much as half the population died. An unknown source named "Adams" provides a figure of 100,000 dead. Later authors have cast doubt, claiming these numbers are grossly exaggerated (see Schmitt 1969).

Population Decline

The precipitous drop in population following the arrival of Cook is reminiscent of the societal collapses that afflicted other New World civilizations upon contact with Europeans (cf. Mann 2006, 2012). Archeological evidence suggests that the population of the islands reached a peak of 400,000 by 1650, by which time settlement had expanded from the productive windward valleys to leeward shores (Cho, Yamakawa, and Hollyer 2007). In 1778, Cook estimated the population to be 300,000—a value repeated by Morgan (1948). Other authors, including Hopkins (1862) and Ellis (cited in Twombly 1899), considered Cook's numbers too high, placing the population closer to 200,000 and 225,000, respectively. By the 1820s, estimates begin to show consistency around 140,000, and by 1836, Morgan's (1948) count of 107,000 reflects the result of an official census. If these estimates are right, Hawaii's population had declined by 63 percent as of 1820.

By this time, Western authors noted long-standing changes in settlement: "In most places, the population was not more than one-fifth of what the land would advantageously maintain . . . traces of deserted villages, and numerous enclosures formerly cultivated, but now lying waste, are every where to be met with" (Hopkins 1862, 8). Hopkins suggests several possible causes, including disease (particularly influenza and venereal disease), infanticide, and moral decline. With respect to infanticide, Hopkins (1862, 370) estimates that two-thirds of children were killed because of the "work" of having a large family and to "preserve the mother's personal charms." More recent scholarship has disputed arguments that infanticide—commonplace in societies of this period—led to population decline (cf. National Research Council 1982). As for "moral" decline, it has been de rigueur for Western historians to cite vice as the reason for social collapse. Results from a survey of prominent haole in 1846 attributed depopulation to "indolence, deceit, lewdness, intemperance" and "evil" from "illicit intercourse with men from Christian countries" (Hopkins 1862, 371). Beyond offering the opportunity to moralize, it is not clear how well early claims of infanticide or vice contribute to an understanding of Hawaiian demographic change.

Morgan (1948, 115) offers a slightly different take, citing four contributing factors: (1) disease, (2) continuing wars, (3) a decline in overall morale due to the use of alcohol and "the wasting away before the superior prestige of the foreigner of native institutions and mores," and (4) foreign interference in taking labor directed to subsistence and shifting it to production for external demand. As for the second factor, most historians believe that large-scale warfare effectively ended after 1804. The third factor is a direct reflection of Morgan's theoretical framework and ultimate thesis—essentially, that locals became lazy and discouraged because they had no way to amass wealth like the haole they encountered. For Morgan, the perceived downfall of the Hawaiian feudal system justified free market capitalism, not just in modern Hawaii but across the developing world. That said, the final factor he cites—a redirection of labor from subsistence to production for export—speaks directly to key transformations in Hawaiian political economy and the tangle of conjunctures from which the sandalwood famines emerge.

Sandalwood

What furs were to the North West Coast, sandalwood was to the Hawaiian Islands.

—Kenneth Porter, *John Jacob Astor and the Sandalwood Trade of the*
Hawaiian Islands, 1816–1828

By Kamehameha's death, Hawaii was linked through trade to political and economic conditions in China, Russia, the East Indies, and the Philippines. It was the subject of a geopolitical tug-of-war between London and Washington. At the center of this web was sandalwood, a slow-growing tropical evergreen once abundant on all the major islands. The numerous species of sandalwood in Hawaii—all of which belong to the genus *Santalum*—grew on both leeward and windward slopes at elevations ranging from 500 to 10,000 feet. At the upper limits of this range, sandalwood grew as a low shrub (Bryan 1915). All species were considered valuable during the 1800s and must have been present in large numbers: at the peak of the trade, as much as $400,000 worth of timber was extracted each year, an amount that suggests sandalwood existed as entire forests or in "pure stands" (St. John 1947, 19). Today, sandalwood can still be found on the islands but in small numbers and in remote parts of the interior.

Until the Pacific Trade, sandalwood did not play a significant role in Hawaiian cultural or economic practice. The wood (*laau ala*) was sometimes ground into a fine powder and sprinkled on cloth to scent it (St. John 1947). On occasion, the timber was cut for firewood (Ellis 1826) but this practice was rare—sandalwood produces charcoal of poor quality. St. John (1781, 18) notes that its aromatic properties led to sandalwood being burned as "mosquito punk." But this was certainly a late development: after all, mosquitoes were not introduced to the islands until 1826 when the ship *Wellington* emptied its larvae-filled bilge at the port of Lahaina (Alexander 1891, 326).

It was a different matter in Asia. Sandalwood was central to religious practices in China, Burma, and India where it was used to make joss sticks, ornamental boxes, and various utensils (St. John 1947). In some cases, the wood served as fuel for funeral pyres. The oil was distilled as a medicinal salve, a perfume, and an ingredient in other cosmetic products. Sandalwood seeds were pressed to extract a denser oil for use in lamps. Throughout the 1700s, most sandalwood extraction took place in Timor and the Lesser Sundas in the Dutch East Indies. But by 1790, the sandalwood supply in Southeast Asia was beginning to diminish. Eventually, growth in the price of timber made it profitable to ship the wood from greater distances (St. John 1947). By 1800, China-bound merchants with shiploads of fur were already stopping in Hawaii for provisions. The discovery of sandalwood on the islands was the perfect complement for the burgeoning Pacific Trade.

By 1818, the trade was in full swing (Daws 1968). Different historians (cf. Alexander 1891; Morgan 1948) offer different dates for the peak of the trade—sometime between 1810 and 1825. Nevertheless, sources agree that the trade quickly expanded under Kamehameha's leadership. During these early years, sandalwood traded for between $8 and $10 a picul, or approximately $120 to $150 a ton (Morgan 1948). Merchant houses worked to develop relationships with chiefs who could requisition labor to collect the wood. Indeed, Kamehameha saw foreign interest in sandalwood as a boon for his newly consolidated kingdom: "He ordered men into the mountains of Kona and Ka'u [Hawai'i] to cut sandalwood, paying them in cloth and in *tapa* material, food, and fish" (Kamakau 1961, 204). With the timber, the king purchased "boats, guns, ammunition, ships and cargoes," among other luxuries (Bingham 1855, 50). Many of these luxuries were stored in warehouses and never used (Jarves 1843). Others were consumed by the chiefs and never benefited the common people: "Tons of the sandal-wood were exchanged for such commodities as useless tobacco, and pernicious alcohol" (Bingham 1855, 50).

Growing demand for sandalwood and royal desire for luxuries resulted in large-scale requisitions of labor to support extraction. According to the historical record, sometime between 1811 and 1817, these demands led to a general neglect of farming resulting in "early and widespread famine throughout the islands" (Kamakau 1961, 204). In his narrative of the crisis, Kamakau (1961) describes how the collapse of food production forced people to eat herbs and tree ferns during this period. There are no mortality estimates, no specifics on when the crisis started or ended, no information on which locations were most seriously affected, and no details of what crops failed or who starved.

What *is* widely recorded, however, is Kamehameha's response. Upon his return to Hawai'i, the king is said to have noticed the impending famine and imposed an immediate monopoly on sandalwood extraction (Twombly 1899). With control in his hands, Kamehameha proceeded to regulate the trade by setting limits on extraction, constraining the authority of chiefs to conscript labor, and imposing conservation measures. Kamakau (1961, 204) describes the king's actions: "[Kamehameha] declared all sandalwood to be the property of the government and ordered the people to devote only a part of their time to its cutting and to return to the cultivation of the land." Prior to the crisis, it was general practice for chiefs to help themselves to a commoner's holdings to acquire taro tops for planting in their own fields. Kamehameha prohibited this practice and set an example for his subordinate chiefs by laboring in the taro fields himself—a clear break with tradition. As Alexander (1891, 158) notes: "Kamehameha set his retinue to work in planting the ground, and also set an example of industry himself. The piece of ground which he tilled is still pointed out."[13] By monopolizing the trade, the king eliminated competition between chiefs and forced merchants to deal directly with him. Finally, Kamehameha made it kapu to cut young sandalwood trees, "observing that such wood was to be preserved for his successors" (Jarves 1843, 200). This attempt at resource conservation is regularly cited as an example of Kamehameha's wisdom and foresight.

It is not clear how well monopolization and labor controls succeeded in averting disaster, though observers and historians broadly assume that these efforts worked. There is documentary evidence that by 1817, Kamehameha's constraints on the sandalwood trade were having a short-term effect. Peter Corney, a Pacific trader during this period, observed that there was never enough sandalwood at any single landing to fill a ship's hold. On his voyage to Hawaii in 1817, Corney's ship had to load sandalwood on Kauai and at three separate ports on Oahu before heading to China (Corney and Alexander 1896).

If Kamehameha's protectionism succeeded in preserving Hawaiian bodies and trees, it also preserved the trade in sandalwood: after all, constricting the supply boosted the price of timber and increased pressure on production. By monopolizing—instead of *reorganizing*—the trade, Kamehameha ensured that the social relations of production stayed the same, preserving the possibility of a future crisis for the next leader. Indeed, when Kamehameha died in 1819, merchants across the Pacific hoped Hawaii's new leadership would loosen the constraints on trade and expand opportunities for profit. They were not disappointed.

Liholiho: New Trajectories

In fact his majesty was so "essentially corned" as they say in Hampshire, that he would not have known his own father, if he had risen out of the grave to reproach him with his degeneracy.

—Charles Hammatt, upon meeting Liholiho for the first time in 1823,
Ships, Furs, and Sandalwood

In 1819 and at the age of 22, Liholiho, son of Kamehameha, was crowned the new king of a unified Hawaii. Five years later he would be dead. In that short time, his reign permanently altered the course of Hawaiian society and deepened the economic connections linking the islands to the edges of the Pacific. Though he was crowned king, his ascendancy was unusual from the outset. Unlike Kamehameha's regency (and the singular authority of every chief before him), Liholiho was not an absolute monarch. In a dramatic turn of events on Liholiho's coronation day, Kamehameha's politically influential widow, Kaahumanu, established herself as executive officer (*kuhina nui*) and coruler of the kingdom (Jarves 1843). In fact, before his death, Kamehameha had prepared the way for Kaahumanu to assume greater control alongside his son (Daws 1968), reflecting, perhaps, a fear that his son could not yet be trusted.

The differences between Kamehameha's government and that of his son were stark. Whereas observers note the virtue and social consciousness of Kamehameha, Liholiho is described as "indolent, and pleasure-loving" (Hopkins 1862, 161). Kamehameha's leadership is characterized as humane and rule-based, while his son "did not have to rule by ritual and he did not know how to rule by law

. . . so he ruled by whim, alternately despotic and delinquent" (Daws 1968, 69). As for the delicate accord that established suzerainty between Kauai and the monarchy, Liholiho made it irrelevant when he secretly kidnapped the king of Kauai and appointed himself ruler of the island. The deposed king would die under house arrest in 1824 (Alexander 1891). Foreign emissaries and merchants were shocked by the number of times Liholiho was late or absent from official events, usually from intoxication (Hopkins 1862). In fact, Liholiho's alcohol addiction is one of those rare points in the historical record around which all sources seem to agree.

By 1823, the new king was beginning to lose control over the powerful chiefs. He had relinquished the upper hand in negotiations with merchants, many of whom had lost confidence in his ability to conduct trade and provide sandalwood. "The King cannot command a man, or obtain a stick of wood without the assistance of Pitt [governor of Oahu] or some of his clan," writes Hammatt (1999, 18) on June 4, 1823. While intoxicated, the king was fond of making large purchases, especially ships (Kamakau 1961). These and other luxuries purchased on credit sent the monarchy spiraling into debt. Not only was Liholiho's personal debt assumed by the government, the escalating debts of his chiefs and retinue compounded the monarchy's growing liability to foreign interests. By the end of Hammatt's June 4th journal entry, he speculates that the king will either be overthrown or will take his own life (Hammatt and Wagner-Wright 1999, 18).

But the reign of Liholiho would not end with such intrigue. Near the end of 1823, the king and his wife commissioned a whaling ship and departed for England to meet King George IV (Daws 1968). It was to be the first official visit between Hawaiian and British heads of state. But within weeks of arriving in London in the summer of 1824, both Liholiho and his wife contracted measles and died within days. Kaahumanu assumed control of the islands until the remains of Liholiho were returned in May of 1825 and Kauikeaouli (the second son of Kamehameha) was proclaimed king.

Arguably the most significant moment in the transformation of Hawaiian culture occurred five months into Liholiho's reign. Encouraged by Kaahumanu and supported by the high priest, Liholiho gave the order to abolish the kapu system along with its governing authorities and idols. Overnight, beliefs and practices that had governed Hawaiian society for centuries were made defunct. Temples (*heiau*) and idols were destroyed, ritual practices were outlawed, and the priesthood was disbanded. The missionary Gerard Hopkins (1862, 180) enthuses about the development: "It is that of a people rising up, and at a blow destroying the religious system in which they and their ancestors had lived, sweeping away their idols, casting them to the moles and to the bats."

Kapu had permeated every aspect of Hawaiian life. Its sudden demise shocked foreign observers and became a subject of considerable debate among later analysts. Some authors feel that the end of the kapu system was a long time coming. Hopkins (1862, 213) attributes the change to a growing skepticism of idolatry, noting that people were regularly breaking kapu rules during Kamehameha's reign, with households eating together and women eating coconut. Punishments for such transgressions were being meted out less frequently and consistently. Forty years of interaction with foreigners since Cook had reduced the strength of belief in traditional idols and eroded support for the priesthood (Daws 1968). Essentially, Hawaiians had grown accustomed to Western ways. Daws (1968, 59) argues that distrust of the priesthood grew as it became obvious that haoles lived in a "happy state" without the kapu system. In a similar, essentialist vein, Morgan (1948) claims that the success of haole institutions prompted Hawaiians to overthrow their own systems of governance.[14]

Other authors note that the end of kapu was concomitant with the advancement of women into positions of leadership—particularly the rise of Kaahumanu to joint regent. After all, the practical restrictions of kapu fell most harshly on women: kapu banned women from every forum in which political and religious decisions were made. Even the wife of the king couldn't formally exercise power on the basis of her sex (Daws 1968). Ellis (1826) and Jarves (1843) note that Kaahumanu was responsible for persuading Liholiho to declare an end to kapu—a monumental transformation she may have found impossible under the rule of her late husband.

For his part, Kamehameha, like all previous chiefs, was bound by the edicts of the system during his ascent to the throne. By the time of his death, he had amassed the political power to overthrow the priesthood and outlaw kapu. But by then, kapu had become a useful system of rituals and social discipline, not to mention a convenient means to both encourage and regulate the trade in sandalwood (Daws 1968). And, so, the system persisted, until Liholiho and Kaahumanu brought it to a sudden end in 1819. Remarkably, Hawaii's first social revolution succeeded without major violence. Minor rebellions from lesser chiefs on Hawai'i were put down within weeks (Hopkins 1862).

The end of kapu—like the system itself—is described in totalizing terms. Western writers invariably see 1819 as a watershed between savage innocence and enlightenment: the groundwork for a modern state in which feudalism is rejected and religion stands separate from politics. The anti-kapu revolution is portrayed as a wholesale renovation of social relations, cosmological beliefs, and everyday practices. Without a doubt, the destruction of religious orders and abandonment of kapu dramatically altered Hawaiian society, but not because it changed everything that came before it. As described in later sections, the social revolution of 1819 was highly selective, eliminating certain relations of production as it reinforced others. Its transformative power came from the different ways it treated long-standing reciprocal relations between the nobility and common people. The so-called end of the kapu system didn't bring an end to feudalism—rather, it created a new and dynamic interface between Hawaii and a globalizing world, one that enabled Hawaii's feudal society to endure. It is precisely at this interface that the sandalwood famine of the 1820s emerges.

Arrival of Missionaries

The first missionaries to Hawaii, sent by the American Board of Missions, were on their way to the islands when Liholiho ordered the idols destroyed. Though they could not claim responsibility for the demise of the old religion, the missionaries certainly took advantage of it. Upon arrival and consultation with the king, the group was given a year's "probation" before being allowed to start work building churches and schools (Daws 1968). During this time, they built relationships with the royal family and chiefs on Oahu and Hawai'i where efforts were to be focused. In their letters and journals from the period, these first evangelists found chiefs and commoners broadly receptive. On this point, Hopkins (1862, 197) once again finds a way to sully the compliment: "Mentally, [the Islanders] were in a condition to accept as readily that or any other faith which should be proposed, as their bodies were to receive any new epidemic."

As expected, the American mission's encounter with the Islanders resembled other missionary encounters from this period, bearing similar tensions and challenges. The topic that most often brought missionaries into controversy (and occupied a significant quantity of mission correspondence) concerned the chastity of local women, especially the relationship with foreign crews. For years, chiefs had been trying to regulate such liaisons as a way to charge sailors for access to women. Missionaries tried to convince the chiefs to be strict with these regulations, while foreigners encouraged chiefs to be more lenient (Daws 1968). For their interference, missionaries quickly became the target of merchant wrath: in 1825, the crew of the *Daniel* became incensed when local chiefs—at the urging of Bingham—prohibited women from visiting the ship. They assaulted Bingham, whose life was saved by the intervention of his parishioners (Jarves 1843).

Expansion of the mission and growth in trade brought increasing numbers of merchants and missionaries into conflict during the 1820s and 1830s, deepening the mission's resolve to discipline women for the good of Hawaiian salvation. Hopkins (1862, 378) argued that the only way to save women was to educate them in the Christian religion, a challenge that entailed taking girls away from home at an early age, to be "educated in the ways of chastity and religious adherence." Here, again, missionaries took advantage of the collapse of the kapu system, neatly replacing one form of bodily discipline with another. Whereas the old system justified its impositions on women as a way to protect and preserve society at large, the new system justified itself by way of individual purification and salvation. Indeed, the taboos handed down by Bingham and other men of the cloth would have fit perfectly with the kapus these same men readily condemned.

To be sure, the mission was one of the only foreign institutions that could reasonably claim to champion the common people, and to this end, its network of churches and schools was well positioned to detect and respond to social calamities, even if its methods for doing so seem bewildering today. But the church's obsession with *behavioral* infractions like licentiousness, indolence, and intoxication distracted missionaries from true, *material* crises of public health and well-being. When the famine struck, missionaries were too busy fighting foreign merchants in the ports to confront the chiefs sending people into the mountains.

Sandalwood Entanglements

While it lasted, this wood was a mine of wealth to the king and chiefs, by means of which they were enabled to buy guns and ammunition, liquors, boats, and schooners, as well as silks and other Chinese goods, for which they paid exorbitant prices.

—William De Witt Alexander, *A Brief History of the Hawaiian People*

The royal monopoly on sandalwood and Kamehameha's policies of conservation abruptly ended with the coronation of Liholiho. In short order, the new king gave away trading rights to his favorite subjects, thereby reintroducing competition among the most powerful chiefs (St. John 1947).[15] The elimination of central control also brought an end to any labor protections. Chiefs quickly mobilized commoners to collect as much sandalwood as possible for foreign exchange. Hammatt and Wagner-Wright (1999, xxi) observe that with the end of the monopoly, all ahupua'a chiefs effectively became competitors in the sandalwood trade, "turning their attention to the role of consumers, emulating the royal warehouses of New England trade goods."

During Kamehameha's reign, demand for sandalwood had grown dramatically. Between 1810 and 1825 the price of sandalwood fluctuated between $8 and $10 a picul. Between 1825 and 1827, it climbed to between $10.50 and $18 a picul (St. John 1947). Higher prices drove extraction and labor exploitation. Competition among merchants became so fierce that traders allowed chiefs to buy goods on credit (Porter 1930). In exchange for the luxuries they sought, chiefs signed contracts in which they promised delivery of specific quantities of sandalwood at a later date. As sandalwood became increasingly difficult to find and chiefs failed to deliver on time, the monarchy's debt grew. When sandalwood payments could not be made, merchants levied interest in the form of higher prices for luxuries, perpetuating the debt cycle.

Not to be deterred, chiefs continued to purchase Western- and Chinese-made goods in exchange for promises of sandalwood. By 1823, the nobility's taste for luxuries was becoming conspicuous. "The chiefs were often clothed in civilized garb, and their houses had some costly furnishings" (Twombly 1899, 179). Observers note that many of these items were never used—simply bought "in a reckless profusion" and then left to deteriorate in warehouses (Porter 1930, 501). On his 1823 tour, Alexander writes, "Great quantities of these costly goods, however, were never used, but being stored away in unsuitable storehouses were allowed to decay" (cited in Twombly 1899, 179).

As conspicuous consumption grew and debts mounted, chiefs turned (once again) to labor to bail them out. Alexander (1891, 186) observes: "This trade greatly increased the oppression of the common people multitudes of whom were obliged to remain for months at a time in the mountains searching for the trees, felling them, and bringing them down on their backs to the royal storehouses." With respect to the size of this labor mobilization, some reports from the period seem almost implausible. Ellis (1826, 397) claims "almost the whole population" was sent into the mountains to search for wood. Kamakau (1961, 252) reports that all commoners were involved and that "none was allowed to remain behind." In a possible repeat of earlier claims, St. John (1947, 7) notes that "all the inhab-itants able to go were ordered into the hills in search of the precious wood . . . the trees were cut down and chopped into logs 6–8 feet long . . . men and women tied the logs to their backs . . . and trudged to the measuring pit or to the shore."

Eyewitness accounts provide context for these sweeping claims. William Ellis, traveling through Hawai'i in 1823, offers much needed detail. Through interviews with cutters he encountered in the northern part of the island, Ellis learned that commoners were required to commit anywhere from three days a week to an entire month at a time, to sandalwood collection (Ellis 1826, 56). Later in the trip, Ellis observed villages in the Kohala peninsula that had been entirely evacuated to collect sandalwood. Villagers had been requisitioned to the neighboring district of Waimea: "Though we had numbered . . . 600 houses, we had not seen anything like four hundred people, almost the whole population being employed in the mountains" (Ellis 1826, 375). Still later, Ellis counted 2000 to 3000 men passing his encampment carrying sandalwood, each man car-rying from one to six pieces of timber, cut to between four and six feet long and about three inches in diameter.

Conditions in the mountains were harsh. Wilkes (1845, 214) reports that "the chiefs would dispatch their dependents to the mountains, with nothing to eat but what they could gather from the forest of ferns, the core of whose trunk supplied them with a scanty and precarious subsistence." These wild foods could only be collected "in the intervals of their toil" (Wilkes 1845, 502). In addition to the lack of food, there were no permanent shelters. Laborers accustomed to conditions at lower elevations found themselves exposed to environmental extremes for weeks at a time (Dibble 1843). On Hawai'i, where the great volcanoes exceed 13,000 feet in elevation and sandalwood grew as high as 10,000 feet, timber collection in the montane interior subjected cutters to extreme cold and heavy rain. "In this exposed situation, many of the poor people died, as the numerous graves at the places of their encampments clearly indicate" (Dibble 1843, 191).

So long as Kamehameha controlled the trade, commoners could expect some return for their labor in the form of food, usually provided directly by their ruling chief (Wilkes 1845). But during and after Liholiho, commoners were expected to survive using their own resources. This shift—the first step toward a commodified labor system—was another break with the kapu system's tradition of reciprocity: chiefs were no longer obligated to provide subsistence support for their subjects, even when those subjects were being called away from their own subsistence production.

The elimination of support for conscripted labor eventually led to popular resistance, though it is not clear exactly when such resistance started, or how extensive it was. Wilkes (1845, 214) reports that trees "not cut down for sale . . . were destroyed by the natives, to prevent impositions being practiced upon them." Resistance to the chiefs could result in severe penalties. Those commoners who did not submit to the demands of conscription would either have their homes burned or all their property seized and their household expelled from the chief's land (Porter 1930, 502). These draconian penalties of the old kapu system were clearly retained, even as the reciprocal impositions on chiefs to support commoners were drastically reduced.

But conditions would deteriorate further. By 1824, the royal debt was $300,000—more than the entire year's export of sandalwood in 1821 (St. John 1947). Meanwhile, the large stands of sandalwood were gone and cutters had to travel greater distances to satisfy demand (Daws 1968). To make up the difference, the king and governors—those carrying the greatest debt—found new ways to accumulate wealth. It was decreed that lesser chiefs were required to bring gifts when visiting their superiors (Jarves 1843), an imposition that lesser chiefs readily passed down to their own subjects. To make matters worse, when Liholiho left for London, he delegated responsibility for his debts to his governors. Upon his death, the governors—confronted with angry traders looking to collect—fought amongst themselves over responsibility for the late king's debts, further aggravating the relationship between chiefs and merchants.

The debt problem became so severe that in 1826, the warship USS *Dolphin* was dispatched to the islands to resolve the matter under the threat of force. After consultation with the chiefs, it was decided that the outstanding debt amounted to 15,000 piculs of wood, or between $120,000 and $160,000 (Morgan 1948). The burden of paying the debt would fall to the common people in the form of a new tax: "To provide for the payment of these claims an edict was issued, December 27th [1826], that every able-bodied male subject should deliver half a picul of sandal-wood or pay four Spanish dollars before the 1st of September, 1827" (Alexander 1891, 197). Other sources report slight variations on these conditions. Chamberlain (March 2, 1827) adds "one dollar on every female above the age of thirteen years . . . each [male] is allowed to choose whether he will go into the mountains & cut the wood, or remain at home and pay cash." Morgan (1948, 66) adds that "every woman was to bring a mat, a piece of tapa, or a Spanish dollar." The vast majority of commoners at the time would have been unable to pay the monetary equivalent provided in the law, effectively forcing them into the hills to hunt sandalwood. The laborious nature of timber collection and the fact that by 1827 the wood was increasingly hard to find led Dibble (1843, 91) to conclude that "the tax was probably one of the heaviest ever imposed upon the people."

This switch from conscripted labor to a head tax on sandalwood was transformative. Under the *corvée* labor regime, chiefs competed with other chiefs to collect sandalwood, using crews assembled from their own subjects. With the imposition of the sandalwood tax, individual laborers were placed in competition *with each other* to locate and extract the diminishing resource. The corvée labor regime placed penalties on individuals for failure to *participate*. But under the tax, penalties were levied on individuals for failure to *produce*. From a commoner's perspective, the effect of labor allocation was critical. Under traditional conscription, you worked as much as you were told. While this imposition may have been severe at times, reciprocal relations between chiefs and commoners (and between rival chiefs) tended to discourage abject brutality. Under the tax, you worked until you satisfied the production requirement. For many—particularly the old, infirm, or unlucky—this requirement might never be met.

Once again, the incomplete dismantling of the kapu system played a key role in the exploitation of labor. With the establishment of the sandalwood tax in 1827, chiefs relinquished the traditional right to recruit labor, while retaining (and reaffirming) their right to capricious taxation. Chiefs eliminated the traditional economies of scale associated with collective effort, while reasserting the long-standing feudal practice of production for the nobility. Commoners could no longer benefit from large teams of workers to assist in the laborious process of locating, cutting, and carrying timber. Instead, the tax discouraged collective effort, pitting commoners against each other in a race to secure the last stands of sandalwood.

The suggestion for a universal head tax to pay sandalwood debts came from George Byron, an admiral in the Royal Navy representing the interests of the British Crown in Hawaii. In wide-ranging conversations with Kauikeaouli in 1826, Byron also recommended laws against "villainry" and the separation of church and state (Jarves 1843, 260). He reassured Kauikeaouli that England would recognize the Islanders as "free and independent people," and would not interfere in Hawaiian affairs (Jarves 1843, 260). With Byron's assistance, new, universal laws prohibiting murder, theft, and debauchery were implemented alongside the sandalwood tax. It is possible that Hawaiian leaders would have levied a similar tax without Byron's council—after all, taxation was commonplace in the history of Hawaiian government. Nevertheless, it is a cruel irony that such an effective mechanism for human exploitation was abetted by a man pledging noninterference.

In 1829, with debts still outstanding, a second U.S. warship was sent to the islands to confront the chiefs. This time the debt was calculated at $50,000 or 4700 piculs of timber (Alexander 1891). The monarchy promised to pay the debt in full within nine months, but by then, sandalwood had become so rare—and labor so depleted—that large-scale extraction was effectively impossible. The remaining claims were not settled until 1843 (St. John 1947), at which point the sandalwood trade was all but over and the dead long since buried.

American missionaries were in an ideal position to observe and report excessive exploitation of labor by the chiefs. By the late 1820s, missionaries could have taken advantage of friendly relations with governors and high-ranking chiefs to make their concerns known. However, it is not clear that any such intervention occurred. Letters and journal entries from the period make it obvious that missionaries were well aware of commoners being forced into the mountains. In numerous instances, pastors complained about the drop-off in church attendance due to sandalwood extraction.[16] In several cases, mission schools were temporarily closed because of declining attendance. Missionaries on Hawai'i noted that parishioners had left for the mountains for periods of up to "two to three months" (Chamberlain March 2, 1827, 585).

Some authors, like Culliney (2006, 334), interpret the church's silence as "acquiescence" to the monarchy's "sandalwood slavery." Though there is no indication that missionaries expressed approval for either the sandalwood tax or the use of corvée labor, it seems clear that the church made little effort to stop these measures. After all, missionary activities were conducted at the mercy of powerful chiefs who could revoke such licenses on a whim. From the perspective of church leaders, it was imperative that missionaries avoid upsetting the political hierarchy. Indeed, the relationship between missionaries and Hawaiian leaders was, at times, quite close, even with respect to the timber trade: documentary evidence indicates that boats belonging to the mission were used by the governor of Oahu to transport sandalwood (entry for May 16, 1826, from the journal of Levi Chamberlain, 24). In hindsight, missionaries saw the sandalwood trade as having a lasting, negative impact on Hawaiians. Writing in 1855, Bingham (1855, 212) reflects on missed opportunities: "Something was needed here, different from the arbitrary edicts of secular power, which could send 20,000 men to the mountains to cut sandal-wood for traders, who were never heard greatly to object to that mode of using the prerogatives of Hawaiian sovereignty."

By 1826, sandalwood was becoming increasingly hard to find.[17] As the easily accessible stands of trees were removed, cutters had to travel greater distances into the interior to find timber (St. John 1947). Out of desperation, some locals set fire to grassland and secondary forest in parts of Oahu to locate hidden supplies of sandalwood: the smell of the smoke served to indicate the presence of standing or fallen logs (Porter 1930). Of course, fire also served to kill any sandalwood saplings or seeds.

The steady removal of sandalwood inland from the shore was accompanied by another agent of change working outward from the interior. In the 1790s, European explorers like Vancouver brought gifts of goats, horses, cattle, and other livestock to the islands. Without a tradition of husbandry or ranching, locals allowed many of these animals to roam free. For several years during Kamehameha's reign, it was kapu to keep or use cows and horses (Cordy 1972). By 1819, wild herds roamed free in the grassy interiors of the major islands. Hopkins (1862, 38) reports that there is "almost a plague of horses on Oahu" and suggests that it would be beneficial "to destroy 9/10ths of the horses on the island because they destroy fences [and] trample crops." As for wild cattle, rapid population growth led to overgrazing in upland areas of Hawai'i, above the limits of agriculture. St. John (1947) speculates that cattle expansion may have prevented regrowth of trees—including sandalwood—in the upper margins of the island's forests. If St. John is correct, extensification of timber extraction deep into the interior (assuming such a thing was possible) would have run headlong into areas denuded by wild cattle. Not only would such forays have demanded more time, they would have yielded less timber.

Changes in the Weather

Overall, Hawaii experiences consistent seasonal temperatures and rainfall. However, the islands are affected by large-scale climate teleconnections like those associated with El Niño and La Niña events. An extensive climatological analysis by Chu (1995) models the effect of El Niño on Hawaii's seasonal weather patterns. During the summer and fall months of a normal year, the North Pacific high-pressure zone moves to the north, following the sun. This movement brings strong and steady northeasterly trade winds to the islands along with abundant rainfall on windward slopes. During the winter months, the North Pacific High moves towards the equator, sending the trade winds south of Hawaii. As a result, rainfall during the winter and spring (usually on leeward slopes) tends to come from more synoptic weather conditions, like frontal systems. By contrast, during the winter and spring months following an El Niño year, the Hadley circulation of the central North Pacific tends to elongate towards the east, interfering with front formation and disrupting the synoptic causes of rainfall (Chu 1995). The result is often drier-than-normal conditions to leeward during the winter and early spring—the prime growing season for sweet potato.

In fact, historical mentions of drought on Hawai'i show some correspondence with putative El Niño events (see Chu 1995; Chenoweth 1996). In 1825, the year after a powerful El Niño, the missionary Artemas Bishop recorded a severe drought in the Kona region of Hawai'i that lasted nine months. He writes, in the Report of the American Board of Commissioners for Foreign Missions (1826, 81), "the whole country was overrun by fire. The famishing people, after their ordinary food was exhausted, betook themselves to fern roots for a subsistence; and when these failed, were obliged to disperse into different parts of the island." Pressure on agricultural labor due to the sandalwood trade may have exacerbated the impact of these climatic stresses.

In 1815, Mt. Tambora—a stratovolcano in the eastern part of the Indonesian archipelago—erupted, devastating nearby islands and releasing 100 cubic kilometers of ejecta (Briffa et al. 1998). The eruption of Tambora remains the largest in recorded history. The plume, estimated to be over 20 kilometers high, pushed material into the stratosphere where high-altitude winds carried volcanic ash around the globe. The resulting occlusion of solar radiation led to the coldest global temperatures since 1400 (Briffa et al. 1998). In 1816, the northeastern parts of the United States and Canada received several feet of snow in mid-June, earning 1816 the moniker of "the year without a summer."

On the leeward coast of Hawai'i, there is evidence of strong winds and severe flooding in April of 1816, a possible consequence of Tambora's climate-altering effects (Chenoweth 1996). But proving this connection is difficult: 1815 was also an El Niño year. The spring months on Hawai'i following an El Niño are usually drier than normal due to a disruption of normal front formation (see Chu 1995). Chenoweth (1996) suspects the ash cloud may have interfered with the elongation of the subtropical jet stream; in effect, disrupting the "normal" post–El Niño pattern. Sweet potato, the primary staple on the leeward slopes of Hawai'i, was vulnerable to flooding. Unlike taro which enjoys heavy rainfall, sweet potato tubers quickly rot under inundation. An unseasonable flood like that described in 1816 could have severely impacted sweet potato production and produced a localized food crisis.

Beyond such speculation, there is no other evidence in the record of eyewitnesses to suggest that Tambora had any effect on the islands. In fact, in all the 19th-century documentation collected for this study, there is no mention of Tambora or its effects. Nevertheless, there are two reasons to suggest that the climate impacts from the 1815 eruption reached Hawaii. First, the reduction in solar insolation caused by stratospheric ash had severe—and well-documented—agricultural impacts throughout the Northern Hemisphere, including widespread crop failure across North America, famine conditions in Ireland and Germany, typhoid epidemics in southeastern Europe, and disruption of the Indian monsoons that led to a famine in Bengal in 1816 (Oppenheimer 2003). On balance, it seems more likely that Tambora had *some* impact on Hawaii, even if the magnitude was negligible.

Second, research into the effects of Mt. Pinatubo's 1991 eruption has shown that stratospheric ash from archipelagic Southeast Asian volcanoes can produce appreciable decreases in solar insolation in Hawaii (Self et al. 1999). Pinatubo is only 2500 kilometers from Tambora and erupted at the same time of year. Furthermore, the quantity of ejecta released by Tambora was ten times that of Pinatubo. In the absence of compelling historical data, it is impossible to assess the material impact of Tambora on Hawaiian agriculture. However, contemporary analogues and data from other regions suggest that the 1815 eruption added environmental stress to an already vulnerable production system.[18]

Food System Stress, Reorganization, and Collapse

Many of them suffered for food; because of the green herbs they were obliged to eat they were called "Excreters-of-green-herbs" (Hi-lalele), and many died and were buried there.

—Samuel M. Kamakau, *Ruling Chiefs of Hawaii*

Writers of Hawaiian history describe the sandalwood famine in uncomplicated terms: sometime during the height of the sandalwood trade, powerful chiefs redirected labor from agricultural production to timber extraction, and as a result, cultivation was neglected, food became scarce, and people starved. There is no mention of where the famine occurred, how many it affected, when people started to die, nor when the crisis ended. Beyond this rudimentary description, no explanation is offered for how or why the most advanced food provisioning system in Polynesia collapsed on contact with foreign markets. Based on a synthesis of primary and secondary historical records, archeological research, and agricultural modeling, we can now piece together a more complete narrative of Hawaii's first "economic" famine.

Two Crises

The famine associated with sandalwood extraction was not a single event but two separate food crises spanning nearly 20 years. The first occurred sometime between 1811 and 1815. Kamehameha and his powerful chiefs directed commoners into the forests to collect sandalwood in support of growing foreign demand. This redirection of labor away from cultivation led to an immediate decline in food availability, resulting in starvation. Compounding factors may have included environmental stressors like El Niño and the eruption of Mt. Tambora in 1815, though the impact of these events is unknown. The crisis was mitigated through the swift action of Kamehameha who took control of the sandalwood trade, imposed regulations limiting the use of labor, and prohibited the extraction of young trees. The consistency with which Kamehameha's response is praised in the historical record suggests that his efforts succeeded in reducing the impact of the shortage.

The second crisis occurred between 1823 and 1830, accompanied the decentralization of the sandalwood trade, and was intensified by the imposition of the sandalwood tax in 1827. The death toll from this crisis likely exceeded that of the first. Once again, commoners were forced into the mountains, this time through a variety of sociopolitical mechanisms made possible by the collapse of the kapu system. Several circumstances exacerbated this crisis. A history of population decline had reduced the productivity of agriculture, especially labor-intensive cultivation. Years of heavy extraction had reduced sandalwood availability, making it harder to find timber. With the decline of the kapu system and the end of Kamehameha's protections, commoners were exposed to labor conscription without relief from long-standing practices of reciprocity. In the end, most of the deaths occurred in the interior from a combination of starvation and exposure, and most of these deaths occurred on Hawai'i.

There are two reasons to believe that most deaths occurred in the interior. First, Dibble (1843) and Kamakau (1961) report that people died and were buried near their encampments in the mountains. Second, if a significant number had died at home or around their villages, one would expect reports of mortality from missionaries and other foreigners well placed to witness starvation firsthand. There are no such reports. In fact, eyewitness accounts mention the *abandonment* of villages and a slow decline in population. Such observations are consistent with mass starvation away from home.

There are five reasons to believe the crisis was centered on Hawai'i. First, as workers were directed away from agriculture, labor-intensive cultivation systems would have been the first affected. In any system, labor is divided into seasonal cultivation and the production of landesque capital. During the extensification of such systems, a higher percentage of labor is directed toward field construction, irrigation, and other forms of fixed capital. But by the 1820s, systems across the islands were already at or past peak extensification. With landesque capital placing relatively few demands on labor, any large-scale imposition on the labor supply would have disproportionately affected seasonal cultivation. Dryfield systems required twice as much seasonal labor per hectare as irrigated systems (see table 1), and of the major islands, Hawai'i was the most dependent on dryfield cultivation: the big island had 25 times more high-potential land for dryfield than land for irrigated cultivation (see table 2). Hawai'i's dependence on a cultivation system with extraordinary seasonal labor demands increased its vulnerability to a large-scale labor crisis.

Second, the duration of conscription was a function of the proximity of sandalwood to human settlement. As such, in places where sandalwood was distant, labor had to be conscripted for longer periods to achieve the same extractive returns. On the smaller islands with more accessible interior forests, commoners might be recruited for a span of days. For example, Beckervaise's (1839) story of mountain cutters assembled for a single night of work takes place on the southeast shore of Oahu. But on Hawai'i, evidence from Kamakau (1961) and eyewitness accounts from Ellis (1826) indicate that work parties were assembled for weeks to months at a time, sometimes from distant parts of the island. Longer travel times to and from sites of sandalwood extraction—more common on Hawai'i—would have exacerbated the impact on agriculture.

Third, the quantity of labor needed for extraction was—in part—a function of the proliferation and density of sandalwood in the interior. In places where sandalwood was rare or otherwise hard to find, more labor was needed to locate and extract sufficient timber. On Hawai'i, eyewitness accounts from Ellis (1826) and Tyerman and Bennet (1832) record the largest work parties—as many as 3,000 men in one instance. Mission correspondence from Hawai'i contains repeated references to people being away from church activities, in some cases entire congregations.[19] Hawai'i's considerable size (the island is double the combined area of all the other islands) would have made it more difficult to locate timber as it became scarce. Greater area may have introduced doubt over how much timber remained: on Molokai (1,547 square kilometers), the task of determining the amount of remaining timber is relatively simple compared to Hawai'i (10,433 square kilometers). Meanwhile, reports suggest that horse and cattle herds had expanded in the interior and were affecting forest growth (Hopkins 1862; see also St. John 1947). In this way, the ecology and geography of Hawai'i increased the labor needed to achieve productive sandalwood extraction, especially in the later years of the trade.

Fourth, on Kauai, Oahu, and Molokai, women had been prohibited from agricultural work. With the end of the kapu system in 1819, these islands could now employ women in the fields as a reserve labor pool. But on Hawai'i, the labor-intensive nature of dryfield cultivation already required both men and women to work in the fields. As such, the end of kapu did not supply additional labor to cultivation. When commoners were drawn away to hunt timber, there were no bodies left to replace them in the fields.

Finally, environmental stresses—like drought or flood—were more likely to occur on the leeward slopes of Hawai'i, precisely where the island's large-scale dryfield systems were located. We know that these weather events continued to affect agriculture into the 1820s: for example, in 1824, Bishop reported a drought in Kona, Hawai'i, that lasted nine months and may have severely affected dryfield systems already impacted by reductions in labor (Report of the American Board of Commissioners for Foreign Missions 1826). More predictable weather and less vulnerable cultivation systems—like those present on other islands—would have reduced the overall impact of environmental stress.

Beyond these inferences, there is little else to directly support the claim that the crisis struck Hawai'i the hardest. Indeed, one of the challenges of this historical reconstruction is that the geographical extent of the famine cannot be easily pinpointed. However, a comparison of population estimates from the major islands is highly suggestive (fig. 3). The data for this chart, compiled by Cordy (1972), shows the estimated population of each island for three points in time, 1778, 1823, and 1831. All islands show a decline in population between 1778 and 1831; however, stark differences between the trajectory of Hawai'i and the other islands between 1823 and 1831 are worthy of consideration.

Did the second sandalwood famine cause Hawai'i's dramatic population decline between 1823 and 1831? The historical record makes little mention of catastrophes that might otherwise explain the decline. For example, there is no record of

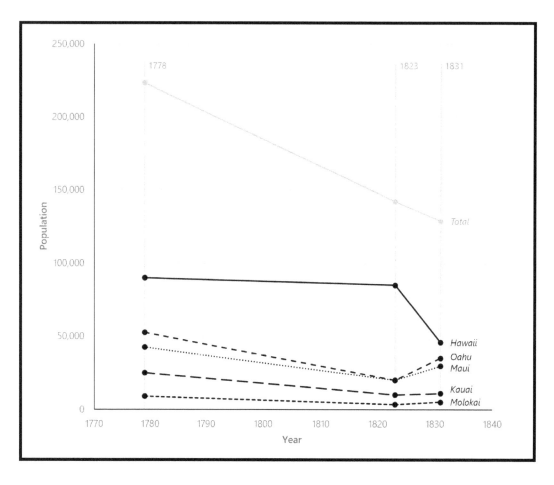

Figure 3. Population decline by island for years 1778, 1823, and 1831. (Data source: Cordy 1972)

any major disease outbreaks during this period, on Hawai'i or elsewhere. The only major drought—in Kona in 1824—lasted nine months and led to extensive wild-fires (Report of the American Board of Commissioners for Foreign Missions 1826). But based on the author's description and the lack of corroboration from authors in other locales, the effect of this event may have been limited. In-migration to Hawai'i from the other islands before 1823 followed by out-migration after 1823 could explain the different population trajectories. But no historian or observer mentions migration on this scale between islands. Furthermore, Cordy (1972) reports that there is no evidence of migration during this period.[20] In fact, other than the movement of armies during war, large-scale transhumance appears to play little part in the history of the islands. Growth in the port city of Honolulu could explain some of the increase in the population of Oahu between 1823 and 1831 (see Morgan 1948, 407), however, there is no evidence that new migrants to

Oahu came predominantly from Hawai'i. In fact, population growth on the other four islands after 1823 could be attributed to a rebound in the birthrate following the *mai okuu*, the mysterious epidemic in 1804 that—according to Kamakau (1961)—killed half of all Islanders. Of course, if Hawai'i also experienced an increased birthrate after mai okuu, its population decline after 1823 becomes even more remarkable.

The lack of alternative explanations supports the possibility that some (if not most) of Hawai'i's population decline between 1823 and 1831 was related to sandalwood extraction. If that is the case, the second sandalwood famine claimed the lives of approximately 41,000 people living on the big island—46 percent of the population—in a span of only eight years.

Population Decline and Economies of Proximity

For reasons that are not entirely clear, Hawaii's dramatic population decline may have started before the arrival of Cook and Western epidemics. As previously noted, a decline in population does not necessarily entail a decline in available food: after all, in systems of rotating (or swidden) cultivation, a decrease in population density has been shown to increase fallow times, improve soil nutrients, and reduce labor per calorie (Hanks 1992). But in sedentary systems like the irrigated and dryfield complexes of Hawaii, a decline in population may negatively impact cultivation in three ways. First, abundant labor is necessary for the production of landesque capital and the maintenance of agricultural infrastructure. If sufficient labor cannot be mobilized, the canals, dams, field boundaries, and rock mulch necessary for high productivity may break down. Hawaii's cultivation systems had already reached peak extensification, reducing the demand for new landesque capital. Nevertheless, population densities may have dropped below the point at which existing capital could be properly maintained.

Second, the transition from a dense and well-connected cultivation system to a patchy one may decrease productivity due to a breakdown in spatial integration—a phenomenon related to the ecological concepts of edge effect and fragmentation (see Haila 2002). In a large mosaic of fields, each field receives benefits from its neighbors. This is most obvious in an irrigated overflow regime where water is directed from one field to another. Lower fields benefit from the continued operation and maintenance of upper fields: should upper terraces fall into disrepair, the productivity of the entire system may suffer. In dryfield cultivation of sweet potato, fields receive numerous benefits from their neighbors, including soil moisture control, erosion control, and pollination. If neighboring fields are no longer mulched or otherwise covered, overall soil moisture may decline and runoff from heavy rain may flow into neighboring fields. Furthermore, tropical sweet potato flowers are self-sterile—that is, a single plant cannot pollinate itself. This means that reproduction usually requires animal pollinators, invariably bees. If the fields in a large agricultural mosaic begin to fragment, plants in isolated fields may suffer from lack of contact with pollinators. Adjusting the arrangement of fields to reduce fragmentation may require impractical outlays of labor. In fact, historical accounts of field abandonment—in both irrigated and dryfield regimes—between 1811 and 1830 suggest that this form of fragmentation may have been involved in both sandalwood famines and across all dryfield systems. If the population of the big island fell rapidly after 1823 (based on Cordy 1972), these spatial disintegration effects may have hit the large dryfield systems of Hawai'i suddenly, reducing opportunities for adaptation and exacerbating the consequences of the second famine.

Finally, population decline may inhibit the transmission of agricultural knowledge if experienced members of the household die or are killed before such knowledge can be passed on to descendants. This effect has been observed in cases where a disease epidemic disproportionately impacts working adults over children (see de Waal 2006 for the example of HIV/AIDS in Africa). Unfortunately, we have no reliable information to indicate how different demographic groups or cohorts were affected during the period of population decline; and until we identify the disease behind the mai okuu in 1804, we won't know if this widespread epidemic disproportionately claimed Hawaii's technical experts.

The effect of population decline on the food provisioning system is one of *pressurization without reorganization*—that is, the conjuncture decreased the *effectiveness of an existing process* (cultivation) by reducing the quality or quantity of inputs like labor and by limiting economies of proximity. Population decline did not, by itself, force a reorganization of relations within Hawaii's spaces of consumption or production. Of course, this conjuncture was both cause and effect: as agriculture became less productive, food production suffered, total food availability declined, people began to starve, and more people died. The relationship between population decline and agricultural production became one of parasitic feedback.

Foreign Trade

Another conjuncture with parasitic feedback was the growth in foreign trade. As the Pacific Trade expanded in the early 19th century, increasing numbers of ships began to arrive in the islands to exchange manufactured goods and luxuries for sandalwood. More merchant activity meant more food provisions directed toward ships: fruits, vegetables, and pigs that could have otherwise fed local households were exchanged for goods that ultimately filled the warehouses of the nobility. More ships also entailed greater recruitment of Hawaiian men as crew members, further depleting the agricultural labor pool. By the 1820s, the booming port cities were attracting labor away from agriculture with new opportunities in ship provisioning and trade. During this period, growth in conspicuous consumption among the chiefs became an end in itself. Morgan (1948, 73) notes: "Before the *haole* conspicuous consumption had held only a minor place in the native economy: most goods spoiled rapidly, and the chiefs generally demanded no more than they could use. Now a long list of foreign goods, useful only for war or ostentatious display, was desired by the chiefs." Growth in the availability of luxuries drove the desire for luxuries, a cycle of feedback that externalized its costs on common labor.

The introduction of foreign trade added new sources of wealth to Hawaii's political economy: the production of commodities for export, notably, sandalwood. In the early days of the Pacific Trade, this had little influence on commoner consumption and production—there was almost no trade in food and the demands of ship provisioning were minimal. But its greatest impact was on the chieftain class. By dealing directly with chiefs (or the king, during Kamehameha's reign), merchants provided the nobility with new ways to accumulate wealth. To obtain foreign luxuries, chiefs expanded their means of wealth production to include sandalwood and those processes necessary for its extraction. Through these new channels of accumulation, chiefs were free to relinquish some control over agriculture and crafts—the primary forms of wealth generation prior to sandalwood. But this did not liberate commoners from feudal impositions. Instead, it served to *disentangle* chiefly livelihoods from agriculture. Before sandalwood, when food production suffered, tax revenues and chiefly wealth suffered with it. After sandalwood, food production could collapse without affecting chiefly well-being. No longer were chiefs motivated to support subsistence agriculture.

Sandalwood

Two simultaneous conjunctures helped disentangle chiefs and commoners. The first was the commodification of sandalwood. At the interface between merchant capitalism and Hawaiian feudalism, foreigners sought an island product that could be exchanged for an abundance of manufactured goods. Between 1778 and 1819, this trade took the form of weapons and trinkets: in the hands of Kamehameha, the weapons were used to consolidate control over the islands and establish the material basis for a monopoly. After 1819, the trade served up increasingly extravagant and expensive luxuries to chiefs. To pay for this, the market established a common value for all sandalwood, regardless of where the timber was cut, who cut it, and at what cost. For the merchant, timber sold for $10 a picul in Canton. If the chiefs could be convinced to trade a picul of wood for a dollar's worth of whiskey, all the better for the merchant. Of course, from the chiefs' perspective, the labor for timber extraction was essentially free.

The commodification of sandalwood eliminated many of the socioecological protections built into Hawaiian land division. Ahupua'a were established to provide a roughly equal valuation for land: windward areas that could produce more resources per hectare were divided into many, small ahupua'a, while leeward regions with less primary production were apportioned into few, large divisions. By balancing productivity between ahupua'a, the system of land division helped balance populations, taxation, and chiefly influence. But with the commodification of sandalwood, the market broke apart these forms of equivalency. An ahupua'a with abundant sandalwood could reap higher rewards for its chief than one without sandalwood. Chiefs with roughly equal wealth and authority abruptly found themselves moving in opposite directions on the spectrum of political influence.

Historically, the intended self-sufficiency of each ahupua'a was critical for preventing large-scale production failures: with little movement of labor or food across ahupua'a boundaries, subsistence crises in one watershed were less likely to spread to others. The breakdown of the ahupua'a system eliminated the protective influence of these boundaries: labor could be moved vast distances at the behest of increasingly powerful chiefs, without a concomitant movement of food or food production. Starvation could now occur in an ahupua'a for reasons unrelated to local environmental stress or warfare; and such starvation could quickly spread to neighboring areas simply through the movement of bodies. The commodification of a single forest product (with an uneven spatial distribution) destroyed existing equivalencies, destabilizing a system that had protected agricultural production and balanced chiefly power for centuries.

Prior to sandalwood, chiefly wealth came with social obligations. Through Makahiki ceremonies, chiefs returned a measure of taxed goods and food to commoners. The kapu system protected the rights of commoners to move between ahupua'a and appeal charges. The political standing of a chief depended on the productivity of his land and the size of the army he could amass for war—measures that encouraged investment in landesque capital and discouraged excessive brutality. But with the sandalwood trade, the wealth returned in exchange for timber came with no social obligation: there was no requirement to distribute the luxuries acquired through trade back into the hands of commoners. Political standing was no longer a function of agricultural production or a healthy population. Instead, the eminence of chiefs rose and fell on the power to negotiate terms of trade and compel labor toward the forest.

At the interface with foreign trade, the ability of Hawaiian labor to extract a natural resource and pass value up the political hierarchy was translated into a commodity that fit the parameters of merchant capitalism. In return, the interface provided abundant personal wealth to the top of the hierarchy: wealth that was not retranslated back into goods, services, or capital that could benefit commoners.

The Decline of the Kapu System

The second conjuncture that helped decouple chiefs' livelihoods from agriculture was the decline of the kapu system. Early growth in the Pacific Trade established new forms of valuation that benefited merchants and chiefs, undermined those valuations that protected commoner livelihoods, and helped initiate the first food crisis between 1811 and 1816. However, Kamehameha's consolidation of the sandalwood trade under a royal monopoly temporarily delayed calamity. The monopoly eliminated competition between chiefs and prevented merchants from playing chiefs against each other. It also gave the king full authority to impose restrictions on conscripted labor and timber extraction. Chiefs could only take labor away from agriculture for short periods and were not allowed to cut young trees. Kamakau (1961) notes that the king paid commoners for timber extraction with food (though the actual "wage" is not reported), and refocused corvée labor on improvements to infrastructure.

Through these policies, Kamehameha effectively "nationalized" the sandalwood industry, albeit without being recognized as a sovereign state. Some of the value realized through the export of sandalwood was returned to commoners through food. The king alone could influence the price of timber by controlling the quantity sold. Most importantly, agricultural production was preserved through the conscription limits placed on chiefs. None of these measures would have been possible without the custom of absolute authority granted to the monarch; indeed, the king succeeded in controlling the trade by taking advantage of Hawaii's strict hierarchy of chiefdom, a system of governance maintained by the politico-religious kapu system.

With the coronation of Liholiho and the decline of kapu, it was inevitable that the royal monopoly, limits on conscription, and conservation measures would end. The detrimental impact on labor, however, was exacerbated by two factors. First, the exploitative relations of sandalwood production that were in effect before Kamehameha's monopoly were not altered during his reign. The willingness of merchants to sell luxuries to the chiefs enabled the nobility to amass wealth outside of agricultural and craft production, effectively decoupling chiefs' livelihoods from commoner production. With the end of the monopoly, powerful chiefs regained control of the trade at the precise moment demand was driving the price to unprecedented heights.

Second, the kapu system did not entirely disappear. Feudal land tenure was broadly retained, with commoners obliged to obey the demands of conscription and taxation, or face expulsion. But the ties of reciprocity that moved material wealth from chiefs to commoners were generally abandoned. Many of these welfare practices—like Makahiki—had been associated with religious doctrine and maintained by the priesthood. Unfortunately, it was the religious part of the politico-religious system that largely came to an end in 1819. Without the benefit of a judicial priesthood, penalties for transgressions fell to the whim of each chief. By the onset of the second crisis in the 1820s, the cycle of taxation and welfare that had linked chiefly wealth production with commoner food consumption was effectively gone.

Like the dismantling of kapu, Liholiho's decentralization of the sandalwood trade was also incomplete. With respect to exchange, chiefs could now compete with each other to negotiate the best terms of trade. But two decades under unified rule had changed the spatial scale at which absolute authority resided.

Before unification, lesser chiefs acted at the behest of their immediate superiors: a regional chief or the king who ruled the island. Labor was recruited and armies conscripted at the scale of the ahupua'a or, in rare cases, an entire island. After unification, the concept of conscription evolved to include the entire island chain. Commoners could now be drawn away from their homes at the whims of distant (and powerful) chiefs that they had never served. Kamehameha used the monopoly to justify sweeping labor policies that applied everywhere and to everyone. Even though Liholiho eliminated the monopoly and devolved the benefits of trade to individual chiefs, he insisted that labor could still be conscripted at the scale of whole islands. This expansion of scale allowed powerful chiefs to take advantage of subjects outside their territory, especially regarding sandalwood extraction and the payment of royal debt. By supplanting the authority of the ahupua'a as the unit of labor enrollment, Liholiho broke the lock on limited food crises and introduced the possibility of widespread provisioning failure. Famine was no longer isolated to drought-prone valleys in leeward districts. Like labor, it could travel almost anywhere.

The Sandalwood Tax

One of the most basic forms of protection was the kinship network through which households exchanged food, shelter, and labor in times of crisis. Early visitors frequently commented on the willingness of commoners to open their home to visiting family members who had fallen on hard times. Unlike other forms of reciprocity that disappeared with the kapu system, these kinship practices were maintained throughout the 19th century, offering some measure of stability during this period of social upheaval. But after 1826, the effectiveness of kinship exchange was severely undermined by the monarchy's most significant imposition: the universal head tax on sandalwood.

Kinship exchange worked by spreading risk across multiple households and multiple geographical environments: if crops failed in one region, villagers traveled to in-laws or other relations in places where food was still abundant. If circumstances ever reversed, the favor was gratefully returned. Kinship exchange could fail if every household experienced the same stress. When no one has surplus shelter, food, or labor, pursuing relief from relatives becomes fruitless and costly. The sandalwood tax of 1827 required every male to provide a half-picul of timber or pay four Spanish dollars, and every female to pay one Spanish dollar or the equivalent in craftwork. As such, the tax created an identical (and sizeable) stress on every household, substantially reducing the efficacy of kinship exchange.

By forcing individuals to supply sandalwood, the tax contravened the need for collective labor. Indeed, the tax placed commoners in competition with each other to locate and collect the last remaining stands of timber. In other trades, where most work can be performed by a single person, the elimination of collective labor may have had little or no effect on productivity. But sandalwood extraction was different: locating, felling, and cutting a tree to size involved many people. Carrying the timber to shore—a journey that might take several days—could be accomplished more quickly when others shared the burden. These tasks benefited from the economies of scale that came with shared effort. As such, it is possible that the elimination of collective labor substantially increased the human effort needed to produce a picul of timber.

Competition between individuals also initiated a new and important conjuncture that would alter the trajectory of the economy and influence Hawaii's eventual annexation by the United States. By placing commoners in competition with each other, the sandalwood tax helped reproduce Marx's (1970) fourth form of alienation: the alienation of laborers from each other. Competition for material survival slowly dissolved remaining lateral networks of support, making laborers increasingly dependent on the wage economy for social reproduction. With the sandalwood tax, the monarchy unwittingly set the stage for a more complete commodification of labor that would emerge to support the sugar industry later in the 19th century.

As with decentralization and the end of the kapu system, the sandalwood tax is an example of the monarchy's selective and contradictory dismantling of existing systems. First, Liholiho declared an end to the sandalwood monopoly (a case of disaggregation) but retained a definition of conscription that protected the centralized coordination of labor (a case of aggregation). Second, the monarchy declared an end to religious control over practices that benefited commoners (disaggregation) but preserved the system of land tenure and conscription that benefited chiefs (aggregation). Finally, the monarchy imposed a universal tax to pay royal debts (aggregation) and in so doing, discouraged collective labor and pitted commoners against each other (disaggregation).

This analysis has concerned itself primarily with those activities, materials, and relationships that were present and operating at each phase in the evolution of Hawaii's sandalwood famines. However, it is also important to consider what was not present. Hawaii's 900-year-old agricultural tradition had a long history of adapting to crises. But in the 1820s, it didn't. The reasons may have much to do with what was missing. Without intervention from prominent missionaries or diplomats, broad resistance to the chiefs could not be mobilized. Without imports of food or new staple cultivars, food consumption could not diversify. Without new technologies, agriculture could not intensify. And without additional labor, production could not reclaim abandoned fields and overcome the effects of fragmentation, nor could it expand into more productive areas. Indeed, if one thing contributed the most to Hawaiian agriculture's resilience in the face of war, drought, and disease, it was the remarkable ability of laboring bodies to squeeze every available calorie out of every available hectare. By the 1820s, labor, too, had gone missing in the mountains.

Conclusions: Sandalwood and Feudal–Capitalism

The starvation and exposure that claimed Hawaiian lives between 1811 and 1830 was caused by a decline in total food production and the forced displacement of bodies away from sources of food. Underlying these two conjunctures was sandalwood: Hawaii's first export commodity and the force behind sweeping changes to the islands' political economy. Driving the growth in sandalwood was the burgeoning Pacific Trade, the U.S. banking crisis of 1819, and the loss of welfare relations once protected by kapu. Meanwhile, population decline, disappearing timber, El Niño events in 1815 and 1824, and the eruption of Tambora may have added pressure to already precarious agricultural production.

Stories like this are found throughout the late colonial period, and though the economies and geographies differ, the basic narrative remains the same: in the collision between subsistence production and global markets, it is the global market that inevitably wins. It does so by reforming the local economy to suit the interests of capital through the elimination of social protections, the creation of new dependencies, and the redirection of local economies toward production for exchange. According to this narrative, at the interface between capitalism and a traditional economy, capitalist relations of production colonize and break down existing networks of exchange, exposing producers to increased risk. We find this story retold through the Victorian famines of India (Davis 2002), the Qing dynasty famines of China (Mallory 1926; Edgerton-Tarpley 2008), and post-independence famines throughout sub-Saharan Africa (Meillassoux 1974; Franke and Chasin 1980; Watts 2013).

But what *actually* takes place at this interface? By what means does one system of valuation and exchange supplant another? Do the verbs *supplant*, *replace*, or *colonize* reflect what is taking place? The structural reorganization that triggered the sandalwood famines was connected to broader transformations initiated through foreign contact and trade. As such, to better understand the famine is to better understand the dynamic nature of this encounter between modes of production.

Merchant capitalism attempted to extract value from Hawaiian production through a variety of mechanisms. The first was ship provisioning, whereby weapons and metal trinkets were exchanged for agricultural products that could be consumed during long voyages across the Pacific. In this way, the value of Hawaiian labor was used to satisfy the immediate subsistence needs of foreign crews. But with the discovery of sandalwood, Hawaii became a trading destination in and of itself. Foreign merchants quickly expanded their interests to include the tree, processes of timber collection, and the chiefs who controlled its extraction. In their holds, ships already carried the Chinese and Western merchandise with which to trade for sandalwood. All the merchants needed were chiefs willing to buy such extravagances. On the Hawaiian side, kings and chiefs took advantage of this new opportunity, expanding forms of wealth production to include exchange with foreigners and processes of sandalwood extraction. The importance of food and craft production to chiefs began to decline, decoupling chiefly livelihoods from commoners, and eliminating the incentive to protect agriculture.

Through this transformation, the interface between capitalism and feudalism opened up a second interface: between chiefs and commoners. This interface was not new; the long-standing relationship between these classes had been governed by the kapu system. But with the partial dismantling of kapu, chiefs were free from obligations to commoners while commoner obligations to chiefs were reinforced. Indeed, the point of opening the interface between chiefs and commoners was to reform the feudal economy's internal systems of equivalency in ways that benefited capital.

As with capitalism, feudalism operates through systems of equivalency that determine what and how much can be exchanged. Processes of translation at the interface convert valuations from one system to another (see Tsing 2015). In Hawaiian feudalism, commoners provided a percentage of their labor and production to the nobility. In exchange, the nobility granted commoners usufruct rights to the land, small contributions of food and material, and various processes of redress. This exchange may not have been fair (in a Western sense), but it protected food provisioning by linking chiefly wealth to agricultural production. To increase profits, chiefs and merchants modified this system to their advantage.

Another system of equivalency that protected commoner livelihoods was Hawaii's tradition of land division. Ahupua'a were established to balance production, population, and chiefly power across units of land. To make the sandalwood trade work, this system had to be replaced with one that permitted island-wide conscription and extraction. Kamehameha unwittingly assisted this process by unifying the islands and monopolizing the trade.

This case study differs from the portrayal of other capitalist-feudalist encounters in one key regard. In Hawaii, as traditional equivalencies collapsed, capitalism did not replace them with its own. There was no market penetration; no "colonization" with capitalist logic. No corporations were established to extract timber, no wages were paid, no labor market was created, and no commoners were given ownership of land. Merchants and diplomats were content to let the chiefs take care of the messy business of timber extraction: after all, a free market for labor (employed through local enterprises) would have threatened merchant profits. Feudalism was good for business so long as it could be tweaked, and this meant breaking it—and resetting it—in specific places.

The most obvious example of this fractured transition is the absence of trade in food. With labor directed away from agriculture and toward production for export, food shortages could have been alleviated through imports. Indeed, modern resource booms that occur in free market contexts tend to produce a steady resource-for-food exchange.[21] This principle forms the basis for import substitution and agriculture-led economic takeoff (Norton, Alwang, and Masters 2014). But in Hawaii, no food imports took up the slack as people starved. The Pacific

Trade was never interested in moving food to Hawaii: the value of the islands had always been the ability for ships to *acquire* food, not to exchange it for other goods.

The Hawaiian conjuncture with global capitalism did not destroy and rebuild the islands' economy; rather, it drove the selective reorganization and repurposing of existing relations. Feudalism fractured but did not completely disappear. The hybrid *feudal-capitalist* economy that emerged helped chiefs and merchants amass enormous wealth while thousands died. Contrary to the dreams of responsible diplomats and proselytizing missionaries, Hawaii's first encounter with global markets did not produce a more modern and civilized society. Instead, the first step out of feudalism was, for a time, a step into slavery.

———————

It is hard to die from hunger, a fact that remained true in a unified and peaceful Hawaii a decade into the 19th century. Drought and warfare brought occasional famine, but the social and agricultural systems perfected by Islanders over the centuries demonstrated a remarkable ability to absorb stress and support population growth within environmental constraints. Indeed, it is worth noting that it took unprecedented pressure from foreign governments and global trade, the sudden abandonment of social safety nets, and the co-option of the Hawaiian ruling class before mass starvation settled in. By necessity, this has been a story of food system failure, but it is also a story of remarkable resilience in the face of inexorable change.

Sandalwood was all but gone by 1830, thanks in part to the wild descendants of Vancouver's hungry cows. With it went the timber trade and the worst of the food crisis. Twenty years later, in a dark twist of history, Hawaiians found solidarity with another working class a world away. At the height of the Great Irish Famine and again during the Lancashire Cotton Famine, Hawaiian congregations took up a collection and sent money to help starving Europeans (Donne 1866). The goodwill between Hawaiians and haole that Vancouver and Kamehameha had worked so hard to cultivate—unlike so much else—was still very much alive.

CHAPTER 2

Madagascar's "Cactus War": 1924–30

When the raiketa gasy vanished, the strong men left to live elsewhere. They went to Diego, Majanga, Morondava, and other places in the North. They left because it was difficult to live without the raiketa gasy. The land here is no longer blessed (raty tanana) and those without patience must leave because there is no water. That is the reason why we are so few now. We are hungry; we are thirsty. There is no water. There is no food. We have rags for clothing. Those who have cattle sell them for food and clothes; those who don't have cattle starve and wear sadia (loin cloths) . . . There are no lazy people here, for they all have died.

—Edward L. Powe, *The Lore of Madagascar*

For cactus pastoralists, the famine that consumed southern Madagascar in 1930–31 marks a watershed in their relationship with the French colonial government (Kaufmann 2011). Local Karembola speak of this watershed as dividing the "time of the ancestors" from "foreign time" (Middleton 1999, 69). Before 1930, in the time of the ancestors, southern pastoralists like the Karembola, Mahafale, and Antandroy were territorial and isolationist. Locals resisted foreign trespassers and ignored growing demand for wage labor. Tribal populations grew steadily alongside expanding herds of cattle and abundant cactus. After 1930, during foreign time, tens of thousands were forced to leave for work on northern plantations, making southern Madagascar the "most important source of cheap, unskilled wage labor" for French businesses on the island (Middleton 1999, 218). Large herds fell into decline as the cactus that sustained them vanished. Repeated famines and epidemics led to a precipitous decrease in population, leading some colonial administrators to worry that these ethnic groups might disappear entirely (Middleton 1999). Indeed, as the French pushed Madagascar into the mid-20th century with their *mission civilisatrice*, the cattle-herding cultures of the "deep South" became more vulnerable to food system failure, not less (see Kaufmann 1998).

At the heart of these changes was the collapse of the South's pastoral economy and system of food provisioning—a collapse initiated by a single insect plague. *Raketa gasy* (or simply *raketa*) is the local term for a spiny variety of prickly pear cactus that used to grow throughout the arid South. Before 1930, herders practiced what came to be known as "cactus pastoralism"—a method of cattle rearing that maintained the animals on a partial diet of raketa. The abundant cactus not only supplied fodder for cows and people, it provided corrals for livestock and security for villages. Dense thickets of cactus kept humans and cattle safe from rustlers, tax collectors, and French soldiers. In late 1924, a colony of cochineal—a tiny, scale insect known as a source of red dye—was released into the cactus-rich South. Five years later, raketa was gone.

Cochineal (*Dactylopius tomentosus*) multiplies prodigiously, travels well on favorable winds, and quickly consumes its sole source of food: prickly pear. As swarms of cochineal females and nymphs eat the broad, ovate "leaves" of the cactus, they secrete a distinctive white wax that covers the colony and protects it from predators and the elements. A mere five years after its introduction, the ensuing plague had cleared 64,370 square kilometers of raketa in the pastoral south, an area one-sixth the size of France (Kaufmann 2000). Among the Mahafale, this swift and near-complete transformation of pastoral ecology came to be known as *ty toan' pondy foty*—the "years of white poison"—in observance of the white wax that suffocated the South's once-abundant cactus (Kaufmann 2011, 134). In the short term, the destruction of raketa led to a local collapse of cactus pastoralism and a famine that killed as many as 300,000 cattle and 30,000 people.[1] In the longer term, the years of white poison bent southern Madagascar's mode of production toward colonial objectives, from an economy that exported beef to one that exported people.

Plagues of insects, usually locusts, have long been associated with subsistence crises (Lockwood 2009). In such cases, a confluence of "natural" events creates ideal conditions for the rapid expansion of an insect population that destroys staple crops. For example, a locust plague triggered by unusually high desert rainfall and strong winds is blamed for exacerbating the 1915–18 famine in Lebanon and Syria (Foster 2015). Furthermore, the late colonial period is rife with examples of accidental species introductions that had disastrous impacts on agriculture (Long 1981, 2003; Crosby 2004).

But Madagascar's cochineal plague is different. The colony of *D. tomentosus* that destroyed raketa did not arrive in the South through an unusual weather event or as a biotic stowaway but was deliberately released into a stand of cactus outside Toliara in late 1924 by the renowned botanist Henri Perrier de la Bâthie. The release marked the culmination of a long-standing debate among French scientists and administrators over the best way to tackle the problem of raketa and southern development—a decades-long controversy shaped as much by the contours of power in Paris as by the demands of colonial consolidation in Madagascar.

Depending on the commentator, Bâthie's act falls somewhere between gross negligence and state-sanctioned biological warfare. After the famine, historians debated questions of colonial responsibility: could the French have predicted the ensuing mass starvation? How much did economic motives drive the decision? Who brought cochineal to Madagascar in the first place? For our purposes, to understand the famine requires an analysis of the slow-emerging structural transformations taking place on both sides of the South's raketa fences. On the Malagasy side, this includes a long history of adaptations by herders who converted from traditional pastoralism to cactus pastoralism; on the colonial side, a steady shift in French perspectives on the colony and the people of the South. The collapse of southern food provisioning was shaped as much by centuries-long sociopolitical conjunctures as by a handful of transformative moments, including the opening of the Suez Canal, the Franco-Prussian War, and a chance encounter between would-be revolutionaries in a Paris apartment. Woven into this tapestry is an environmental history of cows, cactus, and cochineal: a network of material interdependencies and social practices developed to sustain human settlement in a land that receives less than 12 inches of rain per year.

As with Hawaii's sandalwood famines, Madagascar's Cactus War is a story about labor; in this case, a "civilizing mission" intent on extracting taxes and producing plantation workers, confronted with a subsistence economy ready to resist wage labor at all cost. But unlike in Hawaii where labor could be expropriated through the reorganization of feudalism, Madagascar's colonial architects needed first to reorganize the *socioecology* of the South, a task that required France to sever the pastoral dependence on cactus and remake the South's ecological landscape. In the end, a botanist with a matchbox filled with bugs succeeded where decades of military might had failed.

This is also a story about *involution*: a doubling down on historical patterns of decision-making during times of pressure. The classic example of involution describes a colonized society becoming increasingly dependent on traditional strategies of production in response to growing imperial demand (Geertz 1963; Boonstra and de Boer 2014). Over time, it becomes harder to break with tradition: opportunities for beneficial reorganization gradually disappear until, eventually, the system can no longer withstand external pressure. The growing pastoral dependence on cactus up to 1925 is a prototypical example of involution leading to collapse. But involution wasn't confined to Malagasy herders. Among the French, perceptions and policies surrounding cactus and colonists experienced a similar inward-turning. Positions became entrenched as old ways of thinking crowded out alternatives. Political and capitalist imperatives drove the selection of governors as influential colons cultivated powerful connections to bolster personal enterprises. In Paris and Antananarivo, the colony's "politics of ecology" became increasingly entangled with its ecology of politics. By the mid-1920s, the prospect of a biological war against southern pastoralism—at one time merely a thought experiment—had been elevated to a necessity.

Finally, based on the historical data collected in this study, it is possible that most of the human and animal victims of the 1930–31 famine died from dehydration, not starvation. If this is the case, the collapse of the South's food system was also—critically—a collapse of water provisioning. Of course, like insect plagues, failures in water provisioning are frequently associated with famine. Drought and flood have long been considered prototypical natural disasters driving subsistence failure through the destruction of primary production (see Dando 1980). But in this case, causation was reversed: the sudden loss of primary production may have been responsible for the disappearance of water. To understand this inversion, we must examine the hydrology of the South, the biology and ecology of prickly pear, and the physical demands of the human body.

At the porous interfaces between bodies, cows, and cacti, 150 years of steady socionatural change prepared the way for food system collapse. At the apex of this transformation, the French unleashed a biological invasion that initiated mass mortality, permanently altered the South's economy, and condemned the next three generations of Madagascar's pastoralists to unrelenting hunger.

This chapter is organized into four sections. The first provides a brief history of mass starvation in Madagascar's deep South, the challenges involved in interpreting colonial writings, and the role of critical environmental history in explicating social and ecological change. The second section describes cactus pastoralism leading up to 1924: diets and staple crops, social organization, herding practices, and the environmental history of raketa. Section three traces the history of this food system between 1769 and the release of cochineal in late 1924. This history includes the growth of raketa, the arrival of the French in Madagascar, colonial efforts to consolidate the South, and the response from pastoralists. The final section assembles these pieces to identify the socioecological transformations that led the French to embrace imperialism-by-plague at the precise moment when the ecology of southern food provisioning was most vulnerable.

Famine Histories of the Deep South

Since the arrival of Portuguese explorers in the early 16th century, Western writers have focused primary attention on the landscape, history, and people of Madagascar's central plateau. This densely populated region, known as Imerina, is the traditional home of the Merina ethnic group. The area around the capital, Antananarivo, was the historical seat of the Merina kingdom, a succession of powerful monarchs that conquered large areas of Madagascar and deterred foreign conquest until the French invasion of 1895. Throughout the 1800s, British, French, and American dignitaries and merchants traveled to Antananarivo to set up diplomatic missions and establish trade (Brown 2000). For many of these travelers, the rainy, mountainous interior was the only part of Madagascar they saw, and the rice-cultivating Merina were the only ethnic group they observed.

As such, many Western-authored histories of Madagascar written during this period are essentially histories of the Merina kingdom. Ethnographies of the Malagasy are largely ethnographies of the Merina people, while geographical surveys of Madagascar are often limited to descriptions of the central plateau. Sweeping claims about Malagasy agriculture, cultural practice, and religion tend to exclude the diverse ethnic communities on the periphery of Merina control, especially in the sparsely populated South. For example, Copland's *A History of the Island of Madagascar* (1822) makes no mention of southern populations other than a brief note about early French occupation of Fort-Dauphin. More recently, Campbell's (2005) ambitiously titled *Economic History of Imperial Madagascar, 1750–1895*, fails to mention cactus or cactus pastoralism—the key form of subsistence and economic production in the South. Even when authors venture beyond the central highlands, Madagascar's other places and cultures receive little attention (cf. Campbell 1889; Cousins 1895). Such Merina-centrism in the literature makes it challenging to reconstruct the historical relationship between famine and pastoralism in the deep South.

European environmental perceptions provide an additional challenge. The so-called Spiny Desert, located at the island's extreme southern tip, is the driest part of Madagascar and arguably the least hospitable for human settlement. European impressions of Madagascar's southern people during the colonial period were colored by the harshness of this arid and isolated landscape. The Antandroy and Mahafale pastoralists who lived and raised cattle among the thorny xerophytes impressed visitors with their ability to eke an existence out of nothing. To these visitors, such an inhospitable place must have demanded special characteristics from its inhabitants: living "close to nature" surely forced local cultures to accept the specter of early death, dehydration, and starvation. Well into the 20th century, French commentators still considered famine to be a "way of life" for Madagascar's southern people. Deschamps (1959) expresses this environmental determinism:

> It is not these famines . . . that led Antandroy to emigrate. They were part of [Antandroy] tradition. They were the celebrated dates of [Antandroy] history . . . *Hunger was an ancestral custom*; the country had molded men in its own image. They did not dream of fleeing from it, knowing and desiring no other. (emphasis added)

This naturalization of hunger as a feature of the southern landscape served an important function for a colonial government attempting to make sense of the South. First, it offered a rationale for the seemingly desperate and "uncivilized" condition of local people, even as it reproduced such perceptions: the harshness of the environment and proximity to starvation must have prevented the pastoral savage from social and technical advancement. Second, it justified the intervention of France's civilizing mission: Christianity and European values surely offered—at the very least—freedom from the perpetual insecurity of subsistence among the thorns (see Petit 1929). Finally, so long as famine could be explained as a natural feature of the landscape, mass starvation was apolitical. No act of government, as questionable as it may seem, could be held responsible for famine so long as hunger was built into the very nature of the South. Should starvation happen, explanations came easily: the South was arid, prone to severe drought, lacked any infrastructure to support consistent agriculture, and lacked a population capable of technological advancement (for example, see Bâthie 1934).

So long as the South—by its very constitution—was deemed famine-prone, colonial-era commentators remained rather nonchalant about hunger and its causes. French writing on famine during this period tends to be sparse and short on details. As Middleton (1999, 218) notes, most histories of the region "devote no more than a few lines to the subject." But downplaying famine was not limited to colonial writers: Harold Nelson's (1973) *Area Handbook for the Malagasy Republic*, a guide written for members of the U.S. military and foreign service, makes no mention of any famines in the South despite noting the frequent occurrences of drought, locust plagues, typhoons, and leprosy. And when authors do raise the subject of famine, these discussions tend to assume natural—not political—causation.

Despite these shortcomings, an important body of work in the historical record *does* address the overlapping concerns of cactus, pastoralism, and famine. Three categories of authors contribute to this body of work. First, notable French administrators and scientists participated in lengthy and heated debates over cactus pastoralism, both before and after the release of cochineal. The writings of Henri Perrier de la Bâthie (1925, 1934, 1955), Georges Petit (1929), Raymond Decary (1925, 1928, 1930, 1947), Claudius Frappa (1932) and others offer insight into the peculiarities of colonial policy-making and the way southern economic and demographic "problems" were framed.

Second, English and American scholars in the mid-20th century investigated the collapse of cactus pastoralism through an interest in anticolonial movements and the post–World War II expansion of communism (cf. Stratton 1964; Heseltine 1971; Covell 1987). For these commentators, responsibility for the famine is broadly attributed to an ill-advised colonial government desperate to bring the South under control. The collapse of cactus pastoralism and the ensuing diaspora serve as a backdrop for resistance to colonial rule during the 1950s and eventual independence in 1960.

Finally, recent work in colonial history (Finch 2013), species introduction (Larsson 2004), and environmental development (von Heland and Folke 2014) has reinvigorated academic interest in Madagascar's Cactus War. Indeed, the history of raketa gasy's eradication has become especially relevant today as environmentalists, development agencies, and policy makers struggle with another species of invasive prickly pear (Middleton 2012). In this category, two scholars in particular—Karen Middleton and Jeffrey Kaufmann—have conducted extraordinary research on the 1924–30 event and its long-term consequences for local pastoralists (cf. Kaufmann 1998, 2000, 2001, 2008, 2011; Middleton 1999, 2009, 2012). Through a combination of archival investigation, interviews, and ethnographic research, these two anthropologists have assembled a body of work essential for an investigation of this kind. In the analysis that follows, I rely heavily on their contribution.

Most interpretations of the 1924–30 event focus on the choreography of colonial politics and its immediate impact on subject peoples. As such, these narratives fit well within a vast body of work on colonial history that interprets such struggles within a larger framework of North conquering South (see Loomba 2015). But as an analysis of food provisioning, this study must concern itself with sociopolitical and socio*natural* subjects on both sides of the colonial divide. For these reasons, my approach to historiography tends to be more consistent with critical environmental histories (cf. Crosby 2004; Butzer 2005; Hornborg, McNeill, and Martinez-Alier 2007; Beinart and Hughes 2009) than classical colonial ones.

Indeed, to provide adequate context for the famine requires, at a minimum, a partial reconstruction of the environmental history of southern Madagascar. Acquiring the data for such a task is particularly challenging in an imperial context because, for the most part, French authors were only interested in local ecology insofar as this nature pertained to colonial objectives. In the case of Madagascar, the French did not fully consider such objectives until 1895 when they gained control of the island. Even then, French interest in the South grew slowly. As such, much of the environmental history of the South before 1895 is missing from the documentary record and must be constructed from the notes of early travelers and analogues of pastoral practice in other parts of southern Africa (see Kaufmann 1998).

This partial reconstruction must span at least 150 years: in the same way that the South's vulnerability to current food crises can be traced to the destruction of raketa in the 1920s, the destruction of raketa can be traced to structural transformations taking place in the 18th and 19th centuries. After all, cactus pastoralism was not a traditional practice in the South, but an adaptation to the arrival and rapid spread of raketa gasy. In fact, the species of prickly pear that dominated the landscape and upon which pastoralism depended did not arrive in Madagascar until 1769: raketa gasy was an invasive species, just like the cochineal deployed 150 years later to destroy it. In a fitting irony, both raketa gasy and cochineal were released into the wild by the French, and both were intended to help bring the South into submission. The first biological invasion enlarged pastoralism and human settlement throughout the South. The second nearly destroyed it.

Food Provisioning in the Pastoral South

*Truly no land has been made so beautiful as this, so full of possibilities for develop-
ment and enjoyment, without a people capable of developing and enjoying it.*

—Belle McPherson Campbell, *Madagascar*

Madagascar, the fourth largest island in the world, lies in the Indian Ocean, 250 miles off the coast of Mozambique. Known as the Great Red Island for the color of its laterite soils, Madagascar's geology, ecology, and demography have attracted attention from European writers since its "discovery" by Portuguese explorers in the 16th century. Situated on the nautical routes between the Cape of Good Hope and the East Indies, strategic interest in Madagascar grew during the 18th and 19th centuries as Dutch, British, and French governments sought to protect their overseas territories. Beyond geopolitics, Madagascar's unique natural environment drew the attention of geologists, zoologists, and botanists, just as its diverse—mostly animist—population piqued the interest of missionaries. As with Hawaii, Madagascar's geography fit European fantasies of tropical island paradises: its people uncorrupted, its riches unexploited, and its nature untamed.

Overall, Madagascar experiences a tropical marine climate but with significant variations in temperature and rainfall between coasts and interior, and between east and west sides of the island. Easterly trade winds ensure that the east coast sees abundant rainfall for most of the year; as much as 10–18 inches of rain per month (Bâthie 1934). The rain shadow created by the mountainous central highlands mitigates the effect of the trades and ensures that the western half of the island experiences a dry season of several months. In the central plateau, the dry season is generally short and maximum temperatures are considerably lower than on the humid coasts (Nelson 1973). The south of Madagascar is the driest part of the island and experiences some of the greatest variations in rainfall. This is especially pronounced in the southeast near Fort-Dauphin, where humid easterlies run headlong into the Beampingaratra Mountains: "stands of rainforest on the eastern face of a narrow mountain range are within ten miles of semi-desert vegetation on the western slopes" (Bâthie 1934, 39). Toward the west and south, desert environments receive less than 12 inches of rain per year.

November through April mark the rainy season and bring the warmest temperatures. By contrast, cool, dry weather tends to prevail from May through October. The South experiences the highest overall temperatures, while the central highlands tend to be coolest: in Tsihombe, near the southern tip, peak daytime temperatures in March may reach 34°C, while nightly lows in June and July rarely drop below 18°C. Antananarivo in the central highlands may experience freezing temperatures in July (Nelson 1973). Rainfall in the south varies significantly between seasons. Between June and September, it is common to receive less than an inch of rain per month; as much as four inches per month may fall between October and January. During the colonial period, the timing and amount of rain during these months invariably determined the success or failure of small-scale cultivation in the South (Decary 1921).

The arid region that was home to cactus pastoralists and abundant raketa gasy occupies approximately 5000 square kilometers in the extreme south of the island (see fig. 4). From east to west, four rivers transect this region: the Mandrare,

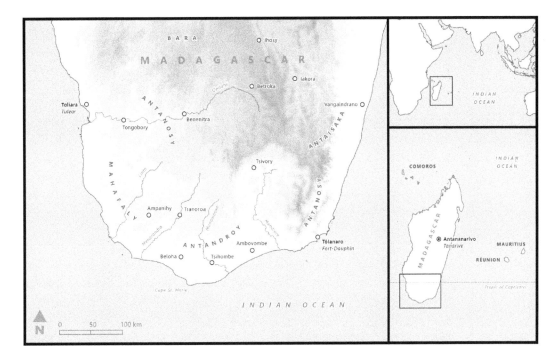

Figure 4. Overview map of southern Madagascar. Wherever colonial-era place-names differ from modern ones, colonial-era names are indicated in italics. General location of ethnic groups is indicated with curved text.

Manambovo, Menarandra, and Linta. Historically, these rivers offered a convenient means for understanding the distribution of tribal groups and pastoral practices. Antandroy considered the land between the Menarandra and the Mandrare their ancestral homeland, while Mahafale occupied land to the west of the Menarandra (Deschamps 1959). Although pastoralism was the dominant form of economic production throughout this region, cactus pastoralism was concentrated around the Manambovo, especially south of the Beloha-Tsihombe-Ambovombe line (Bathie 1934). Raketa and its practical use as fodder proliferated throughout southern Madagascar, but it is here in the southern reaches of the Manambovo that the scarcity of water and lack of natural forage made cactus pastoralism a necessity (Decary 1925).

The topography of the deep South is generally flat and offers few consistent sources of water. The major rivers that transect this region have their headwaters in northern mountain ranges. During the rainy season, these rivers carry abundant water, but may cease flowing entirely when the rains end. During the dry season, it is common for these rivers to dry up before reaching the sea. Bâthie (1934) observes that the geology of the region is not suitable for artesian aquifers: thick layers of highly permeable sediment overlay impervious crystalline rock, with no intervening porous rock layer. In large areas of the South, the permeable layer of overbearing sediment is too thick to make wells feasible. Watering holes in this part of the desert are hard to find, and those that provide consistent water during the dry season are usually proximate to one of the major rivers.

Madagascar is widely recognized for its unique ecology. An extraordinary number of plant and animal species are found only in Madagascar, leading to the declaration of the island as a "biodiversity hotspot" (Myers et al. 2000). High biodiversity and ongoing habitat loss—especially deforestation—have attracted considerable attention in conservation circles. Though recent conservation efforts have focused primarily on the forested ecosystems of the interior, the Spiny Desert (or Spiny Forest) is one of the World Wildlife Fund's Global 200 "priority ecoregions" and contains an extraordinary number of endemic and endangered species (Myers et al. 2000).

Unlike the sandy deserts of Arabia and North Africa, this dry, generally flat peneplain is covered in low, thorny shrubs and trees that have adapted to the lack of water. Trees like the baobab (*Adansonia*), large succulents like the Madagascar ocotillo (*Alluaudia procera*), and spiny thickets of *Didiereoideae* and spurges (*Euphorbiaceae*) have evolved to extract precious water from the permeable limestone soils of the South. Many species of cactus and succulent grow sharp spines to reduce transpiration and deter herbivores. *Androy*, the name for the traditional land of the Antandroy people, means "country of thornbushes" and the Antandroy are "the people of the thornbush." (Deschamps 1959; Nelson 1973).

By the mid- to late 19th century, the landscape of the deep South was dominated by raketa gasy, a species of prickly pear cactus (*Opuntia vulgaris*) introduced by the French military during the settlement of Fort-Dauphin in 1769 (Kaufmann 2001). Native to central and western Mexico, prickly pear found the dry, sandy soils of the Spiny Desert much to its liking. As raketa spread, it forced out many endemic florae from the South including a species of *Euphorbiaceae* known locally as *samata*. A short, flowering tree, samata had been the preferred fodder for cattle pastoralism before the arrival of raketa, but its slower rate of growth meant it could never support large herds nor, consequently, extensive human settlement. Most importantly, unlike raketa, there is no evidence that samata was ever deliberately cultivated by pastoralists (Kaufmann 2001). In fact, the human propagation of raketa during the late 1700s and early 1800s was critical to the production of the extensive *région cactée*, that otherworldly landscape of impenetrable spines that both intrigued and antagonized French administrators by the turn of the 20th century.

Bodies

Madagascar is not an island, but an archipelago.

—Malagasy saying, from Maureen Covell's *Madagascar*

The Far-South was a sort of island on the island, a world apart.

—Hubert Deschamps, *Les migrations intérieures passées et présentes à Madagascar*

The people of Madagascar share many linguistic and cultural traits, a fact that masks extraordinary ethnic diversity (Nelson 1973). Decades of control by Merina monarchs helped ensure standardization in many forms of social practice, especially those related to trade and government. But this superficial unity hid significant variations in culture and forms of subsistence. It also masked a deep-seated animosity toward Merina rule.

Two ethnic groups, the Antandroy and Mahafale, occupied the parts of the deep South where cactus pastoralism was commonplace. Located between the Mandrare and Menarandra rivers (see fig. 4), Antandroy communities operated autonomously: there was no central Antandroy authority beyond the establishment of local leadership councils. As in decentralized societies in other parts of the world (see Vergouwen 1964; Scott 1976), Antandroy communities were loosely bound to each other by kinship relations established through marriage. Almost all economic activity centered around the tending of cattle. Prior to the destruction of raketa, no Merina monarch nor French governor had successfully brought the Antandroy to heel. This long-standing resistance to outsiders helped perpetuate the mystique of *Androy* impenetrability—a narrative that would later inflame French obsession with the South.

Mahafale territory extended west from the Menarandra to the Onilahy River (Nelson 1973). Like the Antandroy, Mahafale communities were generally autonomous and pastoral. Following a series of French military expeditions in the late 1800s, most Mahafale groups swore allegiance to the colonial government, though these promises of loyalty invariably meant more to the French than the Mahafale, whose allegiances often shifted (Nelson 1973). Meanwhile, the enforcement of such loyalty was costly for the colonial treasury and the French military (Finch 2013).

Both Antandroy and Mahafale religious practices centered around ancestor worship. "The dead were the guardians of moral codes whose prescriptions must be followed . . . whoever acted against their wishes, whoever disturbed the social order would suffer mystical sanctions" (Nelson 1973, 101). Important decisions, like the timing of key ceremonies and rites of passage, were invariably made in consultation with family ancestors (*vazimba*), usually through a medium (Cousins 1895). There were no sacred documents, nor any priestly class: individual and community fortunes were understood to rest entirely on the inclinations of powerful forebears. The primacy of ancestors in all social matters was manifested in the landscape through the proliferation of family tombs. Nelson (1973) notes that large kinship groups (*foko*) defined their territory by the location of these prominent structures. The ultimate sign of belonging to a kinship group was the promise of burial in the group's common tomb, an honor bestowed by the most powerful person in the kinship group, often a "government employee or wealthy person" (Nelson 1973, 81). But the right to common burial was not guaranteed: in fact, the threat of losing a place in the family tomb was usually sufficient to ensure compliance with codes of conduct.

French travelers and administrators in the South viewed Antandroy and Mahafale pastoralists as conservative, isolationist, and resistant to modernization and foreign ideas. Deschamps (1959, 69) writes: "This independence, fiercely protected by sage and thorn, isolated the Far-South, and especially the Androy, in an almost absolute way . . . The Antandroy distrusted everything that was not his country and was reluctant to leave it." In a similar vein, Decary (1928, 21) writes: "Temporary displacements for the service of authority were extremely painful to [the Antandroy], and couriers were not easily recruited for Fort-Dauphin." Nelson (1973, 92) notes the "extreme prudence" among the Antandroy "concerning new enterprises and the mistrust and fear of originality and innovation . . . whatever is new is charged with danger." Foreign impressions of Southern conservatism, though exaggerated, are not entirely without merit. Conservatism is not uncommon to pastoral societies, especially in arid contexts where unpredictable rainfall requires the maintenance of precautionary measures (Livingstone 1977). Among Southern ethnic groups, ritual taboos were seen as productive and pragmatic guides to survival rather than constraints on personal freedom (Kaufmann 2011). This pragmatic dedication to tradition was reinforced by raketa: after all, the spread of cactus dramatically increased the security of homes and herds.

Cactus Pastoralism

The form of pastoralism practiced by many Antandroy and Mahafale in the arid South relied heavily on the use of raketa as a cattle fodder, human food, and living hedge for animal enclosures and fortifications. Compared to the long tradition of pastoralism, the integration of cactus into existing practices was a recent adaptation. Cattle herding has a long history in Madagascar: archeological evidence of butchered cattle bones dating from AD 1100–1200 have been found at the confluence of the Manambovo and Andranasoa rivers (Kaufmann 1998). By contrast, the variety of prickly pear on which cactus pastoralism depended arrived in

1769, with the progressive inclusion of cactus into pastoral practices taking place over the next 150 years. During this time, the proliferation of raketa encouraged further settlement of the arid South: population estimates for the pre-raketa period are not available, but by 1925, cactus pastoralists in Ambovombe and Tsihombe districts comprised a population of approximately 150,000 people and 350,000 cattle (Decary 1925).

Similar to other pastoral systems, Antandroy and Mahafale pastoralists moved their herds between northern and southern grazing lands to take advantage of seasonal fodder. During the winter months (July through October in the Southern Hemisphere), herders moved most of their cattle north into Haut Menarandra, Kokomba, Ikonda, and Ranomainty in search of pasture. At these higher elevations, summer and autumn rains (January through March) supported the growth of abundant grasses and shrubs for fodder. By the end of the winter and with the depletion of grass, herders began moving cattle back to their southern homes. During the summer months (November through June), cows were primarily sustained on raketa cladodes.[2]

To support human consumption, most communities engaged in limited subsistence agriculture, usually the production of millet, maize, and sweet potato.[3] Cultivation of these staples began after the herds returned to the South, coincident with early summer rains (December to January). As these crops matured, pastoralists gathered and ate the abundant raketa fruit that usually appeared between August and October. Between March and May, staple crops were harvested, stored, and consumed, slowly replacing the consumption of cactus fruit. Sufficient staples had to be stored during the fall and winter months to last through the northward migration: if rainfall was not sufficient between January and March, crop failure could jeopardize the northward migration and force households to look for other sources of food.

Unlike some pastoral societies, cows were not a primary source of food for the Antandroy and Mahafale, who rarely slaughtered their own cattle or consumed cow's milk (Campbell 2005). In fact, southerners consumed more grains than either meat or dairy (Kaufmann 1998). Herds functioned as a form of living savings account in which wealth was amassed as a protection against crop failure or other household adversity (Kaufmann 1998). When family wealth was plentiful, households invested in cattle. Cows were sold when there was a need to engage in exchange—for example, taxation, purchasing food or consumer goods, or paying for religious ceremonies. Cattle were also given away, killed, or sold during funerals, marriages, circumcisions, and healing ceremonies. In rare cases, a cow might be slaughtered as part of rituals for communicating with ancestors.

In this way, cows occupied a unique place in the pastoral economy. Allen and Covell (2005, 44) write: "Cattle represent more than a commodity, but a source and measure of family wealth." Without cows, southern households could not acquire social capital through gainful marriages nor build social standing by hosting important ceremonies. Households without cattle were increasingly isolated from bonds of kinship and dependent on inconsistent subsistence cultivation. As such, cattle ownership established the material basis for both physical survival and for participation in southern religion and culture.

In addition to formalized cattle exchange, cactus pastoralists participated in an extensive moral economy based on the exchange of gifts, especially labor (Nelson 1973; see also Scott 1976). Bonds established through both marriage and descent defined large kinship networks that could be called upon to assist in times of need. Nelson (1973) observes that these networks were activated at different times and places: for example, locals "may identify with their father's group while living in his village but with their mother's group while visiting hers." The flexibility of social identification helped enlarge the overall size of the network and broadened the identification of kin. Indeed, the support and solidarity of kin was considered an important social value in pastoral communities, a sentiment reflected in the Malagasy saying *tsihy be lambanana ny ambanilanitra*: "all who live under the sky are woven into one mat."

Southern kinship networks were reinforced through use: the continuous, bilateral exchange of gifts of labor and material served as a reminder of one's place in the community and the community's commitment to group survival. This fact may help explain the Antandroy and Mahafale disdain for salaried work, a cultural trait repeatedly mentioned by European observers (Nelson 1973). It was considered impolite to expect or receive payment for assistance from kin. For compensation to be offered or accepted was seen as a deliberate rejection of kinship; a conscious assertion of unfamiliarity between giver and receiver (see Mauss 2002). The cultural importance and material strength of these kinship networks may help explain the difficulties encountered by the colony in its attempt to introduce wage labor to the South.

In contrast with this moral economy, cattle rustling and intergroup conflict was a common practice among Antandroy and Mahafale until the 1930s. For the French, these acts of "lawlessness" were one of the most serious problems facing the South (Nelson 1973). The majority of cattle raids did not occur between neighbors but between distant groups that had a long history of animosity, for example, between Mahafale and Antandroy clans, or between Mahafale and northern Antifiheranana (Deschamps 1959; Kaufmann 2001). Neighboring groups that shared other ties of reciprocity usually maintained a *manaka-dia* ("hoof-tracking pact") that ensured any herders who had lost cattle could peacefully reclaim them from neighbors (Esaovelomandroso 1986). To curb cattle rustling, colonial administrators imposed serious punishments for offenders, but these measures were generally unsuccessful. Many herders objected to such severe punishments for something that was considered "a long-standing custom and not an ordinary crime" (Nelson 1973, 71).

During the winter months, cattle were grazed on northern pastures. If adequate rain fell during the summer and fall, these pastures provided plentiful fodder to support large herds. By mid-spring, as the grass was nearing depletion, herders prepared to move their cows back home. During the summer and spring months in the south, pastoralists fed their cattle a diet of raketa cladodes, a process that involved significant labor. The sharp spines of raketa prevented cows from grazing on the cactus in the wild. To remove the spines, herders painstakingly singed each cladode over a small fire. The heat burned off the thorns and softened the cactus flesh without evaporating the cladode's precious water content. Kaufmann (2001, 100) describes this process:

> At an early age boys become skilled with the *jia*, hardwood lances two to three meters long, tipped with a sharp iron point at one end and a cutter at the other. They jab the sharp flat cutting end into the narrow stem joining one pad to the next, slicing off a stem of three to five pads. They pierce the joint with the pointed end and place it carefully on the ground, making sure no thorns break off. They choose other stems that are not too old and hard for the cattle to chew. After they have cut a sufficient number of joints for the number of cattle they are tending, they stab three to four joints with the lance's pointed end and move them to a pile. They then *mandotse* or singe *raketa*: holding several joints over the fire at a time with the long pointed end, burning off the thorns without toasting the green pads, a process that softens the pads by making them "sweat." It is delicate and difficult work. Afterward, one picks up the now thornless joints with bare hands and slices them into piles of narrow strips in front of the cattle with a sharp iron long knife. When slicing the singed articles by hand, if the herder spots an unsinged thorn, he knocks it off with his long knife, thereby ensuring that the cattle will not consume any thorns.

Herders took extraordinary care with cactus harvesting and preparation: spines eaten by cows could perforate stomachs or intestines. Raketa gatherers wore *holits'aombe*, hardened sandals made of thick leather, to prevent loose spines from puncturing their feet (Kaufmann 2001). Even then, injuries to people and cows were common. Beef tongue from the South was considered a hazardous dish to eat due to the fragments of cactus spines invariably embedded there (Decary 1925). Cows frequently suffered or died from intestinal inflammation while some people suffered from lung problems due to the inhalation of small spines (Larsson 2004).

The diets of the Antandroy and Mahafale, like that of the cows they tended, varied over the course of the pastoral year. Upon the return of the herds to the South around October, locals collected the abundant raketa fruit that had started to ripen in August (Kaufmann 2001). The availability of fruit in the wild usually lasted until February, a period in which households worked to cultivate small-scale staple crops. Between March and April, following the harvest, locals began to transition from eating raketa fruit to cooking millet and maize, supplemented with other legumes and vegetables. Surpluses were securely stored in family granaries.

These surpluses would have to support the household—and the traveling herders—through the dry season until the arrival of raketa fruit in the spring.[4]

A common theme in Western narratives of the South was the overall scarcity of food. Based on data collected in the 1960s, Nelson (1973) notes that southern households produce—by way of agriculture—only four-fifths of what they consume. The remainder must be gathered. During normal years, 39 percent of households experience food shortages; for 13 percent of the population these shortages last five months or more. If environmental conditions are not satisfactory for either cultivated crops or wild foods, starvation may occur. Two successive years of poor rainfall invariably leads to severe famine. It is reasonable to assume that in the 1920s an even higher proportion of total food was gathered, based on the proliferation of (and dependence upon) raketa. However, it is not clear if this greater dependence on gathering meant an increased risk of starvation: after all, gathering may have been more reliable in the 1920s due to the proliferation of cactus. Furthermore, cactus fruit could be stored for extended periods, from six months to a year (Larsson 2004).

Nevertheless, food shortages did occur in the cactus region during the early 20th century. Decary (1925, 769–770) writes: "During periods of scarcity . . . there is an average of one every three or four years . . . the [cactus] fruit is the almost exclusive food of many natives. Some poor Antandroy even make it the basis of their diet in normal times." During the height of fruit consumption, two to three meals per day may have been composed entirely of raketa fruit (Larsson 2004). In the event of harvest failure or a shortage of stockpiled food during the winter months when wild raketa fruit was not available, locals sometimes ate the cactus cladodes (Middleton 1999). These fleshy, oblong "leaves" were not as tasty as the fruit, but provided carbohydrates and plentiful water.

As in other arid environments, water collection in the rural South took the largest fraction of household time. In areas deprived of water, or during severe drought, it could take up to eight hours to walk to the nearest well (Decary 1925). Watering holes for cattle were similarly scarce and fiercely protected. Here, the extraordinary water content of cactus fruits and cladodes offered significant benefits for both humans and cows. Table 4 compares the water content of key staples in the southern diet.

Prickly pear fruit and cladodes have significantly higher raw water content than uncooked maize, millet, or sweet potato. Raw maize and sweet potato have high water content, but the need to grill or bake these foods before eating reduces the net water contribution through moisture loss. Millet is generally prepared by boiling one cup of raw grain in two cups of water. Although the grain absorbs most of this water—thereby providing substantial water to the body—this water is coming out of the cooking budget. As such, the net contribution of water from cooking millet, after considering loss to evaporation, is negative. Prickly pear fruit and cladodes are eaten raw or lightly singed, leading to almost no moisture loss. Away from home, herders tapped the trunks of large cactus stands to extract water. It is little surprise that the Mahafale name for raketa is *sakafondrano*, literally, "water-food plant."

During the summer months, cattle were fed raketa cladodes almost exclusively. Accounts of cattle pastoralism from Decary (1925) and more recent work by Larsson (2004) suggest that so long as cattle were fed sufficient raketa, they did not need to be watered. This extraordinary claim—that raketa could satisfy the entire water requirement of an adult cow—seems hard to believe. Like so

Table 4. Comparison of water content for staple foods of Mahafaly and Antandroy regions.

	Water content (%)	Water intake per serving (as % of daily recommendation)	Net water contribution to diet as prepared
Prickly pear fruit	87.1	3.20	Positive
Prickly pear cladodes	87.2	3.51	Positive
Maize (raw)	76.0	3.16	Marginal positive[1]
Millet (raw)	8.0	0.14	Negative[2]
Sweet potato (raw)	77.4	2.78	Marginal positive[1]

Sources: National Institutes of Health Dietary Reference Intakes (DRI), United States Department of Agriculture (USDA) SR-11, and Chitava and Wairagu (2013)

[1]Usually prepared through grilling or baking, which results in some moisture loss and reduces the overall water contribution of the food.

[2]One cup of millet is prepared by boiling in two cups of water. As such, prepared millet contributes water to daily diet, but at the expense of water in the cooking budget. More water is lost through evaporation during cooking than is contributed by the raw grain.

many other stories about Madagascar's cactus pastoralism, one wonders if this was the result of innocent exaggeration.[5] However, in 1914, trials conducted at research stations in West Texas demonstrated that cows could, in fact, survive on prickly pear without supplemental water (Woodward, Turner, and Griffiths 1915). In Woodward's study, dairy cows fed high quantities of prickly pear mixed with sorghum drank five pounds of water per day, while cows fed only prickly pear (no sorghum) did not drink at all. By comparison, cows fed only sorghum drank 95 pounds of water per day. The cactus used in the study, though not mentioned explicitly, was likely *O. ficus-indica*, a species common to the southwestern United States. The water content of *O. ficus-indica* is believed to be comparable to

O. vulgaris, the species that proliferated in southern Madagascar in the 1920s. The cows used in the study were adult dairy cows with substantially higher water intake than African zebu cattle. Woodward's (1915) study animals demonstrated a baseline water requirement of 95 pounds of water per day; zebu cattle need on average only 36 pounds per day (King 1983).

The consequences for pastoral practice are significant. Herders could keep cattle confined behind cactus barricades and avoid the dangers of watering holes. Time and energy expenditures locating water and moving cows were reduced. Most critically, the impact of a drought on groundwater resources was decoupled from the welfare of the herd, so long as raketa remained abundant. Thanks to the extraordinary dryland adaptations of raketa, cows and people could survive with or without rain. The importance of the cactus to water provisioning offers one final twist to the famine story: with the rapid destruction of raketa between 1925 and 1930, it is possible that some (if not most) of the human and bovine victims died of dehydration, not starvation.

Pastoral settlements in the South generally comprised a handful of households organized into small villages, each ringed with cattle enclosures and fields. Raketa barriers were maintained around villages and pens to deter rustlers, foreign soldiers, and other threats (Kaufmann 1998). These thickets of prickly pear could grow 3–5 meters high and tens of meters deep, obscuring any indication of settlement (Middleton 1999). Decary (1930, vi) writes that the cactus "concealed all dwellings . . . the only signs of [village life] were some smoke, barking dogs, a cows' mooing." Raketa was planted and groomed to line trails with high walls behind which villagers could fire upon intruders. French military campaigns in the South contended with winding labyrinths of raketa that forced soldiers to walk in single file and exposed units to ambush (Kaufmann 1998). Army general and colonial administrator Hubert Lyautey described the South as an "almost impenetrable country [which] constituted a veritable citadel . . . for plunderers and cattle thieves" (1935, 114).

The effectiveness of raketa thickets for community defense, cattle enclosures, fodder, and food ensured that the cactus was actively cultivated and propagated. Communities tended the thickets to encourage suitable patterns of growth. Cuttings were planted in planned forms to create spaces for cattle, protect row crops, and establish new defensive barriers. The result of these efforts is a form of landesque capital (Brookfield 1984): an investment in material, attached to the soil, and intended to exist beyond a single productive cycle. Unlike the forms of landesque capital developed in Hawaii, Madagascar's cactus thickets were consumed as food and fodder. In this way, the same material substance had value through consumption and as fixed capital. This dual purpose was both an advantage and disadvantage: on the one hand, raketa simplified pastoral practices. On the other, the eventual loss of raketa was a loss of both material food and a primary input to food production.

The Environmental History of Raketa

The raketa gasy that came to dominate southern landscapes was a species of prickly pear (*Opuntia*), a genus in the family *Cactaceae* that grows on every continent but Antarctica (Britton 1919). Its ability to survive under arid conditions, coupled with rapid growth and proliferation, has ensured its widespread success. Native to Mexico and Central America, prickly pear crossed the world during the early colonial period as a crop of economic importance, thanks to its relationship with cochineal (Greenfield 2009). Cochineal was the primary source of red dye (carmine) until the 1800s. In the early colonial period, the manufacture of carmine was confined to Central America, and the production process was a closely guarded secret. Merchants demanded exorbitant prices for carmine and, for a time, Mexican producers amassed considerable wealth. But by the 1700s, European powers had acquired the secret, the insect, and the cactus on which it depended for food (Greenfield 2009). The French brought prickly pear to Réunion (see fig. 4) to introduce carmine production to the island. These Indian Ocean plantations never proved economically viable nor politically significant until 1769, when a few cuttings of cactus were carried from Réunion to Madagascar in the hold of a French frigate.

The species of prickly pear that made this journey and transformed southern Madagascar was probably *Opuntia vulgaris Miller*, though its precise classification is still debated. Decary claims the plant was *O. dillenii Haw.*, Bâthie claims it was *O. vulgaris*, and Petit argues for *O. monocantha*. This kind of botanical confusion was common during this period, especially in colonial contexts where botanists lacked experience with local flora or were unfamiliar with the expressions of well-known flora in unfamiliar environments (Middleton 1999). Today, there is growing consensus that raketa gasy was *O. vulgaris*, a plant that can grow into thickets "2 to 4 or even 6 meters high, often with a definite trunk, usually with a large much branched top" (Britton 1919, 156). Sharp spines one to four centimeters in length grow from each areole—the small indentations that cover each cladode. Fruit are 5 to 7.5 centimeters long, obovoid in shape, reddish purple in color, and emerge from the top edges of upper cladodes. The plant is widespread: by the 1920s, *O. vulgaris* could be found in Brazil, Uruguay, Paraguay, Argentina, Cuba, India, South Africa, and Australia where it was frequently harvested for its fruit (Britton 1919). Compared to other *Opuntia* species, *O. vulgaris* fruit will remain ripe and attached to the cactus for many months. In the South, this persistence on the plant aided fruit gathering for subsistence.

In 1769, the southern tip of Madagascar was growing in strategic importance for European powers. Since the 1500s, Madagascar had been visited by the Portuguese, Dutch, French, and English who purchased slaves and cattle in exchange for rifles, alcohol, and manufactured goods. As imperial dominions in South and Southeast Asia expanded, European powers became increasingly concerned with protecting trade routes between the Cape of Good Hope and India: with the growth in trade, this stretch of ocean became an active hunting ground for pirates between 1690 and 1720. The British and French made several attempts to establish outposts on the island without success. The longest of these was a French effort in 1643 at Fort-Dauphin that lasted for 30 years, at which time the settlers' fortifications were destroyed by local resistance (Brown 2000; Allen and Covell 2005).

The French would try again in 1766 to establish a presence at Fort-Dauphin, this time with the help of the spiny *O. vulgaris*. In 1769, the Count Dolisie de Maudave, a naval officer, carried several barrels of prickly pear from Réunion to Madagascar to plant "around the part of the fort that looks at the sea and render it by this means impenetrable" (from the journal of M. de Maudave, December 12, 1768, cited in Decary 1947, 456). Maudave's gardening was successful. Furthermore, resourceful locals took cuttings from the fort's natural barricades and planted them elsewhere. On a visit to Fort-Dauphin in 1819, Frappaz notes that "There is a large amount of *raketa* . . . and is used with advantage to surround [village] fields and gardens, thus preventing thieves and animals from entering it" (Lt. Frappaz, cited in Decary 1947, 456). Raketa began to spread as pastoralists planted the cactus around their settlements, animal corrals, and fields (Kaufmann 2001), incorporating the cactus into their daily lives and adjusting pastoral practice to take advantage of the new plant.

Herders carried cuttings of raketa with them during cattle migrations, planting them along the way to establish fodder for future use. This practice accelerated the spread of raketa and created new areas suitable for immigrant pastoralists (Decary 1930). Planted cuttings could provide fodder within two years, while emergent plants responded to pruning by growing thicker and taller—an adaptation that villagers exploited when constructing defensive barriers (Kaufmann 2011). By the time missionaries arrived in Madagascar in 1820, just 50 years since raketa's introduction, the cactus was widespread throughout the South and used extensively for village defense (Ellis 1838). On the eve of its destruction, the spiny cactus covered 50,000 to 60,000 square miles (Kaufmann 1998).

Along the way, raketa displaced many species of endemic, xerophytic fodder, including types of spurges, flowering succulents, and various aloes. Of those that remained, many were toxic. Decary (1925, 46) notes that while varieties of *E. arborescentes* continued to grow in the South, all but two "have toxic and burning latexes." One of the two, *E. arahaka*, was well known to the Antandroy as an alternate fodder but was not preferred, only being used "in default of any other" (Decary 1928, 46). The loss of endemic fodder resulted from a combination of social and environmental processes: as raketa came to be preferred by herders, less time was spent cultivating (or otherwise encouraging) alternative plants. On the environmental side, as raketa began to colonize land once occupied by endemic plants, it became harder for alternatives to compete. For 150 years, the loss of these potential fodder sources had little impact on pastoralism—in fact, herd sizes and population densities increased throughout the 19th century. The full impact of this biodiversity loss would not be realized until raketa, too, was eliminated.

The growth in population and spatial extent of pastoralism during this period is directly related to the spread of raketa. Studies by Kaufmann (2001), Middleton (1999), and Larsson (2004) indicate that pastoralism on this scale could not have succeeded without the proliferation of cactus. Decary (1947, 456) draws the connection between raketa and in-migration:

> It was from Anosy . . . towards the sub-desert Androy, where [raketa] was to find its preferred habitat [and] spread in the second half of the eighteenth century. This period also corresponds to the actual populating of the country. It was then that many current groups descended into the Far South, following unhappy wars or internal quarrels. The Antanosys . . . made known the advantages offered by [raketa] as a means of defense. [The cactus] then multiplied rapidly as the country became more populous. The native found therein a favorable food for himself and his herds, and the oxen in their turn helped the propagation, for the seeds of the "figs," absorbed and digested, then germinated with remarkable facility in the scattered droppings left by the animals.

Raketa's proliferation solved three key problems for Southern pastoralists: access to fodder, access to water, and protection against intruders. With respect to the last, the primary security threat to villagers in the 18th and 19th centuries were cattle thieves. But by the 1890s, the primary threat was foreign soldiers. During the French campaign to capture Antananarivo in 1895, soldiers discovered ramparts of prickly pear surrounding Merina villages in the central plateau: the southern strategy of natural fortification had spread to the interior in the intervening years (Corlay 1896). It is ironic that the same cactus brought to Madagascar by the French as a defense against the Malagasy turned into the perfect Malagasy defense against the French.

Colonial Influence on Food Provisioning

Three decades after seizing control of Madagascar and on the eve of Bâthie's release of cochineal, the French colonial government still had only minimal influence on food provisioning in the South. Cactus pastoralism and small-scale agriculture continued as it had for decades. In fact, the social and cultural inertia that opposed colonial plans was at an all-time high.

Assisted by raketa, Antandroy and Mahafale communities resisted colonial intervention into local affairs. In 1896, an agreement was reached in which many Mahafale pastoralists swore allegiance to the colonial government in exchange for nonintervention. But this agreement had little effect: the French continued to increase military and civilian control over pastoral territory while Mahafale ignored colonial mandates and continued to antagonize French patrols

(Deschamps 1959). Southerners widely ignored the head tax imposed in 1901 and readily skirted visits by census takers and tax collectors. There was occasional armed resistance to military incursions, but the overall impact of these skirmishes was limited. Raketa had effectively stopped French progress.

In the decades leading up to the release of cochineal, the French tried various strategies to increase the colonial government's influence. Recognizing the lack of political cohesion between Antandroy and Mahafale, military strategists played the two groups against each other, exploiting historical disputes and internal divisions for political gain. French soldiers occupied watering holes and stole cows. The government imposed a tax on funerary ceremonies knowing that funerals were essential to local cultural identity (Kaufmann 2001). Through it all, the Southern strategy of avoidance—assisted by raketa—effectively forced a stalemate. But the stalemate would not last. Forces were amassing in Paris and Antananarivo that would transform the socionature of cactus pastoralism and bring the South's stubborn peoples to heel.

Transformation: 1769–1924

The history of Madagascar's long and tumultuous encounter with Europeans has been documented elsewhere and will not be re-narrated here (see Cousins 1895; Heseltine 1971; Brown 1979, 2000; Campbell 2005). Instead, I focus on the conjunctures and events that had the most significant impact on southern food provisioning leading up to 1924. These conjunctures fall into three broad time periods: 1769–1890, a period of competition between European powers for influence in the island; 1890–1905, the conquest of the island by the French; and 1905–24, the consolidation and expansion of French power.

Competition: 1769–1890

Count de Maudave's introduction of *O. vulgaris* to Madagascar was one of several attempts to secure a French foothold in the arid South. Fort-Dauphin had been the site of continuous struggle between locals and European occupiers, primarily Jesuit missionaries, dating back to 1643. In response to French actions in 1660, Malagasy chiefs refused to provide supplies to the Fort-Dauphin settlers, leading to the starvation of the fort's inhabitants (Copland 1822). Such difficulties eventually led to French abandonment of the fort in 1671. During the 28 years of occupation, as many as 4000 French settlers were killed. The Malagasy death toll is unknown.

Growth in trade to India during the early 1700s brought growth in piracy (Thomson 1996). For some time, the abandoned fort was the center of a pirate colony that launched attacks on European merchant ships transiting the Cape of Good Hope. By mid-century, French and British governments were interested in establishing their own military and civilian outposts on Madagascar to protect growing concerns in South and Southeast Asia (Brown 2000), cultivating another site of competition between these long-standing European rivals. In 1766, the French reestablished the outpost at Fort-Dauphin: political and religious interest in the South had not waned in the intervening years. As part of renovations to the fort, *O. vulgaris* was planted around the seaward sides to discourage attack. Local herders quickly realized the benefits of prickly pear and began to reshape social practices around it.

As raketa spread through the South, imperial interests turned to the central highlands and the Merina kingdom. Merina monarchs had ruled central Madagascar since 1540 (Brown 2000). This kingdom, dominated by members of the Merina ethnic group, maintained control over the central plateau and large parts of the eastern half of the island. But to the north, west, and south, Merina authority was frequently contested, and in the deep South, Merina kings and queens never held sway. Indeed, southern groups like the Antandroy and Mahafale actively despised the Merina and fiercely resisted numerous attempts by highland monarchs to capture traditional lands (Deschamps 1959). Even though the Merina controlled only part of the island, Western diplomats considered the monarchy to be Madagascar's de facto rulers (Brown 2000). To European eyes, the kingdom operated as a republic: it maintained familiar bureaucracies and authoritarian titles, controlled most of the island through a standing army, established and enforced laws, requisitioned labor for public works, and—for a time—sought diplomatic and trade relations beyond its borders. From 1820 on, the Merina government in Antananarivo was considered the authority on matters concerning the Red Island, regulating all trade and authorizing the work of foreign missionaries.[6]

Between the 1820s and 1880s, geopolitical tensions between Britain and France over control of Madagascar increased. These tensions were exacerbated by the diplomatic maneuvering of the Merina monarchy and France's 1871 defeat in the Franco-Prussian War. With British and French attention focused on the island, the Merina monarchs of the mid-19th century quickly recognized that survival depended on being able to play the two powers against each other. To that end, figures like King Radama II (1861–63), Queen Rasoherina (1863–68), and Prime Minister Rainilaiarivony (1864–95) skillfully balanced the competing military and economic interests of Britain and France with the interests of Merina society (Brown 2000). A long history of attempted invasions and intimidations by the French led the Merina government to conclude that the French were more dangerous than the British. To counter the constant and thinly veiled threats of a French attack, Rainilaiarivony made regular overtures to British diplomats and succeeded in negotiating a supply of weapons and military advisors. British companies were given preferential treatment and succeeded in dominating trade with Madagascar. In 1886, the island's exports totaled $6 million, of which 60 percent was controlled by Great Britain and most of the remainder went to the United States. France received only a small fraction of the island's economic output (Campbell 1889).

For the government in Paris and the business interests in nearby Réunion and Mauritius, the expropriation of Madagascar's wealth into Anglophone economies was an ongoing humiliation.

France's defeat in the Franco-Prussian War increased pressure on the government to win Madagascar for France (Kaufmann 2011). During the 1870s, Paris and colonial capitals saw growing criticism of French imperial strategy and a questioning of French national identity. As a result of the war, France lost the territories of Alsace and Lorraine—meanwhile, Britain and the Netherlands were expanding colonial holdings in Africa and Asia. Germany and Italy were making headway in East Africa, and Belgium was developing plans for a colony in the Congo River basin. Over the next three decades, the newly minted Third Republic attempted to keep pace by doubling down on its imperial projects, acquiring new possessions in the South Pacific, Indochina, and West Africa (Finch 2013).

In 1895, Madagascar was added to this list. But until then, so long as the British maintained cordial relations with the Merina government, France could not risk a military conquest of Madagascar. From the French perspective, it was reasonable to assume that Great Britain intended to claim Madagascar for itself. If the French had been correct, it is possible that the Merina government could have survived somewhat longer in the balance. Unfortunately for the Merina, French assumptions of a British commitment were grossly overestimated.

The opening of the Suez Canal in 1873 radically altered British geopolitical objectives in the Indian Ocean. The new sea route to India decreased ship traffic around the Cape of Good Hope, effectively eliminating the threat of piracy in the southwest Indian Ocean and reducing the strategic importance of Madagascar. Furthermore, to protect the Suez, Britain turned its attention to Egypt and control of the Nile (Parsons 1999). Diplomatic and economic resources that could have aided the Merina were redirected towards Zanzibar, Uganda, and Sudan. In 1890, Lord Salisbury signed a treaty with France that recognized French accession of Madagascar, effectively removing the last form of support for the embattled Merina government (Brown 2000).

By 1890, all that stood in the way of France was a lightly trained Malagasy military and a Merina kingdom without any powerful allies. Two hundred fifty years after establishing Fort-Dauphin and embarking upon its ill-fated conquest of Madagascar, France was finally poised to wage a decisive war to claim the island.

Conquest: 1885–1905

In the years following the rise of the Third Republic and the humiliation of the Franco-Prussian War, prominent politicians and businesspeople conspired to drive France toward war. Covell (1987, 17) writes: "The activities of a disparate alliance of Marseilles-based commercial companies and deputies from Réunion, who saw Madagascar as a potential area of settlement, pressed successive French governments to 'do something' about Madagascar." Five years after the treaty that guaranteed British acquiescence, the French invaded.

The French expeditionary force of 18,000 soldiers met with little organized resistance on the mountainous route from Mahajanga (on the northwest coast) to Antananarivo. Morale among Malagasy soldiers was low: many of the poorer recruits had been forced to remain away from homes and farms without pay, while officers—wealthy Merina—were given extensive compensation and allowed to escape the worst action (Brown 2000). Throughout the nine-month campaign, Malagasy forces were unable to hold strategic positions or mount decisive resistance due to desertion and poor training: in fact, by the time French forces entered Antananarivo on September 30, 1895, only 20 French soldiers had been killed from enemy action. However, nearly 6000 French soldiers—33 percent of the force—died from fever and dysentery, making the Madagascar campaign the deadliest in French colonial history (Brown 2000). In later years, the perceived human cost of the campaign was often used to motivate violent crackdowns against local dissent. These acts of repression served to reassure the French that lives had not been "lost in vain" (for example, see Corlay 1896).

On October 1, 1895, a treaty was signed between Queen Ranavalona III and General Duchesne that defined the terms of French rule: (1) a French resident-general was to control all internal and external affairs; (2) France had a right to establish any military force deemed necessary, anywhere in Madagascar, for any length of time; (3) the Queen was allowed to remain in her position and rule indirectly; and (4) missionaries were allowed to stay in Madagascar but could no longer teach English, only French. These terms antagonized the majority of Merina still loyal to the queen and the Protestant church.

Within weeks of the treaty, large-scale unrest erupted across the central plateau. Known as the Menalamba rebellion, the popular resistance movement targeted French nationals, business interests, and Catholic churches (Campbell 1992). As chaos erupted across the countryside, French plans for a quick and orderly consolidation of control were quickly put on the back foot as soldiers were set to work reinforcing Antananarivo. Though the Menalamba rebellion failed to recapture territory or reestablish the Merina monarchy, the speed and magnitude of unrest unnerved the French. Only a year after the triumphant march into Antananarivo, the resident-general was called home in disgrace (Allen and Covell 2005).

The person sent to restore order to Madagascar was Joseph Gallieni, a colonel in the French military who had built a reputation for quelling rebellion and extending colonial territory in French West Africa and Indochina. Gallieni decided that the rebellion could not be defeated unless the monarchy was deposed and all remaining British influence eliminated. To this end, he quickly exiled Ranavalona III to Réunion and executed other members of the royal family including the queen's uncle, Ratsimamanga, and the minister of war, Rainandriamampandry (Finch 2013). Judging that any remaining foreign influence was directed through the network of British missionaries, he gave away church property to Catholic interests and encouraged mission workers to leave (Brown 2000). With respect to the Menalamba, Gallieni worked with local leaders to build loyalty to the French cause even as he steadily expanded his military presence and ruthlessly sought out the leaders of the rebellion. Finch (2013, 208) writes: "What this demonstrated was the essential unity of Gallieni's attitudes towards military and political action. Both relied upon a combination of the light and heavy touch . . . And whilst these actions were certainly callous and calculating, Gallieni had made no commitment to being humane."

With the help of his friend and army general Hubert Lyautey, Gallieni established what came to be known as the Gallieni-Lyautey method of colonial conquest (Finch 2013). Gallieni referred to his tactical approach as the *tache d'huile*, or "oil-stain," approach: by gradually establishing military outposts in concentric circles around the center of imperial control, he was able to build a defensive network that progressively "decreased the area within which bandits . . . could act with impunity" (Finch 2013, 180). Over time, military control in a region gave way to "civilian" leadership, a transition that frequently involved appointing army commanders as de facto administrators.

The oil-stain approach worked well to quell rebellion and restore order in the central highlands where the French had accurate maps and could take advantage of existing roads. But progress in the sparsely populated periphery was a different matter. French forces under Lyautey found it difficult to maintain Gallieni's concentric circles of control in places where vast distances separated population centers. In the South, the combination of a migratory population and dense, featureless cactus slowed the acquisition of territory (see Lyautey 1935). Gallieni and the French would have to modify the oil-stain approach if they were to succeed where the Merina had failed for centuries.

The new tactic devised by Lyautey was to hold hostage the cattle of resistant pastoralists until they pledged loyalty to the French. This was accomplished by strategically positioning soldiers at the dry-season watering holes and stealing the cows when the herds arrived (Kaufmann 2001). Lyautey writes: "The only way to act against the Antandroy was to get hold of these immense herds . . . Each time that a tribe aggressed against us or against submissive tribes, its herds would be seized and given back either to the submissive tribes from which they came or to the rebellious tribes after their submission [to the colony]. This method gave excellent results. A great number of tribes submitted" (Lyautey 1935, 117; cited in Kaufmann 2001). Documentary evidence suggest that Lyautey's strategy was effective at achieving verbal pledges of loyalty from many herding communities. However, Kaufmann (2001) and Middleton (1999) note that pastoralists readily abandoned such commitments when no longer advantageous. Furthermore, incursions of this sort motivated herders to stay behind their cactus fences and rely increasingly on the water-bearing properties of raketa.

Once resistance in each area was suppressed, Gallieni implemented *la politique des races*, or "Race Policy." Attempts were made to draw provincial boundaries around each ethnic group and administer each group separately under its own chiefs, a strategy that worked well for the British in India (Brown 2000, 237). Race Policy provided two advantages for administrators. First, it helped distinguish the French from the Merina monarchs who had imposed Merina rulers over all subject ethnic groups. In fact, Race Policy was preferred by many Malagasy communities that had suffered under Merina rule. Second, it helped deter rebellion by perpetuating ethnic division and hindering the development of a Malagasy national identity (Brown 2000).

Gallieni's vision of indirect rule had one unintended benefit for non-Merina. To support the administrative needs of each ethnic province, Gallieni needed literate civil servants—local chiefs and prominent leaders—trained to manage people and interface with the colony's central bureaucracy. To train these public servants, Gallieni established schools throughout the countryside with the express purpose of educating non-Merina in self-governance (Brown 2000). The closure of these schools in 1910 (for economic reasons) drew significant anger from many ethnic groups that had begun to improve their political capital.

If Race Policy distinguished the French from the Merina, the tax regime established in 1901 did the opposite. Gallieni's imposition of a head tax, livestock tax, and market (sales) tax was particularly burdensome for Malagasy who lived outside of the monetary economy—essentially the majority of non-Merina. This burden was intentional: "Gallieni justified the head tax as a form of motivation to get subsistence farmers to shift to production for export or wage labor . . . it also helped the larger plan of getting subsistence growers to work for French plantations, which were expanding" (Brown 1979, 239). During Merina rule, many ethnic groups were taxed by the monarchy. The most severe imposition was *fanompoana*, a policy of forced labor that took peasants away from farms and homes for extended periods. The arbitrariness of fanompoana service and the demands it placed on bodies already struggling to meet subsistence requirements antagonized many non-Merina. Gallieni's head tax, though quite different from Merina levies, reminded many Malagasy of the kinds of impositions they had grown to despise under previous rulers.

In the South, the 1901 tax regime initially led to a spike in the sale of livestock, presumably to provide money for households to pay the tax. But over time, many Antandroy and Mahafale refused to pay and found it convenient to avoid signing onto the tax rolls in the first place (Kaufmann 2001). In 1909, the percentage of the head tax recovered by the colony was 13.63 percent; the next year, it was 4.8 percent. By 1914, only 1.3 percent of the mandated head tax was being recovered (Kaufmann 2001). Raketa provided a convenient refuge from tax collectors: not only did cactus thickets make it difficult (and dangerous) to identify and confront households, the labyrinthian paths and fences made it nearly impossible to assess herd sizes and land holdings.

Despite these difficulties, French officials were committed to making the head tax work. During a severe drought in 1909, many villagers temporarily left the cactus region to seek food and fodder to the south. In response, administrators demanded that everyone be forced back to their homes so they might be successfully tracked and taxed.

Consolidation: 1905–24

Following Gallieni's retirement in 1905, a string of short-term governors held the highest post in Madagascar. Victor Augagneur (1905–10) attempted to impose separation of church and state, abolishing church schools, and generally ignoring the complaints of colons. For these and other reasons, he was widely disliked, especially by those hoping to expand business interests in the colony. Albert Picquié (1910–14) attempted to repair the breech between the colonial government and settlers. He completed the conversion of military posts to civilian government and expanded construction of public works—projects that had been initiated by Gallieni (Brown 2000). Hubert Garbit (1914–17), Picquié's secretary general, took over the governorship at the outbreak of World War I with a mandate to expand resource extraction on the island to support the French war effort.

The extraordinary material demands of World War I, more than any specific policies of Garbit, helped energize the economy of Madagascar, which expanded its exports of beef, rice, leather, and graphite (Brown 2000). At the same time, the war nearly bankrupted the French treasury. Governors and residents-general of all French territories were instructed to increase productivity. In the case of Madagascar, this policy took the form of expanded plantation concessions, protective tariffs, and growth in the wage labor market. The actions taken around this last objective would have a profound effect on Southern food provisioning.

World War I altered the trajectory of Malagasy social history in another, more subtle way. During the war, 40,000 Malagasy soldiers were sent to Europe to fight in the trenches alongside the French. One in ten were killed (Brown 2000). After the war, some Malagasy veterans used the opportunity to acquire an education in France where they were exposed to left-wing politics and philosophy. For the most part, these emerging revolutionaries were members of the former elite Merina: of all Malagasy ethnicities, Merina had the material means to fund long voyages to and from Paris. Furthermore, animosity against the colony was highest among the Merina, who felt that their position of leadership had been usurped by the French. Marxist and anticolonial philosophies resonated with this emerging Merina intelligentsia who were motivated to put these ideas into action upon their return home.

One such veteran, Jean Ralaimongo, was instrumental in what would become the first significant threat to French rule in Madagascar. While in Paris, Ralaimongo founded the "French League for the accession of natives of Madagascar to the rights of French citizenship" and the revolutionary newspaper *Le Libéré*. With the help of his roommate and a network of young activists, Ralaimongo drew attention to the excesses of French colonial rule throughout the world and petitioned for the integration of Madagascar as a full *département*, granting French citizenship for all Malagasy. The organizations he established in Madagascar upon his return in 1923 became the cornerstone of the emerging Malagasy nationalist movement and a source of concern for each successive governor-general (Brown 2000). Decades later, Ralaimongo's roommate in Paris would go on to direct a revolutionary movement of his own, one that helped bring French rule in Indochina to an end. His name was Ho Chi Minh.

Following World War I, parliament appointed another string of governors-general to lead the increasingly restive colony. Schrameck (1918–19), Guyon (1919–20), and Garbit (second term, 1920–23) continued the economic policies of their predecessors, encouraging plantation growth, expanding public works, and developing the wage labor economy. In February of 1924, Marcel Olivier took office, the 11th governor or acting governor in 20 years to lead Madagascar. For Olivier, the policies of Gallieni's successors had been too coddling of native labor and overprotective of native land (see Olivier 1931). Olivier believed the modernization and marketization of Malagasy society was inevitable: it was the duty of the government to push this process forward, even if it proved painful.

One of Olivier's first actions was to claim all untitled land for the state, thereby creating a sizeable pool for the allocation of concessions. Olivier justified this act of dispossession in racial terms: "how could one, without committing a crime against humanity, devote cultivable land to the natives' sloth, technical incompetence, and demographic shortfall?" (Olivier 1931; cited in Middleton 1999, 227). Dispossession advanced two related objectives at the same time. First, it provided land for concessions, appeasing investors and speculators eager to expand cash-crop plantations. Second, it forced cultivators and ranchers to find other sources of income, ideally as plantation laborers. This appeased the large companies that operated plantations, primarily in the north of the island (Covell 1987).

To improve the balance of trade in France's favor, Olivier imposed high tariffs on manufactured products, ensuring that France was the sole supplier of imported goods in Madagascar. Similarly, export tariffs ensured that France was the sole destination for goods produced on the island. In 1895, Great Britain exported £1 million of goods to Madagascar; as late as 1980, that figure was a mere £100,000 (Brown 2000). This protectionism was a boon for French businesses involved in bidirectional trade, but effectively destroyed smaller Malagasy producers who faced higher costs for inputs and lower sale prices at market.

Olivier sought to recover greater revenues from taxation as an impetus to drive the poor toward the wage economy. Aware of the importance of ancestor worship and burial practices to the Malagasy, Olivier imposed a tax on funerary rites and ceremonies (Nelson 1973). This mandate particularly angered Antandroy and Mahafale groups who still practiced ancestor worship: a family that could not afford proper burial ceremonies or prominent monuments lost prestige, social capital, and political voice. By raising the cost of burial, the government further divided the wealthy from the poor. For many southerners under Olivier's government, wealth not only determined your quality of life, it also determined the quality of your death, and with it, the lives and deaths of your descendants.

Perhaps the most controversial of Olivier's programs was SMOTIG (*Service de la Main d'Oeuvre pour les Travaux d'Interet General*), a system of labor conscription for public works. SMOTIG operated like military conscription, requiring men aged 16–60 to provide service to the state for a set number of days a year. The punishment for noncompliance was 15 days in prison (Covell 1987). Olivier (1931, 70 and 105) wrote on the need for conscription to motivate social and economic progress: "to meet [plantation] requirements, colons needed to procure labor outside the zones of colonization; but . . . outside these zones labor was, on the contrary, very difficult to persuade . . . [In the South] thousands upon thousands of men who do absolutely nothing and who are firmly resolved to do nothing, if not by constraint."

Officially, SMOTIG labor was to be used for public works: roads, railways, irrigation projects, and the like. But Olivier's comments—and the historical record—indicate that the official line between public and private projects was deliberately vague. Malagasy nationalists objected to SMOTIG, noting that the projects for which labor was requisitioned invariably benefited French settlers and business interests at the expense of the Malagasy (Nelson 1973). Foreign governments criticized the program, noting that it violated international agreements outlawing the use of forced labor. At its best, SMOTIG redirected laborers, without compensation, from their own economic activity toward the profits of foreign-owned plantations. At its worst, it bore striking similarity to the near-slavery conditions of fanompoana. This resemblance was not lost on the leaders of the Malagasy nationalist movement who saw SMOTIG as an opportunity to build solidarity between ethnic groups.

Ralaimihoatra (1969) observes that programs like SMOTIG were possible in the 1920s because the government (and Olivier, specifically) saw Madagascar as a "political laboratory": an isolated environment in which social and economic experimentation could be conducted without risk (see also Middleton 1999, 227). This may be true; after all, the government had a history of tinkering with economic policy. For example, the French never settled on a consistent program for cash-crop production, repeatedly contradicting earlier directives (Covell 1987). At first, Malagasy were encouraged to grow cash crops; in some cases, it was illegal not to. Later, Malagasy were instructed *not* to grow cash crops (under severe penalty) because colons complained about native competition. The labor situation was equally confusing and contradictory: Covell (1987, 20) notes that "more ordinances regulating labor were passed in Madagascar than in any other French colony."

If the French saw Madagascar as a political laboratory, it was, nonetheless, one that had to produce results. Olivier was driven to make the colony profitable by any means necessary, and his reorganization of native policy around the interests of French capital demonstrate this resolve. But even Olivier was not convinced that labor and land reform alone could transform the deep South. For that, he needed to enlist other allies.

A side effect of the transition from Race Policy to Social Policy was increased attention to the proliferation of cactus in the deep South. Since the start of the 20th century, the debate over raketa had begun to formalize around two opposing positions. The first argued that raketa stood in the way of colonial advancement (generally) and developing the South (specifically): for the mandates of Social Policy to be achieved, raketa had to be eliminated. The second position argued that raketa was essential to the economy of the deep South and could not be removed without seriously impacting productivity and endangering the livelihoods of many pastoral communities. With growing calls to reform the Malagasy mode of production, these positions became increasingly entrenched (Kaufmann 2001).

Raketa stands in the way of colonial advancement—The primary advocates of this position were Henri Perrier de la Bâthie, a renowned botanist, and his friend Georges Petit, a marine biologist with broad interests in biology. Both men were fellows of the Muséum National d'Histoire Naturelle in Paris and maintained powerful political connections in both Paris and Antananarivo (Middleton 1999). Bâthie's primary argument against raketa was built around three claims: the proliferation of raketa led to lost tax revenue, prevented the conversion of nonproductive land to productive agriculture, and pushed out endemic flora and fauna (Middleton 1999). To these basic points, Petit and others within the colonial government and French military added two more: the proliferation of raketa supported pastoralism which, in turn, reduced the plantation labor pool, and hindered efforts to capture rebels and criminals. The imagined connection between raketa and so many colonial "problems" helped Bâthie and Petit build a broad coalition of support. Petit was well known in scientific circles and argued passionately for the environmental benefits of removing "pest pears." The governor-general— the target of complaints from angry colons and bankers—was concerned with expanding the labor pool and increasing available land for plantations. Meanwhile, military leaders attended primarily to issues of colonial security. It seemed the removal of raketa offered something for everyone.

Bâthie's land surveys of the South led him to argue that the arid river valleys could be converted to productive agriculture, particularly in the Linta and Menarandra deltas. Baseline soil fertility was high; what the land needed was to be cleared of cactus and extensively irrigated. Bâthie (1934, 177) notes, "in order to develop [the South], other means must be employed than in other parts of Madagascar, other crops must be cultivated, other cropping methods must be employed, special agricultural management given to them, and, above all, water, the only thing that it lacks to become a rich country." He repeatedly drew connections between the environment and economy of North Africa—where some plantations had succeeded—and Madagascar's arid South. "Are these plants, these cultural practices, those of an ungrateful country, forever doomed to famine and misery? Do they not suggest an area comparable to the richest parts of Morocco and Algeria, with a similar climate, even better, both warmer and cooler? Do they not show that very many of the farming practices in North Africa are likely to succeed here?" (Bâthie 1934, 177). As in North Africa, Bâthie's confident assessment of the South's potential was based on a deeply held belief that any environment could be made economically productive if put in European hands.

As with land, so, too, with labor. For Bâthie, Petit, and many in colonial government, raketa allowed southerners to be lazy and unproductive. In an answer to critics, Petit (1929, 170; paraphrased in Middleton 1999, 237) writes: "The purpose of French colonialism was to 'civilise.' By insisting that cactus was indispensable, certain misguided administrators had 'encouraged sloth among races who were in fact very perfectible.'" Petit (1929, 171) was convinced that Antandroy could "become agricultural workers overnight" if pointed in the right direction. The extraordinary benefits offered by cactus (water, food, fodder, and protection) encouraged laziness. Proponents of raketa removal believed that eliminating the cactus would "reveal" modernity to the South, save Antandroy and Mahafale from their "thorny dependence," allow them to "see the benefits of life without cactus . . . [and seek] ways of making a living outside of a region so short of water" (Kaufmann 2011, 136).[7]

For many in the military, the key issue with raketa was security. A cactus-fortified South was opaque to surveillance and impenetrable to imperial force. It protected current threats and concealed emerging ones. Raketa played directly into an existing psychology of fear that had permeated colonial discourse ever since the Menalamba rebellion in 1895: French authority was vulnerable to territory that could not be controlled and people whose actions could not be anticipated. If this landscape of spiny thickets—and the hostile people it sheltered—could successfully resist Gallieni's *tache d'huile*, what could be done?

Proponents of the security argument felt that raketa placed the South outside of colonial control. Middleton (1999, 232) cites an unnamed administrator: "One still has the tendency to think of the Deep South as an unpacified country where it appears necessary to maintain troops on constant alert." In 1911, the head of Tsihombe District reported on "the difficulty of carrying out adequate surveillance of the Karembola south of Beloha, where our penetration is still imperfect, and the raketa conceal a large number of criminals outside the law and still very resistant to our action" (Middleton 1999, 232). Of critical concern to administrators was the question of rebellion: no one knew if the ongoing increases in tax and labor levies would foment revolution in the South, and if it did, no one knew for sure if the government had the resources to quell it (Middleton 1999).

The narrative of security that prevailed at the time seems to have fixated on the materiality of raketa rather than pastoralism, cultural practices, or people. Grandidier (1902, 120) writes: "These belts of cactus have opposed a terrible and harmful obstacle to our soldiers during the military conquest of this country. Numerous are the miserable who have been shot by an invisible enemy secretly waiting in a cactus cluster during the assault of a village; and while our soldiers were obliged to advance warily, in Indian file, in the narrow path bordered by thorns." Lyautey (1935, 119) notes, "The penetration has been difficult through these inextricable cacti . . . this countryside has cost us great efforts and painful losses." In the imperial mind, cactus stood in for the savage Southern rebel. It came to embody threatening, inextricable, impenetrable, barbaric, disorderly, and uncivilized qualities that were otherwise associated with Southern society. It was cactus that prevented civilization from coming to the South, cactus that killed French officers, and cactus that stole colonial taxes. It was cactus that came to be feared and hated (Kaufmann 2001).

Kaufmann (2001, 88) observes that many of the debates over raketa amounted to arguments over nonhuman agency: "This vegetal 'pest' seemed to 'work against' colonial interests, as if the plant itself had intentions—like humans—and could initiate actions. The plant's long sharp thorns, for example, which protect its water-bearing joints, were seen in teleological terms as 'self-defending armor' at cross-purposes with colonialism." More than any other rationale, this narrative of the cactus as a conscious and antagonistic enemy of civilization motivated and justified decisive action *against the plant itself*. After all, to destroy it was to save French *and* savage lives.

In 1900, the French military experimented with the introduction of a spineless species of prickly pear, probably a variety of *O. ficus-indica* (see Decary 1928; Kaufmann 2000). But the spineless cactus, identified in the French literature as *inerme*, did not spread readily without human intervention and it was not as desirable—to either cows or people—as raketa. In 1921, Bâthie proposed additional introductions of spineless cactus as a substitute fodder for cattle, but these efforts were never realized on a large scale (Decary 1928). In hindsight, local adoption of inerme was never going to succeed so long as the new cactus lacked the defensive qualities most prized by pastoralists. Spineless cactus could not be used as a cattle barrier because cows were more than happy to help themselves, nor could it deter French military incursions. In all likelihood, French plans for converting southern pastoralism to inerme were never serious; as Decary (1928, 457) notes, whereas "in 1921, it might have been possible to undertake this [project], necessity was by no means felt."

Raketa is essential to the economy—The opposing viewpoint, best articulated by Raymond Decary, argued that raketa was a key feature of southern culture and economic activity. As such, its removal would have severe impacts on Antandroy and Mahafale livelihoods. Decary was the chief colonial administrator for Tsihombe district, located in the heart of the cactus region. His surveys and reports on the social and natural environment in and around Tsihombe provide some of the most detailed descriptions of cactus pastoralism in this period (cf. Decary 1925, 1928, 1930). The first to talk about raketa in economic terms was Grandidier (1902), who explained the success of pastoralism in the cactus region in terms of the defensive, nutritious, and water-bearing properties of raketa. Decary (1928) and others argued the plant was so essential to life in the deep South that its elimination would lead to a collapse of cattle herds and potential famine.

Decary (1925) described the relationship between humans and raketa as a type of "socio-botanical unit"—two organisms that share a cluster of interrelated and symbiotic processes necessary for survival. Humans helped spread and nurture raketa just as raketa enabled human life through the supply of food and water. For Decary, the most important feature of the interrelationship was that neither cactus nor human could survive without the other. Decary's concept of a socio-botanical unit is reminiscent of concepts in political ecology that were not articulated until the late 20th century—for example, coproduction. These insights are particularly noteworthy given that Decary was writing at a time when social theory was heavily influenced by Darwinism (see Rogers 1972) and geographers were entertaining environmental determinism (see Peet 1985).

Decary's argument for the preservation of raketa is based on three observations. First, raketa is necessary for the prevention of starvation: "They have repeatedly prevented famines from being severe . . . In 1903, a time of extreme drought, the Anjeka tribe near Ambovombe had been supplied with water for three weeks with only the liquid expressed from the trunks of Raiketa" (Decary 1928, 44). Second, the cactus is essential fodder for cattle herds in the southern part of Androy. Finally, the loss of raketa would lead to the loss of other productive activities. In the limestone region of Androy, villagers maintained fields of millet, corn, and other crops. These fields were "without exception, surrounded by thick fences of Raiketa, indispensable precaution against the wanderings of the herds. [If the] Raiketa disappear, the crops will be invaded by the oxen" (Decary 1928, 45).

The issue of raketa aside, at the heart of the debates between Decary and Bâthie/Petit are deeper questions of how people should be governed and how best to affect the "advancement" of colonial subjects (Middleton 1999). Of course, these issues were not new, nor were they resolved with the destruction of raketa. What the public airing of these viewpoints *did* achieve was to elevate the legitimacy of Bâthie's proposal. With each publication, the public heard scientists and high-ranking officials discuss how to destroy raketa and eradicate the food supply for an entire region. This once-audacious scheme was becoming increasingly reasonable.

The Introduction of Cochineal

We must not deceive ourselves: in two or three years, the Raiketa will have totally disappeared from the Far South; Nothing seems to be able now to stop the invasion of the Scales [cochineal], the quantity of which is so prodigious that the males form, at certain hours of the day, whirlwinds such as they are a real inconvenience to the traveler.

—Raymond Decary, *À propos de l'Opuntia épineux de Madagascar*

According to Frappa (1932, 49), there are two kinds of cochineal: *Dactylopius coccus Costa*, which was commonly used in the production of red dye, and *Dactylopius tomentosus*, a "wild" variety that was not useful for dye but reproduced quickly and spread rapidly on favorable winds. In Madagascar, it seems the confusion over the precise species of prickly pear also applied to cochineal: writings at the time of the plague refer to *D. coccus Costa*, when the insect in question was actually *D. tomentosus*. It may be that those scientists and administrators behind the release of cochineal were similarly confused. And if so, this might go some way to explain their shock at the outcome (see Middleton 1999).

D. tomentosus has a history of destroying prickly pear infestations. It was introduced for this specific purpose in Australia (Queensland), South Africa, and South America. The experiments in Queensland, begun in 1920, successfully cleared over a million acres of *Opuntia* using a pre-release breeding program, teams of surveyors, and an extensive plan for how to control the spread of the insect (Dodd 1940). Bâthie and Petit knew of these experiments, mentioning the successful cases in their writings leading up to 1924. It is possible that the scientists selected *D. tomentosus* for use in the South based on its successful eradication of prickly pear elsewhere. It is also possible that Bâthie or Petit became confused as to the variety in question, or failed to consider this fact at all before proceeding. Either way, there is no historical evidence that Bâthie and Petit evaluated the density of cactus, wind direction, the presence or absence of natural predators, or any other ecological variables considered important by other cactus eradication programs.

In early 1924, Bâthie conducted a small experimental release of cochineal in a stand of raketa outside Antananarivo, in the central highlands. Much to his delight, the insect spread quickly and successfully destroyed the stand within weeks. Bâthie quickly published on this success, noting the potential benefit for the South, and encouraged colons around Toliara—where there had been long-standing conflicts with natives over land and water rights—to consider using the insect (Middleton 1999). By this time, Bâthie and Petit had the ear of Olivier, and it was becoming clear to both sides that the newly appointed governor-general supported transformation of the South. Middleton (1999, 244) observes: "The influence Perrier de la Bâthie and Petit exercised as 'experts' was exacerbated by the political structure of the colonial state. Whereas in Australia the release of insects into the environment was reputedly subject to a formal process of consultation, in Madagascar it rested on an essentially private agreement between the Governor General, Perrier de la Bâthie and Petit." Notably, Decary, whose opinions about raketa diverged from that of the governor, was not privy to this agreement.

There is considerable debate as to the events leading up to the release of cochineal in the South (cf. Middleton 1999; Kaufmann 2001). But there is general agreement that in November of 1924, a small container of larvae, supplied by Bâthie, was released in a stand of raketa on a colon's farm outside Toliara (Frappa 1932). From there, the infestation spread to the east up the Onilahy River basin before expanding to the north and south, moving at a rate of 100 kilometers per year (Larsson 2004) (fig. 5). The spread may have benefited from human assistance: "French soldiers would throw infected branches on the [raketa fields] and the cactus mazes surrounding the village in order to quell resistance and force

113

submission by destroying the food supply" (Powe 1994, 140–41). By late 1926, cochineal had crossed the Menarandra and was consuming raketa near Beloha. By

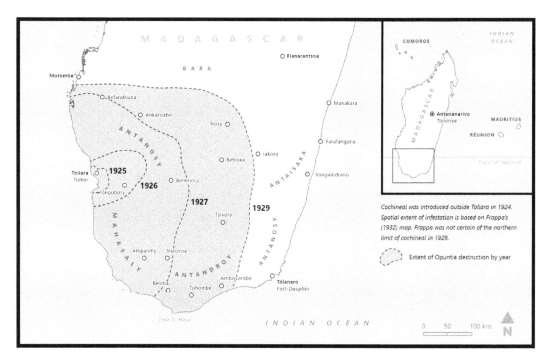

Figure 5. Geographic spread of cochineal between 1924 and 1929. Shading indicates total area where raketa was destroyed. Dotted lines indicate approximate extent of destruction by year. (Data source: Frappa 1932)

1928, it had destroyed cactus throughout Mahafale and Antandroy pastoral areas, including Decary's district of Tsihombe. Frappa (1932, 53) observes: "At the end of 1928 one could say that from Tulear to Fort-Dauphin, from the Mahafale country to the Antanosy country, passing through Androy, raketa had disappeared."

During this period, people traveling through the South reported being "choked and blinded" by swirling clouds of male cochineal (Decary 1930, v). At times, the swarms of insects made travel impossible. Soon after the cactus disappeared, cattle started to die and many people left the area. In April 1929, a prominent newspaper warned of "bovine mortality [which] increases every day" (Middleton 1999, 239). Decary (1935) estimated that as many as 10,000 cattle died in Androy. Meanwhile, Bérard (1951) put the figure at 100,000 cattle in Androy, and Guillermo (1955) estimated 300,000. In the aftermath of the collapse, officials faced significant challenges acquiring information from the region—a situation exacerbated by the contentiousness of the raketa debate. Even if Decary's estimate of 10,000 for

Androy is correct, this toll would have had a serious impact on pastoral life. In all likelihood, Decary was keeping his figures low to protect his job (Kaufmann 2000).

Famine struck quickly as the area of pastoral collapse expanded. Decary (1930) watched as villages in his district emptied overnight. Stratton (1964, 132) cites eyewitness accounts: "The desiccated bodies of the very young and the very old lay alongside the paths where they had stopped for the night but had not got up in the morning to go on trekking to the north." As with the bovine death toll, estimates of human casualties are similarly vague. Decary (1931) says that 500–800 people died in Androy. Deschamps (1959) claims that Tsihombe district alone—60,000 strong prior to the plague—lost more than half of its population. It is not clear how many of these died or migrated. There are no corresponding estimates for the other Androy districts, or any estimates at all for the sizeable Mahafale territories. Figures from these areas would certainly raise the total. We will never have a full accounting of the human and animal cost of the cochineal plague, leading some to argue that focusing on the body count misses the point (see Kaufmann 2000). Indeed, the aftermath of raketa's destruction is best seen in its long-term effect on Southern people and food provisioning, a primary concern throughout the remainder of this chapter.

Twenty years after Gallieni's *tache d'huile* consolidated the central plateau, Olivier deployed an oil-stain of his own. As the concentric circles of cochineal moved out from Toliara, the collapse of cattle herds drove many destitute households out of the cactus region. Of those that survived the exodus, many found themselves far from home and dependent on the new wage economy. In 1928, as cochineal was consuming the raketa in his district, Decary (1928, 44) wrote:

> Now that we are in the presence of a *fait accompli*, we must ask ourselves what will result. Some settlers consider the disappearance of the Raiketa as a good . . . [that] the natives will have to emigrate to more fertile regions where they can employ their arms in the service of the colonists . . . In any case, it has been observed many times that the great displacements of humanity have rarely given good results, especially when it comes to natives very close to nature, such as [the] Antandroy, which, like plants, are remarkably adapted to the desert environment in which they live.

Decary's concern for the people of the South would keep him employed: two years later, he was relocated from Tsihombe to Ambovombe district to manage relief efforts for the ongoing famine.

The Collapse of Cactus Pastoralism

The story of food provisioning failure in Madagascar's deep South is seemingly straightforward: a fast-moving infestation of cochineal destroyed abundant stands of prickly pear, depriving herders of cattle fodder, daily food, famine food, and dietary water. Without fodder, large numbers of cattle died. The loss of cows—combined with the loss of food resources—pushed many households to the point of migration or starvation. The extent of the destruction made it impossible to simply move herds to cactus-rich areas: cochineal succeeded in destroying virtually all raketa south of 21° south latitude, an area over 64,000 square kilometers.

Three aspects of this basic story require clarification. First, it is possible (perhaps likely) that more humans and animals died from dehydration than starvation. Raketa contributed the largest fraction of water to the bovine diet during the dry months, possibly the entire water requirement. It also provided significant water for the human population. Dehydration advances human death faster than starvation: in a hot and dry desert environment, death may occur within a single day. By contrast, it may take weeks to die from starvation, a length of time that depends on age, existing energy reserves, caloric demands, nutritional deficiencies, and vulnerability to disease (Dettmeyer, Verhoff, and Schütz 2014). Witness accounts from the plague note the speed with which victims succumbed. Decary's (1928, 44) description of the 1903 "famine" that affected the Anjeka mentions that the tribe was sustained for three weeks by water from raketa. It is possible that, in general, more victims of Southern famines died from a lack of water rather than food. The same may be true in this instance.

Second, this story has been presented as a famine that broadly affected the deep South. However, Kaufmann (2001, 152) notes significant spatial disparity in the impacts: some areas survived the famine because of a successful sweet potato crop, while "a day's walk away" there was no crop at all. The impact was generally less in Mahafale territory, but a short distance to the east, where cactus thickets were denser, households were severely affected. Bâthie (1934) observed that the village of Bevoalova was hard hit by scarcity, but a mere 10 kilometers to the north, other villages were "prosperous." In other words, as far as spatial extent is concerned, the comprehensive destruction of raketa did not result in a similarly comprehensive food crisis. The local interaction of raketa's disappearance with other variables—for example, the availability of famine foods, local rainstorms, or beneficial kinship networks—affected the spatial distribution of mortality. I offer that this spatial variability is less important than the longer-term consequences for Mahafale and Antandroy societies *as a whole*, for at the decadal timescale, the impact of the loss of raketa was quite consistent.

Finally, the story masks differences in impact based on wealth. Kaufmann (2000) observes that among the Mahafale, those who died tended to be the poorest; essentially, those who lacked cattle. As in other pastoral settings, cows could be sold for food or ritually exchanged to build social networks that provided material support during times of stress. Large herds helped increase prestige and social influence among peers. As such, the loss of cows would have deprived households of material and social safety nets. Younger herders with fewer cows—or those whose herds were heavily affected by the loss of raketa—were the most likely to be forced into migrant labor (Kaufmann 2000). These disparities exacerbated class tensions among the survivors. Decary (1969; cited in Kaufmann 2000) records his observations during famine relief efforts in 1931: "[T]he 'rich' laughed cynically while watching the poor receive their share, refusing to bring them water . . . As they told it, when they slaughtered a cow, the poor received only the odor. Kin fed first; children ate the scraps. Every man for himself."

It is commonplace for famine to disproportionately affect the poor (cf. Edkins 2000; Garenne 2002; Edgerton-Tarpley 2008). Such differences are aggravated in the context of market-based economies that increase food prices during scarcity and decrease the value of savings (like cattle) when there is large-scale liquidation (Davis 2002). Disparities in outcome tend to be mitigated by horizontal or vertical systems of redistribution, such as welfare programs and moral economies (Scott 1976; Edgerton-Tarpley 2008). In the case of Madagascar, the loss of raketa put pressure on limited external sources of food, while the loss of cattle reduced the effectiveness of traditional "welfare" networks by eliminating the primary form of gifted exchange.

Long-Term Ramifications

The famine that took hold of the South during and after the loss of raketa had four significant long-term ramifications for pastoralists. First, the lack of raketa increased pastoral vulnerability to subsequent droughts by depriving humans and cows of fodder, food, and water. In fact, the forms of mobile pastoralism practiced in the South were nearly eliminated during the 1930–31 crisis (Kaufmann 1998). Some authors claim that increased vulnerability led to abnormally high mortality rates in the droughts of 1936–37, 1943–44, and 1957–58 (Nelson 1973; Covell 1987; Kaufmann 1998). As late as 1973, normal seasonal variations were leading to crisis: in the dry months after harvested stocks had been consumed, locals routinely had to seek out "roots and wild fruits in the bush" (Nelson 1973, 96).

Second, the loss of suitable fodder led to a partial collapse of the cattle economy in the South, a primary source of beef for export from Madagascar. In fact, beef exports from the island never returned to their peak of over 700,000 head in 1913 (Kaufmann 1998). The collapse was exacerbated by the global economic crisis of 1929–31 that severely impacted commodity exports (Brown 2000). The colonial-era districts of the South possessed considerable wealth, mostly in the form of cattle, but by 1973, these regions (aggregated into Toliara Province) were the poorest in the country. Instead of herding cattle, smallholders turned to sisal production and the collection of wild products to pay taxes (Nelson 1973).

Third, the ecology of the cactus region was transformed not only by the immediate loss of the dominant flora but also the pastoral response. "Without reserves of prickly pear to feed their hungry herds, pastoralists turned to the native vegetation and cut shrubs, brush, and trees . . . contributing to desertification" (H. Humbert, cited in Kaufmann 2000, 147). Decary (1930) confirmed that herders quickly turned to cutting down any viable forms of fodder in the absence of cactus; an absence that was nearly total. "In the Extreme South there are only a few [cactus trunks] which hardly ever reach adulthood. As soon as they reach sixty centimeters in height, a few mealybugs [cochineal] appear, which cause them to wither and perish" (Decary 1969, 455). Stands of *Euphorbiaceae*, like the once-popular samata, had been crowded out by raketa and were now quickly depleted as pastoralists searched for anything that could support their dwindling herds. Ironically, the same native flora that Bâthie had worked hard to preserve fell victim to his campaign against raketa.

Finally, the collapse of cactus pastoralism drove many Southerners—especially Antandroy—away from home. There were (and still are) two overlapping motivations involved in this transhumance. First, droughts and poverty pushed people out of the South in search of food—a common response to severe famine throughout human history (Gráda and O'Rourke 1997). In the words of the district chief of Ambovombe, "the history of migration is that of hunger" (Deschamps 1959, 83). In years when rainfall was low and subsistence harvests were put in jeopardy, scarcity migration increased. "Emigration now offers the people of the Far-South the necessary valve to balance their economy . . . The expansion of this valve varies in amplitude with the amount of annual rainfall" (Deschamps 1959, 70). This migratory response to environmental conditions caused one colonial official to refer to scarcity migration as "a human evaporation due to drought" (Deschamps 1959, 70).

The second—and related—driver of migration was the growing obligation to participate in the monetary economy. For many, especially young people, wage labor on distant plantations was the only opportunity to raise the money necessary to pay taxes or buy cattle. Remittances helped ensure that households could withstand food stresses and government impositions; for example, tax levies, legal fees, and arbitrary demands. By 1959, 20 percent of all Antandroy were leaving for temporary work on tobacco, sugar, rice, and sisal plantations (Deschamps 1959). Over time, these temporary migrations became permanent: by 1970, 16 percent of all Antandroy had left the South permanently, the largest ethnic diaspora in recent Malagasy history (Nelson 1973).

As Antandroy began to leave traditional land in search of wage labor, small-scale domestic land expropriation started to occur. "As pastoralists worked in towns or on coffee, clove, sisal, and vanilla plantations, saving their earnings to rebuild their herds, [Antanosy] rice cultivators from the southeast appropriated some Mahafaly and [Antandroy] lands around the Onilahy and Mandrare Rivers" (Kaufmann 1998, 133). This slow but inexorable appropriation of land for sedentary cultivation—a move supported by the government—further signaled the end of the South's cactus pastoralism.

Raketa Dependency

Prior to Social Policy, pastoral production overlapped with pastoral consumption: the millet, maize, and sweet potatoes grown in household fields contributed directly to the caloric intake of household bodies. Connecting pastoral production and consumption was raketa: the fruit provided food and water for human bodies while cladodes provided food and water for abundant cattle herds. Cattle could be exchanged for various forms of social capital, reinforcing ties of reciprocity that might be called upon in times of stress. For these reasons, pastoralists sought to build large herds as a form of insurance against disaster. But here, too, raketa was essential: the tall, spiny thickets defended herds from rustlers and protected vulnerable row crops from hungry cows. Households also depended on raketa during periods of ecological or political stress. If harvests failed and raketa fruit was no longer available, people switched to eating cladodes. When the French captured local watering holes, herders relied on raketa in the bovine diet to provide sufficient water, enabling cows to forego watering holes altogether.

In effect, cactus pastoralism was a system of food provisioning predicated on a single point of failure. Even a diversity of cultivated crops could not reduce overall vulnerability so long as these crops were dependent on raketa for protection from cows. Large herd sizes could not function as insurance against stress so long as those herds were dependent on raketa for fodder and water. Indeed, as French interventions mounted, pastoralists responded by increasing their dependence on raketa. By the time cochineal was released in 1924, all food production and consumption depended on raketa in one form or another. This dependency "bottleneck" dramatically intensified the severity of the disaster.

The Coupling of Colonial and Pastoral Production

Famines and misery will disappear forever when there is irrigated land, better crops, products to be exported. Hydraulic works, agricultural improvements and some general measures are the means that will enable us to completely transform the region.

—Henri Perrier de la Bâthie, *Les Famines du Sud-Ouest de Madagascar*

For the French, the emphasis on Social Policy made it seem increasingly obvious that the problem with colonial productivity lay in the South. At the same time, all the problems of the South seemed connected to raketa, which sustained large-scale pastoralism and impeded efforts to alter it. From this perspective, raketa occupied land best placed in the hands of European capitalists, enabled locals to waste their efforts on herding cattle, and threatened colonial stability by sheltering thieves and rebels.

Despite such political discourse, transforming the South into concessions and impelling its people into wage labor was only one of several options. Administrators could have encouraged local ownership of land and production of cash crops. The system of indirect rule partially implemented under Gallieni could have been extended, with ethnic districts empowered to make their own decisions about the forms of production to pursue. Administrators could have ignored the South altogether and concentrated on the concession lands already established to the north. But there is no indication these alternatives were ever seriously entertained. The problem had been framed around the South and its cactus.

The approach promoted by Bâthie and others had the effect of coupling French wealth production with *pastoral* production and consumption. The common material component was raketa: for the French, the cactus stood in the way of imperial progress. For pastoralists, it was essential to food provisioning.

Coupling does not inherently lead to collapse. In the case of Hawaii, the coupling of chiefly wealth and commoner production and consumption (prior to collapse) ensured that chiefs had an incentive to preserve agriculture and commoner well-being. The later decoupling of these interests allowed food system failure to occur. But in Madagascar, colonial interest in raketa was precisely the inverse of pastoral interest. Ultimately, this opposition between pastoral and colonial motives is what drove the conflict: one party wanted the relations of production around raketa preserved while the other wanted them destroyed. Chapter 4 provides a more detailed analysis of these forms of entanglement and the consequences for food provisioning.

The Production of Vulnerability

Under Social Policy, the colonial government sought to make Madagascar economically productive. In the South, this objective was to be realized in two ways: through the conversion of pastureland to cash-crop plantations, and the conversion of pastoralists to wage laborers. With respect to land, plantations could not be established until raketa was removed and pastoral grazing areas relinquished. With respect to labor, the burdens of SMOTIG had set back the objectives of Social Policy by reinforcing pastoral dependence on cactus and enflaming opposition to colonial rule. In the meantime, wage opportunities—available for decades on plantations in Réunion and northern Madagascar—had failed to lure Antandroy and Mahafale away from their ancestral homes. If the wage market was the carrot, the head tax imposed in 1901 was the stick. But this, too, failed to drive locals into the monetary economy. Those who chose to pay taxes sold just enough cattle to acquire the money demanded by tax collectors; those who chose not to pay stayed behind the cactus fences. Thanks to the triangular interdependency linking people, cattle, and raketa, the South seemed impervious to the incursions of western economic markets.

If French plans were to succeed, this triangular interdependency had to be broken and new dependencies established in its place. To pay taxes and buy food, locals would have to sell their labor, not their cows. Plantation owners would buy this labor and extract surplus value in the form of cash crops. These commodities would be sold to France and elsewhere for profit. The means of production for these plantations—fertile land—would be expropriated from pastoralists and divided into concessions. At the top of the pyramid, the colonial government would make money from land leases, head taxes, corporate taxes, tariffs, and profits from its own capital financing arrangements. Finally, the colony would reap the benefits of a landscape made "visible," measurable, and rational; its terrain now open to road construction and its people open to influence (see Scott 1998). The traditional isolationism and self-sufficiency of the Antandroy and Mahafale would be broken by a new dependence on French-controlled markets. After all, by the 1920s, enslavement was no longer an option. Hunger would have to take the place of chains.

The first step in this land-labor transition was obstructed by raketa, a point that Bâthie makes consistently in his pro-eradication arguments. Of course, destroying raketa would make cactus pastoralists exceptionally vulnerable to environmental and social shocks, but from Bâthie's perspective, this vulnerability was necessary and transformative. Writing in 1934 and reflecting on the recent upheaval in the South, Bâthie notes: "the natives of this region were originally shepherds, sometimes living with plunder, when supplies were lacking. Economic development and other causes gradually transform them into sedentary and law-abiding cultivators. This transformation is difficult and we must help them overcome these difficulties" (Bathie 1934, 179). In colonial discourse, such suffering was essential to the modernization of subject peoples, just as modernization entailed the integration of such people into the western economic system (Kaufmann 2008).

The "productive" vulnerabilities emerging in southern Madagascar in the 1930s resulted from the deliberate creation of a new socionature. It may be that all famines emerge from fundamental socionatural transformations, often at the end of long causal chains initiated by policy changes, economic crises, or direct violence. This famine is somewhat unique in that Bâthie's strategy was so obviously ecological in its mechanism. The French didn't break the triangular dependency through legislation or military incursion, but by attacking plants with insects.

The Involution Trap

Writing about the transformation of rice production in Java under Dutch rule, anthropologist Clifford Geertz (1963) uses the concept of involution to describe a particular form of social adaptation to stress. During the 19th century, Dutch administrators placed increasing pressure on Javanese farmers to produce rice and sugar. The response from producers was to improve the efficiency of existing systems through small, progressive adjustments. Over several decades, Javanese wet rice cultivation was fine-tuned to squeeze as much as possible from every available hectare and laborer. Producers adjusted cultivation strategies, planting calendars, crop rotations, tenure systems, and labor relations. For some time, the system successfully increased output and met the demands of the colonial "Culture System." Eventually, however, increasing pressure resulted in subsistence failure and starvation. Geertz (1963) refers to this adaptational strategy as involution: the process of continually adjusting an existing system to meet external demands.

In the Javanese case, involution emerged as a commitment to an existing framework of socioecological practices and relationships, even when that framework could no longer satisfy material needs. This downward spiral of feedback is what Boonstra and de Boer (2014) refer to as the *involution trap*. In the first phase of the trap, a socioecological system emerges that satisfies basic needs and defines available options for growth. As external pressures emerge, the system does not fundamentally reorganize but recommits to existing relations and processes of production. This commitment simultaneously improves overall efficiency and limits alternative pathways. As time passes and pressures increase, possibilities for reorganization dwindle further, ensuring that the system keeps its underlying structure. Ultimately, the system may encounter physical limits to production or diminishing returns on efficiency improvements. In this regard, involution is contrasted with *revolution*—a deliberate (and sometimes violent) rejection of existing relations and processes in favor of new ones.

On the Malagasy side, the commitment to cactus pastoralism between 1769 and 1924 is a prototypical case of involution. The introduction of raketa offered a chance for Southern pastoralists to increase herd sizes and expand settlements. Locals adapted cactus thickets to defend against rustlers, fed cladodes to cattle, and ate the cactus fruit. This commitment came at the cost of alternatives: as raketa spread, other fodder disappeared. Pastoralists no longer tended to samata. Watering holes that could have supplemented moisture-rich raketa were relinquished to French control. As tax collectors and soldiers encroached, villagers planted more cactus. In the late 1700s, raketa emerged as a new source of food, fodder, water, and security; by the eve of the cochineal invasion, it was the *only* source. By the 1920s, abandoning raketa would have exposed Antandroy and Mahafale to exploitative labor markets, the loss of pastoral culture, and starvation.

Involution was not confined to southern pastoralists. In Paris and Antananarivo, failure to subjugate the South and make it economically productive had increased pressure on the government to "do something" about cactus pastoralism. The administrative response amounted to an involution in *thinking* about the South, its ecology and people. This involution consisted of two separate conceptual commitments: a renewed insistence on the conversion of southern land and people to the colonial economic model, and a persistent belief that raketa (the plant) was at the heart of southern resistance. As cactus continued to spread, tax revenues from pastoralists fell, and armed confrontation increased, French commitment to these positions became solidified and alternative views (like Decary's) were discredited.

Two features of the natural and political environment in the 1920s encouraged and accelerated these processes of involution: panacea thinking and the spatial proliferation of cactus. Panacea thinking is the assumption that solutions to environmental or social problems that work in one context will have a high chance of success in other, similar contexts (Ostrom, Janssen, and Anderies 2007). The logic behind panaceas assumes that certain socionatural relationships—like those that connect pastoralists to cows and fodder—tend to hold universally. As such, a conceptual model built on these relationships can be applied to a variety of systems, even when these systems differ in other ways. For panacea advocates, "all problems, whether they are different challenges within a single resource system or across a diverse set of resources, are similar enough to be represented by a small class of formal models" (Ostrom, Janssen, and Anderies 2007, 15176). Panacea thinking has been identified and critiqued in contemporary approaches to international development and environmental conservation; sectors that have a history of applying uniform "protocols" and "strategies" across broad expanses of the Global South (Banuri 1991). Ackoff (2001, 8) refers to panacea thinking as "a diluted form of fundamentalism," offering its adherents a simplification and stabilization of complexity.

The proponents of cactus eradication in the 1920s, especially Bâthie and Petit, applied panacea thinking to their choice of strategy, using successful cochineal introductions in other parts of the world to justify use of the insect in Madagascar. Prickly pear was already considered a scourge in South Africa and Australia where "pest pears" obstructed row agriculture and encroached on pastureland (Middleton 1999). In these colonial contexts, farmers experimented with both physical and chemical control, but plowing down the cactus was time consuming and chemical applications were too expensive. Setting fire to the thickets also proved ineffective. At the turn of the 20th century, Australian efforts to control prickly pear using cochineal met with success. Over the next 20 years, Australia would undertake several waves of cochineal introductions (Pettey 1947). Bâthie and Petit used these successes in their publications as justification for similar experiments in Madagascar: "We ought to follow the example of Australia, a cattle-rearing country par excellence, where the great efforts made to destroy *Opuntia vulgaris* over the past twenty years have been crowned with success" (Bâthie 1924, 222). If it worked in arid, pastoral Australia, why wouldn't it work in Madagascar?

Beyond cochineal, the overall strategy of converting pastoralism to wage labor was justified using "successful" transitions that had been implemented in British South Africa and French Algeria (see Bathie 1934). Bâthie and Petit repeatedly use similarities in climate, terrain, ecology, and social practice from other parts of Africa to advocate for the implementation of similar economic programs in southern Madagascar. These justifications were premised on a fundamental—and dangerous—socionatural determinism: two places that look the same and have similar native populations can be successfully governed in the same way.

In the end, panacea thinking and socionatural determinism prevented a more thorough investigation of the differences between cases—differences that may have been responsible for gross miscalculations of the spread of cochineal. Along the Eastern Cape of southern Africa, cochineal expansion was stopped by aggressive ants. Elsewhere, cochineal was kept under control by diseases and parasites (Pettey 1947). Other environmental factors may have conspired to fuel the spread of cochineal in southern Madagascar, including the specific varieties of cochineal and cactus, the prevailing wind direction, altitude, and climate (Middleton 1999). None of these factors were considered by Bâthie and Petit in their publications. The Australian experiments enthusiastically referenced by Bâthie and Petit were performed under highly controlled conditions as compared to the "wild" release of cochineal in Toliara in 1924.

Kaufmann (2000, 144) argues that the preponderance of unknowns leading up to the release of cochineal ensured that no one anticipated "the success of the insects . . . the devastation was an unforeseen chance event, a contingency that could have ended easily in failure." It may be that some French officials did not foresee the devastation. It may be that the preponderance of unknowns ensured a healthy dose of contingency. But here, my concern is to understand how the *culture of thought* around cactus pastoralism ensured these contextual variables were never fully considered, and why—lacking the appropriate data—Bâthie *still* considered it wise to release cochineal into the wild. Panacea thinking and socionatural determinism helped reinforce and reproduce existing discourses around pastoralism and cacti. Involution in this instance amounted to numerous conscious decisions to double down on environmental perceptions and development policies.

Another driver of involutionary decision-making was the proliferation of cactus itself. The ubiquity of raketa exacerbated provisioning failure in three ways. First, from the Antandroy and Mahafale perspective, the abundance of raketa made it more likely that pastoralists would voluntarily depend on it. Unlike other sources of fodder, raketa seemed limitless and impossible to overuse. The ease with which cactus thickets proliferated across the South, through both human agency and wild propagation, may have created the false impression among locals that raketa had become a permanent feature of the environment or—at the very least—a difficult tenant to evict. Cactus was the core of pastoral environmental perceptions: the name *Androy*, literally "country of the thornbush," didn't make much sense without it.

Second, from the French perspective, the abundance of raketa made it more likely that planners would see the cactus as a problem. Indeed, the more widespread the cactus, the bigger the problem: proponents of eradication needed merely to point to the ubiquity of thorny thickets to magnify the crisis and justify immediate, decisive action. The narrative of raketa being everywhere and touching everything ensured that the cactus was held responsible for every problem taking place in the South. Spiny thickets "concealed" cattle thieves, "abetted" tax evaders, and "sheltered" rebels.[8] If cactus was everywhere, then rustlers, tax evaders, and rebels had to be everywhere as well. Furthermore, the extent of cactus—the spatial magnitude of the problem—helped justify *eradication* over cactus *control*. With cactus covering the South and smothering the land's productive potential, it was no time for half-hearted measures.

Finally, from an ecological perspective, the abundance of raketa made it more likely that an invasion of cochineal could destroy the population completely. Here, the sheer density of the cactus greatly assisted the wind-borne insects in finding food. Had raketa been less prolific, the progress of the plague may have stopped at natural breaks in vegetation or, at a minimum, moved more slowly through the South. A slower rate of infestation may have afforded cactus pastoralists opportunities for adaptation or life-saving out-migration. Furthermore, the 150-year growth of raketa pushed out alternative sources of fodder, like samata. Pastoralists aided this process, not only adapting to the new flora, but actively encouraging its spread. By 1924, cactus pastoralism had become a monoculture dependent on a monoculture. When raketa was eliminated, there was no available substitute to supply the immediate needs of cattle and people.

The proliferation of raketa leading up to 1924 helped encourage involutionary decision-making both materially and discursively. Materially, abundance made it possible for cows and people to subsist on cactus without help from other sources. In this way, abundance deterred systematic revolution by making the diversification of food sources unnecessary. Discursively, for the French, the *symbol* of raketa—representing "backwardness," "imperviousness," and "threat"—was reified through abundance. If cactus posed a problem for colonial security in one district, it surely posed similar problems wherever it could be found; indeed, across the entire South. As "problems" increased and raketa spread, the existing culture of thought around raketa was reinforced and alternative symbolic representations of the cactus were pushed out.

In an interesting twist, abundance *did* promote a revolution in French thinking when it came to eradication: the failure of attempts to introduce inerme and to subdue the South through military means forced administrators to rethink their approach to the cactus problem. By 1924, cochineal had been introduced to destroy prickly pear in other colonial contexts, but no one had attempted to introduce it amidst a human population that depended on cactus. This new use for cochineal— as a technology for social discipline and economic reorganization—was unprecedented in French colonial policy.[9] Of course, this revolution in *approach* did not accompany a revolution in the *interpretation* of raketa (as a symbol). In fact, the policy shift toward eradication was dependent on a recommitment to the belief that cactus was a threat.

The Question of Responsibility

The history of the Cactus War demonstrates the complexity and uncertainty in ascribing blame for colonial-era disasters (Dirks 1992). Documents from the period provide conflicting accounts. Despite historical simplifications, neither pastoralists nor colonists were monolithic categories: there was no essential "French" policy or approach, nor any universal "Malagasy" that antagonized the empire. In historical reconstructions, there is little agreement as to whether the release of cochineal was deliberate or accidental, or whether the fatal consequences could have been anticipated (Middleton 1999). We will never know exactly what was on Bâthie's mind in late 1924 when he set cochineal loose outside Toliara.

In the end, I am not sure it matters. This analysis did not set out to prove the guilt of Bâthie, Petit, Olivier, or others in causing the collapse of food provisioning or the loss of human and animal life: questions of foreseeability, intentionality, and negligence have been argued elsewhere (cf. Middleton 1999; Kaufmann 2000). Rather, this analysis attempts to reveal and examine the larger spatio-historical "logic" that made cactus eradication not only reasonable, but necessary. Such logic did not emerge fully formed on the eve of the plague, but evolved over time. It was shaped by shifting environmental perceptions, racial and class prejudices, and economic imperatives. It was bolstered by imperial "best practices" from North Africa, West Africa, and Tonkin. And it was altered by geopolitical conversations taking place in Paris, London, and Antananarivo. As such, I am less interested in *whether* Bâthie (as a human being and moral actor) committed a crime than in *how* Bâthie came to personify the logic of eradication and mass violence. In the end, the renowned botanist was merely the tip of a very long spear.

On balance, there is evidence to suggest the French knew what they were doing, and evidence to suggest they were caught by surprise. But in the end, I am inclined to think that while Olivier and his government planned to eradicate raketa, they did not anticipate the scale of destruction nor the loss of life. I say this for one practical reason: Social Policy was implemented to convert Madagascar's constellation of local economies into engines of production for France. To that end, it would be counterintuitive for the architects of Social Policy to deliberately engineer a famine in the South. After all, dead bodies can't work plantations.

Conclusions: Madagascar's First Modern Famine

The collapse of food provisioning in Madagascar's deep South between 1924 and 1930 resulted from the sudden loss of raketa, a species of prickly pear that had become widespread and upon which pastoralists depended for fodder, food, water, and physical security. Raketa was destroyed through the deliberate introduction of cochineal, a scale insect known to eat prickly pear. Cochineal was introduced by the French as part of a plan to convert southern land to productive use and push the local population into the wage economy. In the short term, the loss of raketa led to a collapse of Antandroy and Mahafale cattle herds. High bovine mortality led to widespread destitution and famine. Starvation was exacerbated by the fact that raketa was also the primary famine food. In the longer term, the famine led to unprecedented out-migration as impoverished herders sought wage labor opportunities on colonial plantations. Without raketa, local vulnerability to drought increased, leading to elevated mortality in food crises throughout the 20th century. Today, many Antandroy have left the South permanently, while others emigrate on a seasonal basis in search of work. Those who remain are still vulnerable to food crises initiated by drought, locust plagues, disease epidemics, and commodity price fluctuations (Ford 2017).

This case provides an opportunity to reflect on common understandings of famine genesis. In the empirical scholarship, it is commonplace to trace the mechanics of collapse: variations in rainfall, failure of harvests, the movement of markets, or the progress of invading armies. Over the last 50 years, this mechanistic approach has focused almost exclusively on the economics of food production and consumption: prices, markets, and entitlements. In Madagascar, the mechanics of famine are well known. Like a line of fallen dominoes, the desiccated bodies seen by Stratton's (1964) eyewitnesses can be traced back to the release of cochineal outside Toliara four years earlier. The progression from insect plague to dead cactus, to dead cows, to dying people carries an inescapable necessity.

But before the release, there were decisions, and before the decisions, there was collusion: French politicians and scientists worked together to develop and promote a discourse of cactus eradication and pastoral conversion to wage labor. This discourse was built around narratives of colonial advancement, modernization, insecurity, racial inferiority, and retribution. Before cochineal could be released into the wild, it had to become logical (necessary, even) to do so. Decades of evolving French perspectives on the colony—and on "French-ness" itself—helped achieve just that.

On the Malagasy side, for the loss of raketa to initiate a famine the cactus had to first become essential to food provisioning. Once again, there is more than mechanics to this story. Raketa enabled an expansion of pastoralism in the South. For many of the migrants to the cactus region in the 19th century, raketa was the entire basis for their pastoral existence. As foreign interventions increased, cactus helped protect lives and livelihoods. It is no surprise, then, that raketa came to be entangled in discourses of resistance and pastoral identity: herders took pride in being "of the cactus" and saw shared characteristics in themselves and raketa (Kaufmann 2011). Decary's socio-botanical unit is perhaps best expressed in the common Antandroy saying: *Longo ty raiketa sy ty Tandroy*, "the Antandroy and the cactus are kin" (Decary 1921).

Related to these opposing discourses were material realities: for the French, a bankrupt treasury, a humiliating defeat to Prussia, and a costly World War; for the Malagasy, the botanical properties of raketa and the physical geography of the deep South. These kinds of slow-emerging negotiations between physical reality and guiding principles are generally absent from analyses of famine causation. And yet, without them, it is difficult to explain how a biological war against pastoralism became acceptable, or how Madagascar's first modern famine brought such lasting devastation.

In the end, Olivier got his wish: impoverished herders left the South for French-run plantations in Réunion, Mauritius, and other parts of Madagascar. But Bâthie's dream of a "productive" southern landscape did not materialize. There was no rush of colons waiting to convert the South into plantations, nor was there any government interest in Bâthie's dream of desert-wide irrigation. As it turned out, Bâthie could not convince subsequent governors nor investors that the South could be turned green (Middleton 1999). Rearing cattle was also out of the question: with neither raketa nor irrigation, the government acknowledged that large-scale herding was impossible. And as for the hope that eliminating raketa would increase tax revenue, two years after the famine there was still no tax collected (Middleton 1999).

In the 1930s, the government attempted once more to introduce spineless prickly pear to the South. As before, these efforts generally met with failure. Subsequently, several kinds of spiny prickly pear were introduced in a concerted effort to rejuvenate southern pastoralism (Larsson 2004). "For the thirty years until independence, colonial administrators organized the planting of cochineal-resistant *Opuntiae* in the Deep South, ostensibly to provide fodder for cattle but, we may suppose, to feed the people too" (Middleton 2009, 248). These varieties—*raketa mena, raketa sonjo, raketa vazaha* among others—spread rapidly and succeeded in establishing a foothold in raketa gasy's historical home. But none were as desirable to cattle or people as the original (Kaufmann 1998).

Today, raketa mena is considered a pest and has been declared "a primary threat to biodiversity and livelihoods" by the World Wildlife Fund (Larsson 2004, 2). Its proliferation has reanimated debates over how best to control, or even eradicate, introduced "pest pears." It remains to be seen if mercenary cochineal will make another appearance in the South, this time in the service of Western-funded conservation.

CHAPTER 3

War and Reconstruction Famine in Cambodia: 1970–79

By March 1975, Phnom Penh had become a contradiction. For rural refugees desperate to escape the civil war and American bombs, Cambodia's capital city was a place of last resort. Shanty towns and temporary camps materialized in and around the burgeoning city to support the hundreds of thousands who had fled violence in the countryside. With dwindling food and medical supplies, the urban poor relied on aid flights and river convoys for survival. Shells and rockets from insurgent artillery batteries disrupted public services. Rolling power outages—part of a government "austerity program"—left poor neighborhoods, hospitals, and emergency services in the dark and unable to operate (Porter and Hildebrand 1975, 8). When clinics and relief centers were open, lines were hopelessly long, and aid was often nonexistent. A small pediatric clinic operated by World Vision, outfitted with a single exam table and staffed by four doctors, managed to treat an astonishing 600 patients on a single day in March. That same day, it had to turn away 500 who waited in the street (Leslie 1975).

Meanwhile, in other neighborhoods, Phnom Penh's elite relaxed in newly built mansions, surrounded by Western luxuries bought with the profits of a lucrative black market. Government officials and high-ranking military officers had reaped extraordinary personal wealth from Cambodia's civil conflict, turning foreign aid and the spoils of war into conspicuous consumption even as the noose tightened around their regime (Slocomb 2010). In April 1975, an American correspondent for the Baltimore Sun wrote: "For the few privileged elite, the good life of tennis, nightclubs, expensive French meals and opulent brandy-drenched dinner parties went on almost to the very end, while the vast majority of the city's swollen population sank into deeper and deeper misery" (Porter and Hildebrand 1975, 8). A feature of Cambodian society since the time of the French, the urban elite defied the impending storm with denial and extravagance.

The crisis that gripped Phnom Penh in the final months of the Lon Nol regime is perhaps best expressed by its effect on children. In a March 24 interview for the *Los Angeles Times*, relief workers described the state of pediatric care in Phnom Penh (Leslie 1975). Dr. Beat Richner (a Red Cross volunteer) and Dr. Penuy Key (a clinic manager with World Vision) explained that starvation and malnutrition were now commonplace among the children of the city. In 1975, the average child brought in for evaluation weighed 40 percent less than what was considered normal. Many mothers had turned to begging for survival: one lamented that she had not been able to bring her daughter to the clinic because she lacked the 75-cent bus fare. Dr. Key explained that "every child who comes to the clinic should be in a hospital . . . but we're lucky to get one in 10 in." The rest "are sent home with rice and medicine." By mid-March, 90 percent of the children admitted to Dr. Richner's ward were malnourished and nearly half of those admitted to pediatric clinics died there (Leslie 1975). In the last days, relief workers reported widespread kwashiorkor and marasmus, and French doctors recorded evidence of cholera, typhoid, measles, and bubonic plague (Porter and Hildebrand 1975).

As corrupt officials pocketed hundreds of thousands of dollars in U.S. military aid each month and redirected supplies of food and fuel onto the black market, the official price of rice in Phnom Penh soared out of reach for all but the wealthiest (Vickery 2000). As the well-heeled considered whether to stay or flee, impoverished parents were making decisions about which of their children would get food and which would be left to die. "They give up on one person, but they save the others," Dr. Richner explained. "This generation is going to be a lost generation of children" (quoted in Leslie 1975).

In a sinister twist, "letting some die to save others" would soon become an implicit policy of Cambodia's new government (Tyner and Rice 2015). One month later, on April 17, Khmer Rouge forces captured the city, effectively ending the civil war and the contradiction of inequality that characterized Phnom Penh's urban life. The population of the capital and remaining cities were largely evacuated into the countryside to support the demands of rice production and the expansion of irrigation. For the next three years and nine months, the Communist Party of Kampuchea (CPK, also known as the Khmer Rouge) reorganized the country's economy around forced labor, food rationing, and agricultural production for export. To abolish remnants of the "old" society, the CPK imposed draconian restrictions on political expression—incarcerating, torturing, and executing suspected enemies of the state, many from within its own ranks. Indeed, it is *this* history of malnourishment, starvation, and mass murder that has captured most attention. For many, Cambodia's history in this period conjures images of "killing fields" and mass graves. For others, the Khmer Rouge share company with Stalin, Mao, and the communist regimes of North Korea as the purveyors of the 20th century's greatest famines (Eberstadt 2017).

This chapter examines the food provisioning failures that beset Cambodian society in the 1970s, a task that requires tracing historical conjunctures back over 30 years, through four governments and two wars. From this perspective, the starvation that ensued between 1975 and 1979 under the CPK had its origin in a rice-production failure many years in the making, a failure brought on by war and propelled by corruption, black markets, geopolitical intrigue, and a duplicitous U.S. food aid program.

It is also the story of a botched rescue attempt. In the months following the evacuation of Cambodia's cities, the CPK rushed to restart rice production in areas devastated by war. Their plan was based on strategies that had successfully maintained production in parts of the country "liberated" from Republican control during the civil war. It involved steadily increasing both the area under cultivation and rice yield per hectare, a task that required massive labor mobilization and the development of large-scale irrigation infrastructure. These goals were not new to the CPK—rather, they reflected a long legacy of development advice and policy: the French, the United States, and the World Bank had developed similar plans for the reorganization of Cambodia's hydrology (Slocomb 2010). Many administrations before 1975 experimented with large-scale labor mobilization for public works (Chandler 2008). Though the CPK has been portrayed as a backward, anti-urban, and antimodern regime ideologically driven to return Khmer society to the glories of Cambodia's ancient past (see Jackson 2014), this analysis finds the contrary: the CPK were *ultra*modern, not antimodern. The Khmer Rouge dreamed of a Green Revolution for Cambodia at the precise moment when Green Revolutions were all the rage.

It is tempting to see the Khmer Rouge victory and the social transformations of 1975–79 as a complete break from the past—after all, the Khmer Rouge described it as such. But a focus on the structure of food provisioning uncovers a more complex story. As in Hawaii and Madagascar, the history of Cambodia's food system contains both transformation and continuation. As before, it is the interaction between what changed and what stayed the same that is essential for understanding the initial crisis and the failure of recovery. Indeed, like other Green Revolutions, the CPK's rescue attempt contained within it contradictions that precipitated its failure.[1] From a structural perspective, the system that allowed tens of thousands of children to die in Phnom Penh in 1973–75 bears striking similarity to the system that killed many of their parents between 1975 and 1979.

More than either Hawaii or Madagascar, the case of Cambodia demonstrates the spatial unevenness of mass starvation. Under the CPK, some communes lost extraordinary numbers of workers to starvation and exposure, while neighboring communes were well fed and sheltered. The contradiction of Phnom Penh before the war—where the wealthy played tennis as children starved in the streets—came to be played out in the countryside, but with different actors and for different reasons. More than either Hawaii or Madagascar, the famine in Cambodia also demonstrates how enormous wealth can be accumulated through mass starvation.

It illustrates the diversity of powerful actors that have pursued hunger for profit—Party officials, military officers, government institutions, and foreign states. In this way, the *economic calculus of hunger* expressed in Cambodia before and after 1975 offers an important reflection on how starvation remains profitable in today's modern food systems.

This chapter is organized into six sections. The first provides a brief overview of Cambodian history, a comparison of the opposing interpretations of the ascent of the Khmer Rouge and the CPK, and an outline of the analytical approach taken in this chapter. Sections two through four cover the period leading up to the Khmer Rouge victory in 1975. The second section describes the organization of Cambodian food provisioning from the colonial period through the 1960s. The primary focus, here, is on rural rice production: rice has been a central feature of the economy and food system for centuries, and its cultivation was the cornerstone of the CPK's plans for Cambodia. In section three, I trace the effect of large-scale conjunctures emerging from the U.S. war in Indochina, centralized control of rice exports, and growing dissatisfaction among rural producers. This history sets the stage for the fourth section, which outlines how these conjunctures precipitated urban mass starvation on the eve of the Cambodian revolution in April 1975.

Sections five and six cover the four years the CPK was in power. The fifth section describes the CPK's efforts to end the food crisis and transform the Cambodian economy through the abolition of money and private property, the imposition of a food ration, and the forced conscription of labor for agricultural and infrastructural work. The final section outlines how these changes—intended to restart rice production and alleviate hunger—had the opposite effect.

Famine, Genocide, and the "Standard Total View"

Cambodia's postcolonial misadventures have been the subject of abundant scholarship and commentary (cf. Vickery 2000; Kiernan 2002, 2004; Chandler 2008). For the sake of overview, the following is a brief synopsis of the country's political history between independence and 1980. Following 90 years as a French protectorate, Cambodia achieved independence in 1953 under the leadership of King Norodom Sihanouk. During the 1950s and early 1960s, economic growth was hindered by party politics and low-level insurgencies. During this time, Sihanouk welcomed some degree of foreign assistance: U.S., Chinese, and Soviet aid helped build hospitals and highways, prepared irrigation and hydroelectric schemes, and supported scientific agriculture in the form of "improved" seeds, fertilizers, and pesticides. With slow but steady increases in productivity, Cambodia's rice exporting economy began to recover from its post–World War II slump. But as American economic and military intervention in Indochina increased through the 1960s, Sihanouk grew wary of American intentions, canceling all aid and cutting diplomatic ties in 1964. American officials, hoping to support war efforts in Vietnam and concerned with the potential spread of communist insurgencies, sought to establish a friendly government in Cambodia. To this end, the United States exploited political discontent to oust Sihanouk. In 1970, a coup led by then prime minister Lon Nol brought an end to Sihanouk's administration: Lon Nol became president of the new Khmer Republic (KR), inheriting a steadily growing economy and an agricultural system that was producing its highest yields ever (Slocomb 2010).

The coup also led to a sharp escalation in the government's war against insurgents, a war that attracted abundant financial assistance and direct military involvement from the United States. In 1970, the covert U.S. bombing campaigns of the late 1960s became official and were dramatically enlarged. By the time aerial bombardment ended in August 1973, the United States had dropped nearly 3 million tons of explosives on Cambodia, more than the total dropped during World War II. Despite American assistance, Lon Nol's war against the insurgents—now a broad front of communists and Sihanouk supporters—was in trouble. Between 1971 and 1974, Republican forces continued to cede territory to the opposition, increasingly dominated by a well-trained and battle-hardened group known as the Khmer Rouge.

Meanwhile, refugees fleeing from war and bombardment in the countryside sought food and shelter in Cambodia's cities, especially Phnom Penh. Between 1970 and 1975, the population of the capital swelled from 600,000 to over two million (Vickery 2000).[2] With the collapse of rice production and the destruction of the country's transport network, the remaining government forces and residents of Phnom Penh were cut off. By 1975, daily aid flights were the only way in or out of the swollen, starving capital. On April 17, the Khmer Rouge captured the city, ending Lon Nol's government and the civil war.

One of the most widely remembered acts of the Khmer Rouge was one of their first as the new leaders of Cambodia: the evacuation of Phnom Penh and remaining urban areas. City dwellers were moved *en masse* into the countryside where they were organized into labor units and put to work growing rice and building irrigation infrastructure. The Khmer Rouge—now known as the Communist Party of Kampuchea (CPK)—imposed a nationwide ration, abolished private property and currency, and established a quota system for rice production geared toward export. For many Cambodians, especially urban evacuees, labor conditions were harsh and the allotted ration insufficient. Refugees who fled Cambodia during this time reported that deaths from exhaustion, malnutrition, and execution were commonplace.

Over time, CPK leadership became convinced that enemies were amassing against the state. Through a series of brutal purges, the CPK began to turn on itself, executing its own officers for supposed treason, disobedience, or failure to meet production quotas. In January 1979, Vietnamese forces invaded Cambodia and installed a new government, bringing an end to CPK control. In the three years and nine months the CPK managed Cambodia, as many as two million people died.[3]

Two Traditions of Scholarship

Throughout the 1970s, reports of agricultural devastation, mass migration, and social upheaval in Cambodia attracted the attention of diplomats, foreign correspondents, and academics. For many commentators, Cambodia was where the explosive repercussions of the Vietnam War had come home to roost. For others, reports of mass murder under communist rule were positive proof that the Cold War was ideologically justified. From the start, this tension inspired abundant analysis on both sides of the debate.

Scholarship and commentary from the 1970s and 1980s can be broadly divided into two opposing camps. On the one hand, authors like Ponchaud (1989), Jackson (2014), and Carney (1989) focus primarily on the deaths caused by the CPK and minimize the role of U.S. military intervention. From this perspective, mass starvation is understood as communist ideology made real: the motivation behind the CPK policies had less to do with economic necessity than a dogmatic interpretation of socialist revolution. Ponchaud (1989, 152) writes, "a revolution does not follow a logical course; it is an explosion of collective violence, in certain ways akin to a passion: while the leaders might seek to justify their acts through a theory . . . both they and the people more often act out according to unconscious reflexes welling up from the depths of a secular tradition." With respect to the evacuation of urban areas, Ponchaud (1989, 153) continues: "Foreign bred, the cities were akin to cankerous growths that the revolutionaries held as their duty to expunge in order to regain ancestral purity." Authors in this tradition see CPK policies as doctrinaire, fanatical, autarkic (that is, seeking complete self-sufficiency), and rooted in mythologies of Khmer identity. Meanwhile, the role of U.S. military intervention in the humanitarian crisis is generally downplayed; for example, Carney (1989) argues that the refugee crisis emerging in the early 1970s was caused by the civil war and not U.S. bombardment.

By contrast, authors like Porter and Hildebrand (1975, 1978), Shawcross (2002), Haas (1991b, 1991a) and Kiernan (2004) argue that the United States bears significant responsibility for the refugee crisis and the rise of the Khmer Rouge. For these analysts, President Nixon's decision to expand aerial bombing over Cambodia not only dismantled agricultural production and drove the rural population into the cities, the indiscriminate destruction of fields and villages also served as a rallying cry for communist recruiters. For some authors writing shortly after the Khmer Rouge victory (cf. Porter and Hildebrand 1975, 1978), the CPK's evacuation of Phnom Penh and other cities is presented as a necessary response to the spiraling urban food crisis. From this perspective, CPK policy was seen to follow a generally humanitarian logic, and reports of atrocities committed during the evacuation are characterized as exaggerations. As details of malnutrition, starvation, and mass murder began to emerge during the late 1970s and early 80s, much of this scholarship lost credibility. Critics of U.S. policy were labeled Khmer Rouge apologists (see Carney 1989). But the unquestioned brutality of the CPK between 1975 and 1979 drew attention away from the bloody history that preceded it, especially the role played by the United States. This shift in responsibility from American "mishandling" to communist brutality was a welcome change for an American public struggling to understand its place in the world after Vietnam.

Since then, the narrative of Cambodia's war years has been shaped primarily by the former tradition of scholarship, a perspective that Michael Vickery (2000, 36) refers to as the Standard Total View (STV). Under the STV, the policies initiated by the CPK were a deliberate attempt to reform Cambodian society through the extermination of former soldiers, urban elites, and other intellectuals, in particular doctors, teachers, and engineers (Vickery 2000, 36). These policies lacked any logical basis or productive purpose, made unrealistic assumptions, and were implemented by incompetent leaders. At the core of the CPK's mandates was an unwavering commitment to Marxist ideology and the revolutionary goal of creating the first pure, self-sufficient, communist society. According to the STV, the implementation of these policies was universal and "invariant as to time or place; the scenario was true everywhere, all the time, between April 1975 and January 1979" (Vickery 2000, 37). Finally—and most importantly—the STV represents the CPK as unique in world history. Jackson (2014, 4) offers the following characterization of the Khmer Rouge: "their swift sword applied untried revolutionary theories with an appalling literalism that left room for neither pragmatism nor compassion." With regard to the evacuation of urban residents, Jackson (2014, 4) continues: "Since the European revolution, romantics, as well as some revolutionaries, have perceived cities as dens of iniquity, but only the Khmer Rouge emptied every city in the land immediately after victory."

The proliferation of the STV has focused significant—and laudable—attention on the atrocities of the Cambodian genocide. As such, one of the primary benefits of the STV has been to encourage the amassing of detailed and plentiful descriptions of the horrors visited on the Cambodian people. But this descriptive focus comes at the expense of thorough analysis of Cambodia's political economy, especially the everyday practices of rice production and food provisioning (Tyner and Rice 2016). Given the direct impact of war on agriculture (see Darwish, Farajalla, and Masri 2009), the loss of production leading to urban starvation, and the centrality of rice production to CPK reforms, this omission is surprising. To varying degrees, authors from both camps emphasize the mass killings, the Cold War geopolitics that shaped Indochina, and the communist ideology of the Khmer Rouge and other groups. But less attention is directed toward the origin of famine between 1970 and 1979. Mass starvation is almost universally explained in terms of production failures caused by war and misguided CPK policies, but few studies trace the connections between these failures and bodily starvation. To do so reveals startling social and geographical distinctions: the starving and well-fed often lived and worked side by side. Some zones that produced plentiful rice maintained healthy workers while other productive zones did not. Before 1975, it was the urban poor (but not refugees from the countryside) who starved. After 1975, starvation depended significantly on zone, district, region, and commune. As I will show in later sections, these differences in outcome are critical for understanding the processes involved in famine genesis.

Genocide through the Lens of Rice Production

This study looks at changes in the organization of Cambodia's food provisioning system, in particular, the production and consumption of rice. As such, I will spend less time addressing the political and geopolitical spectacle that is a primary part of historical narratives. It is not my intent to rehash debates over the relative contribution of U.S. and Khmer Rouge policies to the Cambodian genocide, nor to "prove" the destructive potential of communism or capitalism: such controversies are elaborated elsewhere. Instead, the focus here is to understand the organization (and reorganization) of a mode of production—one that had to support the demands of war, foreign exchange, elite profiteering, and bodily survival. From this perspective, "communist" Cambodia appears rather un-communist, while "free-market" Cambodia appears rather un-free.

Rice production seems an appropriate starting point for several reasons. First, rice has been essential to both the economy and food consumption for centuries. Seventy-five percent of the calories in the Cambodian diet come from rice, a similar ratio to diets in Vietnam, Burma, and Thailand. By comparison, rice accounts for only 47 percent of the caloric intake in Indonesia and the Philippines, and 46 percent in China (USAID 1977). Though fish, chicken, pork, beef, and various fruits and vegetables are traditional accompaniments, rice has always been the mainstay of Cambodian meals and an essential source of calories.

Second, rice production was the food crop most severely impacted by the civil war and U.S. bombing (Porter and Hildebrand 1975). The destruction of fields and the displacement of labor were key contributors to the collapse of rice production—and, consequently, food consumption—between 1970 and 1975. It was rice production that the CPK sought to rebuild when they took the reins of power in 1975. Exports of rice became the basis of all foreign exchange. With respect to the ration, rice was the only food component that had specific amounts assigned to it; that is, rice was the only rationed food item that was specifically measured and quantified. Through its role as wage and source of foreign exchange, rice took the place of money. In the sections that follow, I will examine the consequences of these changes for the country's political economy.

Finally, the socioecology of rice production places unique demands on land, water, seeds, and labor. In Cambodia, a long history of cultivation has adapted to—and shaped—the physical geography of the country's most productive regions, encouraging the development of novel irrigation technologies, genetic

varieties, and land tenure arrangements (Helmers 1997). Cambodian rice production can be broadly organized into four different cultivation "ecologies" (Javier
1997), each with a unique rhythm of flooding, planting, transplanting, weeding,
draining, and harvesting. Rice cultivation on this scale is an activity involving at
least three primary interests of government: territorial control, allocation of labor,
and the development of public works. For the Khmer Rouge, the environmental
exigencies of rice may have also influenced the timing and trajectory of revolution.
Throughout the 19th and 20th centuries, to govern Cambodia was to govern rice
production, and to govern rice production was to govern Cambodia.

Prewar Food Provisioning

Viewed from the air during the rainy season, it is hard to ignore the influence of
water in the Cambodian landscape. Swollen, silt-laden rivers meander between
clusters of lakes and seasonal wetlands. Discolored sediment from yearly flooding hugs streams and tributaries, each patch of gifted soil greedily carved up
for cultivation. The cadastral polygons of human settlement—fields, buildings,
roads—all seem to obey water's unnegotiable right-of-way. View the same scene
six months later and the mosaic of land and water will have changed.

From the ground, the effect is felt, not seen. The central plain of the country is
exceedingly flat, a shallow plate of iron-rich soil built up from millennia of lacus-
trine deposition. It is here that most of Cambodia's rice production takes place:
a patchwork of large, bunded fields painstakingly tilled and leveled. During the
height of the dry season, water stays confined to stream beds and canals. Under
the hot sun of mid-spring, wetlands slowly dry, leaving a sticky red mud. But by
the start of the wet season in early summer, fields throughout the central plain
turn a dazzling green as farmers transplant young seedlings; by September, water
and rice are nearly everywhere.

In other parts of rice-growing Southeast Asia, notably southern China and
southeastern Indonesia, terraces cling to hillsides in gravity-defying marvels of
terraforming and water control. But not here. Much of the water that fills rice
fields in Cambodia's central plain comes from overland inundation—seasonal
flooding that raises water levels above their topographical constraints. Generous
rivers carve new paths, break their banks, fill lakes, and in some cases, flow back-
wards. It is this unruly hydrology that has made rice cultivation in the central plain
possible. It has also made hydrology a central concern of Cambodian governments
since the 9th century (Helmers 1997).

At the heart of this complex water network is the Mekong River (fig. 6). With
its headwaters in the mountains of southern China, the 6000-kilometer-long
Mekong enters northern Cambodia from Laos and exits into Vietnam to the south,
roughly bisecting the country into eastern and western parts. At Phnom Penh, the
Mekong joins with the Tonle Sap River: during the dry months, the Tonle Sap

drains water from Cambodia's great lake by the same name, a vast floodplain to the northwest of Phnom Penh. As the Mekong passes Phnom Penh, its water is split

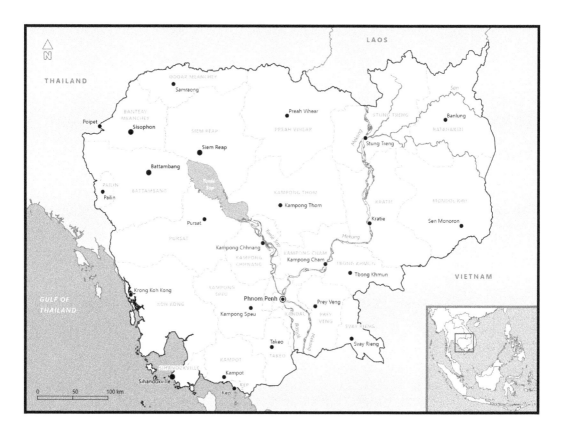

Figure 6. Overview map of Cambodia with modern provinces and major cities.

with the Bassak River before both channels enter Vietnam, the Mekong delta, and the South China Sea. From the delta upstream past Phnom Penh and into Tonle Sap Lake, the basin is extremely flat. Tidal effects can travel 100 kilometers inland from the coast (Biggs 2012). In fact, between the Cambodian border with Vietnam and the north edge of the Tonle Sap—a distance of 300 kilometers—the land rises a mere 10 meters.

During the monsoonal rains that fall between June and October, the level of the Mekong can rise by 9 meters (Nesbitt 1997a). Between July and September, this inundation raises the water level at Phnom Penh above the dry season level of Tonle Sap Lake, forcing the Tonle Sap river to flow backward. The inflow of water from the Mekong expands the area of the lake by a factor of 10. Farmers take advantage of rising water levels by planting "floating rice"—a fast-growing variety with stalks long enough to keep the plant tops above floodwaters. When the rain stops and the level of the Mekong drops, water from the swollen great lake slowly drains back through the Tonle Sap River and to the sea. As the extent of the lake shrinks, farmers use dykes to hold back the receding water. "Recessional" cultivation involves planting rice behind these dykes in temporarily flooded fields. Of course, floating rice and recessional cultivation accompany *rainfed* agriculture, the most common form of rice cultivation in Cambodia.

In the primary rice-growing regions of the country, rainfall averages between 1250 millimeters and 1750 millimeters per year, with most of it arriving between May and October (Nesbitt 1997b). Seasonal variation is strong: monthly averages range from 12 millimeters in January to 312 millimeters in September. Even within wet or dry seasons, rainfall is highly variable: in the 30 years between 1960 and 1990, September rainfall ranged from 185 millimeters (1966) to 458 millimeters (1961). December rainfall for the same period ranged from 9 millimeters (1981) to 185 millimeters (1970).[4] In addition to temporal variability, spatial variations in rainfall frequently determine local outcomes for rainfed cultivation: "mini-droughts" of up to three weeks are common in some locales (Nesbitt 1997b). While the total amount of rain during the growing season is important for yield, it is the timing of rainfall that has the greatest impact on labor, varietal selection, land allocation, and—ultimately—production.

The central plain is ringed to the north and west by mountains. Forested ranges border Cambodia to the east and along the coast to the southwest. Population densities drop with elevation and hilly terrain: Cambodia's largest cities are found in the southern plains or the basin around Tonle Sap Lake, the historical rice-growing regions of the country. Sihanoukville, located on the southern coast, is Cambodia's only deep-water port. During the 1960s, most imports and exports were moved overland to or from Sihanoukville, or loaded onto barges for passage along the Mekong.

Bodies

Throughout history, Cambodia has been a country of rural, agricultural producers involved primarily in subsistence cultivation. Through centuries of feudal, colonial, and capitalist modes of production, rural farmers survived by cultivating household land for personal consumption, with surpluses used to pay taxes and make small amounts of money. The essential crop for most landholders was also the most important part of the diet: rice. According to a recent FAO study, rice accounts for 75 percent of caloric intake in Cambodia, a figure that has changed little in the last 50 years (Helmers 1997). This consumption amounts to 151 kilograms of white rice (approximately 250 kilograms of paddy rice) per year per person, or 1.4 metric tons per year per household.

In addition to rice, the primary source of protein in the diet was fish, followed by poultry, pork, and beef (Helmers 1997). Rural households routinely maintained gardens for supplemental food production: "The area around the house is intensively farmed with various fruit trees, vegetables, and herbs. Farmers often graze cattle, grow pigs, and raise chickens. Their protein intake is also improved with the capture of wild food including frogs, crabs, fish, and insects" (Nesbitt and Phaloeun 1997, 37). In fact, these wild foods may have accounted for up to 40 percent of the protein intake in rural areas (Bolton 1996). Domesticated animals—chickens, ducks, pigs, and cattle—were used to supplement both diets and income. Chickens and ducks were raised primarily for meat and eggs, while pigs and cattle were frequently sold for cash. Manure from household animals was routinely returned to the fields as fertilizer (Nesbitt and Phaloeun 1997).

Most rural households were grouped into small villages, often situated on high ground some distance from the rice fields (Nesbitt and Phaloeun 1997). This arrangement helped protect dwellings from seasonal inundation at the expense of increased travel time to and from tended fields. During the early part of the growing season when intensive weeding demanded frequent trips into the fields, this distance had a pronounced impact. The location of household fields was generally fixed; indeed, most Cambodian farmers retained implicit—and socially enforced—ownership of land. "Land . . . belonged to the tiller; as long as he cultivated the land continuously, and had done so for at least three years, he enjoyed usufruct rights and could bequeath the land to his successors" (Slocomb 2010, 52). During the Protectorate years (1863–1953), the French argued that such implicit ownership did not constitute legal title, and worked throughout the early 20th century to implement an official tenure system that would enable large concessions to be awarded to foreign investors. The new system, established in 1926 and motivated primarily by growth in rubber plantations, helped initiate Cambodia's first large-scale land grab (Slocomb 2010).

The size of the average farm depended on geographical region: farms in the southeast averaged 1–2 hectares; in the northwest, 2–4 hectares (Helmers 1997). With yields hovering around one metric ton per hectare and subsistence demand per household at roughly 1.4 metric tons per year, most smallholders had little left over once the harvest was allocated for taxes and next season's seed. In fact, the difference in average farm size between southeast and northwest parts of the country broadly reflects variations in yield: prior to 1926, the highest rice yields were achieved in the southeast enabling households to subsist on less land. Under traditional tenure practices, children frequently inherited the family farm upon the deaths of the parents. Unlike other tenure-by-descent arrangements in Southeast Asia, inheritance was not limited to the eldest child: households with many children might divide the land into separate plots for each, increasing fragmentation and decreasing the overall size of land holdings.

Until independence, traditional Khmer society was broadly organized into three classes: commoners, government officials, and members of the royal family. Common people worked the fields and paid taxes to officials who provided a portion of the surplus to royalty. At the top, the king served a function that was "quasi-religious and ritual" (Vickery 2000, 12), reinforcing public commitment to the essential nature of Cambodia's class system while keeping officials in line and reaping the rewards of the country's rice harvest. Curiously, traditional Khmer social organization lacked a merchant class, but with the growth of cities and the expansion of trade, a merchant population comprised mostly of foreigners began to emerge (Vickery 2000). As in other parts of late colonial Southeast Asia, Chinese immigrants took over this role, especially in port towns and major cities—a move actively encouraged by French authorities.

Rice Cultivation Prior to Independence

Rainfed rice production in Cambodia's central plain goes back at least 2000 years with the opening of trade routes to India. Archeological evidence suggests technologies for irrigated cultivation were in use 1500 years ago (Helmers 1997). Between the 9th and 14th centuries, the kingdom of Angkor emerged as an economic power centered around Tonle Sap Lake. Large-scale rice production helped to establish Angkor as a regional economic power and the "greatest kingdom in Southeast Asia" (Helmers 1997, 1).

Between the 15th and 17th centuries, for reasons that are not entirely clear, Angkor was abandoned and its population dispersed. For the next two hundred years, frequent conflict between Khmer, Thai, and Vietnamese groups disrupted rice production and prevented the consolidation of territory by any single government. Rural rebellions became the norm as local villages asserted various claims of exploitation against the rulers of the moment. Despite social unrest, rural farming technology made significant advances during this period. Helmers (1997, 2) writes: "Farmers . . . demonstrated their innovativeness, adopting rice production technologies which originated in India and adapting these to the poor soils, erratic rainfall, and complex hydrology of Cambodia." Farmers developed deep-water and recessional cultivation alongside advancements in rainfed and upland rice. Variations in water availability and timing encouraged the breeding of specialized varieties: "Within each farm unit, fields of different water availability (high, medium, and low fields) were planted to varieties of different duration (early, medium, and late)" to spread risk (Tichit 1981; Helmers 1997, 2). By the time Green Revolution scientists began cataloging Cambodian agriculture in the 1960s, farmers were planting 2000 different varieties of rice found nowhere else in the world (Whitaker 1973).

By the mid-1800s, French interest in Cambodia began to grow with the expansion of colonial control in Cochinchina—a territory that includes the Mekong delta region. The possibility of using the Mekong as a trade route into Yunnan, China, sparked French curiosity about Cambodia (Slocomb 2010). But by the 1860s, colonial administrators saw the potential for farmers in the central plains to produce rice for export by way of the French "agroprocessing" complexes established around Saigon (Helmers 1997, 2). In 1863, Cambodia was given protectorate status and joined Laos and Vietnam as part of the French Indochina Union.

To help make Cambodia productive for the Union, administrators encouraged the Cambodian monarchy to implement major agricultural reforms. At the heart of the strategy was the division of rice production into two subsectors (Helmers 1997). The first was comprised of large-scale plantations owned and operated by foreigners. These plantations were created through land concessions established around Battambang in the western reaches of the Tonle Sap basin. Heavily subsidized by the French, the plantations were to be based on "modern" technologies for intensive cultivation. To this end, the colonial administration helped fund the construction of irrigation infrastructure, research stations for plant breeding, and a railway from Battambang to Phnom Penh to speed the transport of harvested rice. From Phnom Penh, the rice traveled by barge down the Mekong to Saigon. By the time of independence in 1953, rice plantations around Battambang totaled 16,000 hectares (Slocomb 2010).

The second subsector comprised the Cambodian peasantry. Local smallholders in family-oriented plots grew rice for subsistence and export using traditional methods, with little colonial involvement in production (Delvert 1994). The colony acquired rice through a direct tax on farmers. There was no French expectation—nor facility for—the introduction of yield-improving technologies and practices into the general farming community: "As with other colonial powers, the French believed that peasants were incapable of developing or mastering innovations" (Helmers 1997, 3). For the entirety of the protectorate era, the colonial administration made no investment in infrastructure for the benefit of Cambodian farmers, despite this subsector contributing the vast majority of rice exported from the country. By 1953, yields remained around one metric ton per hectare, much as they were a century earlier.

Though few farmers benefited from these agricultural reforms, colonial production certainly did; in fact, the rice tax extracted from the Cambodian peasantry was the "largest source of government revenues" in the protectorate (Helmers 1997, 2). Depending on environmental and economic conditions, the total area cultivated under the peasant subsector varied from 0.5 to 1.5 million hectares: 30 to 90 times the area under plantation.

During the colonial period, production demands on the peasant subsector pushed increasing numbers of farmers into debt. To finance improvements or repairs to farm equipment, hire draft animals, or purchase food when taxes required too much of the harvest, many farmers took out loans with village moneylenders at high interest rates. By 1953, chronic indebtedness and uncertain title to land trapped many smallholder households in poverty (Slocomb 2010). Educational opportunities were few: unlike in other French territories, administrators in Cambodia were slow to pursue educational reforms or fund the establishment of schools. Opportunities in rural areas were limited to *wat* (Buddhist temple) schools for boys, with no formal schooling for girls. There was little chance for advancement into government or civil service as these skill positions were filled by foreigners, invariably Chinese, Vietnamese, or French (Helmers 1997).

During the boom years of the 1920s, production improvements and high prices for rice enabled some farmers to make money, but with the collapse of global markets in 1930 and a 60 percent drop in the price of rice, these gains were lost. Farmers adjusted by reducing the area under cultivation by two-thirds: because the tax paid by each household was based on cultivated area (not production), peasants were able to mitigate the effect of the market collapse by concentrating their labor on only the most productive land. But less production also meant less food to eat. In other parts of Southeast Asia during this period, rural rebellions disrupted colonial rule and helped inspire nationalist movements (Kiernan 2004). But beyond scattered protests for tax relief, the Cambodian peasantry remained remarkably calm. Chandler (2008, 163) notes, "the French were pleased to notice that disturbances in Cochin China . . . aroused no echoes in Cambodia" where the response to colonial stresses was decidedly "well-mannered."

By the mid-1930s, rice production was rebounding in both sectors. Cultivated area reached an all-time high of 1.7 million hectares—an expansion in lockstep with rapid rural population growth. By 1940, Cambodia was the third largest rice exporting country in the world despite no substantial improvements in yield (Helmers 1997). Growth in rice production during this period resulted entirely from expansion of cultivated land: between 1900 and 1950, the total area under rice increased by 340 percent (USAID 1977). Meanwhile, export profits were being used to fund increasingly extravagant urban lifestyles (Vickery 2000). In the cities, the largely non-Khmer merchant class amassed extraordinary wealth while Cambodian farmers continued to suffer under heavy debt and high interest rates. By independence, nearly all peasants still farmed for subsistence.

Cultivation Ecosystems

Centuries of agricultural production in the complex hydrology of the central basin led to the development of four different cultivation "ecosystems": rainfed lowland rice, deepwater rice, recessional rice, and upland rice. In those parts of the plain that do not experience seasonal inundation, farmers cultivate *rainfed lowland rice*. Fields are bounded by bunds (earthen dykes) that allow the field to hold water. Field size is usually a function of soil fertility, labor availability, and topological gradient: in places where the land is flat and labor is abundant, larger fields are preferred. Higher fertility encourages denser planting but requires more labor during planting and harvest. In certain areas, rainfed rice systems can be "improved" through irrigation. Irrigated rice follows the same principles as rainfed rice except for the supply of water. Supply canals direct water into fields before planting and during the first few months of the season to nurture the young rice plants and deter the growth of weeds. Channels are cut through the bunds to allow water to enter or exit the field at specific times, a pattern of flooding and parching that is manipulated to maximize yield (White, Oberthür, and Sovuthy 1997).

Deepwater rice cultivation takes place in areas that are regularly flooded during the rainy season—primarily along the banks of rivers or in the wide swath of land around Tonle Sap Lake. At the end of the dry season when water levels are at their lowest, fields are seeded with varieties of "floating rice." This fast-growing plant develops long stalks that allow the top of the plant to stay above rising floodwater; some varieties can grow up to 4 meters in length at a rate of 30 centimeters a day (Nesbitt 1997a).

Recessional rice cultivation takes place at the opposite end of the growing calendar and involves the control of receding floodwater from seasonally inundated areas. As water levels begin to drop at the start of the dry season, water is trapped behind previously constructed earthen dykes to form large reservoirs. Rice is first seeded in the shallower parts of these temporary "recession ponds" before being transplanted into deeper areas (Nesbitt and Phaloeun 1997, 37). As the season proceeds, water may be pumped back up the slope to supply drier fields. Like deepwater rice, recessional rice cultivation involves precise timing and considerable luck: heavy rains in January when plants are still young may destroy crops or damage already burdened water control structures.

Finally, *upland cultivation* involves growing rice on sloping terrain in unbunded fields. Of the four cultivation ecosystems, this strategy is the least used, though it is frequently applied in the hilly north and northeastern parts of the country. Upland rice is often included in mixed cultivation systems where it is grown alongside various legumes, millet, cassava, maize, and sweet potato (White, Oberthür, and Sovuthy 1997). Fields are frequently left fallow for several seasons after a harvest, following patterns of swidden cultivation common to many low population density regions of Southeast Asia (see Hanks 1992).

By 1967, Cambodia had 2.5 million hectares under rice cultivation. Of this, over 77 percent was rainfed, 15 percent was deepwater, 7 percent was recessional, and less than 0.2 percent was upland (Javier 1997). In the sections that follow, I focus primarily on cultivation practices for rainfed and irrigated lowland rice, the most common cultivation system in Cambodia and the one that was central to the CPK's agricultural plans.

Rainfed and Irrigated Cultivation

By April or May, field preparation has begun across Cambodia's central plains. The soil, hardened by months of abundant sunshine and low humidity, starts to soften with the onset of the spring rains. In most cases, small nursery fields are established first: it is here that rice seeds selected from last season's harvest are densely planted while the main fields are prepared. As the seedlings grow, oxen and water buffalo are used to plough the main fields to break up the hardened soil and contribute fertilizer (Nesbitt and Phaloeun 1997). Between one and three months after the seeding of the nurseries, the young rice plants are transplanted into the now softened main fields. This labor-intensive process involves painstakingly replanting each seedling into saturated soil at a precise depth and distance from other plants. If nursery fields are not used, farmers employ "broadcast" seeding. Through broadcasting, seeds are dispersed by hand into the soil of the main field. This strategy conserves land by making nurseries unnecessary and saves labor by eliminating the need for transplanting. However, yields tend to be lower than in nursery-based fields due to the lack of control over plant spacing. Because the field must remain dry from the time of broadcasting until the plants have sprouted, this strategy generally requires more weeding (Nesbitt and Phaloeun 1997).

The flooding of fields tends to inhibit the growth of weeds, though some hand-weeding is usually required throughout the growing season. Generally, the longer the field sits without water, the more weeding is required. In an average season, rainfed fields will be weeded between one and four times (Javier 1997). In locations where rain is the only source of water, dry growing seasons decrease the amount of time the field is flooded, increasing the labor required for weeding. In irrigated fields with a satisfactory supply of water, labor costs for weeding can be substantially reduced.

By December, the rains have given way to the start of the dry season and the rice is ready for harvest. Harvesting is performed by hand using a small sickle, a labor-intensive task that usually requires farmers to enlist help from neighboring households and nearby villages. The cut stalks are stacked into large bundles and left on the bunds to dry. After two-to-three days of drying, the bundles are carried to the farmer's house where the stalks are threshed (to separate the seeds from the stalk) and winnowed (to remove the chaff from the seed). Some producers will thresh and winnow progressively throughout the dry season. After winnowing, the seed is left to dry in the sun for several days before being stored in granaries. Excessively wet weather post-harvest can delay the processing of the rice stalks, exposing the harvest to damage from rodent pests and mold (Jahn et al. 1997).

Traditional rice cultivation is well suited to the management of household animals. Farmers usually leave the uncut stubble in the field as fodder for oxen and water buffalo (Rickman, Pyseth, and Sothy 1997). The rice stalks that remain after threshing are collected into a pile and stored as feed for livestock during the next rainy season. Oxen and water buffalo not only provide traction for field preparation, they are a primary source of manure for fertilizer. This human-plant-animal interdependency has distinct advantages for farmers who would otherwise need to acquire separate fodder for draft animals or rent someone else's animals at an added cost. But this interdependency also increases the long-term consequences of catastrophic failure: the complete loss of a harvest puts pressure not only on household food reserves (through lack of rice) but also animal survival (through a lack of stubble and stalks). Should a farmer lose a draft animal due to starvation or weakness, subsequent harvests may be jeopardized. With the onset of civil war and U.S. bombardment, large parts of Cambodia stopped cultivating rice. The consequences of such an agricultural collapse for oxen and water buffalo—essential inputs to rice production—have yet to be fully explored.

Rice cultivation requires abundant water and precise control over its application, and for rainfed fields, the availability of water depends on the vagaries of the weather. The water requirement means that much of the risk associated with farming centers around getting the timing right—when to prepare fields, when to plant, and when to transplant. Field preparation begins after the first rains have softened the soil. If the spring rains come early (for example, April), farmers can get a head start on preparation and begin seeding nurseries. Labor allocation is easier because farmers in the same geographical area can better distribute when they need to requisition help. If the spring rains are late (June–July), field and nursery preparation is delayed and the collective need for labor is compressed into a shorter period of time as farmers scramble to get their crops planted. If the onset of rain is late enough, farmers who would ordinarily use nurseries may be forced to switch to broadcast seeding, reducing yields and increasing the labor needed for weeding.

Once the crop is established, the most important rains are those that fall between September and October (Nesbitt 1997b). These months tend to bring the strongest storms and contribute the most water to rainfed fields where inundation stifles weed growth and reduces the influence of some insect and rodent pests. Flooding is also necessary for the rice plants to flower and develop seed: severe drought mid-season can drastically reduce yield, in some cases ruining an entire crop.

Most years, the end of the wet season comes quickly, usually in mid-November. By December, the rice has reached full maturity and harvesting begins. Once again, the demand for labor increases as farmers try to bring in the crop before it can be eaten by pests or damaged by strong winds. Between February and March, abundant sunshine and low humidity are useful for drying the stalks before threshing. These months are also the windiest, the wind aiding the drying process through increased evaporation (Nesbitt 1997b). Unseasonable rain between January and March may impact the ability to process the harvest by limiting drying time. But the consequence of these rains is insignificant when compared to the strong negative impacts of rainfall anomalies at other times of the year.

Over the centuries, farmers bred varieties of rice with different maturation rates to reduce risk. Early, medium, and late maturing varieties allowed planters to stagger the planting schedule (and subsequent harvesting schedule) based on the availability of labor and the timing of rain. Farmers would frequently plant different types of seeds in different plots to distribute risk. When used in conjunction with deepwater and recessional cultivation, this agro-biodiversity provided farmers with an invaluable tool for maintaining survival in a complex and unpredictable environment.

The strong seasonality of rainfall over most of Cambodia restricts rice cultivation to a single growing season each year. For farmers with land that can take advantage of receding floodwaters, a dry season crop of recessional rice can help boost profits, but everywhere else, the only consistent way to grow a second (or third) crop is to develop irrigation infrastructure to keep the fields supplied with water year-round. Where such infrastructure was available, farmers used early maturing varieties and started planting in December and January, immediately after the primary harvest. By March, the bulk of the harvest was being collected (USAID 1977).

The impossibility of multiple growing seasons was one of the fundamental limitations on total production. In rice cultivation, total annual production is a function of the amount of land under cultivation, the amount of rice grown per hectare each season (yield), and the number of growing seasons per year. Generally poor soil quality and few technological improvements during the colonial period ensured that yields remained low: approximately one ton per hectare. For comparison, in 1973, Thailand and South Vietnam achieved yields of 1.8 and 2.4 tons per hectare, respectively (USAID 1977). In Cambodia, the growth in total rice production resulted almost entirely from extensification: the conversion of non-agricultural land to rice production. As the rural population increased after 1900, increasing amounts of land were converted to agriculture but yields remained static.

Extensification has limits. Topography, soil quality, and hydrology can make some land unusable. Forest clearing is labor intensive and time consuming, and the development of remote unpopulated areas may require human resettlement. But annual production can increase if existing fields can produce more than one harvest per year, a revolution that can only be accomplished through irrigation. This fundamental constraint is partly why French, Cambodian, and Khmer Rouge administrations all made irrigation a central concern of government.

Traditional rice cultivation in Cambodia was labor intensive: by the 1960s, tractors were beginning to appear in the countryside, but these forms of mechanization were confined to the rice plantations around Battambang and were not a feature of smallholder agriculture. At the end of the 20th century, growing rice in Cambodia was still done largely by hand. A study by Rickman, Pyseth and Sothy (1997) in the 1990s calculated that each hectare required 110–130 person-days of labor. Heavy mechanization (e.g., tractors) could reduce this to 60–65 person-days. Another study in the 1980s found figures of 85–114 person-days per hectare (Tichit 1981). Of course, these labor requirements are not distributed evenly throughout the growing season: up to 50 percent of the total labor used by a farm was taken up by transplanting at the start of the season and harvesting at the end (Rickman, Pyseth, and Sothy 1997).

The forms of intensive rice production common to Cambodia required surplus labor to be available to farming households at specific times during the year. Some agricultural historians have argued that the administrative requirements of wet rice cultivation—and the need to organize around common landesque capital—drove the emergence of centralized government in Southeast Asia (cf. Hanks 1992;

Bray 1994; Rindos 2013). In Cambodia, cultivation was organized around collective labor and shared inputs. For example, in West Svay, an agricultural region near Phnom Penh, approximately one-third of households owned no more than one ox or water buffalo in 1970. Two of these animals are needed to pull a traditional plow. As such, a significant percentage of households in this region had to negotiate the use of resources with others just to complete field preparation (Vickery 2000). Irrigation systems invariably supplied water to multiple fields, requiring cooperation between producers to get the fields flooded. Under times of water stress, these cooperative arrangements could become contentious given that "irrigation techniques for moving water from one field to another required the permission of all the owners" (Vickery 2000, 16). Labor and capital disputes aside, by independence in 1953, the social organization of Cambodian rice production had achieved a rather remarkable feat; namely, it had survived the last 50 years of French control, without a significant food crisis, under the highest taxes in Indochina (Chandler 2008).

One traditional feature of Southeast Asian rice cultivation is the use of traction animals. In Cambodia, oxen and water buffalo are considered essential forms of capital for land-owning agricultural households. Animals provide manure for fertilizer, pull plows and harrows, break up hardpans caused by excessive drying of the soil, and balance soil pH by overturning the top layers. In most cases, ploughing involves two animals attached to a traditional "moldboard" plow. For these purposes, water buffalo are regarded as stronger than cattle, though the Brahmin-based breeds used in the South and Southeast have higher heat tolerance than buffalo (Rickman, Pyseth, and Sothy 1997).

Studies in the 1990s show that a pair of draft animals can plow 0.2–0.25 hectares per day, with an average area of 2–5 hectares worked per pair, per season (Rickman, Pyseth, and Sothy 1997, 93). With farms averaging between 1 and 4 hectares, two to three draft animals could supply the needs of most households. In the 1990s, the national average was 3.4 traction animals per household, but this number hides considerable variation: up to 21 percent of households did not own any traction animals and had to rent them from neighbors.

Challenges

Cambodia's systems of rice production at the time of independence bore remarkable similarity to the systems that had fed the population (and exported surpluses) since the 1800s. Indeed, producers responded to agricultural reforms and colonial impositions during this period by doing what they had always done: expanding the area under cultivation, breeding new varieties, and applying myriad strategies for water control and labor mobilization. The challenges faced by farmers in 1953 were much the same as they had always been: rainfall variability, poor soils, availability of labor, and heavy taxation.

Rainfall variability has been identified as one of the key impediments to productivity in Cambodia (Javier 1997). Today, the country has the lowest rice yields in Asia and the highest percentage of land under rainfed cultivation. These two statistics go together: rainfed rice systems exhibit the lowest yields among major cultivation systems due to the reliance on both total precipitation and timing. Before, during, and after the growing season there are critical points where too much or too little rain—too soon or too late—can impact production.

The hydraulic interconnections between Tonle Sap Lake and the Mekong add an additional variable. The timing and quantity of snowmelt in the mountains of southwest China and rainfall in the watersheds across Laos impact the hydrology of deepwater, recessional, and irrigated fields in the central plain. Combined with rainfall variability, the interaction of this water "space-time" with agricultural demands can be complicated. Javier (1997) provides a modern example of this vulnerability: In 1995, Cambodian farmers planted 1.9 million hectares of rice. Of this, 216,000 hectares were affected—and 138,000 hectares were destroyed—by flooding. That same year, 15,000 hectares were affected—and 9000 hectares were destroyed—by drought. There are few rice-growing regions as small as Cambodia that can claim crop losses from both too much and too little water at the same time.

Under ideal conditions, labor surpluses and labor demand align to help get fields prepared, seeds transplanted, and harvests brought in. But variations in the timing of the spring rains can create unanticipated burdens for smallholders looking for assistance. Field preparation and nursery seeding cannot begin until the early rains have softened the soil. Once the fields are ready, farmers will stagger the planting of early, medium, and late maturing varieties to distribute risk and spread out the demand for labor. But if the rains are delayed, all the fields will need to be planted at the same time (Javier 1997). Under these circumstances, a lack of available labor may force poorer households to cut back on cultivation.

Over time, these challenges have been answered through a diversity of cultivation strategies and plant breeding. By independence in 1953, Cambodian farming had demonstrated a historical tolerance for environmental stresses. But it was about to be tested by sweeping social change. In fact, the same system that had evolved four different cultivation ecosystems and bred 2000 varieties of rice was particularly vulnerable to declines in available labor, loss of traction animals, and the destruction of distribution networks. By 1970, Cambodia was experiencing all of these.

Organization of the Economy

The underlying orientation of the Cambodian economy changed little between the colonial years and independence. Under the French, producers in the peasant sector sold surplus rice to acquire money with which to pay taxes (Slocomb 2010). From this exchange, the government received revenue from rice exported through Phnom Penh and Saigon, and monetary revenue from the tax. After independence, the Sihanouk government continued to tax the peasant sector and benefit from the foreign sale of rice. To increase profits on this exchange, the domestic price offered to farmers for their harvests was kept artificially low despite rising global prices.

By the mid-1960s, in response to low domestic prices, many producers were making a profit selling rice on the black market to Vietnamese buyers or members of the National Liberation Front (NLF). Not only did these sales deprive the Cambodian government of foreign exchange, it irritated U.S. strategists who believed that through these illicit exchanges, rural Cambodians were aiding the communist insurgency in Vietnam (Porter and Hildebrand 1975). As Cambodia became increasingly entangled in the second Indochina War and as Sihanouk grew increasingly wary of Washington, the United States turned its attention to the internal politics of Sihanouk's government to seek out—and nurture—a successor.

Wartime Transformation: 1967–1975

During a visit to France at the turn of the 20th century, Prince Yukanthor, son of then King Norodom, created something of a scandal when he declared to the French people: "You have created property [in Cambodia]; and thus you have created the poor" (Chandler 2008, 147). Yukanthor was hoping to shed light on French abuses in his country; in particular, the economic exploitation of the peasant class.[5] His claim was not entirely glib: France was pushing the Cambodian monarchy to reform agricultural production through the codification of land tenure, a move that would enable the government to appropriate vast tracts of arable land for conversion to plantations. Taxes on the peasantry were the highest in Indochina—an imposition the French were convinced they could get away with thanks to Cambodian "docility" (Chandler 2008, 158). Meanwhile, sporadic rural rebellions were being quickly dispatched by French and Vietnamese soldiers.

But the legacy of French involvement in rural agriculture is complex. On the one hand, administrators sought to implement reforms that increased taxation and encouraged Western ownership of the means of production. On the other, French policy in Cambodia was committed to indirect rule: that is, allowing existing relations of production to operate at the local level without interference. For many rural producers, this meant that taxes were paid (and labor was donated) to the same government officials that had been authorized by the King. Unlike in other colonial contexts, the French had little interest in reorganizing Cambodia's peasant subsector or redirecting the poor into plantation labor. "By the 1920s, in the eyes of French officials, Cambodia had become a sort of rice-making machine," and many administrators were loath to mess with a good thing (Chandler 2008, 139).

Indirect rule aside, French policies did establish important precedents that became recurring themes in later administrations. First, and most obvious, the levying of taxes on rice producers was retained after independence by Sihanouk and later by Lon Nol. Second, the French expanded the right of the government to requisition peasant labor for public works. Mandated corvée labor was employed as a punishment for failure to pay taxes: farmers who owed money to the government were required to work up to 90 days at the discretion of officials (Vickery 2000). Corvée labor was used extensively to construct roads and railways, mostly to help transport rice from the plantations. Between 1900 and 1930, 9000 kilometers of roads were constructed and a 500-kilometer stretch of railroad between Battambang and Phnom Penh was completed (Chandler 2008; Slocomb 2010).

Third, under indirect rule, the French felt no obligation to invest in rural agriculture. Administrators made little effort to advance the livelihoods or production potential of peasant farmers, unlike the heavily subsidized plantation sector. While plantations benefited from investments in irrigation and scientific agriculture, no such improvements were made available to smallholders. Of course, the labor to complete the irrigation schemes was supplied by farming households under the corvée system, so that in effect, it was the peasant subsector that subsidized private, Western-owned businesses. This discrepancy continued into the 1960s with the influx of foreign aid: plantation cultivation in the northwest benefited from USAID-funded irrigation and scientific agriculture projects as peasant sector improvements languished (Helmers 1997).

Finally, profits from rice exports in the 1930s (and again in the 1950s to 1960s) flowed into the pockets of merchants and the burgeoning urban elite (Slocomb 2010). The steady growth in inequality between city and country may be the most important legacy of French policies. The aristocracy that emerged from the colonial period, now grafted to the remains of the traditional monarchy, became the de facto leaders of Cambodia upon independence. By the time the Khmer Rouge started recruiting peasant soldiers, there was abundant populist anger to work with.

Sihanouk and the Nationalization of Rice Production

The history of King Sihanouk's post-independence Cambodia (1953–70) is well documented elsewhere (cf. Chandler 2008; Slocomb 2010).[6] As in other former colonial territories, Cambodia's post-independence years were tumultuous. A mix of both positive and negative social developments, fierce party politics, and the persistence of French influence increased uncertainty for the new state as it entered a world increasingly divided between communists and capitalists. With growing instability in nearby Vietnam, Sihanouk tried to maintain a neutral line, declaring Cambodia a nonaligned nation (Haas 1991a). But this neutrality effectively ensured that his government was opposed on both sides, by rebel groups like the communist-influenced Khmer Issarak and the anticommunist

Khmer Serei. Through it all, the organization of rural rice production stayed remarkably intact.

With the opening of U.S. aid after 1955, Western development agencies began to draw up ambitious programs for infrastructural development. Upon independence, the Cambodian government took control of the plantations in the northwest and looked to continue the expansion of irrigation started by the French. Flush with aid dollars, "irrigation schemes, barrages, canals, and reservoirs were constructed in Siem Reap, Kampong Cham, Kandal, and Kampot provinces" (Haas 1991a, 4). Development assistance was not limited to infrastructure: by 1960, USAID's Rice Production Program had set up six research stations to conduct experiments with yield and seed improvements (Munson 1968). By the time the program ended, USAID claimed that 20 percent of the Cambodian rice crop was using improved strains bred from traditional varieties (Helmers 1997).

Between 1954 and 1968, irrigated rice cultivation expanded from 34,762 to 79,926 hectares, approximately 3 percent of the total area under rice (Slocomb 2010). At the same time, the total area under cultivation grew from 1.7 million to 2.2 million hectares, an expansion that generally aligned with rural population growth (USAID 1977). To address persistent indebtedness among farmers, Sihanouk created the Office of Royal Cooperation (OROC) in 1956 to extend credit lines and assist those in default. The government opened agricultural extension programs and launched several institutions in 1960 to train government workers in agronomy (Helmers 1997). The long-term effect of these programs on the peasant sector is difficult to quantify—average rice yields did increase but more slowly than extensification. When development programs first started in 1955, average yields were 1 metric ton per hectare; when the programs were canceled ten years later, yields were up to 1.1 tons per hectare (Helmers 1997). Despite abundant foreign investment in agriculture, Cambodia saw no real increase in productivity, especially in the peasant sector. Rice production was growing as it had throughout history: by getting bigger, not more efficient. Meanwhile, the wealth gap between rural producers and the urban elite continued to widen.

Over time, Sihanouk became increasingly concerned about U.S. economic involvement in Cambodia. The United States was contributing more aid than China and the Soviet Union combined—ostensibly to further the fight against communism—and Sihanouk sensed the risk of becoming an American client state. Across the border in South Vietnam, U.S. Central Intelligence Agency (CIA) involvement in the death of President Diem helped persuade Sihanouk that the United States was more interested in "proxy, not independent rulers" (Haas 1991b, 6), and his discovery that the United States was secretly supporting the Khmer Serei—a rebel group seeking Sihanouk's overthrow—confirmed his suspicions. In 1964, Cambodia canceled U.S. aid and cut diplomatic ties. That year, the government nationalized control over all foreign trade through the newly created *Société Nationale d'Exportation et d'Importation* (SONEXIM). SONEXIM handled the sale of exported rice and purchased foreign-sourced agricultural inputs like fertilizer, pesticides, and farm equipment, while OROC was made responsible for purchasing rice from producers and processing it for export (Helmers 1997).

The first year under the new system set records: Cambodia exported 500,000 tons in 1964 and 1965, from a total crop of over 2.5 million tons (Helmers 1997). But the price paid to farmers did not improve. In fact, just like earlier purchasing arrangements, the nationalization of agricultural production maintained healthy state profits by suppressing the domestic price of rice. And just like previous administrations, the response from farmers was to find buyers "outside the system." Dramatic growth in black market sales to Vietnamese smugglers and members of the National Liberation Front (NLF) occurred in 1966–67: "In this unofficial market, farmers could obtain prices three times the official sale price through SONEXIM" (Helmers 1997, 5). By some estimates, one-third of the export crop in 1966 was "redirected" through illegal sales (see Osborne 1978). The 500,000 tons of exported rice in 1964 was cut to 250,000 tons in 1966—a result of black markets and a poor national harvest.

In 1967, the government crackdown began. Rice collections at the official price—about one-third the black market price—were now enforced by the military (Slocomb 2010) and farmers found to be selling rice illegally were severely punished. The reaction from farmers was swift: peasants in Samlaut organized a series of protests against government exploitation. The newly appointed prime minister directed the government's response: "hamlets were surrounded, the inhabitants gunned down, the houses destroyed, and a few hundred survivors were led to safety in the forests by Buddhist monks. Those who were captured were executed with clubs 'to save on cartridges,' while the wounded were thrown from a cliff and left to die" (Porter and Hildebrand 1975). The new prime minister and mastermind behind the bloody crackdown was Lon Nol.

By 1969, the United States was eager for regime change in Cambodia. North Vietnamese and Việt Cộng units were now operating in Cambodian territory near the border with South Vietnam, using the hilly and forested terrain to conceal transit routes for material and sanctuary bases for soldiers (Shawcross 2002). Strategists hoped to secure a government in Cambodia that would assist in the fight against a widening front of communist groups. Notably, the United States sought official permission to expand its bombing and defoliation campaigns into Cambodian territory, operations that had been covert—and illegal—up until 1970. To this end, the CIA established contact with possible power brokers in Phnom Penh to exploit divisions in Sihanouk's administration (Haas 1991b). When the coup occurred in March 1970, wealthy and powerful members of the urban elite, eager for the return of lucrative foreign aid, offered their support. Lon Nol assumed the role of head of state and demanded the withdrawal of all North Vietnamese and Việt Cộng forces from Cambodian territory. In April, one month after the coup, U.S. and South Vietnamese ground troops crossed the border into Cambodia, and in May, the U.S. Air Force inaugurated heavy bombardment of the countryside through Operation Freedom Deal.

On the eve of the coup, the structure of rice production was fundamentally the same as it had been on the eve of independence from France. Nearly all rice farmers cultivated for subsistence using traditional techniques and animal traction (Helmers 1997). According to the International Bank for Reconstruction and Development (IRBD), 1500 tractors were operating in Cambodia in 1969, but almost all were in the plantation sector. Pesticide and chemical fertilizer use was paltry, despite a decade of foreign aid to agriculture (Whitaker 1973). Yields remained low compared to neighboring Thailand and Vietnam, and yet—buoyed by extensification and infrastructural improvements to plantation agriculture—the national harvest had grown considerably: the 1969 growing season produced 3.8 million tons, the largest rice harvest in history. But the upward trend was about to disappear: the next harvest this size would not arrive for another three decades (Helmers 1997).

Lon Nol and the Civil War

Within weeks of Lon Nol taking control, Cambodia's simmering civil conflict burst to life. Sihanouk, exiled to Beijing, "granted legitimacy" to the communist rebel groups arrayed against the new Khmer Republic that were organized under the National United Front of Kampuchea (FUNK) (Girling 1972; Slocomb 2010, 132). The incursion by U.S. and South Vietnamese forces, intended to support Lon Nol's fight against the communists, only served to push Việt Cộng positions deeper into Cambodia where they received support from the Khmer Rouge and a peasantry increasingly frustrated with U.S. bombardment. In early 1971, hoping to capture the upper hand, Lon Nol launched a large military offensive against the growing insurgency. His forces, mostly untrained recruits, were badly defeated despite U.S. financial and material support. From this loss forward, Republican forces would be on the defensive until the eventual loss of the capital in April 1975. According to Chandler (2008), U.S. bombardment and the influx of military aid is the primary reason it took another four years for the regime to collapse.

Despite foreign assistance, the Khmer Rouge continued to capture territory. By 1973, the Khmer Republic consisted of the area surrounding Phnom Penh and a corridor linking Phnom Penh to Battambang and extending west to the Thai border (Slocomb 2010). The country was shrinking. As rice-producing regions were gradually overtaken by the rebels, the republic slowly lost the ability to feed its own people. The influx of refugees fleeing the countryside, a rural-to-urban migration that had been ongoing since the expansion of aerial bombardment in 1970, continued unabated until the war effectively cut off the remaining cities from the rest of the countryside. In January of 1973, the United States and North Vietnam signed the Paris Peace Accords, initiating the last phase of the Vietnam War. The Khmer Rouge refused to participate in the Accords and in response, Nixon turned the full force of the U.S. Air Force's strategic assets from bombing Vietnam to bombing Cambodia (Slocomb 2010).

The Aerial Bombardment of Cambodia

President Richard Nixon justified the expansion of the aerial campaign against Cambodia in three ways. First, he declared that Pol Pot (leader of the Khmer Rouge) and North Vietnam were allies. Thus, the logical extension of war against North Vietnam was war against the Khmer Rouge. Second, Nixon argued that the Lon Nol regime had brought peace to Cambodia and deserved to be defended. Finally, the President insisted that communist insurgents were highly organized and opposing them would require immediate and substantial intervention (Haas 1991a).

Nixon was wrong on each point. North Vietnam and Pol Pot were not allies; in fact, some of the first purges conducted by the Khmer Rouge within their own ranks were intended to remove Vietnamese influences. The Lon Nol regime had not brought peace to Cambodia; rather, through a string of questionable decisions dating back to his tenure as prime minister in 1966–67, Lon Nol's policies had increased civil unrest and exacerbated the country's rural-urban rift through growth in inequality and direct violence (Vickery 2000). As for the strength and organization of the insurgents, the Khmer Rouge may have been the best organized of the groups in FUNK, but this was hardly an indication of strength: on the day the Khmer Rouge won the war, rebel forces numbered a mere 60,000 (Jackson 2014).

Ultimately, Nixon needed a way to buy time as the United States decreased its presence in Vietnam. To this end, Nixon's efforts focused on providing Cambodia with enough weaponry to hold off a communist victory until U.S. troops could leave the region. Of course, these intentions were not presented to the Cambodian leadership, many of whom believed until the republic's final days that the United States would rescue the country (Carney 1989). Poole (1976, 23) writes: "President Nixon had done his best to build a back-fire in Cambodia in 1970 in order to gain a 'decent interval' for U.S. withdrawal from Vietnam. The United States had given the Cambodians the means to fight each other, but had given them nothing to fight for, not even a promise of continued U.S. support . . . With South Vietnam's 'decent interval' about to end, thoughts in Washington turned from supplemental aid to evacuation."

Between 1965 and 1970, U.S. aerial bombardment operations were covert, but after 1970 with the start of Operation Freedom Deal, the spatial extent and intensity of the bombing dramatically increased. After the signing of the Paris Peace Accords in 1973, the intensity increased again. That year, led by B-52 heavy bombers, the U.S. Air Force dropped the equivalent of 1.5 million tons of TNT on Cambodia, slightly more than the previous three years (1970–72) combined. The total tonnage dropped between 1965 and August 1973 when the campaign ended is a staggering three million tons: more than was dropped on Europe, by all parties, during World War II.[7]

The bombing campaign killed indiscriminately and destroyed villages, fields, water control systems, and livestock. By some estimates, 10–15 percent of the rural population were killed between 1970 and 1973 (Porter and Hildebrand 1975), though it may be impossible to separate those who died from falling bombs with deaths from other civil war consequences. Many of those who experienced and survived the airstrikes were compelled to flee the countryside for Phnom Penh and other cities; one-third of the rural population had fled the countryside by 1975 (Porter and Hildebrand 1975). For others, the indiscriminate nature of U.S. "imperialism" became justification for joining the revolution. Many peasants gave up farming to enlist with the Khmer Rouge which had been, to that point, "an insignificant force of a few thousand" (Haas 1991a). The bombing also targeted trails and roads, destroying infrastructure necessary for transporting food from surviving rice-producing areas to the population centers. Between 1970 and 1974, the area under rice cultivation in the Khmer Republic declined by 77 percent and total production decreased by 84 percent.

The humanitarian and environmental consequences of American air operations over Cambodia between 1965 and 1973 are difficult to comprehend and impossible to quantify. What we know of the short-term impacts—death, mass migration, and starvation—is distressing by itself. But the long-term legacy should not be forgotten: unexploded ordinance (UXO) dropped during this period continues to claim limbs and lives. Casualties from UXO in Cambodia are now three times higher than casualties from land mines. In 2005, Cambodia ranked third in the world in the number of mine and UXO casualties, with up to 800 reports per year (Wells-Dang 2006).

Economic Collapse

The rapid expansion of civil war and aerial bombardment sent economic production into steep decline. Not only did the republic lose agricultural land to the advancing rebels, yields declined due to the destruction of farm machinery, the loss of traction animals, high input prices, and the death or migration of farmers. But agriculture was not the only sector impacted by the war: loss of territory and the capture of ports and roads constrained the supply of industrial inputs, driving up prices for basic commodities like cement and fuel. Between 1969 and 1974, industrial production had shrunk by 58 percent (Slocomb 2010).

With the downturn, inflation soared. From 1970 to 1974, the consumer price index (for all goods) in Phnom Penh rose 360 percent. A kilo of rice in December 1971 cost 10 riels; three years later it cost 300 riels (USAID 1977). The price increase encouraged hoarding. Incoming food aid was often redirected away from distribution centers and sold on the black market, usually to Vietnam and Thailand (Slocomb 2010). The purveyors of this trade—military and government officials— amassed extraordinary wealth: with only months left before the end of the regime, new neighborhoods in Phnom Penh were being developed with mansions for the burgeoning urban elite (Porter and Hildebrand 1978). Many of the upper class, glad to be rid of Sihanouk, spent their wealth in lavish fashion and in ways that did not benefit the Cambodian economy: "expensive foreign products, frequent trips abroad, hard currency bank accounts, and the construction of amenities modeled on those of Paris and New York" (Vickery 2000, 22).

Meanwhile, military expenditures rose dramatically with growing need for arms, ammunition, and salaries for soldiers. The demands of the military quickly outpaced the republic's available wealth: in 1974, total military expenditure was 69 billion riels, approximately 150 percent of the "total liquid assets in the hands of the public" (Porter and Hildebrand 1975, 2). To support the war effort and the conspicuous consumption of his generals, Lon Nol became intractably dependent on U.S. aid.

Refugee Crisis

As conditions in the countryside deteriorated, rural residents sought shelter in Cambodia's swelling cities, especially Phnom Penh. In 1970, the population of the capital was 600,000; five years later it had grown to at least 2 million (Vickery 2000). The rapid rate of increase made planning difficult: the figure of 2 million is based on official government estimates, but some foreign observers put the population at 2.4 to 3 million in the last days of the war (Porter and Hildebrand 1975). So many people sought refuge in Phnom Penh that the government had to reorganize the city's administration around new neighborhoods and new funding mechanisms (Slocomb 2010). Refugee camps and other informal settlements emerged in and around the capital as the Khmer Rouge cordon tightened.

The seriousness of the refugee crisis, even by 1971, was apparent in some official responses. The Mixed Economic Commission initiated regular truck convoys to transport rice from Battambang to Phnom Penh, moving more than a million sacks of rice (approximately 50,000 metric tons) by the end of that year. A system of barges loaded with rice regularly traveled up the Mekong to the capital. These barges returned with exports destined for Singapore and Hong Kong—one of the few ways the republic was able to receive foreign exchange (Slocomb 2010). Meanwhile, Lon Nol's administration had hoped that normalization of relations with the United States would quickly restart former IMF and World Bank aid programs. But U.S. officials were slow to act, deliberately delaying aid to encourage Lon Nol to reprivatize rice production, foreign trade, and other government monopolies (Slocomb 2010). This was structural adjustment at the point of a gun.[8]

When American aid did arrive, it was earmarked almost entirely for the military. Humanitarian aid was too late and too small to meet demand. In 1974, the director of USAID, Norman Sweet, reported that U.S. food aid to the city was approximately 500–700 metric tons per day, but the amount needed was closer to 1000 (Porter and Hildebrand 1975). As roads and rail lines became impassible, ad hoc "airlines" started to fly food into Phnom Penh from remote rice-producing areas still under Republican control. By January 1975, the rebels had captured the port at Sihanoukville and cut off the Mekong, effectively preventing any resupply of Phnom Penh except by air. What had been a dire situation in the capital was now an emerging disaster.

The Paradox of PL-480

With most of the country's agriculture obliterated or in enemy hands, and its transportation network largely destroyed, the besieged Cambodian population needed food. For Lon Nol's military to keep fighting, however, the government needed something else, namely, revenue. Without money from rice exports, the government could not pay the salaries of soldiers or afford necessary shipments of arms and ammunition. For U.S. strategists—whose primary interest was delaying a communist victory—financing the Republican military became a high priority. This objective was achieved, in part, through a curious piece of American legislation.

The food aid sent to Cambodia from the United States was "donated" through Public Law 480 (PL-480), also known as the "Food for Peace" program. Under PL-480, food aid could take two forms. The first form, called Title I, was intended as a revenue-generating program for foreign governments. It provided food "to a government for sale through commercial or official channels to generate local currencies for military spending" (Porter and Hildebrand 1975, 11). The second form of aid, Title II, had no such constraints and could be freely distributed to the hungry without obligation. Despite the perception that U.S. food "aid" was a charitable gift, in the fiscal year starting July 1974, the United States spent $72.5 million on Title I food and a mere $1 million on Title II. In the final weeks before the revolution, USAID allowed private organizations to distribute larger quantities of Title II aid, but these improvements were negligible. Porter and Hildebrand (1975) estimate that on an average day, a mere 50 tons of rice were distributed free of charge, out of 545 tons total. As such, the vast majority of U.S. food aid that arrived in Phnom Penh was sold to the hungry—not given away—and the proceeds went directly to the government.

The consequences of PL-480's "aid-for-sale" program are important and appalling. With high demand and insufficient supply, the price of rice in Phnom Penh rose dramatically. According to an International Monetary Fund study, by September 1974 the average household did not make enough income to feed itself (Porter and Hildebrand 1978). By February, the government established a "subsidized" price to increase access for the urban poor, but this cheaper rice came with a proviso: each person was limited to 2.75 kilograms every 10 days, barely more than the ration imposed by the CPK three months later. Furthermore, the subsidized price was still beyond what many poor households could afford.

Histories of this period detail the extravagance of American spending in Cambodia and Lon Nol's complete dependence on U.S. aid: indeed, by 1974, 95 percent of the republic's revenues came from the United States in the form of weapons and food (Porter and Hildebrand 1975). But the attention to American money misses an important point: PL-480 financed Lon Nol by exploiting Cambodia's own, desperate population. Thanks to the proliferation of Title I aid, it was the urban poor who spent their last savings to support Lon Nol's military, and it was the starving who sacrificed their children to preserve America's geopolitical dignity.

Starvation and Excess

Through the "Food for Peace" program, the government generated cash to support the war effort, albeit at the expense of its own people. But much of this cash never reached the military. Generals and officers fabricated enlistment rolls to inflate the number of soldiers involved in the war effort. More soldiers meant more U.S. aid was paid out for salaries. The U.S. Government Accountability Office (GAO) estimated that Cambodian military commanders pocketed between $750,000 and $1 million each month from paychecks for "phantom" soldiers (Porter and Hildebrand 1978, 7). Shipments of arms, ammunition, and fuel were sold on the black market, sometimes ending up in Khmer Rouge hands. Corruption in some government and military positions was so lucrative that leaders often rotated officers through these posts to help "spread the wealth."

On the humanitarian side, much of the rice contributed under PL-480 never reached distribution centers. Like other forms of aid, it too was hoarded and redirected into black markets by government officials. In February 1975, the Controller General for aid disbursement reported that up to 46.3 percent of the rice intended for distribution in a neighborhood of Phnom Penh had been lost "due to diversion" (Porter and Hildebrand 1975, 3–4). Despite the mandated maximum of 2.75 kilograms per person every 10 days, by March 1975 officials in Western Phnom Penh had only enough rice to distribute 1.6 kilograms every 10 days. According to the World Health Organization (WHO 2017), 450 grams of rice per day is considered the minimum to meet nutritional requirements. At the rate of 160 grams per day *for sale* at government distribution centers, wasting and starvation were imminent.

Declining food availability, corruption, and the aid market impacted urban residents in different ways. For the elite who could afford rice at the unsubsidized price, starvation was never a consideration—those who profited from hoarding and aid redirection enjoyed increasing luxuries in the last months of the regime. For those who had arrived from rural areas and registered with refugee organizations, food and medical attention was difficult—but not impossible—to find. Services were stretched thin, but when free rice was available, it invariably went to refugees. The greatest suffering fell to Phnom Penh's urban poor who were left to compete for whatever rice was available for sale. Deputy administrator of USAID, John Murphy told Congress, "Ironically, it is the population, the regular population of Phnom Penh that is suffering, because they are not on the list of registered refugees and are not eligible for AID and must buy whatever they eat . . . And the money to buy the rice that is there is just not in the people's hands" (Porter and Hildebrand 1975, 11).

By January 1975, Western reporters and aid workers observed increases in kwashiorkor and marasmus, Vitamin A and Vitamin B1 deficiencies, and a sudden spike in child deaths (Porter and Hildebrand 1975). In March, a doctor with Catholic Relief Services estimated that hundreds were dying each day. There were no official attempts to calculate the death toll from starvation, but based on eyewitness accounts from journalists and interviews with doctors and aid workers, Porter and Hildebrand (1975) estimated that as many as 8000 people died from starvation in the month of March. To put this number in perspective, the mortality rate from *hunger* at the end of the Lon Nol regime (0.44 percent) was almost the same as the mortality rate from *hunger, exposure, and execution* under three years and nine months of the CPK (0.47 percent).[9]

As reports of urban mass starvation began to surface, some in the U.S. government went on the defensive. "U.S. officials explained their lack of concern with the plight of refugees by arguing that in Cambodia, relatives and friends would take care of refugees" (Porter and Hildebrand 1975, 10). It is not entirely clear how relatives and friends were supposed to care for refugees when food was materially out of reach for all but the wealthy. Other officials complained that it was physically impossible to supply the city with sufficient food through airlifts, especially when aircraft could come under fire on approach to Phnom Penh. It may have been impossible to provide sufficient food, but more aid could have been delivered: of the 1010 tons of aid flown in each day, 565 tons was ammunition (*Washington Star*, March 5, 1975).

That statistic is perhaps the most succinct reflection of U.S. priorities in Cambodia. Kissinger, Nixon, and Ford were not interested in preventing a communist victory so much as propping up Lon Nol long enough to get the United States out of Vietnam. From 1970 on, decisions about military operations, aid programs, and diplomatic support all reflect a tepid concern for civilian lives. As civil war and aerial bombardment propelled the humanitarian crisis, PL-480 provided an efficient mechanism for turning that crisis into capital accumulation. Smedley Butler, a Major General in the Marine Corps, once said of such profiteering, "war is a racket . . . it is possibly the oldest, easily the most profitable, surely the most vicious . . . It is the only one in which the profits are reckoned in dollars and the losses in lives" (Butler 2016 [1933], np). The racket that was America's war in Cambodia was abetted by another age-old swindle: the exploitation of the hungry.

Spatial Differences

As the territory and economy of the republic collapsed around Phnom Penh, the Khmer Rouge were reorganizing production in "liberated" parts of the country. Up until mid-1973, captured territory was organized around two different

160

strategies. Under the first, families retained the right to cultivate their land, but labor for harvests was provided communally. All harvested rice belonged to the community: members of the leadership decided how much would be kept for consumption by the population and how much would be "sent elsewhere to support the war effort" (Twining 1989, 125). Family ownership extended to livestock and small animals.

Under the second system, land was owned by collective, interfamily groups. As with the first system, all labor and products of the harvest were shared. Families could still own large and small livestock, and small animals could be eaten without permission, but larger animals could not be slaughtered without the consent of the commune (Quinn 1974).

In places that had been liberated early in the war—usually areas where the Khmer Rouge enjoyed the most support—rebel leaders generally implemented the first, family-based strategy. But in territories captured later in the war, especially Republican regions that had mounted stiff resistance, the Khmer Rouge imposed the second, communal strategy. It is likely that the existence of the two strategies is a legacy of long-standing debates in Party leadership over how to handle land tenure. Hu Nim, a politician and communist intellectual, observed in 1962 that the distribution of land among farmers was skewed toward the wealthy: 30.7 percent of all farming households had less than 1 hectare (5.18 percent of all owned land), whereas 4 percent of all farming households had more than 4 hectares (21.45 percent of all owned land). This inequality was the primary argument for agrarian reform; for some in the Party, this justified the collectivization of all title. At the same time, Nim warned that "the Cambodian peasant is very attached to his plot of land and his right to it must be respected . . . only by persuading—not ordering—peasants to exchange land could progress be made toward that goal" (Twining 1989, 113).

Evidence suggests that in 1973, Khmer Rouge leadership decided to implement the collective strategy in all newly liberated territory and slowly phase out the family-owned system. From this point on, collectives were only allowed to trade through barter, a decision that made monetary exchange with Republican merchants obsolete (Carney 1989). With the capture of Phnom Penh on April 17, 1975, all currency and private property was abolished and the remaining family-owned systems were collectivized. Throughout the South and West, communes were instructed to prepare for the impending influx of urban evacuees. There is evidence that rural communities under Khmer Rouge control may have tried to maintain stockpiles of rice from the 1974 harvest in preparation for the arrival of urban evacuees (Porter and Hildebrand 1975; Slocomb 2010). Even if these stockpiles were insufficient for the task, the situation in the capital was worse. In one report, Western and government officials declared that there were "only a few days left of rice" in the city (quoted in Goodfellow 1975).

The Cambodian death toll during the war years is difficult to calculate: rural-to-urban migration and out-migration to Vietnam and Thailand complicate population and mortality estimates. Research by Craig Etcheson (2000) offers the following approximations: for combatants, 100,000 to 800,000 dead; for noncombatants, 50,00 to 300,000 dead; and from U.S. bombardment, 30,000 to 500,000 dead. These numbers are astonishing, even at the low end of each range. The high values are a sobering reflection on the magnitude of the social upheaval wrought between 1970 and 1975. By itself, this period would mark a watershed in Cambodian history. But these numbers would be dwarfed by the upheaval to come.

Food Provisioning Failure on the Eve of Revolution: April 1975

As it has in nearly every major 20th century famine, war played a central role in the starvation of Phnom Penh's children. The unraveling of Cambodia's food provisioning system during the early 1970s can be traced to the expansion of U.S. bombing and the violence of the republic's civil war against communist insurgents. Conflict and military defeat led to the loss of land under cultivation, the destruction of landesque capital and draft animals, the displacement of labor, and the breakdown of distribution through the destruction of the transportation network. With insufficient food to meet demand, the price of rice skyrocketed, jeopardizing food availability for Phnom Penh's urban poor. Higher prices led to increased hoarding while PL-480 ensured that food aid had to be sold when it could have been distributed for free. Figure 7 shows the breakdown of food provisioning through various economic measures. From this perspective, the 1970 coup stands out as a key moment—it marks the start of large-scale U.S. bombing, the loss of land under cultivation, declines in yield and production, rising prices, and a precipitous fall in the caloric intake of Cambodians.

Production Failure

The food provisioning failure that led to the starvation of thousands in 1974–75 appears, on first consideration, to emerge from a collapse of production. Violent conflict initiated the collapse of food production in three, interconnected ways. First, the direct and indirect *environmental* consequences of war reduced culti- vated area and yields. The destruction of bunded fields, channels, and control structures prevented effective water control and rendered fields useless for rice cultivation until they could be repaired. The deformation of land through cra- tering and the creation of hazard through UXOs—particularly bomblets—made fields unusable. Food storage systems, like Cambodia's raised granaries, were especially vulnerable to incendiary munitions. Forest defoliation from agent orange may have impacted yields in neighboring areas by driving rats into the fields (Jahn et al. 1997). Rice cultivation in Southeast Asia relies on natural

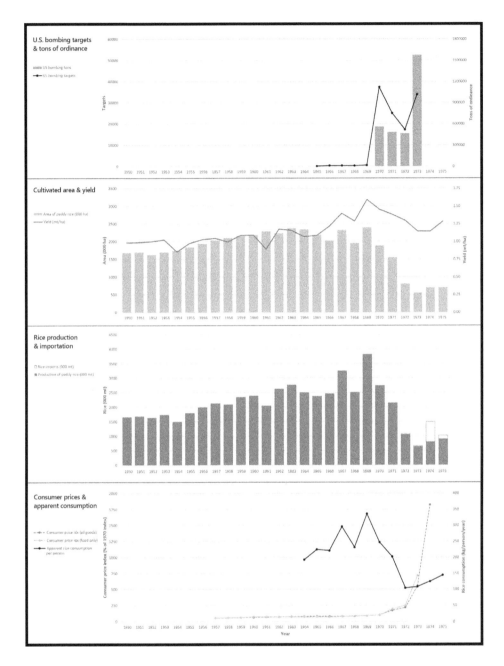

Figure 7. Time series showing correlation between U.S. bombing, agricultural production, and economic consumption. No data for bombing before 1965 or after 1973. Rice imports from 1972–73 are from multiple exporters; imports from 1974–75 are from U.S. only. Consumer price indices are given as a percentage of 1970 values (1970 = 100%). Apparent consumption is calculated based on rice sales, not dietary consumption; as such, rise in apparent consumption from 1973–75 may be due to hoarding. (Data sources: UN FAO, USAID, Genocide Studies Program, MacMillan Center for International and Area Studies, Yale University)

predation to keep pests under control (Oka 1979) and forest loss would have deprived such pest-eating predators of habitat.

Second, the direct and indirect *social* consequences of war impacted the allocation of labor to production. The most obvious and direct impact was bodily injury or death resulting from explosions or UXO. In other contexts of historical bombardment, exposure to heavy metals in the environment has resulted in increased incidences of low fertility, birth defects, and schizophrenia (Wong, Li, and Thornton 2006)—it is possible that such consequences were experienced here. In the short term, indiscriminate heavy bombing instills fear for oneself and one's family, encouraging the abandonment of homes and villages to secure physical safety elsewhere. Over the long term, such exposure may produce post-traumatic stress disorder (PTSD) (Somasundaram 1996).

The spatiality of social networks also played a role. The destruction of a village school (for example, see Strangio 2017) may have impacted many more families than the bombing of a rice field: whereas a field belongs to a single household, a school aggregates the most precious resources for an entire community. The common dependence on collective labor for rice transplanting and harvesting meant that only a few households in a region had to leave before rice cultivation was severely impacted. Once there were no longer enough people to perform necessary collective activities, other farmers would have been forced to leave. Finally, the enormous spatial extent of the bombing and the civil war forced refugees to travel long distances to reach safety and suitable public services, making it costly and risky for refugees to return quickly to home villages and restart production.

Third, there are interactions between these consequences and long-standing historical and spatial patterns. The most heavily bombed agricultural land (in the south and east of the country) was owned by smallholders, not plantation companies. As such, most households that were displaced by war had depended on their own production for subsistence—that is, the rice they grew was also the rice they ate. For these families, giving up agriculture meant depending on non-household sources of food. If the aerial bombardment had occurred over Battambang's rice plantations instead of peasant farms, food availability for the rural masses would have been substantially better; in all likelihood, many more would have stayed home and farmed.

From the standpoint of the state economy, the decline in rice production was catastrophic. Dating back to the days of the French protectorate, the Cambodian government made money from taxes on rice production and export sales. When rural agriculture collapsed in 1970–75, with it went tax revenues and income from foreign exchange. The result was a government increasingly dependent on foreign aid to survive. Notably, this aid was directed toward the military and not economic development. One could argue this was an exigency of war, if it was not also an exigency of American *realpolitik*.

This arrangement of interacting processes ensured a rapid collapse. What started out as many small and localized production failures quickly expanded through progressive, large-scale shortfalls of labor. Declining production led to declining national revenues, increased deficit spending, and growing reliance on aid. Of course, U.S. assistance was designed to keep the war going: it was never sufficient for victory, nor did it accompany any realistic diplomatic efforts at peace (see Haas 1991b; Shawcross 2002). By 1973, this cycle of feedback had left the Republic of Kampuchea in a desperate situation. Fearing the too-early collapse of Lon Nol's administration, the United States tripled the intensity of the bombardment, driving more peasants out of the countryside and adding fuel to the crisis.

Consumption Failure

Compounding the loss of production was a complex consumption failure: the ineffectual performance of systems intended to get available rice to the hungry. With refugees flooding the cities, survival depended increasingly on food distribution networks at the urban scale and incoming supplies of rice from the parts of the countryside under Republican control. As the war progressed, these systems experienced increasing stress. Urban distribution was impacted by shelling, inconsistent food supplies, and power outages that were part of a government attempt to save money (Porter and Hildebrand 1975). Meanwhile, the supply of rice from the countryside was constrained by roads made impassable by bombing, rebel action, and shortages of fuel. Food imports arriving by ship were eventually blocked by the rebel capture of Sihanoukville, and barges carrying food to Phnom Penh via the Mekong were turned back when rebels gained control of river traffic in January 1975. This left daily aid flights as the only way to satisfy the city's food requirements, and half of these flights were filled with ammunition, not rice.

Supply pressures led to soaring inflation, not just for rice but all consumer goods (see fig. 7). Inflation encouraged hoarding, which further restricted supply. Inequality and high food prices have long been associated with famine in market settings (Sen 1981; Davis 2002; Garenne 2002): in locations with marked income inequality, high food prices often starve the poor while the wealthy continue to eat. If prices are high enough and the wealthy are rich enough, this deadly combination can be sustained for some time: sellers will not be impacted so long as sales to the rich counter the loss of poor consumers (through death or an inability to pay). Meanwhile, the wealthy may choose to make money through hoarding. In limited markets, hoarding pushes up the price of food, which increases profits for hoarders. Indeed, it has been suggested that these dynamics of inequality are a common characteristic of urban starvation (Garenne 2002).

One reason why this dynamic can persist is that the movement of food in market-based systems tends to follow the contours of power. In the words of Naomi Hossain (2017, 25), "The intersection of malnutrition with other forms of inequality reflects how the food system amplifies the economic, social, and political disparities that already divide societies." In Cambodia, the inequalities being amplified were the result of two historical conjunctures: a legacy of colonial policies that suppressed peasants and nurtured the urban elite, and a war that pushed these two classes into the *same city* and the *same market* for rice.

Declining food supplies were exacerbated by growth in black markets and illegal "redirection" of aid rice. Black markets, corruption, and other extralegal activities have been associated with forms of social breakdown and civil unrest (cf. Le Billon 2003). In such cases, the loss of governmental control makes illegal activity less likely to be prosecuted and, thus, "worth the risk." But the forms of redirection that contributed to food system failure in Cambodia suggest a more nuanced analysis. First, rural producers had been selling rice illegally to Vietnamese and Thai traders since the French implemented agricultural reforms in the early 20th century (Chandler 2008). This trade ebbed and flowed in response to the farmgate price demanded by the Cambodian government: when the price paid to farmers was high, black market sales declined; when it was slashed (for example, in 1966), sales increased. In this way, extralegal sales served as a temporary, systematic reaction to what were unjust terms of exchange. Even if it was possible for farmers to trade in this way for an extended period, it is not clear these agrarian black markets could have produced a large class of wealthy aristocrats.

By contrast, the corruption and black markets that proliferated in urban areas during Sihanouk's and Lon Nol's administrations did exactly that. From the falsification of salary rolls to the illegal sale of U.S.-supplied weapons, commanders found myriad ways to steal from their own institutions for personal gain. Unlike incidents of peasant crime, high-ranking officials encouraged their subordinates to take advantage of the situation. Porter and Hildebrand (1975, 8) write: "The trafficking in goods became so important to the governmental elite that there was an unspoken understanding that there would be a rotation of the individuals in the most lucrative posts every few months. Thus, Phnom Penh observers spoke of the 'merry-go-round' of executive positions." It is ironic that Lon Nol—who, in 1966, killed farmers and burned their villages as punishment for selling Cambodian rice on the black market—would later preside over an administration that promoted the pillaging of the country's wealth.

Finally, the PL-480 program exacerbated the food crisis by codifying the government's exploitation of its population. Through Title I aid, PL-480 essentially imposed a food market on the city and forced the poor to pay for rice that could have been given away for free. The government was allowed to charge whatever it wanted, so long as the rice was sold. Under PL-480, not only *could* the government run the food program like a for-profit business, it was *obligated to*. The result was a clear example of the relationship between inequality and food markets: even though the rice cost nothing to the government, the official price was set so high that an average household could not afford to feed itself. Once again, the ironies run deep: the same American administration that pressured Lon Nol to end government monopolies, enabled Lon Nol to run a monopoly rice program in the name of humanitarian relief.

On April 17, 1975, Phnom Penh's rice-for-revenue circus came to an end with the capture of the city by the Khmer Rouge. In the following sections, I trace the subsequent transformation of Cambodia's system of food production and consumption by the CPK. At one level, parts of this system would soon look radically different; for instance, the imposition of food rationing, forced labor, and communal living and eating. But at another level, fundamental relations of production and consumption stayed the same. Phnom Penh's famine of the early 1970s emerged from an arrangement of producers, sellers, buyers, and consumers that extracted enormous wealth from ordinary Cambodians. By the mid-1970s, the actors playing these roles had changed, but the script was essentially the same.

Transformation under the CPK: 1975—79

Within hours of the capture of Phnom Penh on April 17, 1975, Khmer Rouge commanders began ordering the evacuation of urban residents. Many details of the evacuation had been planned as far back as 1973 and previously tested in other cities captured during the war (Quinn 1989). Residents in different "sectors" of Phnom Penh were evacuated to different locations, with the majority moved toward agricultural areas to the south of the city. Evacuees were forced to abandon their belongings, travel long distances on foot, and sleep in the open. Eyewitness reports of the exodus are surreal: hundreds of patients were forced to leave Phnom Penh's hospitals in wheelchairs and gurneys, some still attached to their IVs; many of the old and infirm were abandoned along the way; Republican soldiers were executed in front of family members (Carney 1989). Within the first days and weeks, exhaustion, starvation, and exposure to disease claimed many lives already weakened by months of malnutrition. Time Magazine (1976, 9) reported that a cholera outbreak among evacuees south of the city killed 100,000 people while other reports indicate widespread dysentery and malaria (Quinn 1989). By some estimates, the death toll from the evacuation was in the hundreds or thousands (Dawson 1975). Other authors claim as many as 400,000 died (Barron and Paul 1977), though this figure is an outlier.

The lived experience of upheaval, physical exhaustion, and terror is not in question here: it is difficult to read survivors' accounts of this historical moment without feeling a deep sense of unease, despair, or outrage. Indeed, the evacuation of Phnom Penh seems to condense an incomprehensible amount of brutality into a remarkably short period of time, encouraging reflections on the human capacity for cruelty. But at the same time, it is important to note the limits of historical reconstruction around this event. First, primary data is exceedingly limited as the sizeable variations in mortality estimates attest. These were not the actions of an established government bureaucracy: the evacuation of two million people was being conducted by rebel units that had spent the last several years fighting a guerrilla war in the countryside—paperwork was not a high priority. Second, the data available to historians comes primarily from a handful of survivors, most of whom were included in the particularly harsh southern evacuation. As such, it is dangerous (though commonplace) to generalize on the whole evacuation experience from these limited reports (see Vickery 2000).

Finally, it is important to remember the historical and geographical context in which the evacuation occurred. To be sure, these were terrifying moments, especially for wealthy urban residents who were the target of rebel frustration and for whom the relations of power had been recently overturned. But these days and weeks capped several *years* of grinding hunger for the urban poor, many of whom had watched family members starve or die of curable diseases mere blocks away from opulence and excess. From their perspective, the arrival of rebels in the city might have been cause for cautious optimism.[10]

In this analysis, my primary concern is with the *material logic* of revolution, that is, the social and economic motivation behind the reorganization of Cambodia's mode of production. From this perspective, I am less concerned with the psychology of mass violence (see Hinton 2004) than its political economy (Tyner and Rice 2016). Underlying the tumultuous evacuation of Phnom Penh were two unavoidable truths: Cambodians were starving, and the country's rice production was in shambles.

Agricultural Reorganization as Centerpiece

During the first wave of migration in April 1975, many of the refugees that had sought shelter in Phnom Penh during the war returned to their rural homes where they were enrolled in local communes and work units (Slocomb 2010). A second round of migration, in September 1975, involved city dwellers that had been relocated south of Phnom Penh. Most of these people were moved to the northwest where they were put to work on rice plantations and building irrigation infrastructure. Conditions here were harsh—many of the most brutal stories of life and death under the Khmer Rouge come from those forced to labor in the Northwest Zone (Twining 1989; Slocomb 2010).

Over the next three years and nine months, movements of labor like this— albeit on a smaller scale—would serve as the CPK's go-to strategy for jumpstarting rice production in the countryside. To that end, the CPK established two primary objectives. The first was to "serve the people's livelihood, and to raise the people's standard of living quickly, both in terms of supplies and in terms of other material goods" (Party Center 1976/1988b, 51). This objective can be understood as an attempt to respond to the immediate post-war crisis of insufficient food. The second objective was "To seek, gather, save, and increase capital from agriculture, aiming to rapidly expand our agriculture, our industry, and our defense" (Party Center 1976/1988b, 51).

The capital growth called for by the CPK would be accomplished through agriculture-led economic "take-off." Agricultural products were to be sold to other countries and the foreign exchange obtained from these exports was to be used to import agricultural and industrial inputs. According to central planning documents, rice exports were to make up 93 percent of foreign exchange, rubber would provide 5 percent, and the remainder was to come from other agricultural products (Party Center 1976/1988c, 106). Over the next four years, China would become the primary client for all exports, though the CPK also established trade with Japan for kapok and continued protectorate-era trade with Madagascar and several West African countries for rice. Rubber was traded to China and Singapore (Slocomb 2010; Mertha 2014). Some authors writing in the STV tradition have claimed that the CPK sought to establish an autarkic, self-sufficient state closed off to all foreign influence (Jackson 2014). These claims fail to account for the foreign trade that took place during the tenure of the CPK and the fact that production for exchange was the basis of the planned economy.

The capital acquired through rice exports would eventually be directed toward industrial growth: "We can only expand industry by standing on agriculture. Later on, once we have rice, the [Western] Zone could grow its own jute and build its own jute factory to make sacks. The same goes for a textile factory" (Party Center 1976/1988a, 29). In principle, the CPK's approach followed the same economic logic as strategies of agriculture-led economic takeoff that have been promoted to developing countries since the 1950s (cf. Rostow 1956, 1963). Cambodia was faced with production crises in both agricultural and industrial sectors resulting from the war and U.S. bombardment. It had a surplus of labor in the form of urban evacuees. Due to the influx of refugees into Phnom Penh, the urban evacuee population was a representation of the Cambodian population as a whole: as of April 1975, most people living in Phnom Penh were from the countryside and had direct agricultural experience. Directing this labor back into agriculture made economic sense.

Furthermore, traditional Cambodian rice cultivation did not rely heavily on industrial inputs: the primary requirements for rainfed cultivation were land and labor. The state acquired labor by eliminating private property and organizing the population into communes. It acquired land by winning the war. Indeed, with the defeat of Republican forces, the CPK claimed all Cambodian territory, including the plantation lands around Battambang that had remained under Republican control into 1975. Until yield improving inputs like chemical fertilizers and pesticides could be produced domestically or acquired from abroad, it made economic sense to reestablish production under traditional, low-input practices of cultivation.

The CPK's Four-Year Plan to expand rice production was built around three primary goals. First, wherever possible, administrators would try to produce two or more rice crops per year. In 1969, only 5 percent (74,000 hectares) of land under rice produced a dry season harvest; by 1980, according to the plan, 37.7 percent of all rice land was to produce two or more harvests. The only way to increase the number of harvests per year in rainfed systems was to develop irrigation infrastructure, a project that would require extraordinary investment in time and energy if it was to meet the plan's objectives. Second, the total area under cultivation was to be expanded through the conversion of nonagricultural land to rice production. This would be accomplished primarily through the "clearing of forest lands" (Helmers 1997, 6).

Finally, CPK planners declared that rice yields were to be increased to a national average of three tons per hectare per harvest. Historical averages for Cambodia demonstrate the audacity of this objective: yields for rainfed cultivation had stabilized at—or just above—one ton per hectare. Peak yield was 1.6 tons in 1969, but more recent harvests affected by the war (1974–75) produced yields around 1.2 tons. The production increases established in the plan were to be accomplished through improved fertilizer use, growth in the application of chemical inputs, scientific breeding, mechanization, and improved water control through the expansion of irrigation.

The production improvement strategies outlined in the CPK's Four-Year Plan were not new—these strategies were the best recommendations of Western development agencies. Since the influx of aid in the 1950s, development organizations had been encouraging yield increases through improvements in irrigation and the use of "scientific" inputs (Helmers 1997). Organizations like USAID funded agricultural research to develop new strains of rice and supported growth in markets for fertilizers, pesticides, and herbicides (Benge 1991). The U.S. government and the World Bank proposed large-scale irrigation and hydroelectric schemes on the Mekong and in the Tonle Sap basin. Development funds were directed toward rice milling equipment and tractor factories (Rickman, Pyseth, and Sothy 1997). According to the IMF, Cambodia would be best served if rice production was directed toward foreign exchange and industrial expansion through export. In this light, the CPK's Four-Year Plan was not a fundamentally socialist, communist, or "Maoist" revolution—as some narratives under the STV suggest. Rather, the CPK's plan followed the playbook of the *Green* Revolution. It would transform agriculture using the best agronomic and scientific practices available. In foreign trade, it would apply economic principles of comparative advantage and import substitution. As the authors of the plan expressed it, Cambodia's revolution would convert the country's "backward" agriculture to "modern" agriculture in 10–15 years (Party Center 1976/1988a, 27).

The "revolutionary" part of the plan—and the part that consumes the attention of most commentators—concerned the reorganization of labor. With the end of private property, the population of Cambodia became subjects of the Party's system of labor classification and mobilization. Perhaps the most important part of this classification was the distinction between "new" and "base" people. "New" people comprised primarily urban evacuees, "capitalists and foreign minorities" (Vickery 2000, 81). "Base" people included mostly poor and middle-class peasants and workers. This distinction would become the basis of significant differences in labor assignment and treatment: base people received better food and shelter, could occupy positions of leadership, and were assigned primarily to agricultural work. By contrast, new people received less food and were forced to work the most labor-intensive jobs. Though casualty statistics are not available to make a comparison, reports from observers and survivors indicate that new people suffered the most. It is likely that most deaths under the CPK from direct violence and neglect were new people.

In addition to the new/base distinction, the CPK classified people by labor potential (weak strength and full strength) and organized them into working units using a military-style hierarchy. The basic work unit (*pouk*) consisted of three people: a leader and two followers. Three of these units were grouped together into a squad (*krom*) of 10–11 people, usually led by a worker with agricultural experience. At each level, it was common for the leader to be a base person; at higher levels, leaders were usually former Khmer Rouge soldiers. Leaders frequently adjusted the constitution of these groups in response to the work that needed to be completed (Twining 1989).

Laborers were assigned a quota for the work that had to be accomplished each day. This quota varied considerably depending on the task at hand, labor classification, sex, whether the unit was made up of new or base people, which administrative level the unit was attached to, and the discretion of leadership. In agricultural contexts, quotas were often defined in terms of spatial area; for example, a *kong toic* of 33 women assigned to cut rice had to reap two hectares per day. In other cases, physical units or volumes were used: men assigned to rice threshing had to beat 300–500 bundles of rice per day, while laborers working on irrigation projects frequently had to move 1–3 cubic meters of earth per day (Vickery 2000). Those who failed to meet their quota could suffer a range of punishments, including execution.

To feed the population and manage the supply of rice for export, the CPK imposed a statewide food ration. For the first few months, the daily ration was defined as one can of uncooked rice (250 grams) per person per day, a diet that yields approximately 912 calories. According to the WHO (2017), daily requirements for adults range from 1600 to 3000 calories depending on sex and level of physical activity; and from 1000 to 2000 calories for young children. For adults, borderline malnutrition occurs around 1000–1400 calories and starvation begins when intake drops below 500–800 calories. A traditional Cambodian diet prior to 1970 provided approximately 2500 calories, 75 percent of which came from rice.[11] Assuming the quantity of rice was the *only* change under the CPK—that is, the absolute quantity of fish, vegetables, and other items in the diet stayed the same—then the caloric intake under the ration came to 1537 calories, still below the acceptable adult range. A more likely scenario is that the absolute quantity of other foods was severely restricted. In fact, some survivor accounts from the first few months suggest that rice was the only consistent part of the ration: supplemental foods were rarely provided (Carney 1989). Under such circumstances, the daily ration would have provided just over 900 calories, leading to severe malnutrition, wasting, and eventual starvation.

As with the labor quota, the real-world food ration exhibited substantial variation. Base/new status, labor categorization, local production, and the whims of individual leaders all factored into the amount of food laborers received. For example, in Kratie Special Region 505, survivors reported a ration of 50 cans per month, or 416 grams per day (1500 calories), while in parts of the Northwest Zone, rations for new people dropped to "1 can for 6, and then 8, people" per day (Vickery 2000, 115). According to one survivor, as many as one-third of the 5000 people in his area had died by December 1975. CPK cadre who moved from the Southwest to the Northwest Zone in 1977 reported that they had "never seen such misery at home as they did in Pursat and parts of Battambang" (Vickery 2000, 118–19).

According to the Four-Year Plan, the ration was intended to be graduated based on labor classification, with three cans (750 g, 2700 calories) for laborers doing the most strenuous work, down to one-and-a-half cans (375 g, 1350 calories) for "weak strength" workers (Party Center 1976/1988b, 111). In some of the better-fed regions and districts, this more substantial allocation may have occurred, but survivor accounts consistently indicate that such amounts were never realized in the worst areas (cf. Twining 1989; Vickery 2000). Furthermore, planning documents indicate that there was to be no increase in the rice ration over time: meals were to consist of the measured amount of rice, two side dishes, and a dessert for each person. The only change was an increase in the frequency of dessert, from once every three days in 1977 to daily by 1979. The ration was one of the only forms of social welfare that did not increase each year: over the same period, the plan established modest spending increases under the categories of "medicine" and "household, hygiene, and culture" (Party Center 1976/1988b, 88).

The CPK did not hide the larger economic motivation for the fixed ration: the allocated amount of rice would allow the state "To break even [in production] . . . but we do not want only this much. We want twice as much as this in order to have capital to build up the Zone and the country . . . we want more [rice] in order to locate much additional oil, to get ever more rice mills, threshing machines, water pumps, and means of transportation, both as an auxiliary manual force and to give strength to our forces of production" (Party Center 1976/1988a, 19). From the CPK's perspective, every can of rice eaten in Cambodia was 250 grams that could have been sold overseas to help purchase tractors, pesticide, oil, arms, and ammunition.

The logic behind the ration was to provide the CPK with a mechanism for evenly distributing the country's food resources and managing the availability of surplus rice for export. Assuming a fixed ration and low (or tightly controlled) population growth, the state could increase profits by increasing total rice production. Along with the expansion of irrigation, the CPK declared that scientific agriculture was to play a key role in increasing yields toward the three-tons-per-hectare goal. The plan specified that "an area must be set aside for experiments in order to increase rice production, according to the types of seed chosen, fertilizer, and weather conditions" (Party Center 1976/1988b, 90). Domestic radio reports indicated that research efforts produced three high-yielding varieties: *Pram pi taek*, *Ramuon sar*, and *Champas kok*. Of these, Pram pi taek was reported to yield between 4.5 and 6.5 tons per hectare (Helmers 1997). It is possible that these varieties were not developed domestically but were imported from China—after all, Dalrymple (1986, 6) indicates that agronomic research at the Battambang research station was conducted by "Chinese advisors." Regardless of origin, "improved" varieties of rice were considered an integral part of production improvements.

The plan also mandated the development of chemical fertilizers and pesticides to increase yields. Here, too, Chinese help was needed, first as a direct source of such inputs and later to provide assistance setting up factories to manufacture these inputs locally. In the meantime, CPK leadership sought to develop organic fertilizer production through the collection of animal manure and human waste ("night soil"); in fact, such biological sources were considered a largely untapped resource for agricultural production.

Oxen and water buffalo are essential to Cambodian rice cultivation as a source of power for plowing and harrowing, a means to break up hardened topsoil, and a source of manure. Five years of war and bombardment had severely depleted the population of traction animals (Benge 1991). Some animals were killed directly, some were abandoned by farmers fleeing the countryside, and still others were sold for food to Vietnam or eaten by rebel soldiers. In 1969, USAID estimated that there were 1.2 million draft animals in Cambodia (Benge 1991)—after the war, the CPK estimated the population at 230,000 (Party Center 1976/1988b, 94). The lack of traction for agriculture became a central consideration for the CPK: the Four-Year Plan made explicit the need to improve animal husbandry, expand veterinary medicine, and embark on a systematic breeding program to increase the population of oxen, buffalo, and horses.

The mechanization of agriculture was an explicit goal of the Party: a tractor factory was constructed in Mongkol Borey with the help of North Korea (Twining 1989). According to Party documents, in 1977 the country was operating 400 irrigation pumps, 200 rice mills, 3100 threshing machines, and 200 tractors. By 1980 this was to have expanded to 1600 irrigation pumps, 500 rice mills, 6500 threshing machines, and 1000 tractors, an increase that was to come entirely from domestic production (Party Center 1976/1988b). But until such mechanization could become widely available, rice production was short by a few hundred thousand traction animals.

For as much as the STV represents the CPK as autarkic and insisting on self-sufficiency, the Party's plan to transform the economy was predicated on foreign trade and assistance. Exported rice was the core of foreign exchange and was used to purchase the agricultural and industrial inputs that could not be produced locally. It was also used to finance the purchase of weapons and ammunition used by the CPK's security apparatus. China was not only Cambodia's most important trading partner, it was the primary source of official assistance (Mertha 2014). Shortly after the capture of Phnom Penh, food and technical aid began arriving: during July of 1975, Beijing sent 18,000 metric tons of food aid to the CPK (Mertha 2014, 121). This is the equivalent of 580 metric tons per day, more than the United States provided to Phnom Penh in the last days of the war.

Irrigation

Perhaps the most infamous aspect of the CPK's agricultural transformation was the mandate to develop extensive irrigation infrastructure using forced labor. Irrigation was necessary for achieving both the seasonal yield goal of three tons per hectare and the goal of increasing the amount of land capable of two or more growing seasons. Better water control in existing fields during the wet season would allow for denser plantings and help mitigate the effect of unseasonable drought, while water availability during the dry season could enable a second planting between December and April. To this end, the CPK initiated numerous irrigation projects ranging from large dams and reservoirs to extensive supply canals (Kiernan 2002). Many dams and reservoirs—both large and small—are still operational and continue to provide water for local agriculture. Long supply canals still hold water for local use during the dry season, despite being inoperative for water transport over their full extent.

Many of the worst stories of exhaustion and brutality come from those forced to work on the CPK's irrigation projects (Vickery 2000). The construction of dams, dykes, and canals involved a massive labor force directed to clear land, dig trenches, move earth, and compact the ground using mostly hand tools (Helmers 1997). Many of these laborers were urban evacuees forced into inhumane work quotas and sustained by the most restrictive of rations. Most scholars speculate that the majority of those who died from exhaustion or exposure came from the ranks of irrigation laborers, their bodies often buried in the earthworks.

By the time Vietnamese troops arrived in January 1979, many of the CPK's irrigation schemes were not yet complete. According to some authors, completed schemes were failing due to a lack of technical knowledge about water control and an administrative system that placed local leadership committees in charge of engineering decisions (cf. Pijpers 1989; Twining 1989). Congruent with the assumptions of the STV, there is a belief that the CPK blindly pursued a statewide plan for implementing a one-by-one-kilometer grid of irrigation channels, without regard to topography and suitability for agriculture (Pijpers 1989). Such a claim reinforces the view that the CPK were driven by ideology and lacked the capacity for deliberate planning. But the reality of physical and documentary evidence suggests a different conclusion: gridded irrigation was limited to areas where the land was exceptionally flat (Munro-Stasiuk et al. 2017). Furthermore, Party documents from the period repeatedly caution against wasting effort in places difficult for irrigation; rather, CPK leaders stressed the need to identify the "good" areas for rice cultivation and direct water control resources to these regions (Chandler, Kiernan, and Boua 1988).

This debate over the soundness of CPK irrigation projects is important. The STV tends to assume that the inexperience and blind fanaticism of the Party encouraged leaders to implement an inefficient and disaster-prone system for rice cultivation. The failure of this system resulted in a large-scale shortage of food—a classic case of Food Availability Decline (FAD)—and this shortage, articulated through a brutal food rationing regime, caused people to starve. In this way, the STV connects the CPK's ideological, antimodern propaganda to famine: by "cleansing" Cambodian society of technical experts in the name of social revolution, the CPK was left to feed the country's population with a production system in relapse. As a totalitarian regime willing to reorganize production for revolutionary ends, the CPK is made to stand alongside other dictatorships that starved their people in the name of communism.

The problem with this characterization is that it assumes the existence of a *production failure*.[12] In subsequent sections, I argue that FAD is neither sufficient nor necessary to explain starvation under the CPK. Furthermore, there is evidence to suggest that total production and yields *increased* under the CPK, rather than decreased as the STV suggests. Indeed, the starvation that occurred between 1975 and 1979 is more elegantly explained as a consequence of a fundamental contradiction between the state's demand for wealth and workers' demand for calories, a contradiction that was carried through from the days of Lon Nol, Sihanouk, and the French. Starvation had less to do with the part of the political economy that was "communist" than the part that was still capitalist.

The Organization of Governance

DK was not defined by the negative space of anarchy. It was a state. It was a totalitarian state. It was often a poorly run totalitarian state. It was a state that excelled at fear, death, and hubris far better than anything else. But it was a state defined by a distinctive network of organizations and institutions, not the absence of them.

—Andrew Mertha, *Brothers in Arms*

Like the squads, platoons, and companies the CPK used to organize the workforce, the Party organized the territory of Cambodia around a similarly nested hierarchy of administrative units. At the highest level, the country was divided into nine zones (*phumpheak*): North, Northeast, East, Southwest, West, Northwest, Center, Kratie Special Region no. 505, and Siemreap Special Region no. 106 (Vickery 2000).[13] Each zone was divided into several regions or sectors (*damban*) and each region was further divided into districts (*srok*). Each district contained a mix of communes (*khum*) and cooperatives (*sahakor*). Communes were usually composed of multiple villages (*phum*) and had populations of 200–400, whereas cooperatives were groupings of a few hundred people not necessarily associated with a village.

175

This spatial organization did not correspond to traditional province boundaries; in some cases, old provinces were divided across multiple zones. Nor did the zone boundaries appear to capture other forms of geographic or economic logic: for example, the primary rice-growing region was distributed across six of the nine zones. Instead, zone boundaries were likely the result of political considerations and compromises played out between Khmer Rouge leaders during the civil war (Vickery 2000).

Each administrative unit was governed by a "triumvirate of officials" known as the "committee" (Vickery 2000). These committees held broad power to make decisions for subordinate units, including the movement and allocation of labor resources. Each level of the hierarchy also had its own labor units. Mobile units were established for each zone, region, district, and so on. Each received direction from the corresponding central committee for that level, even when units were mixed together on the same project. For example, in the case of large irrigation schemes, regional mobile units frequently operated alongside commune and collective units.

One of the consequences of the spatial hierarchy was that regional administration was a curious mix of autonomy and centralized control. The CPK intended for cooperatives and communes to be the fundamental basis for all economic activity and, as such, these units were to have significant independence to determine the resources they needed. From the cooperative level up, each administrative unit (district, region, and zone) was to assemble its own maps and statistics (Party Center 1976/1988a, 34). According to the plan, cooperatives were to maintain their own small gardens and livestock, assign tradespeople to tasks deemed necessary for supporting the collective (like blacksmiths to repair agricultural tools), and determine how agricultural produce was to be distributed, including how much of the surplus would be released "up the chain" (Twining 1989). As a result, zones and regions showed considerable variation. Vickery (2000, 68) notes: "no two regions were alike . . . amount of food, its distribution, work discipline and general hardship, numbers of executions and execution policy, even the content and extent of political education differed among zones and regions; while execution policy and food distribution sometimes differed even among contiguous villages."

At the same time, it is clear that the Central Committee (also known as "Party Center") demanded regular reports from subordinate administrative levels and made fundamental decisions about rice production and resource allocation (DeFalco 2013). Some authors (cf. Twining 1989) indicate that basic decisions about when to plant, weed, and harvest were made by central authorities and passed down to each collective. By contrast, other authors (cf. Vickery 2000) note that production units were given broad freedom to determine the best way to cultivate under local conditions. It is likely that here, too, influential leaders at the region or district level shielded subordinate units from central oversight, a circumstance with mixed results for the laboring population.

The extraction and redistribution of rice surpluses followed each step in the spatial hierarchy. Mertha (2014, 35) describes the extraction process:

> The commune's agriculture committee would ask the village, How much do you have? Then they would ask, How much are you willing to give to *Angkar*? The decision was placed upon the head of the village leader. Above the village level, each administrative level would simply combine the output provided by their subordinate administrative levels and send it upwards. The zones would then arrange delivery of the goods to the State Warehouse, which was often the principal locus of direct interaction between the local governments and the functional units of the Center.

From the Center, rice surplus was allocated for export and distribution to parts of the country that needed additional food. According to the plan, mobile units, groups assigned to irrigation projects, and agricultural units that did not make enough to feed their workers were to receive these disbursements. In reality, this process was substantially altered by the political landscape. For example, regional mobile units (commanded by regional committees) were often better fed and sheltered than their cooperative- and commune-level counterparts. Accounts from survivors working on large dam projects reveal the disparities in provisioning, with regional units routinely receiving sufficient rations (three cans per day), while units associated with the local collective often received only rice gruel.[14]

The mix of centralization and decentralization, codified process and arbitrary decision-making in the CPK's spatial hierarchy encouraged corruption at all levels and led to considerable variations in outcome for the working population. Village leaders on up through district heads were motivated to falsify production reports, sometimes to horde food for their starving workers, and other times to give away food and curry the favor of superiors.[15] The result was a dynamic and spatially variable food provisioning system that fed some while starving others.

The Logic of "Total" Transformation

The propaganda of the CPK justified the transformation of Cambodia's economy as a completion of the socialist revolution begun during the civil war. But the economic motivation is nevertheless well expressed in planning documents and in the actions undertaken by the Party after the capture of Phnom Penh. Transformation was motivated by two objectives: first, the immediate need to bring land back under production to supply food for the starving population; and second, the longer-term goal of economic growth through improvements in agriculture. Authors writing under the STV tend to portray the CPK's planned transformations as a complete break from the past: a total revolution in the organization of the state. In fact, the totality and uniqueness of the CPK's plan is frequently used to explain the severity of conditions in Democratic Kampuchea and the eventual demise of the Party.

But there are several reasons to temper the STV's enthusiasm for generalization—reasons that help place the Cambodian revolution into a broader historical and geographical context. First, the challenges of rural-to-urban migration, hunger, and overcrowding were not new. Throughout the 1960s and 1970s, governments and development agencies engaged in debates over how to manage and feed overcrowded cities throughout Southeast Asia. Vickery (2000, 64) notes that in 1976, "anonymous Western social scientists" published a "Blueprint for the Future [of Thailand]" that suggested the Thai government forcibly relocate residents from overpopulated urban areas into the countryside where they could support food production. During this period, Indonesia embarked on a monumental "transmigration" program that forcibly resettled millions of citizens from densely populated Java to Sumatra, Kalimantan, and Sarawak (see Pauker 2015), a solution similar to that employed by the Dutch in the 1870s to 1890s (Geertz 1963). Forced resettlement and collectivization of labor was not unique to the CPK, nor was it unique to Cambodia: cooperative labor arrangements were commonplace at the village level and corvée labor conscription to support royal or colonial projects was standard practice (Chandler 2008).

Second, the transformation of land through extensification and large irrigation projects had historical precedent. In the late 19th century, French engineers employed a one-by-one-kilometer grid system—called the "hydraulic grid" (*réseau hydraulique*)—in the Mekong Delta (Biggs 2012). The plan to increase agricultural production through improvements to irrigation was a common theme among Cambodian administrations and development agencies; as Slocomb (2010, 181) notes, "All postcolonial governments had the same goals with regard to agricultural modernization." Throughout the 20th century, farmers responded to population pressure and increasing production demands through extensification (Van Der Eng 2004). When markets collapsed, farmers cut back on the area under production to reduce their tax and labor burdens. In fact, the socioecology of Cambodian rice production (soil, land, seeds, tenure arrangements, and labor practices) demonstrated a remarkable flexibility that tended to be ignored by Green Revolution policies focused on yield. What the French, CPK, and others recognized in this flexibility was a system robust enough to survive transformation.

Finally, the CPK's goals have been characterized as utopian, but the actual strategies intended to achieve these goals were logical responses to contemporary conditions in the country and abroad. In 1967, Cambodia's ratio of irrigated production to total production was the lowest in Asia. Compared to Vietnam where exports from the well-irrigated Mekong Delta increased 545 percent under the French, Cambodia was lagging behind (Bray 1994). Not only was the strategy of growing the economy through rice exports a well-established development policy in the 1960s, Cambodians had proven it could be done: in 1940, at the peak of

French plantation expansion and on the heels of massive infrastructural growth, Cambodia was the third largest rice-exporting country in the world (Helmers 1997).

Production Improvements, Consumption Failures

It is difficult to determine if the CPK's policies achieved production goals between 1975 and 1979. A fundamental lack of documentary evidence, combined with conflicting and anecdotal eyewitness accounts, prevents an accurate assessment of Democratic Kampuchea's rice production. However, based on the data from several authors (cf. Twining 1989; Vickery 2000; Slocomb 2010) and Party documents, it is possible to construct a speculative overview of rice production for the four harvest years the CPK were in power.

1975–76: The capture of Phnom Penh and the end of the civil war in April was opportune timing for the CPK: in the coming weeks, the spring rains would start softening rainfed fields and labor would be required to prepare the land for cultivation. The CPK started the 1975–76 growing season with an abundant supply of labor in the form of urban evacuees. The most pressing concern was feeding this population while the rice was growing. The capture of Phnom Penh and other urban areas yielded no stockpiles of rice, as the cities were already starving. It is possible that food was stockpiled in the countryside and that this surplus is partly what motivated the evacuation of the cities (cf. Porter and Hildebrand 1975; Slocomb 2010). Such claims are difficult to verify, though it is reasonable to assume that rice production in Khmer Rouge–held areas was functional, as many of these areas had been in rebel control since 1971. Serious and widespread starvation resulted from the urban evacuation in April and the subsequent relocation of urban evacuees in September, but there is evidence to suggest that rice production was not a total loss. Twining (1989, 143) writes of the harvest, "while understandably not large, [it] appeared to be somewhat better than outside observers had expected, all things considered."

1976–77: During the 1976 growing season, starvation continued, and reports of malnutrition and exhaustion-related deaths increased—particularly among new people assigned to infrastructural work. But rice production was on the rebound: according to Party documents, two million hectares of rice were cultivated in 1976, short of the 2.4 million hectares achieved in 1969 but a marked improvement over the war years (Party Center 1976/1988d). Production was uneven, with good harvests reported in the South and East Zones, but with shortfalls in the Northwest. Refugees fleeing to Thailand reported that in some districts, agricultural production suffered from the physical weakness of laborers. It is difficult to estimate total production, though the CPK claimed it had enough to feed the population and still export 150,000 tons. As Jackson (1978a) points out, if this is true, total production was just over one million tons—considerably below the yields achieved in the 1960s. Twining (1989) argues that with all the labor resources being directed toward agriculture, low yields and productivity are somewhat surprising. I am not sure it is: the additional labor directed toward agriculture was not the total evacuated population, but that subset of labor not directed to irrigation and other infrastructural projects. Many of these workers lacked agricultural expertise, reducing their productivity. With an 80 percent loss in traction animals, few tractors and other labor-saving devices, and no significant rebound in the availability of chemical inputs, an output of one million tons might be laudable.

1977–78: By 1977, yields were showing improvement, even in areas with the lowest productivity. Vickery (2000, 158) notes that "there was thus a new possibility of improving conditions of life and further developing the country." Newly constructed irrigation was beginning to have a positive effect on production, and the total harvest was better than anticipated, though Twining (1989) notes that heavy flooding damaged some of the new water control infrastructure. According to the CPK, all citizens were receiving at least 312 kilograms of rice per year, the equivalent of 854 grams per day (3.4 cans, 3100 calories). Reports from refugees indicate this was not the case as many were not receiving near this amount, but the food situation was improving (Twining 1989). As for total production, the Four-Year Plan established in 1976 set a production goal of 5.6 million metric tons for the 1977–78 harvest, based on production in 1976 and the anticipated rate of growth. Built into this was a goal of 1.4 million hectares under single-season cultivation and 217,000 hectares under two-season cultivation, resulting in an average yield of 3.05 tons per hectare per season. Other than the exaggerated claims of the CPK, there is no independent data to suggest that these goals were met. But even if planners were off by 50 percent, the growth in productivity would have been noteworthy, putting rice production in 1977–78 on par with the best years of the 1960s.

1978–79: Production was negatively impacted by warfare associated with the Vietnamese invasion in January 1979—a disruption that impacted labor allocation during the critical harvest period. Nevertheless, production was buoyed somewhat by increases in yield and growth in irrigated area. Reports from foreign visitors in 1978 indicate that successful irrigation schemes were leading to steady production increases. Heavy hoe blades contributed by a Chinese aid program were reported to have made a significant contribution. Some locations in the Northwest and Southwest Zones made three successful plantings that year, a remarkable achievement given that these same locations had managed only a single planting prior to 1975 (Twining 1989).

Based on the preponderance of primary and secondary data, it is reasonable to draw the following conclusions about production conditions during the 1975–79 period: (1) total rice production and yields fell short of CPK expectations, but reached—and may have exceeded—benchmarks set in the 1960s; (2) the successful expansion of irrigation increased the total area capable of producing multiple harvests per year; and (3) after widespread starvation during the urban evacuation, overall incidences of starvation declined during this period, though variability between locations was still extraordinarily high as late as 1978.

Productivity in Cambodia's rice-growing region benefited from relatively consistent rainfall during the four years of the CPK. Historically, negative rainfall anomalies during the spring months tend to delay planting and create bottlenecks for labor allocation; negative anomalies during the summer and autumn months reduce the growth potential of rice and force workers into extra weeding cycles; and positive anomalies in wintertime can damage the harvest. Between April 1975 and January 1979, the most impactful anomaly occurred in Spring 1977, a 50-millimeter reduction in average rainfall that may have delayed the planting of rainfed rice. The drought referenced by Twining (1989) in late 1977 is not likely to have impacted rainfed fields at the end of the main growing season; however, irrigation schemes designed to store water for dry season cultivation may have been affected by a rainfall deficit during these months.

Cambodian agriculture may have benefited from consistent rainfall, but production was still hindered by several material shortcomings, especially the loss of traction animals and traditional rice varieties. The 1975–76 harvests were severely impacted by the lack of oxen and water buffalo, a concern serious enough for the CPK that party leaders called out animal husbandry and systematic breeding as primary objectives in the Four-Year Plan (see Party Center 1976/1988b, 1976/1988a). By 1977, the lack of traction had been somewhat addressed by the inauguration of a new tractor factory in Mongkol Borey and the importation of heavy agricultural equipment from Japan (Twining 1989). The CPK's mandate to introduce high-yielding varieties (HYVs) of rice may have negatively impacted production in some areas. Informants from the North and Central Zones reported that agriculture deteriorated because CPK leaders did not listen to farmers with local expertise. As a result, the seed that was used was not suitable for local soil and water conditions (Nesbitt 1997a; Vickery 2000). This story—of centrally mandated agronomy displacing local knowledge—is repeated elsewhere (Helmers 1997; Javier 1997). It is claimed that loss of production during the civil war, combined with the switch to HYVs under the CPK, led to the complete loss of many traditional rice varieties; in particular, breeds of floating rice which were not favored by the CPK (Javier 1997).

Spatial Variations

Deaths from starvation and exhaustion had two principle characteristics. First, peak death tolls occurred shortly after the evacuation. Most of these victims were new people already weakened by malnutrition over the previous weeks and months. New people were also the most likely to be forced into strenuous labor, shelter under harsh conditions, and be subject to the most severe treatment.

Second, starvation deaths that occurred well after the initial mass migration can be attributed to local variations in production and the governance of consumption. The partial autonomy granted to districts and subdistricts created a political space in which leaders could exert profound influence over bodily survival. "Such extreme differences among contiguous units at that low level seem to have resulted from the personalities and attitudes of the village cadres rather than from factional divergence on policy" (Vickery 2000, 125). The attitudes exhibited by Zonal CPK cadre were often shaped by the pre-1975 history of the zone. For example, during the civil war, the people of the Southwest and East Zones harbored the greatest sympathy and support for the Khmer Rouge. Under the CPK, the cadre in these zones were considered "benign," food was plentiful, and yields were high despite these areas being the most heavily bombed during the war (Vickery 2000, 83). The death toll from starvation in the Southwest and East was low compared to the Northwest Zone which remained in Republican hands until the last days of the war. In the Northwest, cadre had a reputation for brutality, food rations were severely restricted, and production rarely met CPK quotas, despite this agricultural land being generally untouched by war (Vickery 2000).

Not only did variations in governing style between administrative units cause differences in death toll, variations *within* a given unit made some lives more precarious than others. In areas with a preponderance of base people, conditions were generally better than areas that received mostly urban evacuees. In some of the most well-fed and sheltered parts of the East Zone, urban evacuees arriving in base villages in 1975 were given an "introductory period" to help them adjust to hard agricultural labor, followed by two days rest (Vickery 2000, 134). Eyewitness accounts generally report that food was sufficient, soldiers were helpful, and new people "were allowed to set their own pace to get used to the work" (Vickery 2000, 134). Elsewhere, particularly the Northwest Zone, many labor units were comprised entirely of evacuees under the command of former Khmer Rouge soldiers. Executions and other violent excesses were common wherever large numbers of new people were assembled: these work units were also the most likely to be directed into forest clearing and dam construction, tasks associated with the hardest physical labor and the strictest rations.

At the cooperative level, administrative autonomy encouraged some leaders to falsify production reports. In some cases, leaders faked production statistics to prevent food from leaving the cooperative and increase what was available for their own people. In other cases, "zonal, regional, or cooperative authorities, afraid to admit they had failed to meet their quota, robbed their people of food rice to provide [Party Central] with a surplus based on a 3-ton-per-hectare calculation" (Vickery 2000, 157). In either case, falsification of production reports was a risky proposition. In 1977 and 1978, the highly productive East Zone chose not to send any rice to Party Center. Ever since the civil war, cadre in the East had demonstrated significant political influence with the Central Committee, a fact that may have emboldened them to push back against the Party's production quotas. In 1978, this favorable status appears to have ended: the Party Center initiated a purge of East Zone cadre that killed over 100,000 people.

According to the STV, it was the paucity of the universal ration that killed Cambodians. This is only partially true. For some, the food they received under the ration was insufficient for the labor they were forced to perform. For others, food was plentiful. Indeed, it was not the *universality* of the ration— but its *inconsistency*—that killed. For base people, assignment to agricultural cooperatives in the Southwest, East, or Kratie Special Region 505 often provided the best outcomes. For urban evacuees, ideal conditions could be found in cooperatives with a high ratio of base to new people, little class animosity, and productive agriculture. In this regard, Vickery (2000, 99) gives the example of Koh Thom (Southwest Zone), where new people shared homes with peasants and worked "under cadres who were local people." Worst off were those new people tasked with building dams or digging canals, in units filled with other urban evacuees and placed under the command of former Khmer Rouge soldiers. In Pursat (Northwest Zone), the common ration was half a can (125 grams) but was sometimes cut to one can for every six people. One survivor, who was "semi-permanently on burial detail" reported frequent cannibalism and noted that "most deaths were from hunger and illness rather than execution" (Vickery 2000, 117).

Final Days of the CPK

Beginning in 1977, death from starvation began to give way to death from execution. CPK documents and propaganda from 1976 on reveal a deep concern with the threat posed by enemies within the Party, often in alliance with Vietnamese or other foreign governments. The national security apparatus (*Santebal*) was tasked with identifying—and often inventing—such enemies and making examples of them through torture and execution (DeFalco 2013). Workers and cadre alike were incarcerated, forced into confessions, or simply killed for "crimes" ranging from stealing food to treason (Tyner and Rice 2015). Between 1977 and 1979, the Party Center initiated numerous large purges. In 1977, high-level cadre in the Northwest Zone were executed and replaced with leaders from the Southwest. In 1978, a major purge was conducted in the West Zone—the cadre that remained were later moved to the Northwest where they conducted a brutal crackdown (Vickery 2000).

On December 22, 1978, Vietnamese forces crossed into southwestern Cambodia and met only minor resistance. On January 7, 1979, after heavy bombardment of the city, Phnom Penh was liberated from the Khmer Rouge. The retreating forces of the CPK destroyed agricultural infrastructure and set fire to granaries already stocked with the 1978 harvest—acts of brutality that would initiate another phase of mass starvation in 1979 and 1980 (Kiernan 2002).

A report published by the Finnish Inquiry Commission in December 1982 put the total death toll under the Khmer Rouge at one million, but noted that depending on changes in the birth rate between 1970 and 1979, the figure could be closer to two million (Slocomb 2010). The CIA claimed that as of January 1979, 1.2

million Cambodians had been killed, while the Vietnamese government and the newly formed People's Republic of Kampuchea put the death toll at three million. Today, the widely accepted figure corresponds to the Finnish report at 1–2 million.

Food Provisioning Failure under the CPK

The onset of Cambodia's second food provisioning failure began at the apex of its first. By April 1975, Cambodians were starving in the streets of Phnom Penh, a city kept alive only by daily flights of aid. In the countryside, bunded fields lay broken and abandoned—a once-impressive agricultural system knocked unconscious by five years of bombardment and civil war. Hundreds were dying of malnutrition each day in the streets of the capital, many of them children. Contagious but preventable diseases were cutting down the weak and impoverished. At first, the urban poor could not afford the rice, and then there was no rice. Families began making decisions about who would be left to die.

When the war ended on April 17, the Khmer Rouge held in their hands a desperate urban population and a broken economy. There was no food stockpiled in Phnom Penh, and transportation of supplies into and out of the capital was hindered by damaged infrastructure and lack of fuel. As they had at times during the war, rebel soldiers forced urban residents to evacuate to the countryside, an arduous exodus during which thousands died. Pol Pot and the new leaders of Democratic Kampuchea imposed a strict food ration and abolished currency and private property. Former government officials and soldiers, doctors, teachers, and academics were executed.

Over the next few weeks and months, the population of the country was organized into communes and collectives. This workforce was mobilized to cultivate rice, build irrigation infrastructure, and clear land for agriculture. The Party organized units by labor capacity, economic sector, and base/new status. The territory of the country was divided into a nested hierarchy of zones, regions, districts, cooperatives, communes, and villages, each governed by a triumvirate responsible for wide-ranging decisions affecting subordinate units. All rice grown on Cambodian soil became state property with surplus production delivered up the hierarchy. At the top of the pyramid, the state exported this surplus to acquire the foreign exchange necessary to acquire the capital to expand agricultural and industrial production. It is here, from within the CPK's organization of food production and consumption, that Cambodia's second food provisioning failure emerged.

Material Deficiencies of Production

Lack of documentary evidence makes it difficult to determine the total amount of rice produced between 1975 and 1979. Without this total, it is impossible to accurately determine yield. But from the data that is available, it appears that rice production and yields under the CPK rebounded from the war years and may have met or exceeded totals set during the 1960s. Led by both extensification and irrigation-enabled intensification, the CPK began to implement a program to rescue and rebuild agriculture using the best advice of Western development agencies. Given the condition of food production in 1975, the fact that these efforts succeeded at all is noteworthy.

That said, it is likely the CPK could have produced more rice had planners been able to overcome several material deficiencies originating from the first provisioning crisis. As a consequence of the war, production was limited by a lack of draft animals, the loss of technical inputs to production (e.g., improved seed, chemical fertilizer, tractors, and processing equipment), and land made hazardous by antipersonnel mines and unexploded bombs. The loss of oxen and buffalo increased the human labor inputs required during field preparation and reduced the amount of manure available for fertilizer.

It is difficult to establish the effect of land mines and UXO on rice production. In those parts of the country that received the heaviest bombardment (Southwest, East, and Northeast Zones), the dangers posed by UXO could have kept some agricultural land out of production and placed limits on extensification. The CPK may have been aware of this danger: according to the Four-Year Plan, the targets for land extensification in the most heavily bombed zones have the lowest percentage growth, while in the least-bombed zones (Northwest and North), land extensification goals are the highest. To be sure, this variation may have more to do with expected surpluses of land and labor in each zone than the hazards posed by explosives.

By late 1978, despite the appalling conditions of production inherited by the CPK, the country had succeeded in growing a substantial amount of rice. It is unclear whether the Party could have ever achieved the long-term objectives of the economic plan—the Vietnamese invasion brought an end to the experiment before any of the long-term objectives could be realized. In the meantime, perhaps half of the 1–2 million that died under the CPK succumbed to starvation or other causes related to malnutrition.[16] Contrary to the STV, it seems unlikely that FAD is sufficient to explain this mortality; for that, it is necessary to outline the institutional deficiencies around rice consumption.

Institutional Deficiencies

Survivor accounts from the Central and North Zones suggest that leaders in these areas made cultivation decisions without consideration for local knowledge and environmental variation. Cadre were reported to have mandated the use of new HYVs over traditional varieties well suited to local conditions, a decision that may have negatively impacted production. But the consequences of such institutional impacts on production were dwarfed by the institutional impacts on consumption.

More than either the Hawaiian or Madagascar crises, this famine was a case of *partial* food system failure: some districts were sufficiently fed while others starved. Rice distribution under the spatial hierarchy was intended to balance variations in production by distributing rice from surplus-producing areas to regions that had a shortfall. But these policies were not consistently followed. Some leaders found ways to hold back rice from delivery to Party Center to provide sufficient food for local workers. In some cases, village and cooperative leaders falsified production reports to show that harvests had not met the mandated quota. Elsewhere, fear of disappointing the Party drove leaders to inflate production reports and deliver the expected quota even when the harvest was insufficient. In these locales, it was workers that paid the price: severe cuts to the daily ration, like those in the Northwest Zone, eventually pushed already weakened laborers to the brink of death.

The political landscape that encouraged both over- and underreporting of production was shaped by what Mertha (2014, 35) refers to as "the hideous mixture of top-down pressure and extreme decentralized authority." The policy of decentralization—letting communes and cooperatives decide the amount of rice that would be delivered to the Party Center—helped bolster leaders with political capital and motivation to withhold rice. In areas with strong historical support for the Khmer Rouge (like the Southwest and East Zones), leaders withheld sizeable portions of productive harvests. Long-standing ties with high-ranking cadre coupled with a high percentage of base people may have allowed these areas to push back against production quotas for some time without incurring the wrath of central leadership.[17] Despite the rhetoric of communal work for the common good, decentralization forced low-level administrative units into competition for limited material resources and political capital. Successful units were those whose leaders could secure the basic needs of workers, curry the favor of high-ranking officials, and produce sufficient rice to feed the population and meet the quota. Units that failed to do this suffered.

Running crosscut to the policy of decentralization was a strict hierarchy that placed extraordinary power in the central government. Rice-production quotas and disbursement amounts were established by the central committee and passed down the spatial hierarchy. *Santebal*, the national security apparatus tasked with rooting out internal enemies of the state, was directed by the Party Center and made frequent examples of zone and region leaders that did not satisfy the demands of the Party. With the growing threat of internal purges, district, commune, and cooperative leaders were forced to make decisions under extreme duress. The fear of reprisal may have pushed some leaders to deliver more rice to Party Center than the unit could afford, just to satisfy the quota. Still other leaders may have used the demands of the quota as justification to severely cut the ration, particularly for new people (Vickery 2000). As observed in other facets of CPK policy, the central committee may have been inclined to look the other way when such institutional abuse impacted an undesirable class. Workers in these areas found themselves surrounded by rice, but with no more rice to eat.

State Capitalism and Rice-as-Wage

It is difficult to overstress the importance of rice to Cambodia and the CPK. Rice provided 75 percent of the calories needed to keep the population alive, and 93 percent of the foreign exchange keeping the CPK in power. In 1969, rice cultivation took up 63 percent of all arable land and employed nearly 80 percent of the workforce. The taxation and export of rice was the basis for government revenue before and after independence, and its collapse in the 1970s was the basis for mass starvation under Lon Nol. Before the Khmer Rouge victory, rice was Cambodia's most important import; afterwards, it was the country's most important export. And in April 1975, rice became something else entirely: the wage exchanged for human labor.

Partial food system failures are frequently associated with markets. Mike Davis's (2002) analysis of 19th century Indian famines demonstrates how late-colonial market reforms exacerbated production crises. With the onset of crop failure and decreasing supply, rising prices at wheat markets within the region moved grain away from poor consumers and toward wealthy ones, while higher prices on international markets drew food away from the region as a whole. The new rail system built by the British exacerbated the crisis by lowering the cost of transport, decreasing the time to market, and drawing more regions into competition.

At first glance, it appears that starvation under the CPK occurred in the *absence* of markets; after all, domestic markets had been effectively abolished along with currency and private property. This coincidence makes it tempting to assume causation; that is, the elimination of markets, in whole or in part, led to famine. In fact, such an assumption dovetails with elements of the STV that characterize the CPK as a totalitarian communist regime. But this analysis finds a more complex story. The institutional failures that led to mass starvation were propelled, not by the regime's dedication to communism, but by its reliance on state *capitalism*.

With the elimination of private property and the end of labor markets, the CPK captured the means of production and forced all Cambodians to become employees of the state. Through the ration, rice became the wage paid for labor, but unlike other historical economies in which rice served as currency (cf. Vergouwen 1964; Hanks 1992; Bray 1994), without domestic markets, rice could not be exchanged. If the CPK had been truly autarkic—like the STV claims—and eschewed all forms of foreign exchange, all rice produced would have been directed to domestic consumption. In other words, Cambodia would have become a *subsistence state*. Surplus production could have been stored and redistributed and, so long as harvests were sufficient, a ration would not have been necessary. The value of a ton of rice would have been its use value—that is, its ability to feed Cambodian bodies.

But under state capitalism, the foreign sale of rice became the basis for economic growth, and a ration was imposed to ensure healthy state profits. In that moment, rice acquired the ability to provide capital for the state, and with it, *exchange value*. A ton of rice became equivalent in value to a volume of diesel fuel, a quantity of ploughs, and a fraction of an armored vehicle. Of course, rice was still needed to feed the population, a task that now had an *opportunity cost*. The decision to feed a worker was simultaneously a decision to forgo the import of something needed by the state.

In this way, rice became essential to both worker consumption and state production, a fact made obvious in the language of the CPK's plans: rice was the only component of the ration for which quantities were discretely specified. Whereas the plan simply noted that each worker was to receive "two side dishes" and a "dessert" every two-to-three days, the allotment of rice was specified by physical volume (see Party Center 1976/1988b, 111). Unlike other parts of the plan that allocated increases in capital to hospitals and medicine over four years, the ration was fixed. After all, the quantity of rice consumed by the population had to be known and controlled if export surpluses were to be maintained and levels of foreign exchange increased. The consequence of rice becoming the national wage was that nutrition became a matter of state accounting: every excess grain of rice eaten by Cambodians was capital lost to the country.

It is here that the economic logic of "letting some die so to save others" is most clearly realized. The CPK used rice surpluses to purchase everything from factory parts to fertilizer—the capital base for economic growth. Labor-saving agricultural inputs like tractors, herbicides, and rice mills could only be acquired because of a ration that promoted rice surpluses. If the ration was too strict and too many workers died, production would drop and the surplus would disappear. If the ration was too lax, not enough rice would be left for export. At a given point—which the CPK specified as three cans per day (750 grams)—the ration was deemed sufficient to keep most workers alive and still leave a profitable surplus.

The key point is that the ration did not need to keep everyone alive: if the inputs purchased with the surplus were labor-saving, the loss of some workers would not immediately impact the economy. In fact, so long as labor efficiency increased faster than the loss of labor through death, the CPK could let workers die and still grow the surplus. And if those that succumbed to starvation were members of a class broadly despised by cadre members, economic efficiencies and cultural reform could proceed hand in hand.

As far back as the French Protectorate, rice was the lifeblood of the state economy. Up until 1975, administrations repeated the same pattern of purchasing rice from farmers to sell on international markets. Each government had its own variation on the same theme, from the laissez-faire days of French "dual economy" to the military-enforced extractions of OROC and SONEXIM. But the underlying relations of production—and the profit motive of the state—remained the same: pay local producers as low a price as possible and sell as high as possible.

Meanwhile, farming households ate the rice they produced and sold the surplus to the government. When environmental and labor conditions enabled harvests to meet the nutritional needs of the household, survival was generally assured. The sale of rice to the government brought monetary income to pay debts and taxes, purchase inputs to production, and acquire supplemental food and household goods. When harvests did not provide sufficient surplus to pay taxes or purchase inputs, farmers took out loans. Over time, indebtedness became an economic purgatory for many rural smallholders.

When the Khmer Rouge took over in 1975, many of these fundamental relations remained the same. As before, the state sought to export rice for profit. To do this, the CPK needed a surplus, and to extract the surplus, it imposed a ration and directed the population into the production of rice and landesque capital. The combination of production quotas and the food ration enabled the state to quantify both profits and costs, aiding centralized planning and surveillance. Meanwhile, the profit motive dictated downward pressure on costs and improvements in overall efficiency—for example, the three-tons-per-hectare goal that bears the hallmark of previous administrations and Western development proposals. From the perspective of the state's space of production, little had changed in the half-century that spanned the French, Sihanouk, Lon Nol, and Pol Pot.

For farming households, the changes were more significant. Farmers became "workers": they still produced rice for the state but were no longer allowed to retain part of the harvest for personal subsistence. All rice became CPK property and, in exchange for labor, the state paid each worker a wage in the form of the ration. For some impoverished farmers in districts with good leadership, the reliability of the ration may have been an improvement over subsistence cultivation (Vickery 2000). At the same time, these new relations of production would have eliminated the burden of past debt: indeed, the notion of a monetary debt disappeared under the CPK. But for wealthier farmers and city-dwellers, forced labor and the rice ration would have severely impacted livelihoods.

For ordinary Cambodians, the vulnerability of household food provisioning before 1975 was a function of rainfall, the price of rice, and the demands of taxation. Failure to grow sufficient rice could result in household hunger, but more often resulted in spiraling indebtedness to lenders or punishment for failure to pay taxes. After 1975, vulnerability was a function of where one was situated in the spatial hierarchy and within the CPK's labor classification. The success or failure of a commune to produce sufficient rice could determine local hunger, but more often, survival depended on the political capital and personal temperament of local leaders. The absolute consequences for ordinary Cambodians certainly deteriorated with the CPK: indebtedness and impoverishment under Sihanouk was still better than death from starvation under Pol Pot. But the presence of the trap and its organization around the poor remained unchanged.

The reorganization of Cambodia's food provisioning was not a fundamental rearrangement of the relations of production: contrary to both the STV and Party propaganda, the CPK did not usher in a classless society in which state profits were equally shared. Instead, the Cambodian revolution preserved historical forms of expropriation—it merely changed who reaped the rewards (table 5). From the early 20th century until 1970, rice flowed out of Cambodia where it was sold to foreign buyers. The government and a growing urban merchant class collected the profits while poor peasants suffered under debt and military crackdowns. Between 1970 and 1975, rice flowed *into* the Republic of Kampuchea under PL-480 where it was sold to the poor in the name of food aid. The Lon Nol government and urban elites reaped the profits while the urban poor starved under food markets designed to extract public wealth. Finally, between 1975 and 1979, rice once again flowed out of Cambodia under export contracts. The profits were amassed by the state and distributed through the spatial hierarchy. But this distribution was uneven, following contours of power established years earlier during the civil war.

In each phase, the economy was organized in a way that trapped the poor and powerless in debt, malnutrition, or both. Such "poverty traps" (Field and Piachaud 1971) have been a common way for Western development agencies to explain lagging growth in postcolonial economies (see chapter 4). In fact, development organizations at the time proposed agriculture-led economic take-off as a way to *break* the trap: with improvements in farm productivity and growth in agricultural exports, the state could amass capital for reinvestment in industry, eventually pushing labor out of agriculture and into manufacturing. Recognizing how the poverty trap had exploited peasants and the urban poor throughout the 20th century, it is no surprise that the CPK chose this solution. The irony is that such a distinctly Western, modernist, and technocratic strategy would be adopted by a state that proclaimed itself the enemy of such values.

Conclusions: The Economic Roots of Famine

During the Cambodian civil war and subsequent reconstruction, the country's food provisioning system experienced two major, interconnected failures. Between 1970 and 1975, as the war and U.S. bombardment drove rural households away from homes and fields, the system experienced a severe decline in absolute food availability propelled by the loss of farm labor and the destruction of agricultural capital. By 1974, traditional interdependencies between landholders and labor, combined with the complex timing of rice planting and harvesting, helped push production declines into full-scale collapse. Unable to supply food to the millions of refugees crowded into Phnom Penh and other urban centers, the Lon Nol government began to depend increasingly on U.S. aid. But the food aid that arrived between 1972 and 1975 under the PL-480 program came with a stipulation: it had to be sold. Indeed, the intent behind the PL-480 program was to extract revenue for Lon Nol's administration. It extracted this wealth from the most desperate: those urban poor who did not qualify for refugee status and lacked the political capital to get help through other means. For the powerful, food aid created an opportunity to accumulate wealth through hoarding and black market sales.

With the capture of Phnom Penh in April 1975, the Khmer Rouge ended the Lon Nol regime and began the transformation of Cambodia's economy. The CPK abolished all private property and currency, imposed a strict food ration, evacuated the urban population into the countryside, and redirected Cambodian labor

---

Table 5. The evolution of capital accumulation between French Protectorate and CPK periods.

Period	Sources of surplus value	Accumulators of capital	Black market beneficiaries
Colonial govt up to 1954	Rural rice producers	State, merchant class, urban elite	Producers and local Cambodian officials
Sihanouk 1954–70	Rural rice producers	State, merchant class, urban elite	Producers, but subject to severe penalties
Lon Nol 1970–75[1]	Urban poor	Military, high-ranking government officials, urban elite	Military and high-ranking government officials
CPK 1975–79	All workers, but especially new people	High-ranking cadre, influential leaders[2]	Local cadre, but subject to severe penalties

[1]This period witnessed the shift from rural rice production to dependence on U.S. aid.

[2]This capital belonged to the state, but its material realization was limited to CPK elite.

---

toward agricultural production. These actions were intended to serve two purposes: to satisfy the immediate dietary needs of a starving population, and to reorganize Cambodian society and economy around a vision of state capitalism. The result was a second provisioning failure compounded by the material aftermath of the first. This time, the imperative of foreign exchange put downward pressure on food access. Units of urban evacuees, usually tasked with building irrigation infrastructure, suffered brutal cuts to the daily ration. With insufficient nutrition and exposure to unrelenting physical demands, hundreds of thousands succumbed to starvation. As the CPK became increasingly wary of internal and external enemies, the Party embarked on a series of brutal purges. By the time Vietnamese forces captured Phnom Penh in 1979, 1.7 million Cambodians had died.

Many of those victims were executed by the CPK. But for those that died from starvation, it is impossible to know if their circumstances would have improved under different policies. What would have happened if the CPK had not abolished private property, but allowed peasants to retain ownership of fields and animals, as the Khmer Rouge had debated prior to 1973? What if the CPK had been more autarkic, temporarily restricted exports of rice, and allowed the entire harvest to be directed to local consumption? An argument could be made in either case that food provisioning would have improved, though it is impossible to know for sure.

By comparison, it is easier to imagine what would have happened if the United States had not bombed Cambodia between 1965–1973. Aerial bombardment pushed many impoverished Cambodians—already critical of Lon Nol's coziness with the West—into the arms of the Khmer Rouge. With each B-52 sortie, the United States fed the communists even as it starved ordinary Cambodians. The bombardment helped justify the Khmer Rouge, the Khmer Rouge justified Lon Nol's civil war, the war justified PL-480 aid, and the influx of aid justified the feeding frenzy of corruption. In this way, the reactive sequence initiated by U.S. expansion of the Vietnam War can be followed directly to Phnom Penh's child victims. When asked about the mounting pressure on aid workers in March 1975, Dr. Penuy Key (quoted in Leslie 1975) lamented, "The greatest pediatrician would be the man who is able to stop the war." By then, of course, American eyes and ears had closed. Thirteen days after the Khmer Rouge capture of Phnom Penh, Saigon fell to North Vietnamese and Việt Cộng forces.

Contrary to the STV, the ensuing revolution was not total. The form of state capitalism implemented by the CPK retained Cambodia's rice export orientation and adopted the best guidance of Western aid agencies. By dangling the promise of autonomy to low-level administrators—and then executing those leaders who failed to cooperate—the CPK reproduced long-standing patterns of corruption and favor-seeking. Most importantly, the elimination of currency made rice the national wage. As both the state's source of income and the body's source of nourishment, rice became the measure of labor's value to the state. The distribution of rice adhered to the arrangements of political power in the CPK's spatial hierarchy, and the withholding of rice from the dying reflected economic expediency. Through the valuation and selective exchange of rice, genocide revealed its economic roots. It is hard to die from hunger, but when the food you eat is literally state property, whether you live or die is a question of fiscal responsibility.

———————

Today, Cambodia continues to work through the legacies of war and social upheaval from the 1970s: slow economic growth, low agricultural yields, and landscapes made deadly by slumbering bombs and mines. As if these challenges were insufficient, in May 2017, the U.S. government insisted that Cambodia pay back $500 million in food loans from the 1970–75 war, an amount that includes $230 million in accrued interest (National Public Radio 2017; Strangio 2017). In response, the Cambodian government has noted the obvious irony—the nation that bombed Cambodia into civil war and famine now wants to be reimbursed for the cost of causing chaos. Embassy spokesperson Jay Raman defended the State Department noting that it "lacks the legal authority to write off debts for countries that are able but unwilling to pay," admitting—in essence—that it is an accounting problem (National Public Radio 2017). It bears noting that for the Khmer Rouge, the value of life and death were a matter of state finances. Once again, it seems they were following the lead of the West. Maybe the child survivors of PL-480 can take cold comfort in the knowledge that someone in the State Department still remembers their suffering.

CHAPTER 4

Famine in the Remaking: The Structure of Food System Failure

In 1990, as the geopolitical edifices of the Cold War began to crumble and Western governments proclaimed the triumph of free markets, one Caribbean nation—unaccustomed to widespread hunger—found itself on the brink of crisis. Cuba, a once-crucial player in U.S.-Soviet power games, was forced to confront the possibility of mass starvation despite a world-class public health system. The crisis emerged within a modern, highly industrialized agricultural system: between 1960 and 1989, Cuban food production took full advantage of petrochemical fertilizers, pesticides, improved seeds, technical expertise, mechanization, and processing equipment. These inputs were acquired from the Soviet Union and other Soviet Bloc states at heavily subsidized prices, driving out traditional farming practices and encouraging large-scale monocultures under central planning and shared infrastructure. In fact, by 1989, Cuban farms were using more tractors and applying more fertilizer per hectare than the United States, and 25 percent of all cropland was under dedicated irrigation (Wright 2012). Ninety percent of all chemical inputs and 57 percent of all food was imported, purchased in exchange for tropical products. Communist trading partners subsidized the economy by paying a premium for Cuban goods—in the case of sugar, the Soviet Union paid Cuba over five times the global market price (Wright 2012).

The collapse of the Soviet Union in 1989 sent Cuban food provisioning into steep decline. No longer able to receive subsidized prices, sugar producers were forced to compete on the global market at the precise moment when market prices collapsed. The loss of a primary trading partner and the ongoing American embargo strangled the country's access to fossil fuels: the supply of gasoline was cut by 75 percent and diesel by 45 percent. Chemical inputs to agriculture were slashed by 80 percent and food imports were cut in half. The impact on public health was immediate and dramatic as average caloric intake for the population dropped by 30 percent (PNAN 1994; Rosset and Moore 1997). Lacking a strong industrial base and hampered by shortages of fuel and electricity, economic recovery looked bleak.

Faced with the specter of famine, Cuban leadership imposed a state of emergency known as the "Special Period" (Piercy, Granger, and Goodier 2010). The government mobilized scientists and agronomists to develop and scale up production of organic (nonpetroleum) fertilizers and pesticides. Smallholders that had been pushed to the economic and geographical fringes by government-run farms were brought back into the mainstream to contribute agronomic knowledge and heirloom seeds (Rosset et al. 2011). With the help of domestic and foreign experts and extension workers, farms switched from petroleum dependency to widespread use of biological pesticides and fertilizers, pest-resistant crops, intercropping, cover cropping, and other organic best practices (Wright 2012). Cropland once owned and managed by the state was given to smallholders under usufruct rights, with the proviso that farmers must practice organic cultivation. A similar restructuring of land rights occurred in Cuba's cities, where the government decreed that residents could cultivate unused urban land "in perpetuity and free from taxes" (Wright 2012, 5). By 1998, the capital, Havana, had 26,000 urban gardens producing over half a million tons of fruits and vegetables.

The sweeping changes enacted by Cuban leaders during the Special Period altered the course of the crisis and averted mass starvation. Today, proponents of organic food production point to Cuba's agroecological revolution as a success story with broad application in other industrial food systems facing natural resource stress and rising petroleum prices (see Wright 2012). Though the long-term costs and benefits of Cuba's dramatic response to crisis have yet to be realized and analyzed, the short-term benefits of restructuring—and the demonstrated vulnerability of industrial agriculture—have attracted sustained attention from food system scholars (cf. Koc and Dahlberg 1999; Nelson et al. 2008; Altieri and Toledo 2011; Altieri, Funes-Monzote, and Petersen 2012).

As the Cuban experience demonstrates, it is not reorganization per se that causes famine. In fact, on the basis of analyses like Rosset et al. (2011) and Wright (2012), one might convincingly argue that reorganization during Cuba's Special Period was essential to *preventing* starvation. If some reorganizations precipitate collapse and others avert it, the essential question for policy makers becomes distinguishing one from the other. What types of reorganization increase vulnerability to hunger and what types build resilience? What socioecological processes drive these changes, and how do variations in historical and geographical context influence these mechanisms? What interactions take place between mechanisms over space and time? Finally, what are the likely trajectories, indicators of future failure, and points of intervention?

In the following sections, I address these questions through a comparison of the Hawaii, Madagascar, and Cambodia case studies. The chapter begins with a brief recap of the primary causal mechanisms identified in each case: the conjunctures, processes, traps, and cycles of feedback that precipitated food system failure. On this basis, I propose two overlapping frameworks for analyzing famine genesis: a conceptual scheme for understanding the interaction of mechanisms across space and time, and a framework for categorizing causal mechanisms into five classes. Subsequent sections describe these classes, the apparent interactions between mechanisms, and the trajectories for socioecological response. The chapter concludes with a discussion of new crisis indicators for structural vulnerability, correspondence with existing research on socioecological traps, and reflections on individual responsibility and the reorganization of contemporary food systems.

Primary Mechanisms by Case

Hawaii

Hawaii's sandalwood famines emerged within a feudal society divided between powerful chiefs and subsistence producers. By the early 1800s, Hawaii was on the cusp of dramatic social and environmental change as its resources and strategic location made it the target of Western political and business interests. In the years leading up to the crisis, the islands experienced several important conjunctures: population decline, rapid expansion of the sandalwood trade, and growth in conspicuous consumption among the chiefly class. The decline of traditional moral economies and territorial practices—under the *kapu* and *ahupua'a* systems—eliminated otherwise regulating influences. As chiefs directed labor away from cultivation and toward sandalwood extraction, several cycles of positive feedback may have been initiated. With increased fallowing of household fields, the agricultural mosaic of dryfield cultivation would have become fragmented, decreasing pest resistance and reducing the effectiveness of pollinators. As commoners died from starvation, exposure, and European diseases, Hawaii's technically sophisticated dryfield systems would have suffered from the loss of agricultural knowledge. And with the depletion of sandalwood trees, laborers were forced to travel further into the interior to find timber, taking them away from agricultural production for longer periods and exposing weakened bodies to cold and wet conditions at high elevation.

As the crisis emerged, two key decisions on the part of Hawaiian leadership stand out. First, Liholiho's decision to end kapu eliminated many of the traditional practices that bound chiefs to commoners, including customary forms of welfare and food relief in times of crisis. Second, the imposition of a tax requiring each person to pay chiefs a set quantity of sandalwood pitted households against each other in competition for the last stands of timber. These decisions strained Hawaii's traditional patterns of horizontal (household-to-household) and vertical (chief-to-commoner) resource sharing. By the time dryfield production collapsed, support networks that had historically offered relief were compromised.

Meanwhile, the rapid adoption of market practices and Western luxuries by chiefs reinforced social and environmental perceptions among the ruling class that justified exploitation of ordinary Hawaiians. Consumer culture, fueled by the Pacific Trade, dovetailed with long-standing chiefly perceptions of class power and the inferiority of commoners. Indeed, sandalwood extraction translated the logic of capitalism into new forms of social and environmental exploitation—Hawaiian feudalism evolved into an economy based on slave labor and directed toward production for foreign exchange.

Madagascar

Madagascar's Cactus War pitted cactus pastoralists in the island's deep South against French military expansion, Social Policy, and *mission civilisatrice*. After its introduction in the mid-1700s, *raketa* (prickly pear) was readily adopted by Antandroy and Mahafale pastoralists throughout the arid South as cattle fodder, human food, crop protection, and village defense. Raketa's extraordinary water content and its proliferation in the arid environment proved particularly beneficial for local producers who readily embraced the new plant into existing pastoral practices. The effectiveness of cactus thickets in deterring French incursion encouraged pastoralists to fortify their settlements with these living ramparts as external pressures mounted. By 1900, raketa had spread throughout the deep South and pushed out native fodder. Meanwhile, the colonial government grew increasingly frustrated with the lack of "progress" in Southern districts: governors dreamed of new farmland and sisal plantations, while powerful colons demanded cheap local labor. By the 1920s, blame for the impasse was placed squarely on raketa. In 1924, a French scientist released cochineal into the South, destroying nearly all the raketa and precipitating the deaths of thousands of cattle and people.

Before and after the release of cochineal, several cycles of feedback were initiated. The centuries-long proliferation of cactus leading up to 1924 led to an increase in the pastoral population, fueling French appetites for plantation labor and increasing the size of the vulnerable population. As French interventions increased, locals retreated further behind the cactus. After the release of cochineal, the density of cactus exacerbated the crisis as the wind-borne plague found abundant food wherever it alighted. The enormous spatial extent of the infestation meant that traditional patterns of migration might not have provided escape. Instead, transhumance increased resource demands in some locales like Tsihombe. The speed of destruction may have prevented some otherwise successful adaptations (like conversion to alternative fodder sources) while dependence on cactus for water would have pushed many victims toward death from dehydration.

Key decisions by the colonial government exacerbated these cycles of feedback.

Gallieni's "oil-stain" approach in the South involved maintaining control of watering holes and holding the cattle of disobedient herders for ransom. Such interventions frustrated pastoral communities, led to increased resistance, and justified local commitment to raketa. Most importantly, the decision to release cochineal—itself a product of increasingly entrenched socioecological perceptions—set the collapse in motion.

Cambodia

Cambodia's food system failure—initiated by civil war and U.S. bombardment in the early 1970s—was predicated on a long-standing pattern of agricultural exploitation for state profit. Since the colonial period, rice was grown by rural smallholders who sold their surplus and paid tax to the government. The exported rice was used to import Western luxuries and support increasingly extravagant urban lifestyles for Cambodia's elite. Between independence in 1953 and the coup in 1970, rural indebtedness grew, as did disruptions to production caused by the Vietnam War. Following the coup, increased warfare and aerial bombardment destroyed most rural rice production and increased the state's dependence on foreign aid. As refugees flooded the cities, American assistance provided a mechanism for the government to expropriate enormous wealth from its own population, both legally (through the logic of PL-480) and illegally (through hoarding and black markets).

The initial production decline was propelled by several cycles of feedback. In the 1960s, falling farmgate prices for rice pushed many producers to sell their produce on the black market. In response, the government made an example of "criminal" farmers through brutal crackdowns and executions, a decision that did as much to drive peasants into the arms of the Khmer Rouge as it did to curb the trade. Declining rice production and farmer migration, initiated by warfare, led to the loss of traction animals and a breakdown of collective labor arrangements. In the short run, these processes exacerbated the severity of the food shortage; in the longer term, the lack of traction animals continued to impact Cambodian rice production well into the 1980s.

Under the CPK, production rebounded, but uneven and inconsistent application of the food ration—a function of the interaction between local autonomy and centralized control—produced considerable variations in outcome. Survival became a question of rice production, social class, and the personality of local leaders. Base people who worked in communes associated with their former villages often received sufficient food, while new people forced into irrigation projects under oppressive leaders were the most likely to die. Whereas progressive marginalization of peasants under the French and Sihanouk led to grinding indebtedness and destitution, marginalization under the CPK could result in starvation or execution.

As in Hawaii and Madagascar, socioenvironmental perceptions worked to shape food system evolution (or lack thereof). In the colonial imagination, Cambodia was a rice-producing machine with little value beyond its ability to support the export-orientation of Cochinchina. Land reforms could be imposed and extraordinary tax rates levied because of the "docility" of the Cambodian people. This perception of Cambodia—as little more than a soggy rice field and its people as simple, uneducated peasants—remained influential long after independence and well beyond the country's borders. It helped justify later governments' expansion of taxation, helped Nixon justify aerial bombardment, explained the failure of U.S. strategists to understand the extent of the urban food crisis, and influenced the CPK's Four-Year Plan for the economy.

Phases and Causal Mechanisms

These three famines span 150 years of history and occupy different phases in the evolution of global capitalism. On the surface, the causal narratives of starvation in Hawaii, Madagascar, and Cambodia have little in common. But from a structural perspective, the events bear remarkable similarity in causal mechanisms, interactions between mechanisms, and stages of development.

Based on these case studies, famine evolution appears to fall into two, broad phases: formation and progression. In the *formation phase*, long-standing and large-scale conjunctures combine to establish the conditions necessary for food system failure. This may involve the steady deterioration of social or environmental protections, the depletion of necessary natural resources or landesque capital, or the emergence of dysfunctional institutions for food production or consumption. During the formation phase, policy decisions and other forms of intervention may successfully avert a crisis, but over time, the number of viable pathways quickly decreases.

The formation phase is followed by the *progression phase* during which these conjunctures begin to trigger sequences of generally short-lived and smaller-scale cycles of feedback. These cycles quickly transform local environmental and social conditions, often initiating multiple, overlapping resource crises. During the progression phase, options that were viable in the formation phase no longer work. Local adaptations switch from proactive to reactive, often contributing to feedback and accelerating the collapse. Once the progression phase has started, avoiding disaster becomes much more difficult.

Operating within and across these phases are five observed mechanisms: conjunctures, reactive sequences, decisions, exogenous stressors, and socioenvironmental imaginaries (fig. 8). *Conjunctures* are large-scale and slow-moving processes of social and environmental change that may span decades and are generally perceived by those experiencing them. These processes interact throughout both phases of crisis evolution: during the formation phase, conjunctures help establish the preconditions for food system failure. During the progression phase, conjunctures interact with other mechanisms in ways that may accelerate or slow the emergence of the crisis.

Operating at a more situated and context-specific scale, *reactive sequences* are short-lived interactions that rapidly transform local conditions through cycles of feedback. Often, these sequences involve clusters of actors and processes that stabilize the food system under normal conditions, but can accelerate collapse when

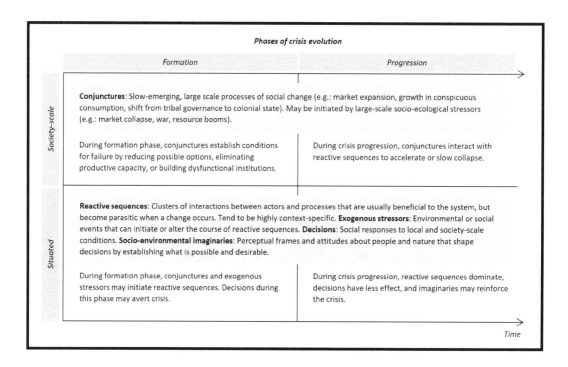

Figure 8. Matrix of scales and crisis phases.

disrupted. For example, communal labor-sharing arrangements in both Hawaii and Cambodia allowed farmers to plant and harvest more food than would be possible with the labor in each household alone. So long as sufficient surplus labor was available to complete the most demanding cultivation task, the production system was supported. However, when available labor dropped to the point where households could no longer plant enough to meet subsistence, the arrangement switched into positive feedback: households abandoned farming to seek other opportunities, further reducing the labor available to the community and accelerating production declines.

Decisions are choices made in response to local- and society-scale conditions. These may include legislative or policy measures (for example, the land reforms instituted by the French in Madagascar and Cambodia) or collective social responses (for example, the adoption and propagation of raketa by cactus pastoralists). Decisions occur throughout the evolution of a crisis: in the formation phase, decisions are often made without awareness of the impending failure and may initiate reactive sequences with positive or negative consequences; in the progression phase, decisions are often conscious attempts to avert or mitigate the now obvious, unfolding food crisis.

Exogenous stressors are environmental or social events, initiated outside of the food system, that impact the course of reactive sequences. Periodic drought, volcanic eruptions, market failures, and war invariably initiate reactive sequences, though such stressors may also alter the trajectory of reactive sequences or conjunctures already in progress. The impacts are articulated through context-dependent structural arrangements: before the loss of raketa, cactus pastoralists survived periodic drought by adjusting the timing of cattle migration and relying on cactus for food and water in the interim. With the loss of raketa, pastoral vulnerability to drought increased markedly.

Decisions and conjunctural processes shape—and are shaped by—*socioenvironmental imaginaries*: discursive frameworks for perceiving and understanding the role of humans, nonhumans, and the myriad "natures" between and within them (cf. Castree 2005; Cutter et al. 2008; Krüger et al. 2015). Like conjunctures, these imaginaries tend to persist, evolve slowly in response to changing conditions, and are readily reinforced through everyday practices. In both phases of crisis evolution, imaginaries play a critical role in shaping decisions by determining what actions are possible, justifiable, logical, and necessary (for example, the introduction of cochineal). At the same time, they determine what trajectories are impossible or beyond consideration (for example, establishing semiautonomy or dual economy in southern Madagascar).

Figure 9 is an idealized schematic representation of the five mechanisms and their interactions across scales and phases. In general, conjunctures influence crisis evolution through both phases while reactive sequences tend to dominate the progression phase. During the formation phase, socioenvironmental imaginaries influence the emergence of influential conjunctures at the scale of society (A). Over time, conjunctures establish many of the preconditions for failure, either directly or through interaction with other conjunctures (B). At a more situated and context-dependent scale, changing conditions introduce reactive sequences that quickly transform local conditions of production or consumption. These sequences may be initiated by exogenous stressors (C), conjunctures (D), or decisions (G). In the progression phase, reactive sequences are responsible for most of the transformations affecting the food system. Contemporaneous reactive sequences may combine in unexpected ways to accelerate or slow down crisis evolution (E).

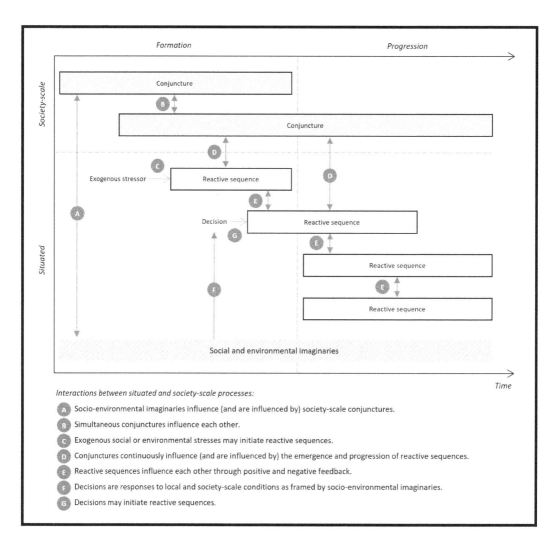

Figure 9. Overview of interactions between situated and society-scale processes across crisis phases.

Socioenvironmental imaginaries shape decisions in both phases by determining what actions are possible (F).

In Hawaii, the formation phase began with the discovery of sandalwood and the expansion of the Pacific Trade—approximately six years before the onset of the first food crisis and 15 years before the second crisis. As the first crisis began to unfold (1816–18), Kamehameha implemented a series of conservation measures designed to protect laborers and remaining timber. These measures temporarily averted the progression of the crisis, but the fundamental conjunctures influencing the food system (the sandalwood trade and growing foreign influence) remained in place. With the ascension of Liholiho and the end of the kapu system, several reactive sequences were initiated that quickly altered the mode of production: chiefs fell into debt through the conspicuous consumption of Western luxuries, conscription increasingly forced commoners into timber collection to help pay these debts, and agricultural production began to suffer through lack of labor.

At that point (early 1820s), crisis could have been averted through labor and environmental conservation policies (like those decreed by Kamehameha), through restrictions on trade, or through a redistribution of Pacific Trade profits back into food production. Instead, the monarchy imposed a sandalwood tax. On the basis of this decision, food system failure was essentially guaranteed, alternative paths disappeared, and the progression phase began. Several reactive sequences emerged to accelerate the crisis: the loss of labor fragmented the dryfield agricultural mosaic, landesque capital fell into disrepair, competition for timber threatened traditional kinship networks, and sandalwood depletion forced commoners away from home for longer periods and into harsh conditions.

In Madagascar, the formation phase began with the introduction of raketa by the French in 1769 and continued until the release of cochineal in 1924. During this time, the steady spread of cactus assisted—and was assisted by—growth in the population of pastoralists who adapted their practices to take advantage of raketa's extraordinary botanical properties. The cactus was an ideal partner for human settlement in the arid South, not just ecologically, but politically: raketa thickets protected villages from French soldiers and allowed herders to avoid French-controlled watering holes. In this way, colonial conjunctures during this period (for example, increased taxation, corvée conscription, and Social Policy) only *encouraged* local adoption of the cactus. By 1924, all the preconditions were in place for failure: the French had access to cochineal and motivation to use it, raketa was prolific, and the local population was entirely dependent on the cactus.

At that point, the French could have averted the impending crisis by not releasing cochineal: as the debates between Bâthie, Petit, and Decary attest, use of the insect to transform the South was not a fait accompli. The colony would have had to commit time and resources to undo the various preconditions established during the formation phase that made pastoralists vulnerability to cochineal—after all, by 1924 any introduction of the insect would have been destructive. But no serious efforts were undertaken in this regard. Instead, the release of cochineal, and the onset of the progression phase, made all other options impossible.

Several reactive sequences initiated by the release ensured the plague would run its course and precipitate widespread famine. First, the density of cactus thickets—a benefit for cactus pastoralists—ensured the wind-borne cochineal could find food wherever it alighted. Second, dependence on raketa for food, water, and shelter meant that its loss created overlapping resource crises for households. As cactus disappeared, laboring time had to be divided between locating fodder and watering holes for cows, finding sources of wild food and water for people, and keeping cows away from surviving crops, demands that quickly took a toll on bodily survival. This famine stands out with respect to the speed of collapse:

whereas the formation phase took over 150 years, the progression phase lasted a mere four.

In Cambodia, the beginning of the formation phase is less clear. On the one hand, the steady exploitation and growing indebtedness of farmers—key drivers of rural dissatisfaction—were firmly established before independence, at least 30 years before the crisis. On the other, warfare, bombardment, and mass rural-to-urban migration did not occur until at least 1967, approximately four to six years before the crisis was underway. Regardless, key colonial-era conjunctures and increasing regional unrest in the 1960s created the preconditions for collapse.

Between 1970 and 1973, these conjunctures combined with wartime destruction to move the crisis from formation to progression. The loss of agricultural production, initiated by war and bombardment, was accelerated by reactive sequences that saw collective labor arrangements collapse, traction animals die or disappear, and millions of rural residents move into the cities. Mass migration triggered additional reactive sequences within urban centers, particularly Phnom Penh, where powerful elites exploited food aid programs through systematic hoarding and illegal sales. As circumstances grew dire and the price of rice skyrocketed, redirection of aid and exploitation of the urban poor by the powerful increased. By 1973, averting the crisis became impossible as the civil war turned increasingly in favor of the rebels and the noose tightened around Phnom Penh. That said, had the Khmer Rouge victory occurred sooner, it is conceivable that food could have been directed to the hungry and production restarted on a national scale before mass starvation set in.

Despite the CPK's rhetoric of total revolution, rice-centrism and export dependence (long-standing features of the Cambodian economy) were reproduced and enlarged after 1975. The reorganization of land and labor under the edifice of state production rearticulated the effect of these conjunctures into different reactive sequences: in some districts, oppressive leaders restricted the ration and imposed demands on labor that led to significant loss of life. This loss of labor impacted unit production and jeopardized quotas, reinforcing Party disapproval and scrutiny. In other areas, some leaders with political capital shielded their workers from the most oppressive demands of the quota system by holding back rice to ensure a sufficient supply of food for laborers. By 1979, localized brutality (an outgrowth of contradictions in the CPKs spatial hierarchy) in concert with an economic model that valorized life through the sale of rice, had killed hundreds of thousands.

Mechanism Interactions

In Hawaii and Cambodia, no single decision, exogenous stressor, conjuncture, or reactive sequence was sufficient to initiate famine. Indeed, a key feature of these famines is the importance of mechanism interactions over the preceding years. Madagascar's famine appears, at first, to be initiated by a single historical event: Bâthie's release of cochineal. But here, too, mechanism interactions were essential for the creation of pre-famine conditions and the development of colonial imaginaries that made the release necessary. Furthermore, mechanism interactions helped determine the trajectory of the crisis and the long-term impacts for southern pastoralists.

Interactions between Imaginaries, Conjunctures, and Decisions

Environmental and social perceptions shape the context in which key decisions are made by defining which actions are deemed possible, logical, or necessary. Throughout both phases of crisis evolution, conjunctures and imaginaries are in conversation. In Madagascar, panacea-thinking and the changing socioecology of the South helped propel increasingly hostile attitudes toward cactus among French administrators. By 1924, moderate voices like Decary's were effectively drowned out by a coalition of scientific and political voices eager to apply ecological principles in the interest of modernization. In Cambodia, colonial-era policies emerged from—and reproduced—long-standing perceptions of the country as a rice "factory." After independence, discourses of "growth through agriculture" were essential to policies pursued under Sihanouk, Lon Nol, *and* the CPK. Finally, in Hawaii, long-standing chiefly perceptions of commoner inferiority dovetailed with emerging discourses of consumption and production for export. These imaginaries helped encourage decisions by the monarchy to end the kapu system, maintain traditional forms of labor conscription, and establish a sandalwood tax. To be sure, such policies were inspired by British and U.S. merchants and politicians who embraced a complimentary socioenvironmental imaginary: one that justified the expropriation of Hawaiian natural resources and the exploitation of a subject population. Indeed, it was this "common ground" between capitalist and feudal discourses on nature and society that helped propel growth in the sandalwood trade and the collapse of food provisioning.

In each case, imaginaries prevented other—potentially beneficial—interventions. In Hawaii, missionaries were well placed to illuminate conditions of starvation let alone act on the population's behalf. But under the mission worldview, commoner's souls were saved by rejecting individual sin, not by destabilizing social structures of violence. As such, mission efforts were directed more toward keeping Hawaiian women chaste than keeping them fed. Among the French in Madagascar, the obsession with cactus as the obstacle to modernism prevented administrators from entertaining options like regional autonomy or dual economy, solutions that had been implemented in other parts of the empire. By the 1920s, the debate was polarized around cactus eradication or preservation, and other options were no longer seriously entertained.

As with all socioenvironmental imaginaries, the imaginaries involved in these cases were associated with the dominant mode of production. In Hawaii and Cambodia, imaginaries that justified resource expropriation and labor exploitation emerged within feudal and capitalist economies. In Hawaii, capitalist discourses found correspondence with traditional chiefly discourses of social stratification, whereas in Cambodia, capitalist discourses found correspondence with the CPK's interpretation of communism through rice production for foreign exchange. In Madagascar, the recommitment of cactus pastoralists to raketa under mounting colonial pressure emerged from a mode of production that valorized conservative management of resources. Securing the well-being of the herd was essential to household survival, and raketa offered better survival odds than any other alternative.

Interactions between Reactive Sequences

Whereas conjunctural mechanisms drive slow but steady transformation of food systems, reactive sequences are responsible for rapid social and environmental changes that characterize the progression phase of food crises. Natural resource depletion, the destruction of landesque capital, loss of access to land, declines in labor availability, falling or rising market prices, and loss of expert knowledge through death are some of the impacts of reactive sequences experienced in the three case studies.

By way of example, a prototypical reactive sequence involved in several 20th century famines begins with an environmental stressor impacting a large population of subsistence cultivators. A drought, flood, or other natural disaster causes a partial collapse of food production, initiating a decline in food availability (FAD). Unable to supply sufficient food, households are forced to make decisions about the allocation of labor and capital. Some may sell property (like cattle and ploughs), commit time to gathering wild famine foods, or migrate. Each of these decisions—and this list is by no means exhaustive—can perpetuate the crisis by extending the effect of the stressor over time: selling cattle, ploughs, and other inputs to cultivation may jeopardize the following harvest; committing time and energy to look for food is time taken away from field preparation and maintenance; and out-migration leaves fields fallow and increases provisioning demands in other locales. Over time, the loss of production from these survival decisions exacerbates FAD, driving more households to abandon agriculture and perpetuate the cycle. These socioecological *traps* are described in greater detail in the Food System Traps section below.

In this example, human actions play a key role in the sequence: by shifting the allocation of resources, households trade labor, capital, and future productivity for immediate survival. Under some circumstances, households may select the course of action from several alternatives, but as the crisis unfolds, the range of options invariably shrinks. One feature of crisis evolution common to all three famines was the steady dwindling of adaptational options during the progression phase. By the time the Hawaiian, Malagasy, and Cambodian food systems were poised for failure, years of conjunctural interactions had eliminated opportunities for commoners, pastoralists, farmers, and states.

But not all reactive sequences involve human choices. The combination of sequences that saw cochineal destroy raketa, deprive cows of fodder and people of food and water, required no human intervention to propel the plague across the arid South. In fact, the dominos had been arranged well in advance of 1924 by decades of conjunctural interaction: French obsession with cactus and increasing pressure to "modernize" the southern economy, and the steady entrenchment of pastoral culture and practice behind raketa thickets. Based on these preconditions, a single decision was sufficient to cause collapse.

Reactive sequences can combine in ways that accelerate or slow down crisis evolution. Accelerating interactions produce cycles of positive feedback that can limit the availability of a common resource, alter the effectiveness of a long-standing socioecological practice, or increase the effectiveness of a threat. For example, the gradual disappearance of sandalwood not only increased pressure on Hawaiians to quickly extract the remaining timber, it also ensured that commoners had to travel farther from home to find trees. In this way, the sandalwood tax and the loss of trees combined to accelerate the loss of agricultural labor. By contrast, decelerating interactions involve cycles of negative feedback. As low rice prices forced Cambodian households deeper into debt, black markets emerged to offer farmers better terms of exchange and more income. Of course, the success of these markets contributed to a subsequent state decision and reactive sequence: brutal military crackdowns served to fuel antigovernment sentiment, rural-urban animosity, and ultimately the Khmer Rouge (see The Black Market Trap section below).

The interplay between reactive sequences can produce unexpected results. In Cambodia, Lon Nol's ill-fated military efforts and the collapse of rural rice production drove increased dependence on U.S. aid. This influx of food and military hardware should have helped stave off hunger and bolster the regime's war effort by providing welfare to the destitute and reinforcing social order. Instead, thousands of tons of aid became the material basis for elite hoarding and black markets. Weapons and ammunition never made it to the battlefield and thousands of tons of rice never made it to the hungry, exacerbating existing shortages and forcing the regime into even greater dependence on the United States. Urban poverty and hunger justified continued aid—the lifeblood of the upper class—while upper class expropriation deepened urban poverty and hunger.

In retrospect, this cycle of feedback produced a curious result: a stalemate. On the one hand, foreign aid prolonged and deepened the food crisis by delaying the inevitable revolution. On the other, this prolonging effect was offset by elite expropriation and a PL-480 program that quickly divested ordinary Cambodians of their money and lives. Between 1973 and 1975, these processes of crisis acceleration and deceleration became synchronized: wealth was extracted and destitution reproduced at a rate fast enough to keep the aid flights coming, but slow enough to prevent social collapse. By April 1975, Phnom Penh's urban poor had been squeezed dry, the United States was pulling out of Indochina, and Cambodia was ready for revolution. Indeed, through the interaction of these reactive sequences, PL-480 and Lon Nol's wealthy friends became the perfect conspirators for Pol Pot.

Interactions between Conjunctures

As with reactive sequence interactions, conjunctures can combine in cycles of positive and negative feedback to accelerate social change. In Hawaii, steady growth in the Pacific Trade brought chiefs and commoners into contact with Western culture and a capitalist mode of production. Meanwhile, the expansion in missionary activity—ostensibly opposed to the corrupting influence of foreign merchants—accelerated the adoption of capitalist relations by helping to dismantle kapu and traditional moral economies. In the formation phase of a crisis, conjunctural interactions help establish the preconditions for failure, initiate reactive sequences, and eliminate options for response. To understand how conjunctures accomplish this, we must first acknowledge the multifunctional character of food systems; that is, the capability of food systems to provision much more than food.

The systems analyzed in this book were complex and dynamic arrangements of actors and processes involved in the production, processing, transportation, marketing, and provisioning of food for human bodies. But food was not the only thing produced, consumed, or managed by these arrangements, nor were the constituent actors and processes dedicated solely to food. Indeed, one of the most important developments in food system theorization is the recent understanding of food systems as intrinsically *multifunctional*: that is, they serve myriad purposes and are imbricated into diverse systems having little to do with supplying needed nutrients (Morgan 2009, 2015). Morgan (2015, 1380) describes food systems as "kaleidoscopic," possessing "multiple prisms—social, economic, cultural, political, psychological, sexual—through which food is viewed, valued and used in society."

To comprehend the Hawaiian food system in the 1820s, then, is to first understand the organization of feudal society and the agro-biogeography of the island chain. Food provisioning among the Antandroy and Mahafale was integrated into the ecological and hydrological processes of Madagascar's deep South, and in Cambodia, the arrangements that produced and amassed rice were the same systems that produced and amassed capital for the state. To understand the success and failure of Cambodian rice production is to first analyze the history of conflict and compromise between capitalism and peasant cultivation. Based on these three cases, it seems clear that multifunctionality is critical to crisis formation; that is, the ability of food systems to serve many purposes and many masters enables forms of conjunctural interaction that increase the likelihood of famine. To this end, three types of conjunctural interactions play a substantial role in famine genesis: collaborative entanglement, antagonistic entanglement, and disentanglement.

Under *collaborative entanglement*, two or more groups of people (or social classes) become dependent on the food system for generally similar purposes, often the provisioning of food itself. Over time, these groups may share resources, work side by side, adopt specialized roles in the system, or become dependent on each other through relationships outside of the food system. Threats to the food system become equal concerns for all groups: even if groups disagree on how crises should be averted, the system's overall effectiveness is a shared value.

Collaborative entanglement is made visible by analyzing each group's interest and participation in the system. For example, in traditional Hawaiian agriculture, the processes involved in commoner food production and consumption overlapped with the processes involved in chiefly wealth production. If drought impacted food production, commoners were motivated to act based on subsistence needs, while chiefs were motivated to assist agriculture to preserve food production and maintain the tax base. The more that subsistence food production and chief wealth production shared common actors and processes, the more each group's self-interest aligned with the interest of the other. As such, collaborative entanglement tends to mediate power asymmetries, at least as far as the food system is concerned. But it can also lead to disentanglement (described below)—a damaging response that can quickly push a food system toward failure.

Under *antagonistic entanglement*, two or more groups of people become dependent on the food system for divergent purposes. One group is usually motivated to maintain the current performance and organization of the system (the *conservative* objective) while another group is motivated to alter the system's structure or behavior (the *transformative* objective). Perhaps the most obvious example of antagonistic entanglement is reflected in modern food commodity markets. Wealthy speculators place bets on the price movements of food markets to which they have no other material connection. Powerful actors may purchase and hoard large quantities of food to drive up prices and increase profits from sale. For hoarders and speculators, profits are made through temporary, high-value fluctuations in food price. Because food price in a market context often determines access, price fluctuations can be disastrous for poor consumers, leading to starvation in some historical contexts (Sen 1981; Garenne 2002). Whereas food consumers benefit from the system continuing to supply inexpensive food, speculators and hoarders benefit from the system's partial failure.

Unlike collaborative entanglement in which many components of the system are critical to each group, antagonistic entanglement usually involves shared interest in only one or two components. For example, in the case of Cambodian rice production under Sihanouk, state wealth accumulation intersected with farmer subsistence at two points: rice purchases and tax payments. Farmers needed the exchange of rice to return enough income to pay taxes, whereas the state sought to pay a low price for rice and extract as much tax as possible. The state—the more powerful of the two actors at these points of intersection—successfully deflated farmgate prices and extracted high taxes, while farmers became increasingly threatened by inadequate harvests brought on by external stressors.

Without intervention, this arrangement might have caused the eventual collapse of food provisioning through subsistence failure: that is, farmers could have been forced to sell their own share of the harvest to satisfy the government, resulting in household hunger. But two reactive sequences emerged to preserve this power asymmetry. First, debt markets expanded to provide loans to the growing population of insolvent farmers. By taking out loans, households could distribute production risks across time, but also became vulnerable to high interest rates. Second, black markets offering higher prices for rice flourished as farmers sought more profitable returns on their labor. As black markets captured an increasing percentage of the national harvest, the state responded with violent crackdowns—a reassertion of its authority over rice exchange.

Finally, antagonistic entanglement may not necessarily precipitate failure. In fact, if power is evenly distributed between groups, or if the system is producing and distributing plentiful food, antagonistic entanglement can be maintained for some time. However, as asymmetries of power grow, vulnerabilities increase: failure (or even the fear of future failure) can initiate a reactive sequence in which powerful actors quickly "take what they can get," robbing the system in a frenzy reminiscent of Phnom Penh's aid crisis.

Disentanglement refers to the steady abandonment of food system participation by a group of people (who become dependent on other systems for food), or the bifurcation of a food system into separate systems for each group. Disentanglement is perhaps most obvious in postcolonial economies that have experienced the rapid growth of an urban middle class. Before this demographic transition, all social classes rely on the same processes of rural food production; that is, the food-producing actors and processes for all groups are shared. But over time, as wealth disparities increase, middle- and upper-class households turn to import markets for food and depend less on local producers. Eventually, the rural poor are the only consumers left that depend on local systems of subsistence. Invariably, these systems are now trapped by lack of capital and waning political influence.

With the ascension of Liholiho, the deregulation of the sandalwood trade, and growth in consumption of Western goods, the interests of Hawaii's chiefly class—once well integrated into the food system—became disentangled. Through the Pacific Trade in sandalwood, chiefs could amass enormous wealth without involvement in the food system. So long as luxuries and some food items could be purchased from foreign traders, chiefs were no longer motivated to continue traditional support for agriculture. Of course, disentanglement is rarely total and Hawaii was no exception: to pay for these luxuries, chiefs needed to reinforce their control over the one aspect of the food system that could provide sandalwood:

human labor. In this way, disentanglement frequently accompanies antagonistic entanglement. As the overlap between commoner food production and elite wealth decreases, powerful actors may exert influence over the remaining shared aspects of food provisioning. Groups may be drawn away from a food system through exogenous events and conjunctures, as the example of a growing middle class demonstrates, or forced out of the system entirely, as Cambodian refugees experienced during the civil war.

All three types of interaction can push a system toward failure and all three can help stabilize a system in the early stages of crisis. Which aspect is realized often depends on the character of powerful actors, how equitably power is distributed across the system, and the specific intention each actor has for food provisioning. Before the famine in Hawaii, the food system was governed by an absolute monarch and commoners lacked political voice. Nevertheless, Kamehameha's sensitivity to social concerns ensured the monarchy pursued protective policies, a goal aided by collaborative entanglement. Cambodian rice production under the CPK is another example of substantial overlap and extraordinary power disparities, but here, the Party's interest in food production for state profit produced antagonistic entanglement throughout the spatial hierarchy. In Madagascar, raketa helped ensure that French spaces of wealth production remained disentangled from pastoral livelihoods and food provisioning. To bend the pastoral mode of economy toward colonial goals, administrators needed a way to establish a foothold in the system—that is, to become entangled. Previous attempts at antagonistic entanglement (armed intervention, the capture of watering holes, and taxation) had all failed. But through the release of cochineal, the French succeeded in breaking the social-ecological lock. Cochineal enabled the entanglement of French economic and political interests with food production by removing the keystone supporting pastoral livelihoods. With raketa gone, the food system could be rebuilt along imperial lines.

Entanglement, Regime Type, and Imperialism

In the introduction, I note the ongoing interest in attributing mass starvation to specific forms of government. Famine has variously been blamed on communism (Sen 1999; Haggard and Noland 2007; Eberstadt 2017), capitalism (Albritton 2009; Jarosz 2011), colonialism (Meillassoux 1974; Franke and Chasin 1980), and—according to some of the 19th century European commentators cited in this study—the backwardness of native government. There is good reason for this interest: if blame for starvation can be pinned on one type of institution, it becomes possible to align the humanitarian goal of ending starvation with broader development objectives and political reforms. Today, within the corporate food paradigm, global food security is routinely forwarded as a rationale for trade liberalization and market expansion, devolution of regulation, and the use of genetically modified organisms (GMOs) in food production (Albritton 2009; Lang and Heasman 2015).

But the famines examined here do not suggest such a relationship. Hawaii in the 1820s was an independent kingdom with a feudal class structure. Though Madagascar was a colony of France, pastoral communities in the South actively resisted colonial control and retained traditional forms of governance. Finally, Cambodia was an independent republic. To be sure, it is difficult to generalize from only three cases, but the obvious differences between these polities do not suggest that famine prefers one kind of regime over another.

By contrast, the structural similarities are revealing. Two similarities stand out. First, in all three cases, the causal narrative includes actors and processes operating beyond the spatial boundaries of the food system. To argue that famine is more likely to emerge under a particular form of government is to privilege processes at the state scale; it is to assume that state policies and practices bear the greatest responsibility for starvation. Such an assumption would have downplayed the role of foreign merchants in Hawaii, French politicians and scientists in Madagascar's deep South, and U.S. bombs in Cambodia—actors that were essential to the emergence of starvation. Recently, such state-centrism has downplayed the faminogenic effect of trade embargoes on North Korea, the U.S. destruction of infrastructure on the Iraqi famine in 1991, the collapse of the Soviet Union on Cuba's Special Period, and the Saudi blockade of food on child starvation in Yemen. Of course, exogenous stressors and foreign actors cannot be blamed for every famine; reductionism remains hazardous here. But if we want to know what causes food system failure, our analysis must be sensitive to actors and processes operating beyond the boundaries of the system.

Second, the most similar parts of each causal narrative are those concerning the *interaction* between powerful and less powerful actors. In other words, what all three famines have in common are the contours of power: the orientation of those contours, the magnitude of the power gradient, and the way such power was expressed on and within the food system over time. I have used antagonistic entanglement to describe a relationship in which influential actors participate in the system for motives unrelated to sustaining bodies, usually through an "interface"—a market, taxation, land policy, or other process of labor and resource expropriation. If the demands of the powerful at the interface are minimal, the system may continue to produce and distribute food to those that need it. But as these extractive demands increase, powerful agents may work to bend the system to their benefit or reorganize the system altogether.

Invariably, these transformations are achieved over a period of increasing involvement during which powerful actors widen the interface to gain control over a larger share of the system. For example, the increasing demand for labor to extract sandalwood in Hawaii encouraged the gradual abolition of social protections under kapu. Over time, Hawaiian leaders abandoned ritual forms of redistribution, disregarded the ahupua'a system which had obstructed large-scale labor conscription, and embraced universal taxation. In the first 30 years of the 19th century, the interface between the Pacific Trade and Hawaiian agriculture expanded from the occasional ship taking on food, to the entire Hawaiian ruling class working in lockstep to satisfy a distant market. Once the system is reorganized, success or failure becomes a question of how well the system continues to provide subsistence for those that depend on it, while satisfying the wealth-accumulating demands of the powerful. In Hawaii (after Kamehameha), Madagascar (after cochineal), and Cambodia (under the CPK), the enormous demands of accumulation—expressed through the mass expropriation of labor—pushed the part of the system responsible for subsistence into failure.[1]

Based on these two generalizations—the importance of exogenous actors and the role of antagonistic entanglement—I offer the following general principle: The potential for food system failure increases as powerful external actors become involved in the organization of the system for purposes unrelated to food provisioning. The corollary is that the potential for failure decreases under two conditions: (1) the reorganizational influence of powerful actors decreases, or (2) their purpose for participating in the system aligns more closely with the objective of food provisioning.

This principle suggests that famine is not associated with a form of government. Indeed, food system reorganization by elite actors for profit, political influence, or social control has been a hallmark of capitalist, communist, and feudal economies alike. But the mechanisms that drive dangerous structural reorganization bear a close resemblance to a cluster of well-known conjunctural processes, broadly assembled under the umbrella of *imperialism*. More than any kind of state administration, food system failure is driven by the large-scale and slow-moving processes through which states (and non-state actors) extend their influence and increase their wealth: war, military occupation, settler colonialism, colonization, disease and species introduction, environmental change, cultural imperialism and expropriation, structural adjustment, and market penetration.

The last of these, market penetration, has drawn significant attention among scholars of uneven development and environmental degradation in postcolonial contexts (cf. Franke and Chasin 1980; Harvey 2007; Smith 2008; Watts 2013). In the case of food system failure, I argue that market penetration is not the underlying mechanism, but an indicator of antagonistic entanglement already taking place. Antagonistic entanglement involves the extraction of something nonfood from a food system—for example, capital or labor. One of the ways this has been accomplished is through the valorization of food; that is, establishing a valuation system that enables the exchange of food for other things—money, bullets, or hours of human labor. Markets, like the trade relationships used by the CPK to export rice, offer an efficient means for this valorization and exchange. But a market is not the only way antagonistic entanglement is expressed. In Hawaii, labor was redirected from agriculture to timber extraction first by chiefly fiat, then through the compulsory sandalwood tax. In Madagascar, the French used a wage labor market to push hungry pastoralists onto Northern plantations, but only after deploying cochineal to deprive them of a pastoral livelihood. Under the right conditions, markets can provide an efficient way for powerful actors to extract capital from a food system. But to bring about the right conditions, other violent processes of reorganization may be necessary.

By focusing on the interaction between powerful and nonpowerful actors across spatial and temporal scales, we can begin to identify and account for the role of modern "imperialisms" in the reorganization of today's food systems; for example, the political economy of war and the destruction of agriculture (Darwish, Farajalla, and Masri 2009), embargoes and blockades (McKernan 2018; Mohareb and Ivers 2018), geopolitical posturing (Wallensteen 1976), regulatory regimes for food and GMOs (Zerbe 2004), and destructive food aid programs (Herrick 2008). Since 2000, these forms of antagonistic entanglement have contributed to major food crises in Southern Africa, North Korea, Venezuela, Sudan, Somalia, northern Nigeria, and Yemen. Repairing past damage and preventing future crises demands two concurrent tasks. First, we must find ways to reduce the transformative influence of powerful actors in food provisioning. Growing global inequality, deregulation, increasing market speculation, and the progressive colonization of food systems by corporations and agro-conglomerates is making this task increasingly difficult. Second, we must find ways to better align elite interests with the goal of feeding bodies: we must get powerful states, transnational institutions, social movements, and wealthy donors to care about—and *depend upon*—resilient and healthy food systems, not just profitable ones.

Crisis Indicators

Today, food security and crisis indices are used by governments and aid agencies to request and distribute financial resources, develop and implement crisis plans, and coordinate relief efforts (Howe and Devereux 2006). Indices like the Integrated Phase Classification (IPC) for food security provide a tool for quickly comparing the potential for crisis between regions with diverse livelihood strategies, agricultural and economic systems, and environmental conditions. The IPC classifies food security into five "phases": (1) minimal insecurity, (2) stressed, (3) crisis, (4) emergency, and (5) famine. Classifying a region as experiencing famine (phase 5) is a "technically rigorous process" that requires three specific conditions to be realized (FEWS 2017, np). First, one in every five households faces an extreme lack of food; second, over 30 percent of children under the age of five are suffering from acute malnutrition; and third, daily mortality equals or exceeds two deaths per 10,000.

The Famine Early Warning Systems Network (FEWS NET) is a USAID-funded program that uses the IPC to classify areas of emerging food insecurity and potential crisis. Based on numerous food security conditions and trends,

FEWS NET staff and partners develop scenarios to predict the potential for IPC-classified crises (FEWS 2017). Scenario development is a complex and time-consuming process that must consider a mix of variables across spatial scales. For example, depending on the locale in question, staple food prices, livestock prices, wage levels, labor demand, fuel prices, regional and international market prices, remittance flows, crop conditions, and average temperatures may all be factored into the analysis. The scenario development framework includes the identification of political, policy, and security factors that are likely to change or remain the same, and "shocks" that are likely to impact the system. In the end, the analysis predicts which of the five IPC phases will apply to the area in question over the next few months.

The FEWS NET framework is laudable for its emphasis on site-specific variables, inclusion of both social and environmental factors, and sensitivity to trends. However, scenario development, like the IPC more broadly, is still limited in a variety of ways. For example, according to FEWS NET, scenario development begins with the selection of geographical areas where "acute food insecurity is likely to be most severe or where major changes in food security are expected" (USAID 2012, 3). These areas should be limited to "a livelihood zone or a portion of a livelihood zone," and within these zones, "the typical scenario period length . . . is six months" (USAID 2012, 4). On this basis, for a geographical area to be considered for analysis it already has conditions that make crisis likely, the livelihood strategies for people in the zone have already been deemed vulnerable, and the temporal horizon for prediction is no more than a single growing season.

Site selection bias, a focus on conditions and not relationships, and a short temporal horizon are serious limitations for a framework intended to identify the emergence of phenomena as complex as food crisis. Had sufficient data and the FEWS NET framework been available during each of the famines described in this book, it is not clear that any of them would have been predicted. Hawaii in the 1820s would not have been considered an area of "acute food insecurity" nor a place "where major changes in food security are expected." Furthermore, it is unlikely that scenario development would have detected a significant change in food security until the amount of labor available for agriculture was in steep decline—that is, shortly before the onset of starvation. In Cambodia, the conditions most likely to draw the attention of the model (i.e., variables associated with rural rice production) did not apply in the areas stricken by famine (urban centers). In fact, with essentially no history of urban starvation or dependence on foreign food aid, it is unlikely that scenario development for Cambodia would have considered the right combination of variables. Of course, once reports of food system failure became widespread by 1975, the FEWS NET framework might have successfully anticipated ongoing food insecurity under the CPK. But to do this, scenario development would have needed to overcome issues of spatial granularity—after all, extreme variations in conditions existed between neighboring districts, even neighboring communes. Conclusions drawn from measures aggregated at the region or zone level, for example, would have concealed considerable suffering.

But the most serious limitation of the FEWS NET approach is made obvious in the case of Madagascar. Condition-based prediction would have been blind to the possibility of food system failure until cochineal was already destroying raketa. In fact, on the eve of the plague, standard food security variables for Antandroy and Mahafale households would have indicated a healthy provisioning system and stable pastoral livelihoods. To predict the crisis would have required an awareness of two structural features of southern Madagascar: the vulnerability of pastoralism to the loss of cactus, and the increasing commitment of French officials to cactus eradication. Neither of these features fit into contemporary scenario development.

So long as crisis prediction is intended to support better *relief efforts*, indicators like IPC and modeling systems like FEWS NET will be invaluable tools. But if crisis prediction systems are to be effective for famine *prevention*, new indicators and forms of scenario development will be necessary. These systems will need to account for the arrangements of actors and processes, identify existing and potential vulnerabilities, and recognize dangerous forms of reorganization. The potential for such a structural approach is that possible crises may be identified and evaluated across a much longer time frame: vulnerabilities can be assessed based on structurally *possible* failures, not already emerging ones. Analysts can identify forms of reorganization and take corrective action long before starvation occurs.

Based on the cases analyzed in this project, we can imagine a rudimentary outline of such a process. By analyzing the provisioning arrangements for different groups within a food system, process tracing can identify bottlenecks in production and consumption, ongoing reductions in the diversity of pathways for acquiring food, and growing dependency on dwindling resources. At the conjunctural scale, historical analysis may reveal processes of collaborative entanglement, antagonistic entanglement, and disentanglement that initiate damaging reactive sequences and usher in the progression phase of crisis. Finally, identifying and understanding reactive sequences from past and contemporary famines can train analysts to find and redirect potential cycles of feedback before they happen.

Food System Traps

In the 1960s and 1970s, the concept of a "poverty trap" began to emerge within development studies as a way to explain persistent poverty in structural terms (Field and Piachaud 1971). As the name suggests, the trap metaphor implies that the organization of socioeconomic systems, combined with rational human responses to changing conditions, produces cycles of positive and negative feedback that ensure poor households cannot improve their livelihoods. More recent work has applied the trap concept to socioecological systems to help theorize the relationship between persistent environmental degradation and collective action

(Carpenter and Brock 2008). These "socioecological traps" are "unplanned and unintended processes that come into existence from the interweaving of human actions and environmental changes" (Boonstra and de Boer 2014, 262–63). These processes can "lock systems into unsustainable pathways," putting pressure on limited resources and pushing once-beneficial socioecological interactions toward failure (Stockholm Resilience Center 2016, np). Traps may be obscured by other processes and conditions, making them difficult to find, and often involve "lag effects" that reinforce feedback. In many cases, traps are driven by poverty and motivated by "ecosystem illiteracy and strong identity" (Stockholm Resilience Center 2016, np).

A key feature of traps is the "unusual degree of rigidity of the interaction between social and ecological processes" (Boonstra and de Boer 2014, 260). Rigidity refers to the lack of alternative pathways: the more rigid the interactions, the more resistant the system will be to changes in trajectory. In many cases, rigidity increases at a certain point in the evolution of the trap; for example, the moment an ecological threshold has been crossed or a decision has been made that drastically limits future options (Barrett 2008). Boonstra and de Boer (2014, 263) propose that traps proceed through a sequence of four temporal phases. In the first phase, antecedent socioecological conditions establish the range of possible trajectories for the system. In the second phase, a "critical juncture" forces the selection of one path over others. This juncture may involve an environmental stressor, an unexpected social or economic disruption, or some combination. In the third ("structural persistence") phase, interactions between the chosen path and antecedent conditions produce reinforcing cycles of feedback, and in the final phase, structural persistence initiates reactive sequences that may reinforce or counteract the trap.

Boonstra and de Boer (2014) develop this sequence of phases through an analysis of four case studies, each case exemplifying one of four socioecological traps: agricultural involution, the gilded trap, the dryland poverty trap, and the lock-in trap.

Similarities and Differences

There are important similarities between socioecological traps and the framework for food crisis evolution developed here. The increase in system rigidity over time closely corresponds to the theorized reduction in alternative pathways that occurs between formation and progression phases. As with the food crisis framework, socioecological trap theorization recognizes that key processes (responsible for setting up, triggering, and perpetuating traps) operate across spatial and temporal scales.

There are also important differences. First, the food crisis framework attempts to classify different types of causal mechanisms, each with different behaviors and periods of influence. Second, based on the three famine cases, reactive sequences are not confined to the final phase of trap development, but participate in the formation of the crisis and the establishment of antecedent conditions. Third, whereas the trap literature insists that reactive sequences include human decisions and actions, the reactive sequences that participate in food crisis evolution may be predominantly or entirely ecological, social, or both. For example, cochineal did not require human intervention once it was released into the wild: the plague was able to accelerate based on the spatial distribution of cactus and the insect's metabolic and reproductive strategies. Fourth, a trap may be comprised of other traps operating at different scales. Local, situated traps are triggered and maintained through reactive sequences while conjunctural-scale traps are perpetuated through ongoing dialog with socioenvironmental imaginaries. Constituent traps may operate in parallel or in sequence. For example, the evolution of Cambodian rice production could be seen as a case of agricultural involution at the conjunctural scale, followed by two simultaneous lock-in traps: dependency on foreign aid coupled with aid expropriation.

Put together, socioecological traps and the framework for food crisis evolution offer complementary insights into the role of structural change in famine genesis. By using the framework's five-class categorization of mechanisms, trap theorization can be expanded in two ways, described below. First, based on the three famine cases, I offer that the description of involution in the literature (Geertz 1963; Boonstra and de Boer 2014) is incomplete. Second, the case of Cambodia reveals a new form of trap, what I call the *black market trap*.

Updating the Involution Trap

As described more fully in chapter 1, the involution trap begins with a socioecological system that satisfies basic provisioning needs. This system experiences a critical juncture in which mounting external pressures force producers to make decisions that affect the organization of the system going forward. Producers choose to keep the fundamental structure of the system the same, recommitting to existing relations and processes of production. This doubling down can bring increases in efficiency and productivity; for example, through intensification, improved labor mobilization, and a more equitable distribution of risk. These production improvements lead to increased external demands on the system, driving further commitment to existing structures. Over time, possibilities for reorganization dwindle and the trajectory of the system becomes increasingly fixed. Ultimately, if pressures continue to mount, material limits to production or diminishing returns may cause collapse. In this way, involution is contrasted with *revolution*—the deliberate rejection of existing forms of organization in favor of new ones.

The involution trap describes several aspects of food system failure in the three case studies. In Hawaii, the reproduction of traditional labor requisition practices to pay increasing sandalwood debts and the reinforcement of these feudal relations in the form of the sandalwood tax can be seen as involutionary "moments." In Madagascar, Antandroy and Mahafale increased their dependence on raketa as pressure from the colonial government grew. Meanwhile, colonial frustration with the lack of progress in the South focused increasingly on the cactus. As pastoralists protected their livelihoods from successive French incursions, administrators became committed to cactus eradication, land reform, and labor expropriation. Over time, alternatives for the South were no longer seriously considered.

The involution trap involves a deepening commitment to existing practices and ways of thinking that eventually eliminates alternatives. But the Hawaii and Madagascar cases suggest that this understanding of involution is incomplete. In fact, observed involution in these cases could not have occurred without *revolution* in other parts of the system. In Hawaii, the involution of feudal relations was coincident with chiefs turning to the Pacific Trade and ending forms of welfare protected by the kapu system. By the 1820s, Hawaiian society was undergoing dramatic upheaval; a social revolution that made it possible for one part of the food system to turn in on itself. In Madagascar, the pastoralists who adopted raketa had to abandon long-standing practices around the seasonal movement of herds, row crop cultivation, and the selection and preparation of fodder. Over time, raketa became deeply integrated into pastoral culture, but this integration was only possible because fundamental cultural features and livelihood practices changed or disappeared.

These examples suggest that the discovery of an involution trap depends on the scale of analysis. At one scale, parts of a food system (or socioecological system more broadly) may exhibit a recommitment to existing relations and processes of production. But viewed within a larger context, involution coincides with— indeed, depends upon—destabilization and change. I offer that this relationship is dialectical: destabilization and revolution drive involutionary processes just as involution and recommitment to old ways can motivate change.

The Black Market Trap

The dialectical relationship between stability and change is expressed through a sequence of interactions that affected Cambodian food provisioning leading up to the civil war. As the government increased pressure on producers through falling purchase prices and high taxes, farmers responded by selling rice on the black market. These sales provided temporary relief for households already burdened with debt, but as increasing quantities of Cambodia's harvest eluded state authorities, the government responded with violence. Military-enforced requisitions, executions, and destruction of property drove rural resentment and fueled the cause of revolution. In turn, growing resentment reinforced farmers' participation in black markets.

This black market trap emerges within a food system experiencing strong antagonistic entanglement between a powerful state (dependent on production for exchange) and a large producer class. As the state works to increase its profits from the food system, producers respond by expanding the system *beyond the reach* of the state. This expansion is temporary: the state—losing potential income to black markets and offended by disregard for the law—responds by recapturing control of food sales. The oppression and violence in the state's response increases resentment and motivates additional extralegal activity which, in turn, justifies increasingly severe responses from the state. At some point, a variation in this cycle may emerge in which antigovernment sentiment is sufficiently widespread to initiate political revolution. Resulting war and civil unrest further destabilize the state and create a power vacuum in which black market activity may increase once again.

The state's decision to use violence during the crackdown is a critical juncture in the trap. By the time this decision is made, farmer frustration is high, as evidenced by the presence and use of the black market. Violence is not the only option at this juncture; for example, the state could increase farmgate prices, lower taxes, or provide debt relief. But the decision to use violence reinforces the trap and makes its future use more likely. Driving the trap is the persistent belief among farmers that black market opportunities could disappear at any moment, and state indignation that farmers are flaunting the law.

In Cambodia, the government saw black markets as contributing to the overall failure of food provisioning by depriving the state of available rice. Such blame is undeserved. The adoption and continued use of black markets by Cambodian farmers emerged as an adaptive response to increasingly unfair terms of exchange—terms that were dictated by a government and elite class taking full advantage of antagonistic entanglement to amass wealth. If black markets exacerbated large-scale food crisis, it was only *after* they had helped avert many smaller subsistence crises at the scale of villages and households.

The Question of Responsibility

Since the turn of the 21st century, the famine body count has been in steady decline. In *Mass Starvation: The History and Future of Famine*, Alex de Waal (2017) notes that recent improvements in crisis detection and aid delivery, better public health programs, and more extensive immunization against infectious diseases have dramatically reduced the mortality rate. In the century between 1870 and 1970, 1 million people died from mass starvation each year—today, that yearly toll has dropped by 95 percent. But de Waal (2017, 2018) cautions against claiming victory over famine. With recent, large-scale food crises in sub-Saharan Africa and the Middle East associated with war and civil unrest, de Waal (2017, np) argues that we have entered a new era in mass starvation, what he refers to as "the new atrocity famines." These events "have in common that they occur in virulent and intractable conflicts . . . as the product of wars in which the belligerents deny the right of the other to exist . . . are ready to discount the lives of people—civilians and soldiers alike—in pursuit of their political and military ends" (de Waal 2017, np).

For de Waal and others (cf. Marcus 2003; Edkins 2006; DeFalco 2013), modern famine prevention must involve the criminalization of acts that lead to starvation. "In every case of mass starvation today, what we see is a political culprit who acts with a well-founded sense of impunity, either to inflict intense hunger or to fail to stop it when it is within their power to do so. All are confident that they will not be called to account for their acts" (de Waal 2018, 33). It is argued that if the act of causing starvation—or deliberately failing to prevent it—is criminalized through bodies like the International Criminal Court (ICC), military and political leaders in a position to prevent famine "will unhesitatingly ensure that it does not occur" (de Waal 2018, 34).

I agree that deliberate actions and inactions that precipitate starvation should be condemned and outlawed, regardless of political motivation or military exigency, economic logic or revolutionary ideology. The inclusion of "famine crimes" alongside genocide as a crime against humanity seems a reasonable first step in acknowledging the extraordinary human cost of mass starvation. But the emphasis on bringing guilty perpetrators to justice begs other important and uncomfortable questions. For example, *why* are famine crimes committed? What is it that makes these criminal acts possible, reasonable, logical, or necessary in the first place? What is it about our food systems—and the socioeconomic histories from which they emerge—that makes them a target for political gain? How do those who seek to starve others achieve their goals? And what are the social, economic, and environmental actors and processes that get mobilized to precipitate crisis? These are the concerns I sought to address in this book.

In these three famines, powerful people made decisions that resulted in mass starvation: Liholiho, Henri Perrier de la Bâthie, Richard Nixon, and Pol Pot, among others. It is tempting to blame them for the deaths of millions. But to end the forensic analysis there is to lose sight of the forest for the trees. It is also to let many coconspirators off the hook. The decisions that led to famine in Hawaii, Madagascar, and Cambodia were not made in a vacuum; rather, they emerged within a geographical and historical context that had been shaped over decades and centuries. Most importantly, the decisions that starved millions were considered logical and necessary within this context, not reprehensible. To understand how similar decisions are still being made today demands that we place the complex and slow-emerging socionature of food provisioning—its structure—under analysis.

Criminalizing starvation may be a necessary step to end famine, but it is not sufficient. Laws attempt to establish a degree of semantic precision around the conditions, actions, and consequences they regulate. But semantic precision around famine has been notoriously hard to come by (Pinstrup-Andersen 2009).

How many people must starve for a crisis to be considered a crime? How tightly must we draw the line of causation between the criminal act and subsequent deaths? How much intention or knowledge of wrongdoing (mens rea) is required for a criminal to be held accountable? There is already a long history of state and non-state actors manipulating the definition of famine for political gain (cf. Brunel 2002). As we have seen, precise death tolls are often hard to come by: during a crisis, people die from acute malnutrition brought on by starvation, but they also die from exposure to the elements, lack of medical care for existing conditions, infectious diseases, and bullet wounds.

Human and nonhuman factors often combine to initiate a crisis, further complicating questions of responsibility. For example, if a change in agricultural policy makes farmers vulnerable to a subsequent drought, who is to blame, the policy makers or nature? New laws may provide definitions of what constitutes a famine and a famine crime, but this is unlikely to curb the manipulation of such definitions for political gain. Even if the international community succeeded in developing acceptable definitions, a law would only make a specific set of faminogenic acts illegal; it would not make mass starvation itself unreasonable or illogical.

To end famine demands that the production of hunger becomes irrational and detrimental to its future perpetrators on the basis of economic logic and political expediency—in other words, it demands structural reorganization. Such a reorganization must make the social, economic, and environmental systems that provision our food *hostile* to those actors and actions that would disrupt them. And to do this requires us to first understand how these systems have succeeded and failed to provision food. It is to take our forensic analysis back in history.

Reorganization for Justice

This book set out to examine the origins of three historical famines. To accomplish this, we needed to reconstruct the organization of once-functional food systems, identify the changes taking place to them, and understand the large-scale and slow-moving mechanisms that sent them into decline. Based on this analysis, it is hard to deny that mass starvation emerges—in significant part—from the contested arrangement and rearrangement of actors and processes responsible for feeding hungry bodies: in other words, the structure of food provisioning.

Today, famine is only one of the challenges facing our global food systems. But like mass starvation, many of these challenges have structural roots—malnutrition, obesity, food waste, topsoil loss, agro-biodiversity loss, racial and gender inequalities in food access, and worker exploitation, among others. Exposing and untangling these roots has become a central goal of contemporary food studies research and the food justice movement (Alkon and Norgaard 2009). Growing interest in food system reform has motivated research into the market logics that simultaneously produce starvation and obesity (Albritton 2009; Guthman 2011), the discourses that vie for dominance in food policy circles (Lang and Heasman 2015), the dynamic relationship between culture and food consumption (Mintz 1986, 1996), and the pervasive, racialized spaces of nutritional disparity—what food justice leader Karen Washington calls "food apartheids" (Torres 2017; Brones 2018). From the outset, reform movements acknowledge the multifunctionality of modern food systems, that the challenge of "just" food production and consumption is inextricably intertwined with social and environmental justice at all scales.

It is here, in food system studies, that the food crisis frameworks proposed in this book may provide the most benefit: by directing attention to the ways food systems have been organized, we expose not only the pitfalls that can lead to crisis, but the transformations that can build more equitable and resilient structures for nourishing living bodies. We put famine to work for justice.

Conclusions

It is hard to die from hunger, but if past is prologue, millions more will. Across the globe, climate change is impacting cultivation through increased CO_2 concentrations, variability in rainfall, and more destructive natural hazards. Land grabbing, cash-crop conversion, and farm consolidation are turning traditional agricultural systems into factories for capital, while emerging markets funnel this capital to distant investors. In short, today's food systems are experiencing dramatic and rapid change. They are becoming increasingly connected to each other and to powerful actors with intentions other than food provisioning. As they have been throughout history, food systems are still targets of warfare and mass violence. This picture seems familiar because it bears a discouraging resemblance to the changes that affected Hawaiian, Malagasy, and Cambodian food systems prior to their collapse.

Based on these cases, I offer three insights for policy. First, it is possible to anticipate crises by examining a food system's structural history—we need not wait until conditions trigger warnings and warnings trigger public attention. Second, early intervention saves lives. The formation phase of a crisis is invariably longer than the progression phase and offers a wider range of options for avoiding disaster. Most crisis warnings are not triggered until reactive sequences have altered local conditions, but structural analysis allows us to see the possibility of a crisis before it becomes inevitable.

Finally, and most importantly, the right combination of mechanisms may produce a fate worse than famine: an interminable and inescapable cycle of grinding hunger. A stable trap is more insidious than a sudden collapse because it hides in plain sight. It conjures no images of crowded relief camps, scorched fields, or swollen bellies. Nor does it mark a watershed in social and cultural history; here, starvation is business as usual. I offer that finding and disarming these traps through the structural transformation of food provisioning is a key challenge for modern society.

———————————

In *Unmodern Observations*, Nietzsche identified three modes of historical memory: the exemplary, the monumental, and the critical (Nietzsche and Arrowsmith 1990). Through the critical mode, we examine the past so that we might be liberated, not only from the record of violence and misery but also from the weight of responsibility we bear as the heirs and beneficiaries of past suffering. For Nietzsche, the liberating aspect of critical historiography draws our focus toward the future, to suffering that has yet to happen. It illuminates potential crises from within the universe of future possibilities, clarifies them, traces their future histories, and exposes them to intervention. It is, in essence, "a trauma-driven repudiation of the past in the name of a better future" (Moses 2005, 313).

In the quote that started this book, Nasib Arida laments the impotence of those that witnessed the Lebanese and Syrian famine of 1915–18 when he writes, "The horror has made us all so brave / But moved us only to narrate."[2] The human record of mass starvation invites both Nietzsche's critical historiography and Arida's self-criticism. Like a scalpel opening a cadaver, famines expose the hidden machinery of a once-functioning food system—its dependencies and vulnerabilities, its stressors and adaptations, its winners and losers. The attention that famine brings to human hunger is invaluable for understanding not only why starvation *has* happened, but why modern food systems continue to reproduce it. The first step in building tomorrow's just and resilient food systems, then, falls to critical history—to the relentless examination of those elusive mechanisms that have produced hunger in all its forms. The next step is to turn that narration into action.

Notes

PREFACE

1. This number reflects only famine deaths. The total number who died from hunger during the 20th century is unknown.

INTRODUCTION

1. There are notable exceptions within food system studies, for example, Ericksen (2008), who analyzes food system interactions at a global scale and bridges social and natural science perspectives.
2. For an example of this reasoning, see Haggard and Noland (2007). Within this literature there is a tendency to conflate communism with authoritarianism and to overlook significant structural differences between communist governments.
3. Jeffrey Kaufmann (1998) used "Cactus War" to refer to the extended period of colonial violence—and threatened violence—surrounding cactus pastoralism and efforts to bring pastoralists under colonial control.
4. It may be argued that the case of Cambodia has already received abundant attention in the literature and should not be characterized as a less analyzed case. It is true that significant scholarship has recounted the rise and rule of the Khmer Rouge. However, much of this work assumes this history constitutes a brutal reign of terror for which famine was an unintended consequence. In contrast with the extant literature, this analysis puts the failure of food provisioning at the center of analysis and works outward. This prevents top-down generalizations about regime type (e.g., "totalitarian," "autarkic," and "communist") being the cause of failure.

CHAPTER 1

1. The toponym *Hawaii* may be written in its traditional form with the glottal stop indicator (*Hawai'i*) or in its modern form without the indicator. Following Sahlins (1990), I use the traditional form when referring to the island of Hawai'i, and the modern form when referring to the Hawaiian Islands as a whole.
2. *Precontact* here refers to the period prior to the arrival of Captain James Cook at Kauai in 1778.
3. In this regard, the famine bears strong similarity to other crises. Schmitt (1970, 115) observes the complete lack of mortality data for Hawaiian famines and epidemics, noting "Contemporary descriptions and traditional accounts are so vague or questionable as to be worthless as a basis for statistical analysis."
4. There is some debate as to whether Cook was the first European to visit the Islands. Some authors (cf. Kane 1996) argue that the first Europeans were Spanish plying the "Manila Galleon" route between Mexico and the Philippines.

There is some documentary evidence that Ruy Lopez de Villalobos and Juan Gaetano may have observed the island of Hawai'i in 1555.

5. Bingham is referring to a picul: a unit of weight equivalent to 133 and 1/3 pounds. Piculs were the standard unit of measure for sandalwood.

6. Cook estimates the population of the Sandwich Islands to be approximately 300,000 in 1778. Some later historians believe this number is too high, suggesting a figure closer to 200,000.

7. In addition to irrigated and rainfed systems, Hommon (2013) adds a third type—colluvial cultivation—that combined features of the other two. Colluvial cultivation would have been used in situations where erratic rainfall patterns impeded rainfed agriculture and topography prevented systematic irrigation.

8. Landesque capital may be considered synonymous with Marx's "*la terre*-capital": capital that has been incorporated into land (1977, 618).

9. While root crops like tubers and gourds do respond to environmental conditions with remarkable variations in size, the "great sweet potato" story is probably apocryphal.

10. It is in 1810 that Kauai's governor, Kaumaulii ceded control of the island to Kamehameha. Kauai was the last island to be brought under Kamehameha's control. Some authors prefer a different date for consolidation, given that suzerainty existed prior to 1810.

11. It is not entirely clear what definition of "carrying capacity" is used by Kirch (1994, 2011), Culliney (2006), and Hommon (2013). For a detailed discussion of the different usages of the term, see Seidl and Tisdell (1999).

12. A compelling argument has been made that patriarchal discourses surrounding women and disease are in no way relegated to the past (see Doezema 1999).

13. Twombly (1899, 155) considers Kamehameha's act more for show than a practical contribution to agriculture, noting that the king "did some little digging himself by way of an object lesson to his subjects."

14. By assuming that the encounter with Western "others" produced envy and self-criticism, both Daws (1968) and Morgan (1948) may be guilty of a common postcolonial bias (see Loomba 2015).

15. There is some debate on this point. Daws (1968) argues that some of the chiefs were persuasive and convinced Liholiho to release the royal monopoly. Hammatt (1999) takes this a step further, arguing that Liholiho lost the monopoly to the five most powerful Kona chiefs who had been Kamehameha's favorites.

16. See the Missionary Letters from the Sandwich Islands Mission to the American Board of Commissioners for Foreign Missions 1819–1837, Vol. 2. Archived at the Hawaiian Mission Houses Museum and Archive, Honolulu, Hawaii.

17. For a qualitative assessment of sandalwood's decline, see Porter (1930).

18. Tambora may have had one other circuitous connection to Hawaii. In the early 19th century, sandalwood was being extracted from Sumbawa and other islands near Tambora. It is possible that the devastation of these islands during the 1815 event had an impact on the sandalwood trade. If the eruption constrained the supply of timber, any increase in price would have helped drive extraction in other locations, including Hawaii.

19. See the Journal of Levi Chamberlain, entries from 1826; also, Missionary Letters from the Sandwich Islands Mission to the American Board of Commissioners for Foreign Missions.

20. It is worth noting that Cordy (1972) makes no attempt to explain these divergent trajectories and provides no sources for his data, though his estimates for Hawai'i in 1823 may come from Ellis (1826) who compiled numbers from local chiefs. Chiefs were required to maintain accurate population counts within their territories for the purposes of taxation—a fact that lends credibility to Ellis's numbers.

21. For example, in 2012, petroleum and petroleum products comprised 90 percent of Saudi Arabia's exports. The second largest category of imports was foodstuffs.

CHAPTER 2

1. The bovine and human death toll from this event is contested. See the section The Introduction of Cochineal for a more complete discussion on mortality discrepancies.
2. Months are approximations. Actual periods of migration depended on herder preferences and environmental conditions.
3. In addition to these crops, locals also cultivated groundnuts, Cape peas, manioc, sorghum, and other small-scale legumes and vegetables. Millet, maize, and sweet potato were the most common staple grains and as such, are the three crops (in addition to raketa) that are factored into this analysis.
4. Authors do not agree on the exact timing of pastoral migration, cultivation, or food consumption. This may be due, in part, to real-world variations. Kaufmann (2001, 89) refers to the fruiting period of raketa between August and February as the dry season. Decary (1925, 769) refers to this same period as the wet season. Historical climate data for Tsihombe indicates this period receives the most rainfall, suggesting Decary is accurate.
5. For example, Stratton (1964) claims that the water holding properties of raketa raised the water table across the cactus region, ensuring that rivers never ran dry. There is no other evidence to suggest this was the case, or even possible.
6. Between 1835 and 1861, diplomatic and missionary relations between Madagascar and Europe effectively ceased under the leadership of Queen Ranavalona I who is perhaps best known for the purges and executions of Malagasy Christians under her rule. This period of "martyrdom" was used by Protestants to justify the reestablishment of mission activity upon her death and became a central narrative in church history (see Cousins 1895).
7. The argument for raketa removal presents a curious paradox. On the one hand, the elimination of raketa is intended to encourage locals to leave an arid, hostile place. On the other, its elimination is supposed to reveal an underlying fertile terrain for colonization.
8. Kaufmann (2001) observes that an underlying theme in many of the debates during this period concerned the agency of nature. Proponents of eradication tended to attribute agency to raketa, portraying the cactus as a destabilizing, anticolonial force and an active threat to law, order, and progress. On the other side, Decary and others placed raketa as a passive participant in food provisioning and economic production.
9. Of course, there is a long history of societies using biological agents to bring subject populations under control usually through disease, starvation, or the loss of basic resources. For example, in 1887, rinderpest was deliberately introduced into Eritrea by Italian forces during a military campaign against Somalia. The intent was to bring pastoralists in the Horn of Africa into submission by killing their cattle. It is estimated that the resulting famine claimed one-third of Ethiopia's population (Davis 2002). It is not known if French administrators ever considered introducing rinderpest into southern Madagascar in the 1920s: documentary evidence clearly demonstrates an obsession with cactus, not cows. If rinderpest was considered, it may have been ruled out based on the Italian experience, but this is simply speculation.

CHAPTER 3

1. For examples and analyses of Green Revolution "failures" in other parts of the world, see Griffin (1979) and Singh (2008).
2. Kiernan (2002) and Porter and Hildebrand (1975) put the population of Phnom Penh at three million by April 1975.
3. There is considerable uncertainty and debate over the final death toll under the CPK, a question that is addressed more fully in subsequent sections.

4. From World Bank Group, Climate Change Knowledge Portal; raw observational data from Climate Research Unit, University of East Anglia and International Water Management Institute.

5. As a member of Cambodia's elite, Yukanthor's claims to represent his country's oppressed may be a stretch: the rebellion of 1884 which motivated Yukanthor's trip to France was led by members of the ruling class who felt that growing French involvement in the countryside would threaten their authority. Yukanthor's adoption of left-wing language may have been more political theater than genuine concern for Cambodia's peasants.

6. During this period, Sihanouk did not always occupy the same office, though he was effectively Cambodia's head of state for the duration.

7. It is important to distinguish *tons* of bombs from *tonnage*. *Tons* often refers to the physical weight of the ordinance (either imperial or metric). *Tonnage* refers to equivalent explosive power of the ordinance in TNT. The tonnage figure of three million tons, therefore, refers to the explosive equivalent of TNT.

8. Structural adjustment refers to part of the World Bank and IMF's development paradigm in the 1970s to 1980s by which poor countries would only receive aid if they agreed to reorganize the national economy around free market principles.

9. This claim is based on 8000 deaths per month in Phnom Penh, with a population of 2 million; contrasted with 2 million deaths over 45 months in a population of 8 million.

10. Vickery notes that some city dwellers welcomed the Khmer Rouge on April 17, 1975.

11. This is based on data for rice consumption by an average Cambodian farmer (see Slocomb 2010) and composition of caloric intake from rice (see USAID 1977).

12. Other problems with this approach include the tendency to take CPK propaganda as a reflection of both the "reality on the ground" and the basis for leadership decisions (see Jackson 2014). Indeed, an overreliance on the part of CPK propaganda is a primary weakness of the STV (Tyner and Rice 2016).

13. Siemreap Special Region no. 106 was dissolved in 1977.

14. See, for example, "Interview with Chhum Seng," "Interview with Chhay Phan," and "Interview with Lot Suoy," archived at the Documentation Center of Cambodia, Phnom Penh.

15. See, for example, "Interview with Im Chaem," archived at the Documentation Center of Cambodia, Phnom Penh.

16. This estimate is from Kiernan (2002), though it is impossible to precisely determine the relative percentage of deaths from starvation, exposure, and execution.

17. Such political capital did not always last: it should be noted that as many as 100,000 members of the East Zone were killed in 1977 from purges associated with the zone's failure to deliver rice (Kiernan 2002).

CHAPTER 4

1. It is worth noting that in Madagascar, the famine preceded and helped precipitate large-scale labor expropriation, not the other way around. That said, it was French designs on Southern labor that justified the introduction of cochineal in the first place.

2. From Arida's poem about the 1915–18 famine in Lebanon and Syria, published in his magazine *al-Funun* (quoted in Fraser 2015).

References

Ackoff, R. L. 2001. Fundamentalism and Panaceas. *Systemic Practice and Action Research* 14 (1):3–10.

Albritton, R. 2009. *Let Them Eat Junk: How Capitalism Creates Hunger and Obesity.* Pluto Press. http://books.google.com/books?id=dtgmAQAAMAAJ.

Alexander, W. D. W. 1891. *A Brief History of the Hawaiian People.* American Book Company.

Alkon, A. H., and K. M. Norgaard. 2009. Breaking the Food Chains: An Investigation of Food Justice Activism. *Sociological Inquiry* 79 (3):289–305.

Allen, P. M., and M. Covell. 2005. *Historical Dictionary of Madagascar.* Scarecrow Press.

Altieri, M. A., F. R. Funes-Monzote, and P. Petersen. 2012. Agroecologically efficient agricultural systems for smallholder farmers: contributions to food sovereignty. *Agronomy for Sustainable Development* 32 (1):1–13.

Altieri, M. A., and V. M. Toledo. 2011. The agroecological revolution in Latin America: rescuing nature, ensuring food sovereignty and empowering peasants. *The Journal of Peasant Studies* 38 (3):587–612.

Anderson, B., and J. Wylie. 2009. On Geography and Materiality. *Environment and Planning A* 41 (2):318–335.

Atkins, P. 2009. Famine. In *International Encyclopedia of Human Geography*, eds. R. Kitchin and N. Thrift, 14–20. Oxford: Elsevier. http://dro.dur.ac.uk/7075/.

Bakker, K., and G. Bridge. 2006. Material worlds? Resource geographies and the matter of nature. *Progress in Human Geography* 30 (1):5–27.

Banuri, T. 1991. *Economic Liberalization: No Panacea: The Experiences of Latin America and Asia.* Clarendon Press.

Barnes, J. 2014. *Cultivating the Nile: The Everyday Politics of Water in Egypt.* Duke University Press. https://books.google.com/books?id=Gx7IBAAAQBAJ.

Baro, M., and T. F. Deubel. 2006. Persistent hunger: perspectives on vulnerability, famine, and food security in sub-Saharan Africa. *Annual Review of Anthropology* 35 (1):521–538.

Barrett, C. B. 2008. Poverty traps and resource dynamics in smallholder agrarian systems. In *Economics of Poverty, Environment and Natural-Resource Use*, eds. A Ruijs and R. Dellink, 17–40. Springer.

Barron, J., and A. Paul. 1977. *Murder of a Gentle Land: The Untold Story of a Communist Genocide in Cambodia.* Reader's Digest Press: distributed by Crowell.

Bassett, T. J., and A. Winter-Nelson. 2010. *The Atlas of World Hunger.* University of Chicago Press.

Bâthie, H. P. de la. 1924. Introduction a Tananarive du Coccus cacti ou cochenille du Figuier d'Inde. *Bulletin Economique de Madagascar* 21 (3–4).

———. 1925. Ignames cultivées ou sauvages de Madagascar. *Revue de botanique appliquée et d'agriculture coloniale* 5 (46):417–422.

———. 1934. Les Famines du Sud-Ouest de Madagascar. Causes et Remèdes. *Revue de botanique appliquée et d'agriculture coloniale* 14 (151):173–186.

———. 1955. Notes concernant l'Homme et les Plantes utiles à Madagascar. *Journal d'agriculture tropicale et de botanique appliquée* 2 (5):298–322.

Beckervaise, J. 1839. *Thirty-Six Years of a Seafaring Life: By an Old Quarter Master*.

Beechey, F. W. 1831. *Narrative of a Voyage to the Pacific and Beering's Strait: To Co-operate with the Polar Expeditions: Performed in His Majesty's Ship Blossom, Under the Command of Captain F.W. Beechey . . . in the Years 1825, 26, 27, 28 . . .* H. Colburn and R. Bentley.

Beinart, W., and L. Hughes. 2009. *Environment and Empire*. Oxford University Press. https://books.google.com/books?id=4zZPPgAACAAJ.

Bellwood, P. S. 1987. *The Polynesians: Prehistory of an Island People*. Thames and Hudson.

Benge, M. 1991. *Cambodia: An Environmental and Agricultural Overview and Sustainable Development Strategy*. Washington, D.C.: USAID.

Bérard, H. 1951. Le problème agricole du ravitaillement des populations dans l'extême-sud de Madagascar. *L'Agronomie Tropicale* 6.

Biggs, D. A. 2012. *Quagmire: Nation-Building and Nature in the Mekong Delta*. University of Washington Press.

Bingham, H. 1822. Sandwich Islands Mission correspondence, March 19, 1822. Archived at the Hawaiian Mission Houses Museum and Archive, Honolulu, Hawaii.

———. 1855. *A Residence of Twenty-One Years in the Sandwich Islands*. H. D. Goodwin.

Blaikie, P., and H. Brookfield. 1987. Approaches to the study of land degradation. *Land Degradation and Society / Piers Blaikie and Harold Brookfield with contributions by Bryant Allen . . . [et al.]*. http://agris.fao.org/agris-search/search.do?recordID=US201301749562 (last accessed 7 November 2016).

Blaney, D. L. 1996. Reconceptualizing autonomy: The difference dependency theory makes. *Review of International Political Economy* 3 (3):459–97.

Bolton, M. 1996. *Report on Exploratory Survey of Wild Food Usage by Rural Households*. Manila: IRRI.

Boonstra, W. J., and F. W. de Boer. 2014. The historical dynamics of social–ecological traps. *AMBIO* 43 (3):260–274.

Boserup, E. 2005. *The Conditions of Agricultural Growth: The Economics of Agrarian Change Under Population Pressure*. Aldine Transaction. http://books.google.com/books?id=t6dv9ufX9_cC.

Braudel, F. 1982. *On History*. University of Chicago Press.

Braudel, F., and I. Wallerstein. 2009. History and the Social Sciences: The Longue Durée. *Review (Fernand Braudel Center)* 32 (2):171–203.

Bray, F. 1994. *The Rice Economies: Technology and Development in Asian Societies*. University of California Press.

Briffa, K. R., P. D. Jones, F. H. Schweingruber, and T. J. Osborn. 1998. Influence of volcanic eruptions on Northern Hemisphere summer temperature over the past 600 years. *Nature* 393 (6684):450–55.

Brinkman, H.-J., S. de Pee, I. Sanogo, L. Subran, and M. W. Bloem. 2010. High food prices and the global financial crisis have reduced access to nutritious food and worsened nutritional status and health. *The Journal of Nutrition* 140 (1):153S-161S.

Britton, N. L. 1919. *The Cactaceae: Descriptions and Illustrations of Plants of the Cactus Family*. Carnegie Institution of Washington.

Brones, A. 2018. Food apartheid: the root of the problem with America's groceries. *The Guardian* 15 May. http://www.theguardian.com/society/2018/may/15/food-apartheid-food-deserts-racism-inequality-america-karen-washington-interview.

Brookfield, H. C. 1984. Intensification revisited. *Pacific Viewpoint* 25 (1):15–44.

Broughton, W. R. 1804. *A Voyage of Discovery to the North Pacific Ocean, 1795–1798*.

Brown, L. R. 2011. The New Geopolitics of Food. In *Food and Democracy: An Introduction to Food Sovereignty*, ed. M. Gerwin. Krakow: Polish Green Network.

———. 2012. *Full Planet, Empty Plates: The New Geopolitics of Food Scarcity*. W. W. Norton.

Brown, M. 1979. *Madagascar rediscovered: A History from Early Times to Independence*. Archon Books.

———. 2000. *A History of Madagascar*. Markus Wiener Publishers.

Browne, G. W. 1900. *The Paradise of the Pacific: The Hawaiian Islands*. D. Estes & Company.

Brunel, S. 2002. *Famines et politique*. Presses de Sciences Po.

Bryan, W. A. 1915. *Natural History of Hawaii: Being an Account of the Hawaiian People, the Geology and Geography of the Islands, and the Native and Introduced Plants and Animals of the Group*. [Printed for the author by] the Hawaiian Gazette Company, Limited.

Butler, S. D. 2016. *War Is a Racket: The Antiwar Classic by America's Most Decorated Soldier*. Skyhorse Publishing, Inc.

Butzer, K. W. 2005. Environmental history in the Mediterranean world: Cross-disciplinary investigation of cause-and-effect for degradation and soil erosion. *Journal of Archaeological Science* 32 (12):1773–1800.

Cahill, G. F., and R. L. Veech. 2003. Ketoacids? Good medicine? *Transactions of the American Clinical and Climatological Association* 114:149.

Campbell, B. M. 1889. *Madagascar*. Woman's Presbyterian Board of Missions of the Northwest.

Campbell, G. 1992. Crisis of Faith and Colonial Conquest: The Impact of Famine and Disease in Late Nineteenth-Century Madagascar (Crise de la foi et conquête coloniale: les conséquences de la famine et de la maladie à Madagascar à la fin du XIXe siècle). *Cahiers d'Études Africaines* 32 (127):409–53.

———. 2005. *An Economic History of Imperial Madagascar, 1750–1895: The Rise and Fall of an Island Empire*. Cambridge University Press.

Carney, T. 1989. The Unexpected Victory. In *Cambodia 1975–1978: Rendezvous with Death*, ed. K. Jackson, 13–35. Princeton, NJ: Princeton University Press.

Carpenter, S. R., and W. A. Brock. 2008. Adaptive capacity and traps. *Ecology and Society* 13 (2). http://www.jstor.org/stable/26267995 (last accessed 24 May 2018).

Castree, N. 2001. Socializing Nature: Theory, Practice, and Politics. In *Social Nature: Theory, Practice, and Politics*, eds. N. Castree and B. Braun. Wiley.

———. 2005. *Nature*. Routledge. http://books.google.com/books?id=qQ8Uwgd MehMC.

Chamberlain, L. n.d. Journal of Levi Chamberlain. Volume VII. Archived at the Hawaiian Mission Houses Museum and Archive, Honolulu, Hawaii.

Chamberlain, L. 1827, March 2. Letter to the American Board of Commissioners for Foreign Missions. In "Missionary Letters from the Sandwich Islands Mission to the American Board of Commissioners for Foreign Missions 1819–1837, Vol 2." Archived at the Hawaiian Mission Houses Museum and Archive, Honolulu, Hawaii.

Chandler, D. 2008. *A History of Cambodia*. Westview Press.

Chandler, D. P., B. Kiernan, and C. Boua. 1988. *Pol Pot Plans the Future: Confidential Leadership Documents from Democratic Kampuchea, 1976–1977*. Yale University Southeast Asia Studies, Yale Center for International and Area Studies.

Checchi, F., M. Gayer, R. Grais, and E. Mills. 2007. *Public Health in Crisis-Affected Populations: A Practical Guide for Decision-Makers*. London: Overseas Development Institute.

Chenoweth, M. 1996. Ships' logbooks and "the year without a summer." *Bulletin of the American Meteorological Society* 77 (9):2077–94.

Chiteva, R., and N. Wairagu. 2013. Chemical and nutritional content of *Opuntia ficus-indica* (L.). *African Journal of Biotechnology* 12 (21).

Cho, J. J., R. A. Yamakawa, and J. Hollyer. 2007. Hawaiian Kalo, past and future. *Sustainable Agriculture — College of Tropical Agriculture, University of Hawaii, Manoa* (SA-1).

Chu, P.-S. 1995. Hawaii rainfall anomalies and El Niño. *Journal of Climate* 8 (6):1697–1703.

Coffee, C. J. 1999. *Metabolism: Quick Look Medicine*. Wiley.

Collet, D., and M. Schuh. 2018. Famines: At the Interface of Nature and Society. In *Famines during the "Little Ice Age" (1300–1800)*, 3–16. Springer.

Copland, S. 1822. *A History of the Island of Madagascar . . . With an appendix, containing a history of the several attempts to introduce Christianity into the island. [With a map.]*. Burton & Smith.

Cordy, R. H. 1972. The Effects of European Contact on Hawaiian Agricultural Systems—1778–1819. *Ethnohistory* 19 (4):393–418.

Corlay, G. de. 1896. *Notre campagne à Madagascar: notes et souvenirs d'un volontaire*. Tolra.

Corney, P., and W. D. W. Alexander. 1896. *Voyages in the Northern Pacific: Narrative of Several Trading Voyages from 1813 to 1818, Between the Northwest Coast of America, the Hawaiian Islands and China, with a Description of the Russian Establishments on the Northwest Coast. Interesting Early Account of Kamehameha's Realm; Manners and Customs of the People, Etc. And Sketch of a Cruise in the Service of the Independents of South America in 1819*. T.G. Thrum.

Cousins, W. E. 1895. *Madagascar of To-day: A Sketch of the Island, with Chapters on Its Past History and Present Prospects*. Religious Tract Society.

Covell, M. 1987. *Madagascar: Politics, Economics, and Society*. F. Pinter.

Crosby, A. W. 2004. *Ecological Imperialism: The Biological Expansion of Europe, 900–1900*. Cambridge University Press. http://books.google.com/books?id=Phtqa_3tNykC.

Culliney, J. L. 2006. *Islands in a Far Sea: The Fate of Nature in Hawai'i*. University of Hawai'i Press.

Currey, B. 1980. Famine in the Pacific losing the chances for change. *GeoJournal* 4 (5):447–66.

Cutter, S. L., L. Barnes, M. Berry, C. Burton, E. Evans, E. Tate, and J. Webb. 2008. A place-based model for understanding community resilience to natural disasters. *Global Environmental Change* 18 (4):598–606.

Dalrymple, D. G. 1986. *Development and Spread of High-Yielding Rice Varieties in Developing Countries*. Int. Rice Res. Inst.

Dando, W. A. 1980. *The Geography of Famine*. Edward Arnold (Publishers) Ltd.

Darwish, R., N. Farajalla, and R. Masri. 2009. The 2006 war and its inter-temporal economic impact on agriculture in Lebanon. *Disasters* 33 (4):629–44.

Davis, M. 2002. *Late Victorian Holocausts: El Niño Famines and the Making of the Third World*. Verso Books. http://books.google.com/books?id=2LjYUY3LHkoC.

Daws, G. 1968. *Shoal of Time: A History of the Hawaiian Islands*. University of Hawai'i Press.

Dawson, A. 1975, July 2. High Khmer toll is cited in Saigon. *Washington Post*.

Decary, R. 1921. Monographie du District de Tsihombe. *Bulletin Economique de Madagascar* 18 (2).

———. 1925. L'utilisation des Opuntias en Androy (Extrême Sud de Madagascar). *Revue de botanique appliquée et d'agriculture coloniale* 5 (50):769–71.

———. 1928. À propos de l'Opuntia épineux de Madagascar. *Revue de botanique appliquée et d'agriculture coloniale* 8 (77):43–46.

———. 1930. *L'Androy (Extrême-sud de Madagascar): essai de monographie régionale. Géographie physique et humaine*. I. impr. Firmin-Didot.

———. 1931. *Rapport sur la famine en Androy pendant la saison chaude 1930–1931*. Tsihombe.

———. 1935. La conquête économique de l'extreême-sud de Madagscar. *La Géographie* 64:369.

———. 1947. Époques d'introduction des Opuntias monacantha dans le Sud de Madagascar. *Revue internationale de botanique appliquée et d'agriculture tropicale* 27 (301):455–57.

———. 1969. *Souvenirs et croquis de la terre malgache*. Éditions maritimes et d'outre-mer.

DeFalco, R. 2013. *Justice and Starvation in Cambodia: International Criminal Law and the Khmer Rouge Famine.* Unpublished master's thesis, University of Toronto. http://hdl.handle.net/1807/67245.

Delvert, J. 1994. *Le paysan cambodgien.* L'Harmattan.

Deschamps, H. 1959. *Les migrations intérieures passées et présentes à Madagascar.* Paris: Berger-Levrault.

Dettmeyer, R. B., M. A. Verhoff, and H. F. Schütz. 2014. Death by Starvation and Dehydration. In *Forensic Medicine,* 261–68. Berlin: Springer. https://link .springer.com/chapter/10.1007/978-3-642-38818-7_16 (last accessed 21 July 2017).

Devereux, S. 2006. *The New Famines: Why Famines Persist in an Era of Globalization.* Taylor & Francis. http://books.google.com/books?id=2jYdfkY8fQUC.

Devereux, S., and Z. Tiba. 2006. Malawi's First Famine, 2001–2002. In *The New Famines: Why Famines Persist in an Era of Globalization,* ed. S. Devereux. Routledge.

Diamond, J. 2007. Easter island revisited. *Science* 317 (5845):1692–94.

Dibble, S. 1843. *History of the Sandwich Islands.* Press of the Mission Seminary.

Dirks, N. B. 1992. *Colonialism and Culture.* University of Michigan Press.

Dodd, A. P. 1940. *The Biological Campaign against Prickly-Pear.* Government Printer, South Africa.

Doezema, J. 1999. Loose women or lost women? The re-emergence of the myth of white slavery in contemporary discourses of trafficking in women. *Gender Issues* 18 (1):23–50.

Donne, M. A. 1866. *The Sandwich Islands and Their People.* Society for Promoting Christian Knowledge.

Drèze, J., and A. K. Sen. 1989. *Hunger and Public Action.* Clarendon Press. http:// books.google.com/books?id=OjCHQR-M0ocC.

Eberstadt, N. 2017. *The Poverty of Communism.* Routledge.

Edgerton-Tarpley, K. 2008. *Tears from Iron: Cultural Responses to Famine in Nineteenth-Century China.* University of California Press. http://books.google.com /books?id=-Pp_EYAI7FgC.

Edkins, J. 2000. *Whose Hunger?: Concepts of Famine, Practices of Aid.* University of Minnesota Press. http://books.google.com/books?id=GUljpjS8F5YC.

———. 2006. The Criminalization of Mass Starvations: From Natural Disaster to Crime against Humanity. In *The New Famines: Why Famines Persist in an Era of Globalization,* ed. S. Devereux. Routledge.

Ellis, W. 1826. *Narrative of a Tour through Hawaii, or, Owhyhee; with Remarks on the History, Traditions, Manners, Customs and Language of the Sandwich Islands.* H. Fisher, Son, and P. Jackson. Hatchard and Son; Seeley and Son; Hamilton, Adams, and Company; Sherwood and Company; and Simpkin and Marshall, London: Waugh and Innes, Edinburgh; and Keene, Dublin.

———. 1838. *History of Madagascar: Comprising Also the Progress of the Christian Mission Established in 1818, and an Authentic Account of the Recent Martyrdom . . .* Fisher.

Ericksen, P. J. 2008. Conceptualizing food systems for global environmental change research. *Global Environmental Change* 18 (1):234–45.

Esaovelomandroso, M. 1986. Millieu naturel et peuplement de l'Androy. In *Madagascar, Society and History,* ed. C. Kottak. Durham: Carolina Academic Press.

Etcheson, C. 2000. Did the Khmer Rouge Really Kill Three Million Cambodians? *Phnom Penh Post* 30.

Fadani, A. 2018. Remembering Hunger. Museums and the Material Culture of Famine. In *Famines during the "Little Ice Age" (1300–1800),* 255–269. Springer, Cham https://link.springer.com/chapter/10.1007/978-3-319-54337-6_13 (last accessed 8 August 2017).

Fagan, B. M. 2009. *Floods, Famines, and Emperors: El Niño and the Fate of Civilizations.* Basic Books.

FAO. 2017. FAO issues alert over third consecutive failed rainy season, worsening hunger in East Africa. http://www.fao.org/news/story/en/item/1023788/icode/ (last accessed 29 July 2017).

FEWS. 2017. Home | Famine Early Warning Systems Network. https://www.fews .net/ (last accessed 31 July 2017).

Field, F., and D. Piachaud. 1971. The poverty trap. *New Statesman* 3:772–73.

Finch, M. P. M. 2013. *A Progressive Occupation?: The Gallieni-Lyautey Method and Colonial Pacification in Tonkin and Madagascar, 1885–1900*. Oxford: Oxford University Press.

Ford, P. 2017. Madagascar skirted famine—barely. Now, it's boosting resilience before drought returns. *Christian Science Monitor*. https://www.csmonitor.com /World/Africa/2017/0725/Madagascar-skirted-famine-barely.-Now-it-s -boosting-resilience-before-drought-returns.

Foster, Z. J. 2015. The 1915 locust attack in Syria and Palestine and its role in the famine during the First World War. *Middle Eastern Studies* 51 (3):370–94.

Franke, R. W., and B. H. Chasin. 1980. *Seeds of Famine: Ecological Destruction and the Development Dilemma in the West African Sahel*. Allanheld Osmun and Company Publishers.

Frappa, C. 1932. Sur Dactylopius tomentosus Lam. Et son acclimatement à Madagascar. *Revue de pathologie végétale et d'entomologie gricole de France* 19:48–55.

Fraser, T. 2015. *The First World War and Its Aftermath: The Shaping of the Middle East*. Gingko Library.

Garenne, M. 2002. The political economy of an urban famine. *IDS Bulletin* 33 (4):55–62.

———. 2006. An Atypical Urban Famine: Antananarivo, Madagascar 1985– 1986. In *The New Famines: Why Famines Persist in an Era of Globalization*, ed. S. Devereux. Routledge.

Gazdar, H. 2002. Pre-modern, modern and post-modern famine in Iraq. *IDS Bulletin* 33 (4):63–69.

———. 2006. Pre-Modern, Modern and Post-Modern Famine in Iraq, 1990– 2003. In *The New Famines: Why Famines Persist in an Era of Globalization*, ed. S. Devereux. Routledge.

Geertz, C. 1963. *Agricultural Involution; the Process of Ecological Change in Indonesia*. Berkeley: Published for the Association of Asian Studies by University of California Press.

Girling, J. L. S. 1972. The resistance in Cambodia. *Asian Survey* 12 (7):549–63.

Goldman, I. 1970. *Ancient Polynesian Society*. Chicago: University of Chicago Press.

Goodfellow, W. 1975, July 14. Starvation in Cambodia. *New York Times*.

Gráda, C. Ó., and K. O'Rourke. 1997. Migration as disaster relief: Lessons from the Great Irish Famine. *European Review of Economic History* 1 (1):3–25.

Grandidier, A. 1902. *Histoire physique, naturelle, et politique de Madagascar: Saussaure-Myriapodes de Madagascar. 2 v*. Impr. Nationale.

Greenfield, A. B. 2009. *A Perfect Red*. Harper Collins.

Griffin, K. 1979. *The Political Economy of Agrarian Change: An Essay on the Green Revolution*. Springer.

Guillermo, L. 1955. Les plantations de raquette inermes en Androy. *Union Francaise et Parlement* 7 (65).

Guthman, J. 2011. *Weighing In: Obesity, Food Justice, and the Limits of Capitalism*. University of California Press.

Haas, M. 1991a. *Cambodia, Pol Pot, and the United States: The Faustian Pact*. ABC-CLIO.

———. 1991b. *Genocide by Proxy: Cambodian Pawn on a Superpower Chessboard*. ABC-CLIO.

Haggard, S., and M. Noland. 2007. *Famine in North Korea: Markets, Aid, and Reform*. Columbia University Press. http://books.google.com/books?id=3WxiBhHRL 4QC.

Haila, Y. 2002. A conceptual genealogy of fragmentation research: From island biogeography to landscape ecology. *Ecological Applications* 12 (2):321–34.

Hammatt, C. H., and S. Wagner-Wright. 1999. *Ships, Furs, and Sandalwood: A Yankee Trader in Hawai'i, 1823–1825*. University of Hawai'i Press.

Handy, E. S., E. G. Handy, and M. K. Pukui. 1972. *Native Planters in Old Hawaii: Their Life, Lore, and Environment*. Bishop Museum Press.

Hanks, L. M. 1992. *Rice and Man: Agricultural Ecology in Southeast Asia*. University of Hawai'i Press.

Heinberg, R. 2011. What Will We Eat as the Oil Runs Out? In *Food and Democracy: An Introduction to Food Sovereignty*, ed. M. Gerwin. Krakow: Polish Green Network.

von Heland, J., and C. Folke. 2014. A social contract with the ancestors—Culture and ecosystem services in southern Madagascar. *Global Environmental Change* 24:251–64.

Helmers, K. 1997. Rice in the Cambodian Economy: Past and Present. In *Rice Production in Cambodia*, ed. H. J. Nesbitt, 1–14. Int. Rice Res. Inst.

Heseltine, N. 1971. *Madagascar*. Praeger.

Hinton, A. L. 2004. *Why Did They Kill?: Cambodia in the Shadow of Genocide*. University of California Press.

Hommon, R. J. 2013. *The Ancient Hawaiian State: Origins of a Political Society*. OUP USA.

Hopkins, M. 1862. *Hawaii: The Past, Present, and Future of Its Island-Kingdom. An Historical Account of the Sandwich Islands (Polynesia)*. Longman, Green, Longman, and Roberts.

Hornborg, A., J. R. McNeill, and J. Martinez-Alier. 2007. *Rethinking Environmental History: World-System History and Global Environmental Change*. Rowman Altamira.

Hossain, N. 2017. Inequality, Hunger, and Malnutrition: Power Matters. *IFPRI book chapters*:24–29.

Howe, P., and S. Devereux. 2006. Famine Scales: Towards an Instrumental Definition of "Famine." In *The New Famines: Why Famines Persist in an Era of Globalization*, ed. S. Devereux. Routledge.

Hugenholtz, W. R. 1986. Famine and Food Supply in Java 1830–1914. In *Two Colonial Empires*, Comparative Studies in Overseas History, 155–88. Dordrecht: Springer. https://link.springer.com/chapter/10.1007/978-94-009-4366-7_8 (last accessed 8 August 2017).

Hwang, H.-S. 1999. A food distribution model for famine relief. *Computers & Industrial Engineering* 37 (1):335–38.

Jackson, K. D. 2014. *Cambodia, 1975–1978: Rendezvous with Death*. Princeton University Press.

Jahn, G., K. Bunnarith, P. Sophea, and P. Chanty. 1997. Pest Management in Rice. In *Rice Production in Cambodia*, ed. H. J. Nesbitt, 83–92. Int. Rice Res. Inst.

Jarosz, L. 2011. Defining World Hunger: Scale and Neoliberal Ideology in International Food Security Policy Discourse. *Food, Culture and Society: An International Journal of Multidisciplinary Research* 14 (1):117–39.

Jarves, J. J. 1843. *History of the Hawaiian or Sandwich Islands*. Tappan and Dennet.

Javier, E. 1997. Rice Ecosystems and Varieties. In *Rice Production in Cambodia*, ed. H. J. Nesbitt, 39–82. Int. Rice Res. Inst.

Kagawa, A. K., and P. M. Vitousek. 2012. The ahupua'a of puanui: A resource for understanding Hawaiian rain-fed agriculture. *Pacific Science* 66 (2):161–72.

Kahneman, D., and I. Ritov. 1994. Determinants of stated willingness to pay for public goods: A study in the headline method. *Journal of Risk and Uncertainty* 9 (1):5–37.

Kamakau, S. M. 1961. *Ruling Chiefs of Hawaii*. Kamehameha Schools Press.

———. 1992. *The Works of the People of Old: Na Hana A Ka Po'e Kahiko*. Bishop Museum Press.

Kaufmann, J. C. 1998. The Cactus Was Our Kin: Pastoralism in the Spiny Desert of Southern Madagascar. In *Changing Nomads in a Changing World*, ed. J. Ginat and A. Khazanov, 124–42. Sussex Academic Press.

———. 2000. Forget the numbers: The case of a Madagascar famine. *History in Africa* 27:143–57.

———. 2001. La Question des Raketa: Colonial struggles with prickly pear cactus in southern Madagascar, 1900–1923. *Ethnohistory* 48 (1–2):87–121.

———. 2008. The non-modern constitution of famines in Madagascar's spiny forests: "Water-food" plants, cattle and Mahafale landscape praxis. *Environmental Sciences* 5 (2):73–89.

———. 2011. Doubting modernity for Madagascar's cactus pastoralists. *History in Africa* 38:123–151.

Keen, D. 1994. *The Benefits of Famine: A Political Economy of Famine and Relief in Southwestern Sudan, 1983–1989*. Princeton University Press. http://books .google.com/books?id=cHaWQgAACAAJ.

Kiernan, B. 2002. *The Pol Pot Regime: Race, Power, and Genocide in Cambodia under the Khmer Rouge, 1975–79*. Yale University Press.

———. 2004. *How Pol Pot Came to Power: Colonialism, Nationalism, and Communism in Cambodia, 1930–1975*. Yale University Press.

King, J. 1983. *Livestock Water Needs in Pastoral Africa in Relation to Climate and Forage*. Addis Ababa: International Research Center for Africa.

Kirch, P. V. 1982. The ecology of marine exploitation in prehistoric Hawaii. *Human Ecology* 10 (4):455–76.

———. 1994. *The Wet and the Dry: Irrigation and Agricultural Intensification in Polynesia*. University of Chicago Press.

———. 2011. *Roots of Conflict: Soils, Agriculture, and Sociopolitical Complexity in Ancient Hawai'i*. School for Advanced Research Press.

Kirch, P., and K. S. Zimmerer. 2010. Dynamically Coupled Human and Natural Systems: Hawai'i as a Model System. In *Roots of Conflict: Soils, Agriculture, and Sociopolitical Complexity in Ancient Hawai'i*, ed. P. Kirch. Santa Fe: School for Advanced Research Press.

Kloppenburg, J. R. 2005. *First the Seed: The Political Economy of Plant Biotechnology*. University of Wisconsin Press. http://books.google.com/books?id=QGx9Ao 2dzckC.

Koc, M., and K. A. Dahlberg. 1999. The restructuring of food systems: Trends, research, and policy issues. *Agriculture and Human Values* 16 (2):109–16.

Kondo, J. 1988. Volcanic eruptions, cool summers, and famines in the northeastern part of Japan. *Journal of Climate* 1 (8):775–88.

Kotzebue, O. von. 1821. *A Voyage of Discovery, Into the South Sea and Beering's Straits, for the Purpose of Exploring a North-east Passage, Undertaken in the Years 1815–1818, at the Expense of His Highness the Chancellor of the Empire, Count Romanzoff, in the Ship Rurick*.

Krüger, F., G. Bankoff, T. Cannon, B. Orlowski, and E. L. F. Schipper. 2015. *Cultures and Disasters: Understanding Cultural Framings in Disaster Risk Reduction*. Routledge.

Kuykendall, R. S. 1938. *The Hawaiian Kingdom*. University of Hawai'i Press.

Ladefoged, T. N., P. V. Kirch, S. M. Gon III, O. A. Chadwick, A. S. Hartshorn, and P. M. Vitousek. 2009. Opportunities and constraints for intensive agriculture in the Hawaiian archipelago prior to European contact. *Journal of Archaeological Science* 36 (10):2374–383.

Lang, T., and M. Heasman. 2015. *Food Wars: The Global Battle for Mouths, Minds and Markets*. Routledge.

Lappé, F. M. 2011. The City That Ended Hunger. In *Food and Democracy: An Introduction to Food Sovereignty*, ed. M. Gerwin. Krakow: Polish Green Network.

Lappé, F. M., J. Collin, P. Rosset, and Institute for Food and Development Policy. 1998. *World Hunger: 12 Myths*. Grove Press. http://books.google.com/books?id =EjNUa56Cy2MC.

Larsson, P. 2004. *Introduced Opuntia spp. in Southern Madagascar: Problems and Opportunities*. Uppsala: Swedish University of Agricultural Sciences.

Lautze, S., and D. Maxwell. 2006. Why Do Famines Persist in the Horn of Africa? Ethiopia, 1999–2003. In *The New Famines: Why Famines Persist in an Era of Globalization*, ed. S. Devereux. Routledge.

Le Billon, P. 2003. Buying peace or fuelling war: The role of corruption in armed conflicts. *Journal of International Development* 15 (4):413–26.

Leslie, J. 1975, March 24. Children victims in Phnom Penh: Malnutrition kills thousands in war. *Los Angeles Times*, A2.

Linton, J. 2010. *What Is Water?: The History of a Modern Abstraction*. UBC Press.

Livingstone, I. 1977. Economic Irrationality among Pastoral Peoples: Myth or Reality? *Development and Change* 8 (2):209–30.

Lockwood, J. A. 2009. *Locust: The Devastating Rise and Mysterious Disappearance of the Insect That Shaped the American Frontier*. Basic Books.

Long, D. C., and D. F. Wood. 1995. The logistics of famine relief. *Journal of Business Logistics* 16 (1):213.

Long, J. L. 1981. *Introduced Birds of the World: The Worldwide History, Distribution and Influence of Birds Introduced to New Environments*. Universe Books.

———. 2003. *Introduced Mammals of the World: Their History, Distribution and Influence*. Csiro Publishing.

Loomba, A. 2015. *Colonialism/Postcolonialism*. Routledge.

Lyautey, L. H. G. 1935. *Lettres du sud de Madagascar: 1900–1902*. Colin.

Lyons, C. J. 1875. Land matters in Hawaii. *The Islander*.

Mackintosh, C. 2011. Orchestrating Famine. In *Food and Democracy: Introduction to Food Sovereignty*, ed. M. Gerwin. Krakow: Polish Green Network.

Maddox, G. 1990. Mtunya: Famine in central Tanzania, 1917–20. *The Journal of African History* 31 (02):181–97.

Mallory, W. H. 1926. *China: Land of Famine*.

Malo, D. 1903. *Hawaiian Antiquities: (Moolelo Hawaii)*. Honolulu: Hawaiian Gazette Company, Ltd.

Malthus, T., and G. Gilbert. 1993. *An Essay on the Principle of Population*. Oxford University Press, UK. http://books.google.com/books?id=pui8Brw3mdMC.

Mann, C. C. 2006. *1491 (Second Edition): New Revelations of the Americas before Columbus*. Knopf Doubleday Publishing Group.

———. 2012. *1493: Uncovering the New World Columbus Created*. Vintage Books.

Marcus, D. 2003. Famine crimes in international law. *American Society of International Law* 97 (2):35.

Marx, K. 1977. *Capital: A Critique of Political Economy*. Vintage Books. http://books.google.com/books?id=bknCAAAAIAAJ.

Marx, K., and F. Engels. 1970. *The German Ideology*. International Publishers Co.

Mauss, M. 2002. *The Gift: The Form and Reason for Exchange in Archaic Societies*. Routledge.

Mayer, J. 1975. Management of famine relief. *Science* 188 (4188):571–77.

McKernan, B. 2018. Yemen: up to 85,000 young children dead from starvation. The Guardian 21 November. https://www.theguardian.com/world/2018/nov/21/yemen-young-children-dead-starvation-disease-save-the-children (last accessed 27 November 2018).

Meillassoux, C. 1974. Development or exploitation: Is the Sahel famine good business? *Review of African Political Economy* 1 (1):27–33.

Mellen, G. 2015. "The Killing Fields": Forty years after rise of Pol Pot, SoCal Cambodian Americans struggle with emotional toll. Orange County Register 13 April. https://www.ocregister.com/2015/04/13/the-killing-fields-forty-years-after-rise-of-pol-pot-socal-cambodian-americans-struggle-with-emotional-toll/ (last accessed 12 December 2018).

Menzies, A., and W. F. Wilson. 1920. *Hawaii Nei 128 Years Ago*.

Mertha, A. 2014. *Brothers in Arms: Chinese Aid to the Khmer Rouge, 1975–1979*. Cornell University Press.

Middleton, K. 1999. Who killed "Malagasy cactus"? Science, environment and colonialism in southern Madagascar (1924–1930). *Journal of Southern African Studies* 25 (2):215–48.

———. 2009. From Ratsiraka to Ravalomanana. *Études Océan indien* (42–43):47–83.

———. 2012. Renarrating a biological invasion: Historical memory, local communities and ecologists. *Environment and History* 18 (1):61–95.

Mintz, S. W. 1986. *Sweetness and Power: The Place of Sugar in Modern History*. Penguin Books. https://books.google.com/books?id=_pefwak9cPAC.

———. 1996. *Tasting Food, Tasting Freedom: Excursions into Eating, Culture, and the Past*. Beacon Press.

Morgan, K. 2009. Feeding the city: The challenge of urban food planning. *International Planning Studies* 14 (4):341–48.

———. 2015. Nourishing the city: The rise of the urban food question in the Global North. *Urban Studies* 52 (8):1379–394.

Morgan, T. 1948. *Hawaii, a Century of Economic Change, 1778–1876*. Harvard University Press.

Moses, A. D. 2005. Hayden White, traumatic nationalism, and the public role of history. *History and Theory* 44 (3):311–32.

Mostert, M., and A. Bonavia. 2016. Starvation ketoacidosis as a cause of unexplained metabolic acidosis in the perioperative period. *The American Journal of Case Reports* 17:755–58.

Munro-Stasiuk, M., C. Coakley, J. Tyner, S. Kimsroy, and S. Rice. 2017. "Documenting the extent and style of the Khmer Rouge irrigation infrastructure, Cambodia." Presentation at the Annual Meeting of the AAG.

Munson, F. P. 1968. *Area Handbook for Cambodia*. U.S. Government Printing Office.

Myers, N., R. A. Mittermeier, C. G. Mittermeier, G. A. B. da Fonseca, and J. Kent. 2000. Biodiversity hotspots for conservation priorities. *Nature* 403 (6772):853–58.

Nabhan, G. P. 2012. *Where Our Food Comes From: Retracing Nikolay Vavilov's Quest to End Famine*. Island Press.

Nally, D. 2011. *Human Encumbrances: Political Violence and the Great Irish Famine*. University of Notre Dame Press. http://books.google.com/books?id=de03Yg EACAAJ.

National Public Radio. 2017. U.S. demands Cambodia repay loan from Vietnam War era. *NPR.org*. https://www.npr.org/2017/05/30/530683478/u-s-demands -cambodia-repay-loan-from-vietnam-war-era (last accessed 5 December 2017).

National Research Council. 1982. *Determinants of Fertility in Developing Countries: An Overview and a Research Agenda*. National Academies.

Nelson, E., S. Scott, J. Cukier, and Á. L. Galán. 2008. Institutionalizing agroecology: successes and challenges in Cuba. *Agriculture and Human Values* 26 (3):233–43.

Nelson, H. D. 1973. *Area Handbook for the Malagasy Republic*. U.S. Government Printing Office.

Nesbitt, H. J. 1997a. *Rice Production in Cambodia*. Int. Rice Res. Inst.

———. 1997b. Topography, Climate, and Rice Production. In *Rice Production in Cambodia*, ed. H. J. Nesbitt, 15–20. Int. Rice Res. Inst.

Nesbitt, H. J., and C. Phaloeun. 1997. Rice-Based Farming Systems. In *Rice Production in Cambodia*, ed. H. J. Nesbitt, 31–38. Int. Rice Res. Inst.

Nietzsche, F. W., and W. Arrowsmith. 1990. *Unmodern Observations*. Yale University Press.

Norton, G. W., J. Alwang, and W. A. Masters. 2014. *Economics of Agricultural Development: World Food Systems and Resource Use*. Routledge.

Ó Gráda, C. 1995. *The Great Irish Famine*. Cambridge University Press. http:// books.google.com/books?id=X0uf6t8VfAsC.

———. 2009. *Famine: A Short History*. Princeton University Press. http://books .google.com/books?id=LoN2XkjJio4C.

Oka, I. 1979. *Brown Planthopper: Threat to Rice Production in Asia*. Int. Rice Res. Inst.

Olivier, M. 1931. *Six ans de politique sociale à Madagascar*. B. Grasset.

Oppenheimer, C. 2003. Climatic, environmental and human consequences of the largest known historic eruption: Tambora volcano (Indonesia) 1815. *Progress in physical geography* 27 (2):230–59.

Osborne, M. 1978. Peasant politics in Cambodia: The 1916 affair. *Modern Asian Studies* 12 (2):217–43.

Ostrom, E., M. A. Janssen, and J. M. Anderies. 2007. Going beyond panaceas. *Proc Natl Acad Sci USA* 104 (39):15176–8.

Parsons, T. 1999. *The British Imperial Century, 1815–1914: A World History Perspective*. Rowman & Littlefield.

Party Center. (1976) 1988a. Excerpted Report on the Leading Views of the Comrade Representing the Party Organization at a Zone Assembly. In *Pol Pot Plans the Future: Confidential Leadership Documents from Democratic Kampuchea, 1976–1977*, ed. D. Chandler, B. Kiernan, and C. Boua. New Haven: Yale University Press.

———. (1976) 1988b. The Party's Four-Year Plan to Build Socialism in All Fields, 1977–1980. In *Pol Pot Plans the Future: Confidential Leadership Documents from Democratic Kampuchea, 1976–1977*, ed. D. Chandler, B. Kiernan, and C. Boua. New Haven: Yale University Press.

———. (1976) 1988c. Preliminary Explanation before Reading the Plan, by the Party Secretary. In *Pol Pot Plans the Future: Confidential Leadership Documents from Democratic Kampuchea, 1976–1977*, ed. D. Chandler, B. Kiernan, and C. Boua. New Haven: Yale University Press.

———. (1976) 1988d. Report of Activities of the Party Center according to the General Political Tasks of 1976. In *Pol Pot Plans the Future: Confidential Leadership Documents from Democratic Kampuchea, 1976–1977*, ed. D. Chandler, B. Kiernan, and C. Boua. New Haven: Yale University Press.

Pauker, G. 2015. The Role of the Military in Indonesia. In *Role of the Military in Underdeveloped Countries*, ed. J. A. Johnson. Princeton University Press.

Peet, R. 1985. The social origins of environmental determinism. *Annals of the Association of American Geographers* 75 (3):309–33.

Petit, G. 1929. Introduction à Madagascar de la cochenille du figuier d'Inde (Dactylopius coccus Costa) et ses conséquences inattendues. *Revue d'histoire naturelle* 10:160–73.

Pettey, D. F. W. 1947. Le contrôle des Cochenilles dans les plantations d'Opuntias inermes en Afrique du Sud. *Revue internationale de botanique appliquée et d'agriculture tropicale* 27 (301):457–60.

Piercy, E., R. Granger, and C. Goodier. 2010. Planning for peak oil: Learning from Cuba's "special period." *Proceedings of the ICE—Urban Design and Planning* 163 (4):169–76.

Pijpers, B. 1989. *Kampuchea—Undoing the Legacy of Pol Pot's Water Control System*. Trócaire.

Pinstrup-Andersen, P. 2009. Food security: definition and measurement. *Food Security* 1 (1):5–7.

Ponchaud, F. 1989. Social Change in the Vortex of Revolution. In *Cambodia 1975–1978: Rendezvous with Death*, ed. K. D. Jackson, 151–178. Princeton, NJ: Princeton University Press.

Poole, P. A. 1976. Cambodia 1975: The Grunk Regime. *Asian Survey* 16 (1):23–30.

Porter. K. 1930. *John Jacob Astor and the sandalwood trade of the Hawaiian Islands, 1816–1828*. Archived at the Pacific Collection, University of Hawaii at Manoa, Hawaii.

Porter, G., and G. C. Hildebrand. 1975. *The Politics of Food: Starvation and Agricultural Revolution in Cambodia*. Indochina Resource Center.

———. 1978. *Cambodia: Starvation or Revolution*. Monthly Review Press.

Potter, N. W., L. M. Kasdon, and A. Rayson. 2003. *History of the Hawaiian Kingdom*. Bess Press.

Powe, E. L. 1994. *The Lore of Madagascar*. Paterson, N.J.: Armchair Travelers, a subsidiary of Dan Aiki Publications.

al-Qattan, N. 2014. When mothers ate their children: Wartime memory and the language of food in Syria and Lebanon. *International Journal of Middle East Studies* 46 (Special Issue 04):719–36.

Quinn, K. 1989. The Pattern and Scope of Violence. In *Cambodia 1975–1978: Rendezvous with Death*, ed. K. Jackson, 215–240. Princeton: Princeton University Press.

Quinn, K. M. 1974. *The Khmer Krahom Program to Create a Communist Society in Southern Cambodia*. Airgram to the Department of State.

Ralaimihoatra, E. 1969. *Histoire de Madagascar*. Imprimerie Société Malgache d'Édition.

Rangasami, A. 1985. Failure of exchange entitlements' theory of famine: A response. *Economic and Political Weekly* :1747–752.

Report of the American Board of Commissioners for Foreign Missions. 1826. Boston. Archived at the Hawaiian Mission Houses Museum and Archive, Honolulu, Hawaii.

Richards, W. 1841, March 15. Letter to C. Wilkes. Archived at the State Archives of Hawaii, Honolulu, Hawaii.

Rickman, J. 1781. *Journal of Captain Cook's Last Voyage to the Pacific Ocean, on Discovery: Performed in the Years 1776, 1777, 1778, 1779. Illustrated with Cuts, and a Chart, Shewing the Tracts of the Ships Employed in this Expedition*. E. Newbery.

Rickman, J., M. Pyseth, and O. Sothy. 1997. Farm Mechanization. In *Rice Production in Cambodia*, ed. H. J. Nesbitt, 93–98. Int. Rice Res. Inst.

Rindos, D. 2013. *The Origins of Agriculture: An Evolutionary Perspective*. Academic Press.

Rogers, J. A. 1972. Darwinism and Social Darwinism. *Journal of the History of Ideas* 33 (2):265–80.

Rosset, P. M., B. M. Sosa, A. M. Jaime, and D. R. Lozano. 2011. The Campesino-to-Campesino agroecology movement of ANAP in Cuba: Social process methodology in the construction of sustainable peasant agriculture and food sovereignty. *J Peasant Stud* 38 (1):161–91.

Rostow, W. W. 1956. The take-off into self-sustained growth. *The Economic Journal* 66 (261):25–48.

———. 1963. Leading Sectors and the Take-Off. In *The Economics of Take-Off into Sustained Growth*, International Economic Association Series., 1–21. London: Palgrave Macmillan. https://link.springer.com/chapter/10.1007/978-1-349 -63959-5_1 (last accessed 5 December 2017).

Sahlins, M. 1990. The Political Economy of Grandeur in Hawaii, 1810 to 1830. In *Culture Through Time: Anthropological Approaches*, ed. E. Ohnuki-Tierney. Stanford University Press.

Sahlins, M. D. 1967. *Social Stratification in Polynesia*. University of Washington Press.

Schmitt, R. 1969. Catastrophic mortality in Hawaii. *Hawaiian Journal of History* 3:66–86.

Schmitt, R. C. 1970. Famine mortality in Hawaii. *The Journal of Pacific History* 5 (1):109–15.

Scoones, I., and J. Thompson. 2011. The politics of seed in Africa's Green Revolution: Alternative narratives and competing pathways. *IDS Bulletin* 42 (4):23.

Scott, J. C. 1976. *The Moral Economy of the Peasant: Rebellion and Subsistence in Southeast Asia*. Yale University Press. http://books.google.com/books?id =qu5KUdN_rDkC.

———. 1998. *Seeing Like State: How Certain Schemes to Improve the Human Condition Have Failed*. Yale University Press. http://books.google.com/books?id =PqcPCgsr2u0C.

Seidl, I., and C. A. Tisdell. 1999. Carrying capacity reconsidered: From Malthus' population theory to cultural carrying capacity. *Ecological Economics* 31 (3):395–408.

Self, S., J.-X. Zhao, R. Holasek, R. Torres, and A. King. 1999. The atmospheric impact of the 1991 Mount Pinatubo eruption. *USGS-PHIVOLCS*.

Sen, A. 1981. *Poverty and Famines: An Essay on Entitlement and Deprivation*. Clarendon Press. http://books.google.com/books?id=cfm0QgAACAAJ.

———. 1999. *Development as Freedom*. Oxford University Press. http://books .google.com/books?id=NQs75PEa618C.

Shaler, W. 1935. *Journal of a Voyage between China and the North-western Coast of America, Made in 1804*. Saunders Studio Press.

Shawcross, W. 2002. *Sideshow: Kissinger, Nixon, and the Destruction of Cambodia*. Cooper Square Press.

Shiva, V. 2016. *The Violence of the Green Revolution: Third World Agriculture, Ecology, and Politics*. University Press of Kentucky.

Singer, P. 1972. Famine, affluence, and morality. *Philosophy & Public Affairs*:229–43.

Slocomb, M. 2010. *An Economic History of Cambodia in the Twentieth Century*. NUS Press.

Smith, N. 2008. *Uneven Development: Nature, Capital, and the Production of Space*. University of Georgia Press. http://books.google.com/books?id=5dfKBaNo UbwC.

Somasundaram, D. J. 1996. Post-traumatic responses to aerial bombing. *Social Science & Medicine* 42 (11):1465–471.

St. John, H. 1947. The History, Present Distribution, and Abundance of Sandalwood on Oahu, Hawaiian Islands: Hawaiian Plant Studies 14. http:// scholarspace.manoa.hawaii.edu/handle/10125/12535 (last accessed 24 August 2016).

Statista. 2017. Global grain production, 2016–2017. *Statista*. https://www.statista .com/statistics/271943/total-world-grain-production-since-2008–2009/ (last accessed 18 August 2017).

Stockholm Resilience Center. 2016. Insight #5 Social-ecological traps—Stockholm Resilience Centre. https://www.stockholmresilience.org/research/insights/2016 -11-16-insight-5-social-ecological-traps.html (last accessed 7 January 2018).

Strangio, S. 2017. The past isn't past. *Mekong Review* (8). https://mekongreview .com/the-past-isnt-past/.

Stratton, A. 1964. *The Great Red Island*. New York: Scribner.

Thompson, E. 2013. *Colonial Citizens: Republican Rights, Paternal Privilege, and Gender in French Syria and Lebanon*. Columbia University Press.

Thomson, J. E. 1996. *Mercenaries, Pirates, and Sovereigns: State-Building and Extraterritorial Violence in Early Modern Europe*. Princeton University Press.

Tichit, L. 1981. *L'agriculture au Cambodge*. Paris: Agence de Coopération Culturelle et Technique.

Time. 1976. Why are the Khmer killing the Khmer? *Time Magazine, Asia Edition*.

Torres, I. 2017. Hungry for Change. *The New School Free Press*. http://www .newschoolfreepress.com/2017/03/25/hungry-for-change/ (last accessed 24 May 2018).

Tsing, A. L. 2015. *The Mushroom at the End of the World: On the Possibility of Life in Capitalist Ruins*. Princeton University Press.

Twining, C. 1989. The Economy. In *Cambodia 1975–1978, Rendezvous with Death*, ed. K. Jackson. Princeton, NJ: Princeton University Press.

Twombly, A. S. 1899. *Hawaii and Its People: The Land of Rainbow and Palm*. Boston: Silver, Burdett and Company.

Tyerman, D., and G. Bennet. 1832. *Journal of Voyages and Travels by the Rev. Daniel Tyerman and George Bennet, Esq: Deputed from the London Missionary Society, to Visit Their Various Stations in the South Sea Islands, China, India, &c. Between the Years 1821 and 1829*. Crocker and Brewster.

Tyner, J. A., and S. Rice. 2015. To live and let die: Food, famine, and administrative violence in Democratic Kampuchea, 1975–1979. *Political Geography* 48:1–10.

Tyner, J., and S. Rice. 2016. Cambodia's political economy of violence: Space, time, and genocide under the Khmer Rouge, 1975–79. *Genocide Studies International* 10 (1):84–94.

USAID. 1977. *World Rice Statistics: Food Production and Nutrition*. Washington, D.C.: USAID/FAO.

———. 2012. Scenario Development for Food Security Early Warning: Guidance for Famine Early Warning Systems Network (FEWS NET) Staff and Partners.

Van Der Eng, P. 2004. Productivity and comparative advantage in rice agriculture in South-East Asia since 1870. *Asian Economic Journal* 18 (4):345–70.

Vancouver, G. 1801. *A Voyage of Discovery to the North Pacific Ocean: And Round the World*. J. Stockdale.

Vergouwen, J. C. 1964. *The Social Organisation and Customary Law of the Toba-Batak of Northern Sumatra*. Los Angeles: The University of California Press.

Vickery, M. 2000. *Cambodia, 1975–1982*. Silkworm Books.

de Waal, A. 1990. A Re-assessment of entitlement theory in the light of the recent famines in Africa. *Development and Change* 21 (3):469–90.

———. 1997. *Famine Crimes: Politics & the Disaster Relief Industry in Africa*. African Rights & the International African Institute. http://books.google.com/books?id=UV3XROXhn5oC.

———. 2006. AIDS, Hunger and Destitution. In *The New Famines: Why Famines Persist in an Era of Globalization*, ed. S. Devereux. Routledge.

———. 2017. *Mass Starvation: The History and Future of Famine*. John Wiley & Sons.

———. 2018. Social nutrition and prohibiting famine. *World Nutrition* 9 (1):31–35.

de Waal, A., and A. Whiteside. 2003. New variant famine: AIDS and food crisis in southern Africa. *The Lancet* 362 (9391):1234–237.

Watson, F. 2006. Why Are There No Longer "War Famines" in Contemporary Europe? In *The New Famines: Why Famines Persist in an Era of Globalization*, ed. S. Devereux. Routledge.

Watts, M. J. 2013. *Silent Violence: Food, Famine, and Peasantry in Northern Nigeria*. University of Georgia Press. http://books.google.com/books?id=vRuvAAAAQBAJ.

Wells-Dang, A. 2006. A regional approach: Mine and UXO risk reduction in Vietnam, Laos and Cambodia. *Journal of Conventional Weapons Destruction* 9 (2):8.

Wemheuer, F. 2014. *Famine Politics in Maoist China and the Soviet Union*. Yale University Press.

Whitaker, D. P. 1973. *Area Handbook for the Khmer Republic (Cambodia)*. For sale by the Supt. of Docs., U.S. Government Printing Office.

White, P. F., T. Oberthür, and P. Sovuthy. 1997. *The Soils Used for Rice Production in Cambodia: A Manual for Their Identification and Management* ed. H. J. Nesbitt. Int. Rice Res. Inst.

WHO. 2017. WHO | Dietary recommendations / Nutritional requirements. *WHO*. http://www.who.int/nutrition/topics/nutrecomm/en/ (last accessed 5 December 2017).

Wilkes, C. 1845. *Narrative of the United States Exploring Expedition during the Years 1838, 1839, 1840, 1841, 1842*. Philadelphia: Lea and Blanchard.

Wittfogel, K. A. 1957. *Oriental Despotism: A Comparative Study of Total Power*. Yale University Press.

Wong, C. S., X. Li, and I. Thornton. 2006. Urban environmental geochemistry of trace metals. *Environmental Pollution* 142 (1):1–16.

Woodward, T. E., W. F. Turner, and D. Griffiths. 1915. Prickly-pears as a feed for dairy cows. *Journal of Agricultural Research* 4:405–51.

Wright, J. 2012. *Sustainable Agriculture and Food Security in an Era of Oil Scarcity: Lessons from Cuba*. Routledge.

Young, H., and S. Jaspars. 1995. Nutrition, disease and death in times of famine. *Disasters* 19 (2):94–109.

Zerbe, N. 2004. Feeding the famine? American food aid and the GMO debate in Southern Africa. *Food Policy* 29 (6):593–608.

Index

accumulation, 71, 160, 191, 209, 213
agricultural involution. *See* involution
ahupua'a, 18; breakdown of, 72, 74, 77, 196, 212; and ecological zones, 34–36; and food production, 36, 43; and political hierarchy, 34–37, 39, 46, 58; and taxation, 37, 41, 71
aid, xi, 152, 155, 164–66, 190–92, 207, 210, 214; and flights, 133, 165, 184, 208, 129; food, 131, 156–59, 162, 174, 190–91, 204, 214–15; foreign, 129, 132, 151, 153–54, 180, 198, 207, 218, 228n8; industry, xi, 4, 220; and military, 130, 154
alcohol, 20, 51, 53, 55, 97
Algeria, 109, 123
alienation, 41, 75
Ambovombe, 87, 91, 112, 115, 118
American Board of Missions, 57
ancestors, 55, 79, 90–91
Angkor, 141
Annales School, 9
Antananarivo, 81–82, 86, 99–101, 103, 109, 113, 122, 126
Antandroy, 8, 79, 83, 101; diet, 93–95; French involvement with, 99, 100, 104–5, 110–11, 219; geography of, 87–89, 115; pastoral practice of, 90–92, 107, 124, 197, 208; plague consequences for, 80, 114–16, 118, 120–22, 127
aristocracy, 151, 166
Augagneur, Victor, 106
Australia, 113, 123–24
autarky, 8, 134, 169, 173, 187, 192, 225n4

barter, 41, 48, 161
Battambang, 142, 147, 151, 157, 164, 169, 172–73
beef, 80, 93, 106, 117, 136, 139
Beloha, 87, 110, 114
Bingham, Hiram, 18, 23, 46, 57, 226n5
Bishop, Artemas, 63, 67
black markets: elite use of, 129–31, 156, 159, 191, 198; farmers use of, 150, 153, 166; as socioecological trap, 207, 218, 219–20
bombardment. *See* bombing
bombing, 8; and agriculture, 145, 156, 164–65, 169, 173, 184–85, 198; casualties of, 162;

and civil war, 154, 192; and refugees, 133–34, 160, 190, 204; and U.S. policy, 153, 155, 199
Braudel, Fernand, 9
bubonic plague, 130
buffalo. *See* water buffalo
bunds, 143, 145
Butler, Smedley, 160
Byron, George, 61

cactus fruit, 91, 94, 122
cactus pastoralism, 80, 83–84, 87–90, 95, 111, 124; collapse of, 80, 100, 115, 118; evolution of, 81, 85, 99, 122; vulnerabilities of, 119, 125
cactus thickets, 80, 96, 97, 105, 110, 116, 119, 122, 123, 124–25, 197, 203
caloric intake, 119, 136, 139, 162, 171, 194, 228n11
calories, 31, 136, 171–72, 175, 180, 187
canals: in Cambodia, 137, 143, 152, 174, 183; in Hawaii, 25–26, 28, 30, 41, 69
cannibalism, 1, 183
Canton, 18, 47, 71
Cape of Good Hope, 86, 98, 100, 102
cash crops, xi, 5, 108, 120–21, 223
cassava, 7, 144
Catholic churches, 103
Catholic Relief Services, 160
cattle, ix, 8, 123; as basis of economy, 89–92, 117, 119, 128; death of, 80, 111, 114–16, 127, 197, 227n9; in Hawaii, 14, 62–63, 67; in religious and cultural practice, 90, 119; as social welfare, 79, 91–92, 116–17, 206; theft of, 92, 99, 104, 198; water requirements of, 94–96. *See also* cactus pastoralism; fodder; oxen; traction; water buffalo
census, 37, 51, 100
Central Intelligence Agency (CIA), 152–53, 183
centralization, 3, 7, 177
ceremony, 23–24, 38, 42, 72, 90–91, 100, 107
chickens, 23, 37, 136, 139, 140
chiefs: and conscription, 18, 27, 53; and conspicuous consumption, 14–15, 48–49, 58–59, 70; and diet, 23; and hierarchy, 35–40, 71–72; and missionaries, 57, 62;

CPSIA information can be obtained
at www.ICGtesting.com
Printed in the USA
JSHW020531190220
4256JS00002B/3

9 781949 199345